TEXTS
and
TESTAMENTS

*Critical Essays on the Bible
and Early Church Fathers*

A VOLUME IN HONOR OF
STUART DICKSON CURRIE

TEXTS
and
TESTAMENTS

*Critical Essays on the Bible
and Early Church Fathers*

Edited by W. EUGENE MARCH

Trinity University Press San Antonio

Grateful acknowledgment is extended to Random House, Inc. for their permission
to quote from *W. H. Auden: Collected Poems,* edited by Edward Mendelson (New
York: Random House, Inc., 1976). Unless otherwise indicated, all biblical quotations in English are from the Revised Standard Version of the Bible, copyright 1946,
1952, 1971, 1973, by the Division of Education and Ministry of the National Council
of the Churches of Christ in the United States, and used by permission.

*Texts and Testaments: Critical Essays on the Bible and Early
Church Fathers* has been prepared under the auspices of
Austin Presbyterian Theological Seminary in honor of Stuart
Dickson Currie (1922-1975). Professor Currie joined the
faculty of Austin Presbyterian Theological Seminary in 1961
as Assistant Professor of Church History. In 1964 he became
Professor of New Testament Language and Exegesis.

Printed by Best Printing Company
Bound by Custom Bookbinders

ACKNOWLEDGMENTS

A volume of essays is special in many ways, but perhaps particularly for the patience and cooperation it requires from so many. First and foremost, a word of appreciation is due the authors. Without the understanding, tenacious, diligent commitment of each of the contributors, this project could not have reached completion. That willing gift of mind and pen cannot be measured.

Many others assisted in the countless tasks involved in forging this book as well. First, there was the steering committee composed of Denis Farkasfalvy, William Farmer, Everett Ferguson, George Heyer, John Jansen, and Albert Outler, which was invaluable in selecting contributors for this volume. William Farmer and John Jansen especially deserve a word of thanks for their willing assistance as part of an executive committee which helped me make numerous decisions. Then there were student assistants, Brett Morgan and Bobbi Kaye Cloninger, who relentlessly pursued bibliographical data and textual references toward the end that accuracy could be achieved. Dorothy Andrews of Austin Presbyterian Theological Seminary and Virginia Cabello of Trinity University Press went well beyond the bounds of duty in typing and retyping manuscripts with speed, accuracy, and goodwill. All their effort is most appreciated.

Gratitude must also be expressed to the administration, faculty, alumni, and friends of Austin Presbyterian Theological Seminary for the many forms of support given to enable the successful conclusion of this undertaking. President Jack M. Maxwell and Academic Dean E. Dixon Junkin were constant in their encouragement and understanding. The faculty never ceased to show interest and concern. The Alumni Association through its officers and members showed its readiness to help with concrete financial assistance.

Finally, a word of thanks to Trinity University Press is much in order. Joe W. Nicholson, Director, and Lois Boyd, Editor, have offered unfailing support and encouragement during the course of this project. Particularly has Lois Boyd shared her professional counsel and assistance through every phase of the editing and publishing process. To her I express in equal measure my deep respect and appreciation.

W.E.M.
1979

CONTRIBUTORS

William Baird
Professor of New Testament
Brite Divinity School
Texas Christian University

David L. Balás
Professor of Theology
University of Dallas

William A. Beardslee
Professor of Religion
Emory University

Thomas W. Currie, Jr.
Pastor
Oak Cliff Presbyterian Church
Dallas, Texas

Denis M. Farkasfalvy
Headmaster
Cistercian Preparatory School
Irving, Texas

William R. Farmer
Professor of New Testament
Perkins School of Theology
Southern Methodist University

Everett Ferguson
Professor of Bible
Abilene Christian University

George S. Heyer, Jr.
Associate Professor of the
   History of Doctrine
Austin Presbyterian
   Theological Seminary

John F. Jansen
Professor of New Testament
   Interpretation
Austin Presbyterian
   Theological Seminary

Abraham J. Malherbe
Professor of New Testament
Yale Divinity School
Yale University

W. Eugene March
Professor of Old Testament
Austin Presbyterian
   Theological Seminary

Thomas H. Olbricht
Professor of Biblical Theology
Abilene Christian University

Albert C. Outler
Research Professor of Theology
Perkins School of Theology
Southern Methodist University

James A. Wharton
Pastor
Memorial Drive Presbyterian
   Church
Houston, Texas

Prescott H. Williams, Jr.
Professor of Old Testament
   Languages and Exegesis
Austin Presbyterian
   Theological Seminary

CONTENTS

The Formation of Canon and
the Discipline of Interpretation

Stuart Dickson Currie: Biography and Bibliography

PREFACE

Texts and Testaments is a collection of essays written in memory of a remarkable colleague who had an unquenchable thirst for knowledge and an unswerving respect for texts—Hebrew, Greek, Latin, German, French, English, Modern, Ancient, Prose, Poetry! Stuart Currie never tired of studying a text, seeking to understand, question, be questioned. The Old and New Testaments were of special interest to him, and he read them with the kind of insight and sensitivity which is achieved only in the course of a long friendship. But texts—all texts—provoked his curiosity. Thomas Olbricht, in reflecting on this insatiable appetite for texts, wrote, "Professor Currie in his eagerness for insight roamed the centuries, but as his published works indicate, felt especially at home in the first and second centuries."* None of those who knew Stuart Currie would question the accuracy of this comment. The "concentration" on but two centuries, however, was a limit posed only by mortality and not by interest.

Those who have contributed to this volume knew and worked with Stuart Currie in a variety of settings. One worked with him as his professor as well as colleague (William Beardslee). Others came to know him most intimately in the context of a Seminar on the Origins of Catholic Christianity conducted in this region for some years now (William Baird, David Balás, Denis Farkasfalvy, William Farmer, Everett Ferguson, Abraham Malherbe, Thomas Olbricht, Albert Outler). Some of us had the privilege of an even closer contact that came with serving on the same faculty with him at Austin Presbyterian Theological Seminary (George Heyer, John Jansen, Eugene March, James Wharton, and Prescott Williams). Finally, one knew him as elder brother and colleague in ministry (Thomas Currie). All of us know ourselves made richer by Currie's life and share, however modestly, his passion for texts and testaments.

*The quotations from Olbricht, Jansen, Outler, and Wharton in this preface are drawn with their permission from private correspondence to the editor.

The materials presented here are aimed at furthering discussion on a wide range of issues. Particular biblical and intertestamental texts as well as patristic sources are addressed. Issues relating to the formation of the canon and the implications of canon for theology are raised. The history of the interpretation of texts and periods also receives attention. The reason for the breadth of subject is Currie himself, for this is an accurate reflection of his interests. Albert Outler wrote, "One of my most cherished memories of Stuart Currie—constant over the long course of our friendship—was the breadth and vigor of his curiosity." John Jansen, on reflecting on the rationale for his contribution to this volume, an essay that moves from Paul to Marcellus to Van Ruler, correctly concluded, "This study in the history of dogma is not inappropriate to the memory of an esteemed colleague whose own New Testament exegesis was enriched by his wide knowledge of patristic literature and who himself stood firmly within the Reformed tradition."

There is one side of our colleague that is difficult to acknowledge properly. Thomas Olbricht described Currie's style as "inimicable country-peppered erudition." Albert Outler commented on Currie's "gracious irreverence...toward the academic 'establishment' in which he was, of course, a fully credentialed and competent member." All who worked with Currie witnessed at one time or another the seemingly simple, homespun, understated logic of Stuart Currie disarm and destroy what had appeared an impregnable position. James Wharton best described this quality in the following words:

> Since a great deal of the scholarly apparatus in biblical studies appears to be devoted to the securing of solutions, and since the authority to condescend to texts and colleagues is often taken as a mark of scholarly distinction, Stuart was always an irregular and improbable member of the scholarly guild. When, as a delicious charade, he chose to play the typical competitive games by the typical competitive rules, he was a terrifying adversary. What an international reputation he might have made for himself if he had turned those awesome talents and energies in the direction of setting the rest of us straight and imposing his own solutions upon us by dint of evidence and argument! Those of us who worked with him will contend forever that it was only the regard he had for himself and for the biblical materials that prevented that course. We lament Stuart's diffidence that largely kept the scholarly world from knowing that a giant had walked among them, yet we treasure his diffidence insofar as it bears prophetic witness against con-

descension toward texts or persons in the work of interpreting the Bible.

For those who knew him well, words are not adequate to express what his absence has meant. Spurred by his memory, however, we continue to quest after insight into texts and testaments. After all, these texts—oh so many texts—are part of a covenantal legacy received by Stuart Dickson Currie and passed along to us. We are grateful to God for him and for them.

TEXTS
and
TESTAMENTS

Biblical and Intertestamental Texts

Ascension and Resurrection: An Intersection of Luke and Paul

William Baird

Considered in light of the Pauline letters, the view that Jesus appeared to his disciples for a period of forty days prior to his ascension (Acts 1:3) is problematic. The apostle was convinced that the risen Lord had appeared to him, but this could not have been possible if resurrection appearances were restricted to a forty-day period. For all his claims to apostleship, Paul did not qualify as "one of the men who have accompanied us during all the time that the Lord Jesus went in and out among us" (Acts 1:21-22).

On the other hand, if Paul's contention was correct that the risen Lord had in fact appeared to him (1 Cor 15:8), then Luke's account of the ascension is called into question. Moreover, the character of the account, replete with proofs and promises, men in white and transporting cloud, has led most scholars to conclude that the doctrine of the ascension is a relatively late and largely apologetic invention. Many would agree with the judgment of Hans Grass that the doctrine of the ascension developed "auf dem Boden der späten Legende."[1]

Over against this apparent impasse, however, is the fact that the understanding of the exaltation of the crucified one at (or by means of) the resurrection is present in the pre-Pauline tradition as texts like Phil 2:9 and Rom 1:4 indicate. Although this idea of exaltation at/by resurrection is different from Luke's ascension doctrine in both time and character, there is a common element—the transportation of the risen Christ to the realm of exaltation. Moreover, Luke's belief that the appearances of the exalted Christ were confined to a particular, limited, time period is not lacking elsewhere in the NT. This seems to be the force of Paul's claim, "last of all...he appeared also to me" (1 Cor 15:8). Although the exegesis is open to other possibilities, many interpreters would agree with Freeman Sleeper that Paul's phrase "has the effect of setting a definite temporal limit to the resurrection appearances."[2]

The purpose of this essay is to investigate the relationship between Paul's idea of a temporal limitation for the resurrection appearances and Luke's doctrine of the ascension. First, the nature, origin and meaning of Luke's doctrine will be analyzed. Then, Paul's understanding of the resurrection appearances will be investigated. Finally, an attempt will be made to assess the meaning and implications of the temporal limitation of resurrection appearances. The thesis is that beneath Paul's idea of the temporal limitation of the appearances and Luke's doctrine of the ascension there is common theological ground: the belief that the resurrection appearances of Christ did not continue indefinitely but were to be understood as essential to the Christ event.

The Lukan doctrine of the ascension has been comprehensively investigated by Gerhard Lohfink.[3] Using a variety of methodological approaches (tradition-historical, form-critical, *religionsgeschichtlich,* redactional), Lohfink was concerned with two main questions: 1) Was Luke's presentation of the ascension a composition of his own, or did it rest on earlier ascension tradition(s)? 2) What is the meaning of the doctrine of the ascension for the theology of the author of Luke-Acts? Lohfink began by arguing that the ascension should be classifed as an *Entrückung,* a "bodily translation." It was not a variation on the ancient motif of the heavenly journey of the soul, but the removal of the individual in bodily form into the heavenly realm. By a thorough study of the Old Testament, Jewish, Greek, and Roman background materials, Lohfink sought to establish his contention. A "translation" narrative was identified as having the following distinctive characteristics: a mountain as the place of ascent, a speech by the one ascending, witnesses present, the viewing of bodily ascent. On the basis of his research and the obvious parallels with the Lukan account, Lohfink concluded, "Die Himmelfahrt Jesu bei Lukas ist eine *Entrückung.*"[4]

Next, Lohfink investigated the NT literature. The earliest concept was not bodily removal by ascension, but exaltation at (or by means of) the resurrection. This understanding of Christ's exaltation was implicit in 1 Thess 1:10, where Paul said that believers who have turned to God "wait for his Son from heaven whom he raised from the dead." The same idea is found in the pre-Pauline material cited in such texts as Rom 1:4 and Phil 2:9. Even a text like Rom 8:34—

Is it Christ Jesus, who died, yes, who was raised from the dead, who is at the right hand of God, who intercedes for us?

—does not in Lohfink's view distinguish resurrection and exaltation.

A similar case is made for the writings of the Pauline school. Eph 1:20, which speaks of what God has accomplished in Christ "when he raised him from the dead and made him sit at his right hand in the heavenly places," indicates that resurrection effects exaltation. To be sure, Eph 4:10 speaks of the one "who ascended far above all the heavens," but, according to Lohfink, this expression represents the author's interpretation of Ps 68:18 (cited in Eph 4:8) and does not constitute the formal concept of a visibly witnessed *Entrückung.* No doubt the author of 1 Peter drew a distinction between resurrection and exaltation, for he declared that after Christ was made alive he "went and preached to the spirits in prison" (3:19) before he departed into heaven. Nevertheless, this action of Jesus was accomplished "in the spirit" (3:18) and thus his translation into heaven was an invisible exaltation, not a bodily ascension. On the basis of this survey, Lohfink concludes, "Nirgendwo finden sich auch nur die kleinsten Indizien einer sichbaren Himmelfahrt beziehungsweise einer Entrückung, wie wir sie von Lukas herkennen....Auferweckung und Erhöhung bilden vielmehr eine innere Einheit."[5]

After concluding that the concept of visible, bodily ascension occurs within the NT exclusively in Acts, Lohfink proceeded to argue that the author of Luke-Acts was the originator of the doctrine of the ascension. To support his case, Lohfink rejected the view that Luke had borrowed the idea from some earlier tradition. For instance, with most scholars, Lohfink accepted the longer text of Lk 24:51, which includes the phrase "and was carried up into heaven." He rejected, however, the theory that the Easter day ascension implied in that text was changed to an ascension forty days later (Acts 1:3) on the basis of another tradition which Luke had received after writing Lk 24 but before writing Acts 1. Lohfink also rejected that notion that the ascension account in Acts represented an editorial interpolation created when a hypothetical original unified-work of Luke was later separated into two volumes.[6] The supposed contradiction between Lk 24 and Acts 1 had been discussed and discounted by Grass,[7] while the forty day interim was better understood as a matter of theology rather than chronology.[8] Thus, Lohfink concluded that a doctrine of ascension was present in both Lk 24 and Acts 1, and that the originator of that doctrine was the author of Luke-Acts.[9]

In Lohfink's view, the striking phenomenon was the persistence in the church of an early doctrine of Christ's exaltation over against Luke's doctrine of the ascension. Where the ascension is affirmed (for example, in the addition to Mark, [Mk 16:9], Barn 15:9, and by Gnostics), dependence on Luke is evident, but the idea of ascension did not triumph over the exaltation doctrine until the second century. Moreover, investigation of Lukan texts besides Acts 1 and Lk 24 indicates that Luke also was fully aware of the earlier exaltation concept. In Acts 2:32-33 we read, "This Jesus God raised up....Being therefore exalted at the right hand of God . . . ." The same idea is expressed in 5:30-31: "the God of our fathers raised Jesus whom you killed hanging him on a tree. God exalted him at his right hand as Leader and Savior." These texts, including the use of Ps 110:1,[10] represent the earlier idea of exaltation at (or by means of) resurrection. Yet Lohfink argued, as the stress on "witnesses" shows (2:32; 5:32), Luke reinterpreted the exaltation motif in terms of an ascension doctrine. That is, Luke took the idea of exaltation and shaped it into concrete, historical form. This is the Luke who presented the risen Christ as one with "flesh and bones," who ate a "piece of broiled fish" (Lk 24:39, 42). This is the Luke whose narrative of the baptism of Jesus describes the descent of the spirit "in bodily form, as a dove" (Lk 3:22). Thus, following his usual method, Luke historicized the exaltation of the risen Christ as a distinct event—an event of bodily ascension, visible to the eyes of witnesses. In Lohfink's words, Luke is engaged in the *"Einbau der Erhöhung in die Geschichte."*[11]

It is not necessary to accept all of Lohfink's historical-critical conclusions in order to appreciate his theological analysis.[12] In general, he agrees with Conzelmann that "The Ascension...is given its place within the whole course of redemptive history."[13] Lohfink, however, detected four main features of Luke's reinterpretation of the exaltation of the risen Christ in terms of the ascension. First, the ascension is the conclusion of the earthly life of Jesus. Not the death nor even the resurrection is the termination of Christ's redemptive work, but his exaltation by the ascension marks the conclusion of this segment of salvation-history.[14] The ascension also shows (perhaps against the Gnostics)[15] that the risen Christ is one with the crucified Jesus, and that his bodily existence, even after the resurrection, is attested by witnesses. Second, the ascension points forward to the *parousia*. The parallels between ascension and *parousia* in Luke's narrative indicate that though the *parousia* had not yet come, it would surely come.[16] In the meantime, the spirit has come and the mission of the church has begun. Third, the ascension affirms the continuity between Jesus and the church. This is expressed by the focus on Jerusalem in whose environs the ascension took place and where the mission of the church began. A period of forty days, an OT symbol, was employed to provide a time for instruction and the announcement of the spirit's coming in preparation for pentecost and the era thereby inaugurated.[17]

Fourth, the ascension is identical with the exaltation. For Luke, the resurrection did not accomplish the exaltation of Christ. Exaltation only happens later, at the ascension. Thus, Christ's appearance to Paul was from heaven after the ascension-exaltation (Acts 9:3; 22:6, 26:13, 19). It was only after the ascension that Stephen could say, "Behold, I see the heavens opened, and the Son of man standing at the right hand of God" (Acts 7:56).

Over against Lohfink's analysis of Luke's understanding of the ascension, Paul's view of the resurrection appearances poses some interesting alternatives. The crucial text is 1 Cor 15:3-8:

> For I delivered to you as of first importance what I
> also received,
>> that Christ died for our sins in accordance with the
>> scriptures,
>> that he was buried,
>> that he was raised on the third day in accordance with
>> the scriptures,
>> and that he appeared to Cephas, then to the twelve.
> Then he appeared to more than five hundred
> brethren at one time, most of whom are still alive,
> though some have fallen asleep.
> Then he appeared to James, then to all the apostles.
> Last of all, as to one untimely born, he appeared
> also to me. (arrangement of lines mine)

Many hold that this text incorporates pre-Pauline tradition.[18] The technical terms "delivered" and "received" indicate the transmission of a tradition. Moreover, the style and structure of the material suggest a confessional or kerygmatic formula which underscores the non-Pauline, pre-Pauline character of the tradition.

Though there is wide agreement that some of 1 Cor 15:3-8 is pre-Pauline, there is debate on the extent of the traditional material.[19] Paul, no doubt, adapted the material to his own use as indicated by reference to his own experience (vs 8) and his comments about the five hundred brethren (vs 6). According to most recent scholarship, the earliest material extends only to vs 5, ending with the appearances to Cephas and the twelve.[20] However, the attempt to identify and delimit the tradition rests on a variety of arguments. The conclusion that the traditional material ends at vs 5, for example, has been supported by the observation that the use of *epeita* in vs 6 constitutes a grammatical change. On the other hand, it can also be argued on stylistic grounds that the key to the composition is the conjunction *hoti,* and that the basic tradition contains four main elements:

> that *(hoti)* Christ died
> that *(hoti)* he was buried
> that *(hoti)* he was raised
> that *(hoti)* he appeared.[21]

The fourth element, the appearances, include an official list, linked together by the adverbs *eita...epeita...epeita...eita*—terms which also represent a definite formula.

Still other attempts to reconstruct the traditional material rely on efforts to find some formal groupings within the appearance list. For example, the parallel character of vs 5 and vs 7 has been frequently observed:

> he appeared to Cephas, then to the twelve.
> he appeared to James, then to all the apostles.

This parallel structure has led some scholars to detect separate traditions of appearances—traditions which reflected the struggle within the early church between the followers of Peter and the disciples of James.[22] Paul Winter has argued for two traditions represented by groups of three:[23]

Cephas	James
The Twelve	The Apostles
Over 500 brethren	All the brethren

This view assumes that the traditions began with individuals and expanded to larger groups, that "the twelve" and "the apostles" are the same, and that Paul has replaced "all the brethren" with himself. While such a conjecture is hardly convincing, it illustrates the lack of certainty with regard to the identification and delimitation of the tradition.

Regardless of the extent of the traditional material, the list of appearances, at least in Paul's understanding, is presented in chronological order.[24] This is shown by the use of the temporal adverbs *eita...epeita...epeita...eita*—a construction which implies chronological sequence. Moreover, whatever else it may mean, Paul's statement that the appearance to him was "last of all," surely indicates that his experience was the latest of those he listed. Apparently Paul believed that the first appearances was to Cephas and the last to himself.

The identification of the appearances is problematic. The appearance to Cephas (Simon Peter) is mentioned in Lk 24:34 and implied in Mk 16:7 and Lk 22:32, but nowhere else described in the Synoptic Gospels. The appearance to the twelve can be supported by Matt 28:16-20 and Lk 24:36-42, but the appearance to the five hundred, despite efforts to identify it with pentecost,[25] affords no obvious parallel. The appearance to James is recorded only in the aprocryphal Gospel of the Hebrews, and the appearance "to all the apostles" is too vague for identification. It is also evident that Paul's list fails to include some appearances narrated in the Synoptics, such as the appearances to the women (Matt 28:9-10) and to the Emmaus pilgrims (Lk 24:13-32). These accounts, however, represent a later stage in the resurrection tradition, a stage which assumed the empty tomb and stressed physical proofs (Matt 28:9, Lk 24:39, 42) and the development of apologetic (Lk 24:27, 32) and liturgical motifs (Lk 24:30).

Paul was convinced that the appearance to himself was of the same character as that to the others.[26] He included himself in the list and used precisely the same term to describe his own experience as to describe those of the others. The term *ōphthē*, which means "to be seen" or "to appear," is used in the LXX for theophanies (Exod 6:3). "The dominant thought," says Wilhelm Michaelis, "is that the appearances are revelation, encounters with the risen Lord who herein reveals Himself, or is revealed."[27] This view is supported by other Pauline texts. In Gal 1:11-17, the fullest account of Paul's revelation-conversion experience, Paul insisted that his gospel came through an *apokalupseōs Iēsou Christou*. The genitive is probably objective, so that the content of the revelation is Jesus Christ. In vs 16 Paul added that God was pleased *apokaluspai ton huion autou* to him. Commenting on this text, Albrecht Oepke has written, "Here 'to be revealed' means much the same as 'to appear.' "[28] Again, that which was disclosed or seen was God's son, Jesus Christ. When Paul noted that the revelation occurred *en emoi*, he may have intended to stress the inward character of the experience, but the construction may simply mean "in my case" or "to me."[29] The purpose of the revelation was not to dazzle Paul with some supernatural disclosure, but to confront him with a commission. God decided "to reveal his Son to me, in order that I might preach him among the Gentiles" (Gal 1:16).

These same motifs are emphasized elsewhere in the epistles. In 1 Cor 9:1, Paul asked, "Am I not free? Am I not an apostle? Have I not seen Jesus our Lord?" Again, stress is placed on seeing, and the word used is another form of *horaō*. This term can describe either physical or ecstatic sight. In this context it suggests that revelation has been received. Like Gal 1, this text indicates that revelation involved a commission. Because Paul had seen the Lord, he was able to claim that he was an apostle. In 2 Cor 4:4-6, Paul referred to "seeing the light of the gospel of the glory of Christ, who is the likeness of God." Finally, he exclaimed, "For it is God who said, 'Let light shine out of darkness,' who has shone in our hearts to give the light of the knowledge of the glory of God in the face of Christ" (4:6). Although Paul was speaking primarily of the disclosure of Christ in the proclamation of his gospel, many commentators believe his conversion experience is implied.[30] The visual imagery, together with the typical hellenistic theme of light and glory as revelatory symbols, makes this clear. Moreover, the object of revelation is more explicit here than in the other texts, namely, the light of the glory of God in the *prosōpon* (face or person) of Christ.

Since Paul claimed to be an eyewitness of a resurrection appearance, his understanding of the resurrection is of utmost importance. Consequently, attention should be given to his discussion of the resurrection body in 1 Cor 15:35-50. Although this text describes the nature of the resurrection body of Christians, Paul's understanding of the resurrection of Christians resulted from his perception of the resurrection of Christ. Elsewhere he wrote, "If we have been united with him in a death like his, we shall certainly be united with him in a resurrection like his" (Rom 6:5). This means that the resurrection body of Christ and the resurrection body of Christians are the same in nature.[31] In 1 Cor 15:42-44, Paul described the resurrection body of Christians, making use of the analogy of seed and plant:

> What is sown is perishable,
> > what is raised is imperishable.
> It is sown in dishonor,
> > it is raised in glory.
> It is sown in weakness,
> > it is raised in power.
> It is sown a physical body,
> > it is raised a spiritual body.
> (arrangement of lines mine)

Debatable, to be sure, is the meaning of Paul's phrase "spiritual body."[32] Nevertheless, he certainly understood the "spiritual body" to be different from the "physical body," for, he concluded dramatically: "I tell you this, brethren: flesh and blood cannot inherit the kingdom of God, nor does the perishable inherit the imperishable" (15:50).[33] Perhaps Paul coined a new phrase, "spiritual body," paradoxical in meaning. The resurrected reality is a new reality, spiritual in nature, yet a bodily reality nonetheless. The old has been changed (15:51), transformed into the new without loss of somatic reality and maintaining recognizable continuity.[34]

The perception of this new reality was understood by Paul to be radically different from his later visionary experiences. For example, in 2 Cor 12:1, he mentioned "visions and revelations of the Lord." Although he claimed an "abundance of revelations" (vs 7), Paul had to reach back fourteen years into his past to come up with an illustration, and the description of this experience stands in bold contrast to his revelation-appearance accounts. Rather than a description in first person of a clear revelation "to me" (Gal 1:16), Paul described in third person the experience of a man caught up to the third heaven in some incomprehensible way (2 Cor 12:2-4). Rather than a commission to proclaim what he had seen (Gal 1:16), Paul's later visionary experience involved "things that cannot be told, which man may not utter" (2 Cor 12:4). These contrasts indicate that Paul did not understand the resurrection appearances to be subjective, ecstatic, on-going religious experiences.[35] Grass has described the appearances as "objective visions"—a phrase which, despite its inadequacies, avoids defining the resurrection as a subjective psychological phenomenon and preserves the transcendent character of the resurrection as an act of God.[36]

Regardless of the difficulty in defining the nature of the appearances, Paul clearly did not understand the resurrection in terms consistent with a visible, bodily ascension. Instead, texts like Rom 8:34 indicate that Paul was in essential agreement with the early church's idea of exaltation by means of the resurrection. The same point is implicit in the hymn Paul quoted in Phil 2:5-11. While this text does not explicitly mention the resurrection, immediately after the reference to Christ's death on the cross the text says, "God has highly exalted him" (vs 9). This suggests that exaltation is identical with resurrection. A similar idea is expressed in the pre-Pauline confession cited in Rom 1:3-4 which states that Jesus Christ was appointed (*horizō*) "Son of God in power...by his resurrection from the dead." The resurrection then is the means by which God vindicated the crucified one. "For he was crucified in weakness, but lives by the power of God" (2 Cor 13:4). According to Paul, and much of the tradition which preceded him, the appearances of the risen Christ were appearances of the exalted one, "appearances of the risen Lord *from* heaven."[37]

If Paul understood the resurrection appearances as revelation of the risen Christ from heaven—in sharp contrast to bodily manifestations of Jesus on earth for forty days prior to his ascension—a question can be raised about the meaning of Paul's conviction that the appearances were limited to a particular time period. The view that Paul advocated such a limitation rests on the interpretation of his phrase "last of all," *eschaton de pantōn,* in 1 Cor 15:8. This could mean, of course, that Paul's experience was last of those listed, or that it was "least in importance."[38] However, most interpreters agree with von Campenhausen that, "It must be presumed that he meant the account of the appearances of Christ, as he gave them, to be complete; in other words, he mentions here all the reliable testimonies and witnesses that he knows."[39] Moreover, Paul, writing some twenty years after his own experience, seemed to presume that others would accept his claim to be the last to perceive a resurrection appearance. If, on the contrary, someone could have demonstrated that there were other appearances after Paul's, the whole argument would have folded like a flimsy tent.

As a matter of fact, the claim to a limited number of appearances within a definite time-frame seems to be well-attested in the early tradition. Although scholars are not agreed on the meaning of Paul's statement in 1 Cor 15:8 that the appearance to him was *tō ektrōmati* (RSV: "as to one untimely born"),[40] the phrase certainly indicates that the including of Paul in the list involved some sort of exception. The fact that Paul apparently felt it necessary to make a case for himself suggests that the tradition before him already acknowledged a limited number of resurrection appearances. Although the NT contains appearances not included in Paul's list, it does not record appearances which took place after his. The author of Acts, creating a problem for the forty-day limit of his own ascension-narrative, presented the exceptional appearances to Stephen (7:56) and Paul (9:17; 22:14; 26, 19). However, this author, who acknowledged the possibility of such post-resurrection appearances from heaven, included no account of a resurrection appearance later than Paul's.[41] Even the Gnostics attested to the persistence of the tradition of the limitation of appearances, though the period between the resurrection and the ascension was sometimes extended (550 days in the Apocryphon of James, twelve years in Pistis Sophia). By accepting the doctrine of the ascension, the Gnostics acknowledged that the period in which the risen Christ dispensed secret doctrine was subject to temporal limits.

The question can be raised as to why Paul and the early church concluded that appearances of the exalted Christ were confined to a limited time and a particular group. Perhaps the early Christians wanted to emphasize their conviction that the resurrection was not a mere hallucination or an on-going subjective experience. Moreover, the close temporal link between crucifixion and the subsequent appearances may have served to affirm (perhaps against proto-Gnostics) that the crucified Christ and the risen Lord were one and the same. Paul, of course, could have used the tradition of limitation as a device to support his own apostolic authority and restrict that of others, although Paul actually seems less restrictive than the author of Acts, who insisted that membership in "the Twelve" required witness of the ministry of Jesus from his baptism until his ascension (1:21-22).[42]

Whatever may have been at stake in the various uses of tradition, Paul considered his inclusion among the limited number who had seen the risen Lord to be foundational for his own apostleship. It is not clear who was included in the phrase "all the apostles" (1 Cor 15:7), but when Paul mentioned "five hundred brethren" to whom Christ had appeared (15:6), Paul recognized that these shared with him the basic qualification for apostleship: they had seen the risen Lord (1 Cor 9:1). This is why Paul's list of resurrection appearances and claim to be "last of all" were so important. Apostleship was dependent upon having seen the risen Lord whose appearances were limited in number and restricted to a particular period of time. Unless the priority of this limited number who alone could testify to the reality of Christ's resurrection was acknowledged, Paul argued, "our preaching is in vain and your faith is in vain" (1 Cor 15:14).

Paul's recognition of the limitation of resurrection appearances, like Luke's doctrine of the ascension, was related to his understanding of redemptive history, or better, his eschatology. For Paul, the decisive eschatological event had occurred in the death and resurrection of Christ. The risen Lord was identical with the crucified Christ so that a continuity between the historical Jesus and the risen Christ was affirmed. Moreover, Paul nowhere presented an account of the actual raising of Jesus—nor did any other NT writer, for that matter. Instead, the resurrection was presented in terms of the appearances. The appearances represent the event of resurrection and are thus an essential aspect of the resurrection event. Although Christ has been exalted by the resurrection, his exaltation is not yet complete. Only at the *parousia* will he destroy "every rule and every authority" (1 Cor 15:24), only then will all things be subjected to him (1 Cor 15:27). For Paul, the present situation of Christians is that they live in the time between, the time of the "already" and the "not yet." The appearances serve to delineate this interim "in between" period. The end of the resurrection appearances points to the termination of the decisive eschatological event, the "already" of Christ's death and resurrection. While the church awaits the "not yet," there are no more resurrection appearances. The exalted Christ "is at the right hand of God" (Rom 8:34), making intercession for those who are "at home in the body...away from the Lord" (2 Cor 5:6). The appearances, though past, point to the future, to the *parousia* when the exalted Christ will come to complete his work (1 Thess 4:16), fulfilling the expectation of the faithful who wait for God's son from heaven (1 Thess 1:10).

If this line of interpretation is correct, the view that Paul and much of the early church understood the resurrection as an "event" takes on added significance. The church viewed the resurrection as an aspect of the total event of Jesus Christ. The Christ-event included the life, death, resurrection, and appearances of Christ. The kerygma of Paul and the church before him probably contained two basic elements:

> Christ died and was buried,
> Christ was raised and appeared.[43]

The appearances belong with the resurrection and are essential to the total redemptive event of Jesus Christ.[44]

In connection with the total redemptive event of Jesus Christ, the Lukan doctrine of the ascension and the Pauline recognition of the limitation of appearances intersect. Luke, in his typical historicizing fashion, presented the total event as literal history—from the baptism of John, through the crucifixion, to the resurrection confirmed by earthly appearances and terminated by bodily ascension. Paul, accepting an older idea of Christ's exaltation to heaven by means of the resurrection, understood the appearances as perception of the accomplished vindication of the crucified one. Paul, of course, did not limit the time span of the redemptive event in terms of Luke's forty days concluding with ascension, but he did insist that the Christ-event had historical limits, that resurrection appearances did not continue indefinitely. To say that the resurrection was an "event," however, does not mean that the early church consistently understood it as an objective happening, factual and provable in nature. Although Luke believed that the resurrection could be attested by "many proofs" (Acts 1:3), he also observed that the risen Christ appeared and disappeared, and that he was recognized only by those whose eyes were opened (Lk 24:31). Paul, on the other hand, made it clear that the resurrection was a unique event, and that the "object" of the appearances was a transformed reality, the "spiritual body" (1 Cor 15:44). Nevertheless, Paul and Luke appear to agree on a significant theological point: the resurrection appearances belonged to the Christ-event. If this understanding of the appearances is valid, then the faith of subsequent Christians is dependent upon witnesses who have historical priority and whose witness is essential to an understanding of the decisive Christ-event.

NOTES

1. "in the context of late legend." Hans Grass, *Ostergeschehen und Osterberichte* (Göttingen: Vandenhoeck & Ruprecht, 1956) 50. See Rudolf Bultmann, *The History of the Synoptic Tradition* (New York/Evanston: Harper & Row, 1963) 290.
2. C. Freeman Sleeper, "Pentecost and Resurrection," *JBL* 84 (1965) 396.
3. Gerhard Lohfink, *Die Himmelfahrt Jesu* (Munich: Kösel, 1971).
4. "For Luke the ascension of Jesus is a bodily translation." *Ibid.,* 75.
5. "Nowhere does one find even the slightest indication of a visible ascension or a physical translation, as we know it from Luke....Resurrection and exaltation, rather, form an inner unity." *Ibid.,* 95. Eduard Schweizer, *Lordship and Discipleship*, SBT 28 (Naperville: Allenson, 1960) 38: "That the exaltation of Jesus really dominated the thought of the early Church is also shown by the fact that the oldest tradition barely distinguishes between Easter and Ascension."
6. See, for example, Amos N. Wilder, "Variant Traditions of the Resurrection in Acts," *JBL* 62 (1943) 307-18. Lohfink's position has been supported by Ernst Haenchen, *The Acts of the Apostles* (Philadelphia: Westminster, 1971) 145-46.
7. Grass, 43-51.
8. P. A. van Stempvoort, "The Interpretation of the Ascension in Luke and Acts," *NTS* 5 (1958-59) 30-42.
9. This conclusion, of course, is not universally accepted. J. G. Davies, *He Ascended into Heaven* (London: Lutterworth, 1958) argued that the ascension is implied in some of the texts discussed above and believed the doctrine of the ascension is important for christology and the idea of redemption. Davies, however, was influenced by later doctrinal developments, and his work lacks historical-critical precision.
10. For the importance of this text for the development of the idea of exaltation, see David M. Hay, *Glory at the Right Hand*, SBLMS 18 (Nashville/New York: Abingdon, 1973).
11. "the structuring of the exaltation into history." Lohfink, 248.
12. Some scholars have supported the idea of an early (pre-Lukan) ascension or assumption tradition. For example, James M. Robinson, "Ascension" *IDB* 1.245-47, saw the ascension as related to the early confession of Jesus as Son of man and that it was already assumed by the opponents of Paul. Reginald H. Fuller, *The Formation of the Resurrection Narratives* (New York: Macmillan, 1971) 129, has written that "there was a very primitive kerygmatic affirmation...that he was assumed into heaven."
13. Hans Conzelmann, *The Theology of St. Luke* (New York: Harper, 1960) 204.

14. The same idea has been expressed by Helmut Flender, *St. Luke: Theologian of Redemptive History* (Philadelphia: Fortress, 1967) 11.

15. See Charles H. Talbert, "An Anti-Gnostic Tendency in Lucan Christology," *NTS* 14 (1968) 259-71, and his *Luke and the Gnostics* (Nashville/New York: Abingdon, 1966) 30.

16. S. G. Wilson, "The Ascension: A Critique and an Interpretation," *ZNW* 59 (1968) 269-81, argued that Luke was struggling against two opposing views: that the end had already come; that the *parousia* would not come at all. Eric Franklin, *Christ the Lord* (Philadelphia: Westminster, 1975) 29-41, understood Luke to shift the eschatological emphasis from the *parousia* to the ascension. See also the same author's "The Ascension and the Eschatology of Luke-Acts," *SJT* 23 (1970) 191-200.

17. This point has been supported by Kirsopp Lake, "The Ascension," *The Beginnings of Christianity*, ed F. J. Foakes Jackson and Kirsopp Lake (Grand Rapids: Baker, 1966) 16-22, and C. F. D. Moule, "The Ascension—Acts 1.9," *Exp Tim* 68 (1956-57) 205-209. Gottfried Schille, "Die Himmelfahrt," *ZNW* 57 (1966) 193, argued (unconvincingly) that Luke's account of the ascension is "eine Kultätiologie für eine Versammlung der Jerusalemer Gemeinde auf dem Ölberg am 40. Tag nach dem Passa...bei welcher man der Himmelfahrt Christi gedachte."

18. Joachim Jeremias, *The Eucharistic Words of Jesus* (Oxford: Blackwell, 1955) attempted to demonstrate that the original tradition was semitic. This view has been refuted by Hans Conzelmann, *1 Corinthians* (Philadelphia: Fortress, 1975) 252-53.

19. The arguments have been well summarized by C. F. Evans, *Resurrection and the New Testament*, SBT, 2d Series 12 (Naperville: Allenson, 1970) 44-46.

20. This view has been supported by Jeremias, *Eucharistic Words*, 129-30, and Hans Conzelmann, "On the Anaylsis of the Confessional Formula in I Corinthians 15:3-5," *Int* 20 (1966) 15-25.

21. See Ulrich Wilckens, "The Tradition-History of the Resurrection of Jesus," *The Significance of the Message of the Resurrection for Faith in Jesus Christ*, ed C. F. D. Moule, SBT, 2d Series 8 (Naperville: Allenson, 1968) 51-76.

22. This older view of Harnack has been more recently developed with variations by Ernst Bammel, "Herkunft und Funktion der Traditionselemente in 1. Kor. 15,1-11," *TZ* 11 (1955) 401-19.

23. Paul Winter, "I Corinthians XV 3b-7," *NovT* 2 (1957) 142-50.

24. See Conzelmann, "On the Analysis of the Confessional Formula in I Corinthians 15:3-5," 23: C. K. Barrett, *The First Epistle to the Corinthians*, HNTC (New York/Evanston: Harper & Row, 1968) 344; Fuller, 12-13.

25. The older view of von Dobschütz has been taken up more recently by S. MacLean Gilmour, "The Christophany to More than Five Hundred Brethren." *JBL* 80 (1961) 248-52.

26. Evans, 55: "Thus, in Paul there is no hint, when he places the appearance to himself alongside those to others, or when he defends his apostleship on the grounds that he had 'seen' the Lord (1 Cor. 9.1) that there was any difference in kind between these appearances to others and that to himself; or, conversely, that he understood the

appearances to others in any other way than he understood his own."
See Fuller, 43.

27. Wilhelm Michaelis, *TDNT* 5. 358.

28. Albrecht Oepke, *TDNT* 3. 577.

29. See Willi Marxsen, *The Resurrection of Jesus of Nazareth* (Philadelphia: Fortress, 1970) 101-102.

30. See Rudolf Bultmann, *Der zweite Brief an die Korinther,* ed Erich Dinkler, MeyerK (Göttingen: Vandenhoeck & Ruprecht, 1976) 111; C. K. Barrett, *The Second Epistle to the Corinthians,* HNTC (New York/Evanston: Harper & Row, 1973) 135.

31. Fuller, 20-21, has refuted Grass's argument that Paul's presentation of the resurrection of Christians cannot be used to interpret Paul's understanding of the resurrection of Christ.

32. Main arguments have been briefly summarized by Conzelmann, *1 Corinthians,* 283.

33. Joachim Jeremias, " 'Flesh and Blood Cannot Inherit the Kingdom of God' (1 Cor 15:50)," *NTS* 2 (1955-56) 151-59, argued that this verse does not refer to the resurrection body, but to the transformation of those who will be alive at the *parousia.* Nevertheless, since both living and dead are to be changed, both are apparently transformed into a body which is not composed of flesh and blood.

34. See E. Schweizer, *TDNT,* 6. 421.

35. See Wilhelm Michaelis, *Die Erscheinungen des Auferstandenen* (Basel: Heinrich Majer, 1944) 97-100.

36. Grass, 248. Fuller, 49, preferred to define the appearances as "revelatory encounters," and John E. Alsup, *The Post-Resurrection Appearance Stories of the Gospel Tradition* (Stuttgart: Calwer, 1975) 271, observed the problem of describing "an event without parallel in human history."

37. Norman Perrin, *The Resurrection* (Philadelphia: Fortress, 1977) 72.

38. Barrett, *First Corinthians,* 344, considered and rejected this possibility.

39. Hans von Campenhausen, "The Events of Easter and the Empty Tomb," *Tradition and Life in the Church* (Philadelphia: Fortress, 1968) 54. This position has also been supported by Conzelmann, *1 Corinthians,* 259; Grass, 105; Fuller, 43.

40. Conzelmann, *1 Corinthians,* 259, has presented a succinct summary of the issues. See also Thorleif Boman, "Paulus abortivus (1. Kor. 15, 8)," *ST* 18 (1964) 46-50.

41. It is possible, of course, to construe Acts 22:17-18 as an account of a later resurrection appearance to Paul, but the description of the vision as occurring while Paul was in a trance *(en ekstasei)* seems more in harmony with the author's typical interest in ecstatic disclosures (10:10; 11:15). We can probably agree with Michaelis, 25, that "weder aus der Apostelgeschichte noch aus den Paulusbreifen etwas bekannt ist über Erscheinungen, die noch nach der Erscheinung vor Damaskus stattgefunden hätten." ("...neither from the Acts of the Apostles nor from the letters of Paul is anything known concerning appearances which took place after the appearance on the road to Damascus.")

42. Although there are a few exceptions (Acts 14:4, 14), "the apostles" in Acts are virtually identical with "the Twelve."

43. See Conzelmann, "On the Analysis of the Confessional Formula in I Corinthians 15:3-5," 15-25.

44. Fuller, 49: "The appearances occurred over a period of some three years or so, the last and definitive one being that to Paul. As such, they belong to the *eph' hapax* of the Christ event."

Medical Imagery in the Pastoral Epistles

Abraham J. Malherbe

The author of the Pastoral Epistles made frequent use of the language of health and disease in polemic leveled at false teachers and their followers. The expressions "sound (healthy) teaching" (1 Tim 1:10; 2 Tim 4:3; Tit 1:9; 2:1), "sound words" (1 Tim 6:3; 2 Tim 1:13; Tit 2:8), and being "sound in the faith" (Tit 1:13; 2:2) appear in the New Testament only in the Pastorals and represent a major theme of the letters, viz., that orthodox teaching alone issues in a moral life. The entire complex of medical terminology in the letters, however, has not received extensive treatment. Commentators have occasionally discussed "sound teaching" *et al.* in brief excursuses, but they have not placed the use of these terms firmly in either their suspected philosophical context or in the argument of the letters themselves.

The use of "sound teaching" *et al.* in the Pastorals presented further evidence to Martin Dibelius that Paul was not their author.[1] The singular use of these terms in the Pastorals, he insisted, could not be explained either as a new designation for the gospel by Paul in his old age or as new terms coined to fight the heresy at hand. The use of the term was as old as Homer and common in the philosophical literature of the author's time. But this terminology should be understood in the contemporary philosophical sense in which it designated rational speech and not in the original poetic sense according to which it would describe the power of the gospel to bring healing and life. While rationality was not a basic part of the structure of Paul's thinking, Dibelius detected "some shifts toward rationalism" in the Pastoral Epistles. The gospel, an established part of the church's teaching, is a rational criterion which can be applied.

Subsequent discussion has generally addressed the issues as identified by Dibelius. Some support has emerged for his claim that the terms were derived from the philosophers referring to the teaching of a rational moral life, but not to teaching whose goal is the health of the soul.[2]

Wilhelm Michaelis, however, rejected Dibelius' position and insisted that the terms should not be understood in a philosophical sense but in the context of a polemic against heresy.[3] On this reading, the teaching is described as sound, not because it is rational or makes the readers or hearers spiritually healthy, but because it is free from the disease of heresy. Such usage was not intended in a philosophical sense.

A mediating position was presented by Ulrich Luck, who with Dibelius insisted that the terminology could be understood only against the Greek-Hellenistic background, but for him that background is not specifically philosophical but represents the "average understanding." We thus have to do, not with a philosophical rationalism, but with "the logical relating of faith and teaching to rational existence in the world." Traditional teaching, in contrast to perverted doctrine, is concerned with "rational and proper life in the world, which as creation is characterised by order and reason."[4] It does not refer to teaching which seeks to make its hearers whole.

The way non-Christian material has been utilized to illuminate the use of the terminology in the Pastorals is unsatisfactory. Dibelius did little more than list some parallels, and Luck did not clearly relate his discussion of the Pastorals to what he considered to be their background. Michaelis and Jeremias did not treat the pagan material at all. Ceslaus Spicq, while citing many parallels indicating that the terminology was not unusual in antiquity, did not present a unified picture that helps in understanding the language.[5] And Robert J. Karris, although he assiduously gathered parallels from ancient philosophers to support his thesis that the anti-heretical polemic of the Pastorals was indebted to the philosophers' attacks on sophists, studiously avoided dealing with the terms describing health and disease.[6]

In order to make any advance in understanding the function of these terms in the Pastorals, all the terms describing health and disease will be considered. Inquiry will be made into the conceptual framework of the Pastorals in which the terminology may fit, and then, in light of these findings, non-Christian material will be investigated for any contribution it may make to understanding the Pastorals' imagery. It is methodologically proper to begin with the assumption that the Pastorals were addressing either an actual situation or one that would be readily recognizable to their readers. Since the language of health and disease was used in the polemic against false teachers, it is reasonable to assume that a particular type of opponent was in view and that it may be possible to sketch a picture of the author's perception of this type.

In using the terminology of health and disease, the author of the Pastorals revealed an understanding of the nature of the church's teaching and also characterized those who opposed it or did not hold to it. On the positive side, the sound words are thought to form a pattern and to have been received from Paul (2 Tim 1:13). Such sound teaching cannot be censured (Tit 2:7). Instruction is given in it, and those who oppose it are reproved so that they might be sound in the faith (Tit 1:9, 13; cf 2:2). It is not said that sound teaching makes its recipient sound; at most that is an inference that may be drawn from these latter statements.

The author was much more explicit in using the terminology polemically to describe the heretics. In using the language of health and disease, the intention was not so much to describe the content of the heretics' teaching as their demeanor and its causes and results. The details about the heretics given in passages containing medical terminology are echoed and sometimes amplified in other polemical passages in the letters which do not employ such terminology. These details are, therefore, not isolated bits of polemic, but form, in the author's perception, major features of the character as well as preaching method of those opposed. In its salient points, the exhortation of the author, frequently in explicitly antithetic form, urges the readers to the exact opposite mien and method, making it clear that the author was operating with a distinct type of person in mind who was to be shunned. The characterization of that type is vivid and polemical.

To begin with, the person who does not adhere to the sound teachings knows nothing (1 Tim 6:4). This theme of obtuseness runs throughout the letters. The heretics' mind and conscience are defiled (Tit 1:15), their conscience is seared or cauterized (1 Tim 4:2), they fall into many senseless lusts (1 Tim 6:9), their controversies are stupid and uninstructed (2 Tim 2:23; Tit 3:9). Those who listen to them and whom they capture are silly little women who are forever trying to learn but never come to a knowledge of the truth (2 Tim 3:7). In contrast to the heretics, the orthodox do have knowledge and understanding (1 Tim 1:7f; 4:3). By applying their minds to what is written by the Apostle, they will receive understanding from the Lord (2 Tim 2:7; cf. 1 Tim 3:15). In other words, their knowledge is derived from tradition and Scripture (2 Tim 3:14ff; cf 2:2; Tit 1:9), and as the grace of God had appeared to instruct them (Tit 2:11f), so the servant of God instructs his opponents with gentleness (2 Tim 2:25).

The intellectual condition of the heretics is so wretched that, in contrast to the soundness of orthodox teachings, it can be said that

they are diseased (1 Tim 6:4).[7] Their minds are corrupt
(*diephtharmenōn...ton noun*) (1 Tim 6:5; cf. 2 Tim 3:8) and defiled
(Tit 1:15), and the teaching they produce will eat its way in their
hearers like gangrene (2 Tim 2:17). Their diseased condition is
exhibited in their demeanor, in their preoccupation with controversies, verbal battles, and wranglings (1 Tim 6:4f) which are
unprofitable and useless (2 Tim 2:14; Tit 3:9). Their harsh,
bellicose, and misanthropic bearing is reflected in other descriptions of them in the letters, especially by the antisocial vices listed
in 2 Tim 3:2-4; they are proud, arrogant, abusive (cf. 1 Tim 6:4),
disobedient to their parents (cf. Tit 1:16), ungrateful, inhuman,
slanderers, fierce, haters of good, treacherous, reckless, swollen
with conceit. Futhermore, they are insubordinate (Tit 1:10), given
to strife (1 Tim 6:4; Tit 3:9), and factious (Tit 3:10).

The contrasting qualities and actions that should characterize the
readers, given in the form of exhortations and in lists of qualifications of various functionaries, frequently in antithetic form, serve
to further delineate the heretical type who is to be avoided. The
readers should avoid useless verbal battles (2 Tim 2:14; Tit 3:2, 9;
cf. 1 Tim 3:3, 23f) and stupid and uninstructed controversies,[8] and
should not be swollen with conceit (1 Tim 3:6), or be arrogant (1
Tim 6:17), quick-tempered; or violent (1 Tim 2:8; 3:3, Tit 1:7). They
are to abuse and slander no one (1 Tim 3:11; Tit 2:3; 3:2), but are to
be gentle to all (2 Tim 2:24; cf. 1 Tim 3:3; 6:11; Tit 3:2), especially in
their instruction (2 Tim 2:25; Tit 3:2), showing all patience (2 Tim
4:2).

The terms describing the preaching and pastoral care of the
orthodox distinguish them from their opponents: they are to preach
(2 Tim 4:2) and speak what befits sound doctrine (Tit 2:1; cf. 15)
and are to charge (1 Tim 1:3; 4:11; 5:7; 6:17), instruct (1 Tim 4:6, 11,
16; Tit 3:14; cf. 1 Tim 3:3, Tit 1:9), correct (Tit 1:5), and remind (2
Tim 2:14) others. They should be careful in chastising those within
the community (1 Tim 5:1; cf. 19, 22), and should rather exhort (1
Tim 5:1; 6:2; 2 Tim 4:2; Tit 1:9; 2:6) and honor (1 Tim 5:3, 17) them.
Only seldom are they commanded to engage in censure (2 Tim
4:20) and severe rebuke, harsh treatments reserved primarily for
those who persist in sin (1 Tim 5:20; cf. 2 Tim 4:2; Tit 2:15) and for
the heretics (Tit 1:9, 13) who must be silenced (Tit 1:11). The
evangelists are to present themselves as examples in their speech
and conduct, in love, faith, and purity (1 Tim 4:12), which requires
that they constantly give attention to their own progress in the
Christian virtues (e.g., 1 Tim 4:12-16; 5:22; 6:11-14; 2 Tim 2:1-8, 22;
3:10, 14; 4:5, 15).

All Christians should strive to live quiet and peaceable lives, godly and respectful in every way (1 Tim 2:2). This demeanor is the exact opposite to that which characterized them once, when they themselves were foolish, disobedient, passing their days in malice and envy, hated by men and hating one another. All that was changed when the goodness and loving kindness of God the Savior appeared (Tit 3:3f).

In addition to the diseased condition that they create in their hearers, the heretics through their harsh verbal battles produce the antisocial vices of envy, strife, slander, and base suspicions, which are summarized as the frictional wranglings of people corrupt in mind (1 Tim 6:4f).[9] They subvert entire households (Tit 1:11; cf. 2 Tim 3:6). But all vice is contrary to sound doctrine (1 Tim 1:10).[10] They have in mind not the good of the people they preach to, but their own gain (1 Tim 6:5-10; cf. Tit 1:11). In contrast, the sound teaching has the life of the orthodox as an ordered community in view. The social responsibilities in which that community is instructed are tantamount to the sound teaching (1 Tim 6:1-3; Tit 2:1-10), and the behavior inculcated further has in view the approval of the Christian community by the larger society (Tit 2:5, 8, 10; cf. 1 Tim 3:7). High value is placed on the home and the instruction that goes on in it (e.g., 1 Tim 2:15; 3:4f, 12; 4:3; 5:1-4, 14-16; 2 Tim 1:5, Tit 1:6), and when the church's leaders are to confront the heretics, it is to stop them from upsetting households (Tit 1:9ff). The teaching of the orthodox always has in mind the benefit of their hearers, never their own profit (e.g., 2 Tim 2:24-26; 1 Tim 1:20f).

The heretics are received by people who do not endure sound teaching,[11] but who in keeping with their own irrational lusts accumulate teachers for themselves who will merely tickle their ears *(knēthomenoi tēn akoēn)* (2 Tim 4:3).[12] Among them are the silly little women who are incapable of grasping the knowledge of the truth (2 Tim 3:7). It is among such people that their teaching will eat its way like gangrene (2 Tim 2:17).

In sum, the author's use of the medical images is part of his overall perception of the heretics. The author describes them as intellectually inferior, having diseased minds which produce violent preaching and contaminate those who accept their teaching. They are antisocial and upset the social order by their preaching. They are motivated to preach by their hope of financial gain. Those who welcome them are likewise intellectually and morally inferior and are infected by them. Contrasted to the heretics are the orthodox who have knowledge and hold to sound teaching, who are generally mild in their own teaching, yet know to be severe when the occasion demands severity, who are socially responsible, who give constant attention to their own moral progress, and always have the benefit of others at heart.

When the historical and social setting of the Pastorals is considered, a certain group of teachers, well known in the early Empire, fits well the description noted above. Among the many kinds of philosophers who wandered about was a group, Cynics of a particular type, who were distinguished for the severity with which they delivered their message. They held a strange fascination for those who heard them, meeting with both acceptance and repulsion. Cor.temporary writers used the medical metaphor and images of the Pastorals in discussing the teaching of philosophers in general, but the language was particularly used in connection with rigoristic Cynics and the questions they raised about the nature of the true philosopher's *parrēsia,* that frankness of speech used in attempting to cure people of their moral illness.

The description of human vices and passions as diseases was widespread, but was especially used by Stoics and Cynics. Stoics, as was their wont, engaged in minute subdivision and definition of the passions as diseases and identified the degrees to which the soul might be subject to them.[13] The soul, they held, might be in a state of war, with its passions and diseases prevailing over its healthy (rational) principles *(tous hygiainontas logous).*[14] When passion in the soul rages savagely and produces itchings and ticklings which arise from lust and indulgence *(knēsmous kai gargalismous ex hēdonēs kai epithumias),*[15] it is cured by drugs, and if some vice spreads *(epinemomenē)* like festering shingles, it is incised with professional skill with the instrument of sharp reason *(logō tomē to kat' epistēmēn temnetai).*[16] After reason has rid the soul of its disease, reason remains in the soul.[17] Such therapy cannot be brought about by eloquence or a specious *parrēsia* which is not genuine or beneficial *(ōphelimon),* but merely tickles.[18] The person who is aware of moral illness should seek and welcome effective treatment. "Why do you tickle my ears?" asks Seneca, "Why do you entertain me? There is other business at hand; I am to be cauterized, operated upon, or put on a diet. That is why you were summoned to treat me!" *(Epistle* 75.6f)

Since philosophy was viewed as intended to cure vices and lead to virtue, it is natural that the philosopher was described as a physician of the soul whose teaching was the means by which the cure was effected.[19] The widespread use of such medical terminology and imagery is not surprising since philosophers (and sophists) were in fact closely related to physicians.[20] The description of the philosopher as a physician became most common among the Stoics and Cynics, although it was by no means confined to them.[21] The

Stoics Seneca, [22] Musonius, [23] and Epictetus[24] frequently made use of the comparison. As the quotation from Seneca reveals, Stoics expected that the philosopher-physician's treatment might need to be severe: not only drugs and diet, but the knife and cautery might need to be used. Epictetus held the same view.[25]

Dio Chrysostom permits the clearest insight into how a Stoic philosopher regarded his own exhortation as analogous to the work of a physician.[26] In *Oration* 77/78 Dio justified the philosopher's "fullest frankness" *(pleistē parrēsia)*. A soul is corrupt *(diephtharmenē)* because of the ignorance, depravity, insolence, jealousy, grief, and the countless other lusts *(epithumiai)* that beset it.[27] Such a condition requires surgery, and especially cautery (43). But the philosopher must first begin, and be as unsparing, on himself as on others (45). The philosopher is not to be indiscriminate in severity but as one who is sound *(hygiēs)* in words and deeds, is to adapt his treatment to the condition of the hearers. By sometimes being severe and sometimes gentle, the philosopher hopes thus to rescue others from foolishness, lusts, intemperance, and soft living.[28] The aim is not to cause dissent, greed, strife, jealousies, and desire for base gain, but to remind others of sobriety and righteousness and to promote concord (38f). The Stoic philosopher-physician is thus concerned with the virtue of individuals, yet takes special care to contrast antisocial vices with social virtues.

The social dimension of instruction in virtue was elaborated by Dio in *Oration* 32, where the medical metaphor was extended to apply to political officials. For the vices, Dio said, the gods have prepared one remedy and cure, namely, education and reason, and a person who employs this remedy throughout life arrives at last at a healthy and happy end (16).[29] The most depraved flee furthest from reason as the most inflamed sore shrinks from touch. Their treatment will need be the most drastic. The treatment of vice and its prevention is twofold. The one treatment may be likened to dieting and drugs and is applied by philosophers who, through persuasion and reason, calm and make the soul gentle, and who are the saviors of those who can be saved by confining and controlling vice before it reaches its final stage. The severity of their speech saves. The other treatment may be likened to surgery and cautery and is practiced by rulers, laws, and magistrates, who remove what is abnormal and incurable. They are to be milder than the philosophers, for one should be sparing in meting out punishment, but not in imparting instruction (17-18). Dio appears to have had difficulty with his metaphors as cautery and surgery, the more severe treatments, ought to belong to the philosophers, if they are the more severe, while dieting and drugs would be the method of the milder officials.[30] In any case, what is to be noted is that the metaphors are used of instruction in virtue within the social order and that there is a stress on the need for different degrees of severity corresponding to the differences in the moral condition of those instructed.[31]

While Dio asserted the need for painful frankness, he had a relatively optimistic view of the human condition which permitted him to adapt his preaching to the condition of his audience.[32] His comparatively rare pessimistic statements on the condition of the masses occur in speeches which show Cynic influence.[33] Stoics in general shared this relatively charitable view of human nature. Musonius, for example, held that humans have a natural disposition toward virtue,[34] and that the majority of wrongs are due to ignorance and misunderstanding which can be overcome by instruction.[35] Epictetus insisted that the philosopher should not be angry at those who err, but should pity them.[36] Such a humane view not only permitted but required that the philosopher temper biting frankness with gentleness.

Some Cynics also viewed human nature in this way. Perhaps in reaction to Cynicism's reputation for harshness, there were those who emphasized that some of its heroes had been gentle in demeanor. Indeed, a milder strain of Cynics can be identified at least as early as Crates.[37] The major representative of this type under the Empire known to us was Demonax who, according to Lucian, was kind, gentle, and cheerful, was everybody's friend, and avoided only those whose error placed them beyond the hope of cure.[38]

More important, however, is the larger company of Cynics, considered more typical of Cynicism in the popular mind, who were not sociable or gentle. Cynics of this type scoffed at the masses[39] and insisted that, since the masses were ignorant, they could not be friends of the philosopher.[40] The true Cynic was an avowed hater of mankind and withdrew from society.[41] While medical metaphors were used by all types of Cynics,[42] our particular interest is that group of stern Cynics.

These Cynics held that it was by virtue alone that the soul could be purified of its diseases and that it was the Cynic who was the physician who could bring about the cure.[43] The human condition was so corrupt that only the most painful treatment, the severest parrēsia, could avail. The letters ascribed to Diogenes illustrate the attitude and manner of preaching. *Epistle* 28 was a severe condemnation of Greek civilization directed at Sinope.[44] Diogenes called their laws the greatest delusion, and excoriated them for doing nothing by sound reason *(hygiē logō)*. By their ignorance and senselessness they had become a mockery, and Diogenes and nature hated them. Diogenes punished them in word, nature did so in deed. They legislated and educated, but to no avail. They were tickled by pleasure *(egargalisthēte hyp' hēdonēs)*. If they continued to indulge themselves, Diogenes warned, the judges elected by the people, whom they called physicians (!), would treat them. They would cut and cauterize and prescribe drugs for the people, but would not be thanked for their ministrations. As for himself, Diogenes would associate only with those who knew his Cynic worth. He would be like Antisthenes, who spoke only with those who knew him, and avoided those who knew neither nature, reason, or truth.

Epistle 29, addressed to Dionysius, tyrant of Sicily, likewise found justification for the Cynic's harshness and antisocial attitude in the putrid condition of society.[45] Diogenes threatened to send Dionysius a hard taskmaster (a Cynic) who would purge him. The tyrant needed someone with a whip, not someone who would flatter him. His disease *(diaphthora)* was far gone, and required surgery, cautery, and medication for healing. Instead, Dionysius had brought in grandparents and wet nurses! The author seemed to be polemicizing against those philosophers who saw the need for occasional gentleness in preaching.

The antisocial Cynics did not, of course, withdraw from society, but lambasted it with unrelenting intensity. That they found audiences at all who would listen to them may be surprising, for the harsh treatment the mobs accorded philosophers in general was frequently recorded.[46] The fact, however, that the descriptions of mob-reaction frequently came from philosophers or professional teachers, persons never quite satisfied with the adulation they deserved, should warn of the hazard of overstressing the animosity with which they were regarded.[47] The moral philosophers obviously did meet certain needs or there would not have been as many of them as there were.[48] And, it was not only those of high moral purpose who were accorded a hearing. Lucian provided ample evidence that, although the wandering preachers did not always have motives and demeanor of the purest kind, they nevertheless had little difficulty in securing an audience. This was also, perhaps especially, true of both those Cynics who had a genuinely pessimistic view of mankind and adopted a correspondingly harsh style of preaching, and of those charlatans who effected such a Cynic style as a cover for their true designs.

Lucian provides the best source for the sharp reaction that such preachers caused. His polemic was explicit and attached itself to the medical images that were in vogue. He was familiar with the metaphors of surgery and cautery as applying to the philosopher's speech and with the description of the philosopher as a healer of the passions.[49] In his polemic against the vagabond preachers he repeatedly mentioned the attraction they had for the masses. In *Philosophies for Sale,* Lucian described the work of the Cynic through the mouth of one such physician of men's ills (8). The man claimed that the Cynic should be impudent, bold, and abuse everyone, for then the people would admire him and consider him manly. Education was altogether unnecessary (10f). Elsewhere Lucian likewise observed that people tolerated the outspokenness of such preachers, delighted in their therapy, and cowered under their censure.[50] Particularly the common, simple people, especially those who had nothing more pressing to do, admired such preachers for their abusiveness.[51] Despite their flailing of others, these preachers themselves were immoral and greedy. The masses, however, were reticent to speak against them, both out of fear and because such preachers were thought to be superior persons by virtue of their belligerence.[52] In his inimitable way, Lucian sketched what would be the disastrous effect on society of such preachers: industry would grind to a halt.[53] While Lucian thus satirically polemicized against these severe charlatans, he recognized that they did have a considerable following—his reason, in fact, for taking both them and their followers to task.

Lucian did, however, see much in true Cynicism that he admired.[54] That is most clearly evident in his tractate *Demonax*, but it also emerges from the picture he sketched of the Cynic in *The Downward Journey.* In the latter tractate a Cynic, appointed an observer and physician of men's ills (7), was being judged. Although the Cynic had been free-spoken, critical, and censorious (13), Lucian did not find fault with him. In the final judgment scene, the Cynic is told that wickedness leaves marks on the soul which only the judge can see, but there are no such marks on the Cynic. Then Lucian used the image of "searing" in a new way. Though no marks of vice are found on the Cynic, there are many traces of searing (*egkaumatōn*) which somehow or other had been removed. The Cynic explains that he had earned them when in his ignorance he had still been wicked, but that when he began to live the philosophic life, after a while he had washed the scars from his soul (24). For Lucian, then, the searing that comes from vice must be removed before a person presumes to correct others.

Another reaction to the upbraiding of the Cynics can be identified. In a context in which every street preacher asserted his right to *parrēsia,* often conceived as the misanthropic railing of the

Cynic, it was natural that serious philosophers would, on the one hand, distance themselves from such preachers, and on the other, give renewed attention to the nature of the true philosopher's *parrēsia*. It became customary for philosophers to describe either themselves or their heroes in an antithetic manner that would make the differences between themselves and the interlopers clear. This can be seen clearly in Dio Chrysostom as well as in other philosophers.[55] We have also seen that philosophers of higher culture and milder mien, when reflecting on the proper method of teaching, carefully specified how verbal cautery and surgery were to be used.[56] Yet they were equally careful to avoid specious frankness.

Plutarch's tractate *How to Tell a Flatterer from a Friend,* which utilized material from discussions of the philosopher's frankness, illustrates the concern of a serious philosopher.[57] True frankness is like a potent medicine, when it is used with moderation (74D),[58] but flattery, at its most insidious, can take the form of a specious *parrēsia* (61D-62C). The flatterer, Plutarch charged, is himself diseased and in need of prudent remedies (62C) but is not thereby deterred from letting his flattery become a pestilence in society (49C). His "frankness" merely titillates (*knā*) and tickles (*gargalizei*) (cf. 51CD, 61B). It adds nothing to the powers of thinking and reasoning, but caters to pleasure, intensifies irrational temper, and engenders a tumor of conceit (cf. 59E). The flatterer's presence is like a growth in that he always assaults the festering and inflamed conditions of the soul (cf. 59C-60B). In criticism of those who open themselves to this specious frankness, Plutarch warned that its vicious, secret attacks would produce in them an itching sore whose scar would remain even after it healed. Such scars or gangrenes lead to destruction(65CD).[59] These scars caused by vice are evidently what Lucian referred to as searings. Like Lucian, Plutarch did not object to frankness when it was properly applied, but demanded that the person who presumed to speak with boldness be without disease lest the listeners become infected.

Genuine philosophic frankness, according to Plutarch, should be employed for the philosopher's as well as the listeners' improvement and should not be used out of a desire for reputation or out of ambition. Using a different metaphor, he elaborated on the subject in his tractate *Progress in Virtue,* in which he warned against that bellicosity which might be mistaken for frankness. "But most of all must we consider whether the spirit of contention and quarreling over debatable questions (*zētēseis*) has been put down, and whether we have ceased to equip ourselves with arguments, as with boxing gloves or brass knuckles, with which to contend against each other,

and to take more delight in scoring a hit or knockout than in learning and imparting something. For reasonableness and mildness in
such matters, and the ability to join in discussions without wrang-
ling, and to close them without anger, and to avoid a sort of
arrogance over success in argument and exasperation in defeat, are
the marks of a man who is making adequate progress'' (80BC).
Those who are insolent and filled with haughtiness and disdain are
uninstructed in philosophy and will change when they train their
minds, apply their stinging criticism to themselves, and in consequence be milder in their intercourse with others (81BC).

This historical and social context, in which the claims of certain
harsh Cynics to be the healers of diseased humanity brought forth
various responses, demonstrates how the language of health and
disease function in the Pastoral Epistles. Like Lucian, the author
accused harsh opponents of being ignorant, abusive, immoral,
antisocial, and charged that they were received only by the ignorant of whom they took advantage. Into this fairly standard picture of charlatans the description of specious *parrēsia* represented
by Plutarch was woven. Contemporary harsh preachers intoned
their own superiority as physicians and found cause for their
pugnaciousness in the diseased condition of their hearers' minds
and souls. The author of the Pastorals, in rebuttal, accused the
heretics, as Plutarch did the flatterer, with being diseased of mind
and morals. Their verbal battles do not eradicate disease in others,
but are the products of their own disease, and will further infect
those who, with irrational lusts, will listen to them with itching
ears which wait only to be tickled. When the author described the
heretics' consciences as seared, he probably meant that they were
still seared with sin, as had been Lucian's Cynic before his conversion to philosophy. Therefore, he implied, they were in no condition to heal others. In light of the popularity of the metaphor of
cautery, however, his use of the image might perhaps have had an
added barb: not only were they themselves still seared by sin, their
sinful condition was so extreme that their own consciences had
been cauterized.

The use of the medical imagery in the Pastorals is thoroughly
polemical. There is no picture, as in the moral philosophers, of the
intellectually and morally ill person who will be cured by reason
through the application of the drugs, surgery, and cautery of
parrēsia. While it is affirmed that the orthodox do have understanding, it was not the rationality of the sound teaching that made them
so, but rather the apostolic tradition. That the ''sound words'' may
bring about health of soul is an inference the reader may be temp-
ted to draw, but it is not part of the function to which the images

are put. That function is polemical.

The contrasting picture of the orthodox teacher as gentle and mild, knowing when to be severe, concerned with personal moral progress, who preached to benefit others, and who promoted social stability, is similar to that sketched by Dio Chrysostom of himself and the ideal philosopher in antithesis to misanthropic, antisocial Cynics. This presentation of the Christian teacher is in harmony with the overall tendency of the Pastoral Epistles to present Christianity as a responsible part of society.

That the author of the Pastorals made use of such typical descriptions does not compel us to conclude that they were not applicable to actual situations confronted. Dibelius was correct in his insistence that the language with which we have been concerned be understood as it would have been by the original readers. Those readers would not only have recognized the language, but the types as well. They could see and hear them in the streets. The literary and polemical traditions we have traced developed in and found application to actual situations. In the absence of compelling reasons to believe the contrary, we would hold the same to be true for the Pastoral Epistles.

NOTES

1. Martin Dibelius and Hans Conzelmann, *The Pastoral Epistles* (Hermeneia; Philadelphia: Fortress, 1972) 29f.
2. E.g., B. S. Easton, *The Pastoral Epistles* (New York: Scribner's, 1947) 234; J. N. D. Kelly, *A Commentary on the Pastoral Epistles* (HNTC; New York: Harper and Row, 1963) 50.
3. W. Michaelis, *Pastoralbriefe und Gefangenschaftsbriefe: Zur Echtheitsfrage der Pastoralbriefe* (Neutestamentliche Forschungen, Erste Reihe, 6; Gütersloh; "Der Rufer" Evangelischer Verlag, 1930) 79-85. N. Brox, *Die Pastoralbriefe* (RNT; 4th ed; Regensburg: Verlag Friedrich Pustet, 1969) 39f, 107f, mentions neither Dibelius nor Michaelis in this context, but represents the latter's view, as does J. Jeremias, *Die Briefe an Timotheus und Titus* (NTD 9; 11th ed; Göttingen: Vandenhoeck und Ruprecht, 1975) 14f.
4. U. Luck, *TDNT* 8 (1972) 312.
5. C. Spicq, *Les épitres pastorales* (EBib; 4th ed; Paris: Gabalda, 1969) 115-117.
6. Robert J. Karris, "The Function and Sitz im Leben of the Paraenetic Elements in the Pastoral Epistles" (Th.D diss., Harvard Divinity School, 1971) and a summary of the first part of the dissertation published as "The Background and Significance of the Polemic of the Pastoral Epistles," *JBL* 92 (1973) 549-64.
7. *tetyphōtai, mēden epistamenos, alla nosōn.* The combination of *typhoō* with words describing the cognitive element in man is common in the literature. Cf. Lucian, *Nigrinus* 1, *anoētos te kai tetyphōmenos;* Polybius 3. 81. 1, *agnoei kai tetyphōtai.* Epictetus was aware that one's great power of argumentation and persuasive reasoning may be an excuse for *typhos* (1. 8. 6f) and it is understandable why, as Julian (*Or* 6 197D)

says, that true philosophers were called *tetyphōmenoi*. The word could also mean to be mentally ill, demented. See Demosthenes, *Or* 9. 20, where it is contrasted with being in one's right senses (*hygiainein*). Plutarch (*Progress in Virtue* 81F) cautions the young man that as he lays firmer hold on reason he will lay aside *typhos,* and he then goes on to expand a medical metaphor. In this light, it is quite likely that *tetyphōtai* in 1 Tim 6:4 is intended to describe mental illness, and that *mēden epistamenos, alla nosōn peri zētēseis* is a further specification of the condition. Cf. Theophylact (PG 125, 77), who, in commenting on the passage, thought that ignorance causes delusion, which he interpreted as a tumor of a diseased soul.

8. For the theme of avoiding the heretics, see further 1 Tim 4:7; 6:11; 2 Tim 2:16.

9. *Diaparatribai* ("frictional wranglings") clearly describes friction. See Polybius 2. 36. 5, *en hypopsiais ēn pros allēlous kai paratribais,* and cf. Athenaeus 14 626E and other references in L.-S.-J., *s. v. paratribē.* Chrysostom (*PG* 62, 392) proposes an alternative explanation: The heretics are like scab-covered sheep which infect the healthy sheep when they rub against them. He thus seems to think that *paratribē* is in some way related to *paratrimma,* which is used by medical writers of (infected?) abrasions. Cf. L.-S.-J., *s.v. paratrimma* for references. In view of the other medical terminology in the passage, the fact that *diaphtheirō* ("corrupt") is also used in a medical sense (see L.-S.-J., *s.v. diaphtheirō, phtheirō,* and see below for the use by Dio Chrysostom and ps-Diogenes), and the analogous view in 2 Tim 2:17, the interpretation is not improbable, despite the caution of Dibelius-Conzelmann, *The Pastoral Epistles,* 82 n.3.

10. The unique formulation of 1 Tim 1:10, *kai ei ti heteron tē hygiainousē didaskalia antikeitai,* should not be overstressed. In function it is not different from such endings to vice lists as *kai ta homoia* (Gal 5:21) and *ta toiauta* (Rom 1:32; 2:3), used to indicate that the list is not all-inclusive. Cf. Gal 5:24, *kata tōn toioutōn ouk estin nomos.* Karris' statement ("The Function and Sitz im Leben", 64), that "no other catalogue of vices employed in Christian writers contains a reference to the 'sound teaching,' " must not include the Pastorals (see 1 Tim 6:4f; Tit 1:9f, and cf. 2 Tim 4:3f).

11. The conjecture by Price (recorded in the Nestle-Aland apparatus), that *anthexontai* should be read for *anexontai* is attractive in light of Tit 1:9, but the latter reading is perfectly intelligible in the context. Cf. Dio Chrysostom, *Or* 33. 15f: Man's ears are dainty when reared on flattery and lies; they cannot endure (*anexesthe*) demanding preaching.

12. "Irrational lusts": The RSV rendering of *epithymias* by "likings" is too mild. The term in Greek philosophy described "the waywardness of man in conflict with his rationality." Cf. F. Buechsel, *TDNT* 3(1965) 169, and see below. The element of irrationality is not absent in the Pastorals. Cf. 1 Tim 6:9, *epithymias pollas anoētous;* 2 Tim 3:6, of the women who learn without coming to knowledge of the truth; Tit 2:12, the divine *paideia* has as its goal the renunciation of worldly *epithymiai;* Tit 3:3, the *anoētoi* were enslaved to their *epithymiai.*

13. See Cicero, *Tusculan Disputations* 4. 10-13, especially 10, 23, 27, 33. Cf. Galen, *De locis affectis* I 3 (VIII 32 Kühn; *SVF* 3, 429); Diogenes Laertius 7. 115 (*SVF* 3, 422); Stobaeus 2. 7. 10 (2, 93, 1-13 W.-H.; *SVF* 3, 421). See I. Hadot, *Seneca und die griechisch-römische Tradition der*

Seelenleitung (Berlin: Walter de Gruyter, 1969) 142ff.

14. Philo, *On Abraham* 223.

15. Cf. 2 Tim 4:3.

16. Philo, *The Worse Attacks the Better* 110. The medical metaphor of the (rational) word as a scalpel is behind Heb 2:12. It is tempting to force 2 Tim 2:17, *ergaten anepaischynton orthotomounta ton logon tes aletheias,* into a medical sense, for example, "a workman unashamed of the word of truth as it cuts straight (correctly)" (?), especially since the medical metaphor is continued in the next verse, *kai ho logos auton hos gangraina nomen hexei.*

17. Musonius, *Fr* 36 (123f Hense); cf. *Ep Pancrat* 3f (137f Hense).

18. Plutarch, *How to Tell a Flatterer from a Friend* 51CD. The medical metaphor is not used in this immediate context, but is applied extensively elsewhere in the tractate where *parresia* is discussed. It is the basic conviction of all moral philosophers that the philosopher and his speech should be beneficial. See, for example, Dio Chrysostom, *Orations* 1. 3f; 32. 2, 5, 12f, 33; 33. 56; Plutarch, *How to Tell a Flatterer from a Friend* 55CD, 68C;Lucian, *Demonax* 63, 66.

19. For references, see S. Dill, *Roman Society from Nero to Marcus Aurelius* (1904; repr. New York: Meridian 1956) 292; K. Holl, "Die schriftstellerische Form des griechischen Heiligenlebens," *Neue Jahrb. f. d. klass. Alt* 19 (1912) 418; G. Bardy, *La conversion au christianisme durant les premiers siécles* (Paris: Aubier, 1949) 75f.

20. Cf. the title of one of the works of the physician Galen: *That the Best Physician Is also a Philosopher,* and see G. W. Bowersock, *Greek Sophists in the Roman Empire* (Oxford: Clarendon, 1969) 19, 59-75, esp. 67f.

21. Once they found their way into the diatribe, medical images were assured of wide usage. See A. Oltramare, *Les origins de la diatribe romaine* (Lausanne: Librairie Payot, 1926) 304 (index), *s.v. Médicin (comparaisons avec le -);* B. P. Wallach, *A History of the Diatribe from Its Origins Up to the First Century B. C. and a Study of the Influence of the Genre Upon Lucretius, III, 830-1094* (Ann Arbor, Mich.: University Microfilms, 1975) 134ff, *passim.* For extensive non-Stoic and -Cynic use of the image of the physician, see, for example, Philo of Larissa, the Skeptic teacher of Cicero, in Stobaeus 2. 7. 2 (2, 39, 19 - 42, 6 W. -H.), Plutarch, who does, however, reflect Stoic ideas on the subject, in *How to Tell a Flatterer from a Friend* 61ff., 73A-D, 74D, and see below in my text.

22. E.g., *Epistles* 22. 1; 27.1; 40. 5; 50. 4; 64. 8; 72. 5f, 94. 24; 95. 29.

23. E.g., 1, 9f; 12, 15ff Hense.

24. E.g., 2. 15. 5; 3. 21. 20; 3. 23. 27f, 30; 3. 25. 7f; *Fr* 19.

25. 3. 22. 72f.

26. Although *Or* 77/78 may be from his Cynic period, it nevertheless shows a milder attitude than that of the type of Cynics with which we shall be concerned. The dating of *Or* 32 to the middle years of Trajan's reign, thus after his Cynic period, proposed by H. von Arnim, *Leben und Werke des Dio von Prusa* (Berlin: Weidmann, 1898) 435-8, is generally accepted. See C. P. Jones, "The Date of Dio of Prusa's Alexandrian Oration," *Historia* 22 (1973) 302-9, for an attempt to place it in the reign of Vespasian, thus before Dio's Cycnic period. In either case, [the oration does not belong to his Cynic period, and in fact shows a definite anti-Cynic bias.

27. Cf. 1 Tim 6:4 and n. 9 above.
28. Cf. 2 Tim 2:23ff.
29. Cf. *Or* 17. 6.
30. For the ruler who practices surgery and cautery like a physician, see Plutarch, *Cato Major* 16.5; Epictetus *Fr* 22.
31. Dio frequently uses the images of surgery and cautery in conection with his own exhortation toward social harmony, and constantly seeks to justify his own severity. Cf. *Or* 33.44; 38. 7; cf. 57. 5. For his persistent use of the image, see J. Oesch, *Die Vergleiche bei Dio* (Diss. Zurich, 1916) 15ff.
32. Cf. *Or* 32. 24-28. See *Or* 13. 13; 17. 2f for his view that the crowd does not do what it knows to be best, and for its ignorance, *Or* 13. 27; 14. 2.
33. Cf. R. Hoistad, *Cynic Hero and Cynic King* (Uppsala, 1948) 169. Dill, *Roman Society* 369, generalizes on the basis of the orations which are influenced by Cynicism.
34. See *Fr* 2 (6ff Hense), and cf. A. C. van Geytenbeek, *Musonius Rufus and Greek Diatribe* (Assen: van Gorcum, 1963) 18, 28ff.
35. *Fr* 10 (56, 3ff Hense).
36. E.g., 1.18. 3, 7ff. But some are impossible to persuade, cf. 2. 15. 13ff.
37. See Abraham J. Malherbe, " 'Gentle as a Nurse': The Cynic Background to I Thess ii," *NovT* 12 (1970) 210f.
38. Lucian, *Demonax* 10.
39. E.g., ps-Hippocrates, *Ep* 17. 26ff, 47ff (301, 304 Hercher).
40. E.g., ps-Socrates, *Ep* 8 (616f Hercher).
41. E.g., ps-Socrates, *Ep* 24 (626 Hercher). On the misanthrophy represented by these letters, see G. A. Gerhard, *Phoinix von Kolophon* (Leipzig-Berlin: Teubner, 1909) 67f, 156ff, 170ff.
42. Antisthenes, already, is said by Diogenes Laertius (6. 4, 6) to have compared a philosopher to a physician. To Diogenes is attributed the statement that he, like a physician, does not spend his time among those who are healthy, but among those who need therapy. See Stobaeus 3. 13. 43 (3, 462, 11-15 W. -H.), and cf. Dio Chrysostom, *Or* 8. 5. For further references, see J. J. Wettstein, *Novum Testamentum Graecum* (1751; repr. Graz: Akademische Druck, 1962) I 358f, on Matt 8. 5. Demonax, according to Lucian (*Demonax* 7), thought that one should pattern oneself after physicians who heal diseases but are not angry at the patients.
43. Cf. ps-Diogenes, *Epp* 27 (241 Hercher); 49 (257f Hercher); ps-Hippocrates, *Ep* 11.7 (293 Hercher).
44. 241-3 Hercher. See Victor E. Emeljanow, *The Letters of Diogenes* (Ann Arbor, Mich.: University Microfilms, 1974) 49, 71f, 136-9; cf. Malherbe, "Gentle as a Nurse," 212 n. 3.
45. 243f Hercher. Cf. ps-Heraclitus, *Epp* 2, 7 (280, 283ff Hercher). For the Cynic debate on whether the true Cynic can associate with rulers, see Ronald F. Hock, "Simon the Shoemaker as an Ideal Cynic," *GRBS* 17 (1976) 41-53.
46. For the reception of the philosophers see L. Friedländer, *Darstellungen aus der Sittengeschichte Roms* (8th ed.; Leipzig: Hirzel, 1910) IV 301ff.
47. See, for example, the endless discussions by such teachers and philosophers on the proper hearing they should receive, e.g., Plutarch, *On Listening to Lectures*; Dio Chrysostom, *Or* 1. 8, 10; 32. 2; 72; Seneca, *Ep* 52. 11ff.

48. Dill, *Roman Society,* 340f; cf. Dio Chrysostom, *Or* 13. 12; 72. 11.
49. Cf. *The Dead Come to Life* 46, 52; *Apology* 2.
50. *The Runaways* 12.
51. *Peregrinus* 18: *The Double Indictment* 11, of Stoics who act in the same manner.
52. *The Runaways* 12; *The Carousal* 12-19; cf. *The Dream* 10f.
53. *The Runaways* 17; cf. *Peregrinus* 18: The wise prefect runs Proteus out of town.
54. See R. Helm, "Lucian und die Philosophenschule," *Neue Jahrb. f. d. klass. Alt.* 9 (1902) 351-69 for what Lucian found attractive in Cynicism.
55. See above and cf. Dio Chrysostom, *Or* 32. 11; 34. 30; 42. 1f; 77/78. 37f; Lucian, *Demonax* 4, 8; Julian, *Or* 6 200BCD. See further, Malherbe, "Gentle as a Nurse."
56. See above and cf. Cicero, *De Officiis* 1. 136.
57. The type of criticism Plutarch applies to the flatterer's supposed frankness is also leveled by the sophist Aristides at the Cynics in *Oration* 46 (2, 398-406 Dindorf), translated into French by A. Boulanger, *Aelius Aristide* (Paris: Anciennes Maisons Thorin et Fontenmoing, 1923) 249-56. The summarizing paraphrase by A. Harnack, *The Mission and Expansion of Christianity in the First Three Centuries* (New York: G. P. Putnam's Sons, 1908) I 500 n. 3, illustrates the parallels between the criticism of harsh Cynics and that of the heretics in the Pastorals: They preach virtue to others but are themselves corrupt, they are avaricious, their outspokenness is in fact maliciousness, they are anti-social and undermine households, etc.
58. Cf. Themistius, *Or* 22 (67, 4-6 Downey-Norman): The *parrēsia* of a true friend is like a physician who uses the proper treatment (drugs instead of cautery and surgery).
59. The comparison with gangrene had already been used by Lucilius, *Fr* 7 Krenkel. Cf. Wallach, *A History of the Diatribe, 276f.*

The Unanswerable Answer:
An Interpretation of Job

James A. Wharton

All the questions of the Book of Job fascinated Stuart Currie: its urgent theological questions about the ways of God and people, detailed questions about the text and its transmission, and the intricate puzzles of its tradition history and redaction. I am also certain he had particular interest in a question that ordinarily goes begging in scholarly discussions of Job. Let us concede that the materials in Job go back to ancient and disparate origins. Grant that at some point an extraordinary human spirit undertook to recast those materials in the form of a series of more or less apposite discourses designed to bring into focus a wide range of questions relating to divine and human justice. Grant further that the work thus achieved has had a complex history of reworking and reformation in transmission in order to reach its present form. Let us concede that some of those who intervened in the text either failed to understand or were inimical to the intentions of the original author.

Granting all that, Stuart Currie would have had, I believe, an inordinate interest in the present, tattered, cluttered book of Job as an entity that has a right to be respected and listened to for its own sake, just as it is. If pressed he might have pointed out, more or less graciously depending on the attitude of his conversation partner, that the present book of Job is the only book of Job we possess. He would have been especially sensitive to the fact that, since the conclusion of its complex history of formation and transmission, Job has functioned in the life of the Jewish and Christian communities as a word of address, the word of God to his people. Even if one did not share that faith, one should recognize that the book as it is represents a unique and complete literary *datum*, a *de facto* entity that has a right to be heard and interpreted on its own terms.

Other studies are unquestionably important but *subsidiary* studies made in the interest of clarifying "why the text is as it is and not some other way." They are all preparatory studies to the really serious work of giving an account of what is said as it ultimately appears on the page, on its own terms.

Among other things this involves recognizing the book of Job as a congeries of failed or distorted human intentions. It is apparent that the inner logic of no single tradition or individual whose impulse is discernible in the book of Job has succeeded in bending the entire work to its purpose. The final book has achieved a baroque unity which no individual seems to have intended. Yet it stands there entire and complete, as palpable as the Münster in Basel with its manifest history of architectural battles between Romanesque, Early, Middle, and Late Gothic plus Gothic Revival. But those who worship in that house are not privileged to worship in a purely Romanesque or Gothic or Gothic-Revival structure. Whatever the Münster does to people it does as its grotesque (for some tastes) self, and not as it might have been. It is simply and irrevocably *there.*

The composite and self-contradictory character of the book of Job is appropriate to its subject matter, given the fact that the questions it addresses are quite "insoluble" in this life. In fact, if Job provided the "answer" to the questions it raises it would be a self-liquidating book. An "answer" to such titanic questions as these would render the questions uninteresting. Yet the power and the fascination of the book has resided in its capacity to focus the questions of divine and human righteousness as they surface in each generation. Every reader is compelled to see the questions as his or her own questions, to plunge into them, to wrestle with them, to try to walk in the direction of resolving them—yet without the comfort of having "resolved" them in the sense of having provided the world with a final solution. For as long as Job-like questions burn—as they do!—in human hearts, it is heartless to speak of resolution.

Each contributor whose hand is discernible in the book of Job has wrestled with insoluble questions, irrespective of whether he may have thought to have "answered" them or not. Every attempt at resolution serves to focus the questions in a slightly different way. In that sense, every turn and quirk in the book enhances the fundamental point at every stage: to delineate and press the questions of divine and human righteousness. This lends to the present work an extraordinary intensity and coherence of purpose that quite overrules the particular intentions of the several minds who have contributed to its formation (or even to its "distortion").

Gerhard von Rad honors this character of the book in a particularly illuminating way when he urges us not to discount everything the "friends" say as if all the speeches of Job were only right and all the speeches of the friends were only wrong.[1] Every line is an invitation into dialogue with elemental questions upon which hinge the meaning of human life and the possibility of God. Insofar as the argument rings true, these elemental questions are raised in one way; insofar as they ring false, in another. What rings true in one heart may ring false in another, and on that level the book of Job goes on pressing its claims and fulfilling its function. From beginning to end, in this book, the question's the thing.

For the interpretation of Job, I take this to mean that every exegete is compelled, out of respect for the material, to become a participant in the dialogue. The interpreter will inevitably be interpreted by the material in terms of his or her response to the questions.

It is on these suppositions that the following remarks are offered as a contribution to a volume designed to honor Stuart Currie. The reader may or may not find them edifying from the standpoint of understanding the present book of Job. In any case, the interpreter will stand exposed and interpreted before questions which will remain gloriously unanswered for as long as the book of Job can be read with profit.

In present form, the book of Job places the following extraordinary demands upon its readers:

1. One must conceive Job initially as "righteous" not merely by his own or other people's judgment, but by the judgment of God (1:8, 2:3).

2. The suffering and loss he undergoes bear no relationship to any failure of integrity on Job's part toward God or any human being.

3. The genuineness of Job's integrity in relationship to God and people is not initially called in question by God or Job or any human being. It is "the *satan*," the "adversary," the "attorney for the prosecution," who presents the hypothetical but testable case against Job.

4. Job passes a two-part comprehensive examination (1:20-22, 2:9f), but somehow, the question is still burning for Job in an interior way. The book moves beyond the *fact* of Job's endurance to the question as to how, by what titanic interior struggle, the bare fact of his endurance is maintained.

5. This leads to the dialogues in which the silence of Job is broken. The contradiction between the prologue and the poem is thrust upon the reader as if it were consistent, as if Job's uncomplaining submission to suffering and loss were somehow

explicated by the most abandoned expressions of outrage against injustice—as if *that* were fidelity.

6. The friends' counsel to quiet submissiveness, on the other hand (i.e., something like Job's response reported in 1:20ff and 2:9f), somehow emerges as *infidelity* (42:7).

7. The crux of Job's appeal is the appeal for the vindication of his integrity (against the witness of his own suffering) and for the vindication of divine integrity (against the witness of the world's suffering). This is one appeal, not two, since Job is presented as the ultimate case. If God vindicates, or fails to vindicate, such a one as Job, then the case for or against the integrity of God is made. If Job is not vindicated, there is no vindication for the innocent sufferer.

8. The outcome is that Job is not only vindicated (42:7), but the blessings of God are restored to him in double measure. This seems to confirm the friends' judgment that fidelity toward God ultimately issues in paradise-like blessedness in this life. It also seems to confirm the *satan's* initial suspicion that human "righteousness" is simply a game people play in order to secure for themselves the maximum personal benefits from God. Yet somehow the whole work forbids this dual confirmation. If those who wrote the epilogue intended to achieve such an effect, the book simply defeats them and demands a different account of what the epilogue may mean as the denouement of the whole work.

9. Job's repeated demand for a hearing *vis à vis* God himself (cf. 9:32ff; 10:2; 13:3, 15f, 20ff; 14:15; 23:3-7; climaxing in 31:35-37) is indeed granted in 38:1ff, an event toward which Job looked with sovereign confidence that when it occurred his integrity would be fully and finally vindicated. Yet the outcome of Job's longed-for encounter with God is a scathing reduction-to-absurdity of any grounds Job might arrogate to himself for questioning the inscrutable wisdom and incomparable power of God in ordering the affairs of the universe.

10. Most devastating of all, Job appears to recant everything he has said in the face of this divine bombast (40:3-5; 42:2-5). He humiliates himself in apparent contradiction to what he has affirmed about his integrity and what God affirms about him from beginning (1:8, 2:3) to end (42:7).

Scarce wonder that generations of exegetes have been driven to account for these disparities and contradictions by recourse to theories of multiple authorship and diverse tradition sources. That approach permits us, within limits, to cluster together materials that have a consistent viewpoint and isolate them from others governed by different viewpoints. Links between the prose framework and the poem can be loosened to the extent that no logical consistency between them is demanded. Even if one feels driven to suppose that the author of the discourses deliberately made use of an extant folktale, it is well possible that he did so more or less off-handedly as a device for staging the dialogues. And it may be that the epilogue has been expanded by later hands to strengthen the dogma that righteousness is rewarded in this life. From there one moves easily to identification of insertions, such as Job 28 and the speeches of Elihu in 32-37, and to reconstruction of the third cycle of discourses and the speeches of God in order to eliminate clumsy repetitions and inapposite passages.

While no one has claimed for these researches that they have made it possible to reconstruct the "original" book of Job, at least they have opened avenues of understanding that do not make it necessary to postulate an incoherent or an inherently self-contradictory author. It has always been less clear how one is to conceive the intentions of later authors and editors who may have contributed to the present confusion. Did some insertions happen accidentally, i.e., without anyone's ever having reflected upon the effect the insertion might have had on the entire work? Or is it possible, for example, that someone scrambled the third cycle of discourses intentionally in order to have it end in a *Katzenjammer* of self-contradictory speeches? Why was no one ever prompted, in the long editorial and transmission process, to make those minor modifications that would have been required to include Elihu in the prologue and the epilogue and remove other small discrepancies between the two (e.g., one misses in the prologue the "brothers and sisters and all who have known him before" of 42:11; and one misses in the epilogue any mention of the *satan* or of Job's wife)?

We are blocked at points like these by the inescapable fact that people who turned their hands to this document, for whatever reason, simply did so without regard for the scholar's demand that gratuitous discrepancies and contradictions be avoided. Whether intentionally or inadvertently they succeeded in adding a minor note of absurdity, for modern tastes, to a set of major questions which, for modern tastes at least, always tremble on the brink of the absurd.

The present question is whether, given the complex and at least partly absurd shape of the book of Job in present form, there are ways of answering the demands placed on the present reader by the text as it is. I must register the opinion that this cannot be done comprehensively and in detail. This would be analogous to endowing a scribal error with some inherently profound meaning. I should not like to be in the position of making sententious judgments as to why the *satan* and Job's wife are absent from the epilogue (least of all on the premise that they are identical or in any case expendable).

At the risk of making only partially dissimilar judgments, however, I would like to explore again the possibility that the sequence from prologue to the voice from the whirlwind to the epilogue is capable of a relatively coherent reading, one that embraces a number of apparent contradictions even if it does not resolve or eliminate them. I am not prepared to contend that a particular author or editor contrived this coherence—only that the combination of materials that has been effected challenges me to think along relatively coherent lines.

Discord and disorder in human affairs appear in the Bible along one major and one minor line. Pre-eminently, when human beings come to grief, whether as individuals or collectively, the misfortune is illuminated as a sign of discord between God and people. Inherent in this view of things is implicit trust that what God intends for people is the fullest and richest imaginable life in fellowship with each other and with him. How such a trust emerged against human experience of life that is "nasty, brutish, and short" remains an extraordinary mystery, especially among people who were forbidden recourse to polytheism or radical dualism as means of accounting for the good and the bad in human life. Yet there it is in the beginning (Gen 1:1-2:4a), the middle (Is 11:1-9), and the end (Rev 21:1-22:5) of the biblical story.

On that view, the major implication of suffering and loss by human beings is that the relationship between God and people is not intact, things are not going in accord with God's overarching intention. The higher one holds the integrity and benevolence of God, the more sharply disorder in the human community calls in question the integrity and benevolence of people. *Fault* is disclosed in disorder, and it is nearest at hand to discover the fault in the unwillingness of human beings to affirm the just and loving order of God. There can be no doubt that the Bible affirms this, or that it affirms it with a breadth and sophistication far beyond the usual caricature of the vengeful deity bent on exacting pain from those who have aggrieved him.

Even those harsh texts that have always provided the raw material for "sinners in the hands of an angry God" carry with them at least a hint of the most exalted thing the Bible has to say at all: namely, that behind and in and through all things there is one whose will is wholly just and wholly loving, and whose purpose in the world is not to be stayed. The alternative to his life-giving way in the world is death. The agents of death appear under the guises of sickness, warfare, pestilence, earthquake, drought, famine, vicious animals, misfortune—whatever operates in the world to diminish or destroy human life. It is possible to be "caught in the snares" of one or the other of these agents, and so to enter the deadly realm, even before death and burial.[2] Thus human suffering and loss are placed in a moral context. The fact of their existence poses the question of human integrity and fidelity *vis à vis* God.

But the moral question posed by human suffering and loss may, on occasion, cut the other way. The integrity and fidelity of God are also called in question when people suffer altogether disproportionately with respect to any faithless act or intention on their part. Given the biblical insistence on God's oneness, God's utter righteousness and perfect love, as well as God's invincible power, the frequency of texts that lay the moral question at the feet of God is astonishing. How can there be human distress that is *not* the result of human failure in a universe governed by the righteous will of God?

The characteristic questions addressed to God on such occasions are "Why?" and "How long?". The first tends to imply outraged innocence, but it may root back in the serious religious enquiry into human "causes" that underlie the suffering, even though they are hidden. Joshua 7:6ff tells of a human "Why? that received an immediate and explicit answer. A human act of disobedience has evoked the present distress. The ritual mourning (7:6) already seems to imply that the fault lay with the people, even though the question to God is put with the anguished intensity of genuine innocence. Moreover, the appeal is made on the basis of God's fidelity to his avowed purpose (7:7-9). It is not that God is being measured by human standards of fidelity and righteousness. Rather, God is being called to account for fidelity to his own revealed character, his own disclosed purpose. Thus, even though the "Why?" addressed to God may receive (and here does receive) an explicit answer, it is not inherently a docile question. At the very least it carries a strong human affirmation of the justice and righteousness of God, fidelity to which is not only a human but a divine responsibility. If there is no adequate response to the "Why?", then God's fidelity and integrity are challenged.

"How long?", on the other hand, introduces the complex notion of a divine delay in meeting the demands of righteousness in human affairs. Apparently it is conceivable that a genuinely unjust and unwarranted state of affairs may continue for a time until

God's intervention or the disclosure of God's purpose rectifies the present injustice. Here one must speak of a human "patience" with God, a patience capable of enduring innocent suffering in the hope of future vindication. Implicit in such "patience" is the idea that God may be "forgiven" the temporary incidence of injustice in the world provided God's just purpose ultimately prevails. Justice delayed is apparently not justice denied in the relationship between God and people. An early instance of this appears in God's answer to Moses in Exodus 6:1 (J). The answer to Moses' "Why?" is not that God's people have incurred guilt sufficiently to justify their distress, but "now you shall see what I will do to Pharaoh; for with a strong hand [I] will send them out, yea, with a strong hand [I] will drive them out of this land."

The logic of such delayed vindication is not at all transparent, by ordinary human conceptions of justice. For us, no amount of later "reparations" is capable of removing the stark fact of injustice. It may indeed be "just" to compensate injured people for wrongs they have suffered as a result of our actions or failure to act. But our canons of justice do not permit us to regard such compensations as any sort of excuse for injustice done, or "justification" for past failures. The very act of compensation or reparation after the fact emphasizes the acceptance of moral responsibility for wrong.

The question "How long?" implies a relational concept of fidelity and integrity between God and people that cannot be comprehended by the usual moral or legal categories. If the quality of relationship proves ultimately valid, even through and beyond unaccountable breaches of it, then the relational claims of justice and fidelity have been met.

An interesting counterpart to this concept of an interim space between justice demanded and justice delivered is to be found in the prophetic promises of judgment. As W. Zimmerli has pointed out, the prophet's word often precedes the event (although sometimes it may follow it as a word of clarification) in order to provide a gracious interim during which relationship may be restored.[3] Sheer justice demands immediate retribution. It is appropriate at any time. The prophetic word is a relational intervention, implying that a new quality of relationship is capable of rendering the "legal" demand for "justice" inoperative. Here one must speak of a divine patience in which injustice is tolerated for a time in the interest of relationship. Through the prophetic word, God affirms to Israel that the covenant relationship is still intact from God's side, that its claims are still operative, that God still stands behind them. God does this not by assuring Israel that all is well, but by the thundering word of judgment and threat. God loves people by holding them accountable for a relationship that cannot ultimately survive on the basis of infidelity. Yet the word of judgment implies that the quality of the relationship is of such an order that, if restored, even at this late date, it is capable of absorbing and rendering void the whole past history of infidelity.

Is it possible that the cry of the innocent sufferer, seen above all in Moses, Jeremiah, the Psalms of lament, and Job, represents a kind of prophetic word addressed by human beings to God? Has Israel been emboldened by its distinctively relational concept of God to make the question of relational integrity a two-way street? Do the passionate words of lament offer to God a gracious interim within which it is possible for God to affirm the integrity of the relationship from his side, perhaps at some future time, before it is too late?

This is not to suggest that the relationship between God and Israel is seen to be bilateral in the strict sense, as if it were established between fully equal partners. Nothing in the Bible encourages such a conception as that. The anguished cries of Moses and Jeremiah and the Psalmists and Job are all predicated on the prior initiative of God in creating the relationship. The appeal for justice is an appeal to *God's* justice, an appeal *to* God, *against* God, on the grounds of God's *own* disclosed character and will. Its indispensable fundament is the record of God's prior grace and favor and God's inviolable promise of fidelity. This is what defines the enormity of a circumstance in which genuinely faithful people meet in human experience all the deadly realities which are taken to be the signs of a breach in the relationship between God and people. The moral question is laid at the feet of God in something like the way the prophetic word lays that question at the feet of human beings, and for something like the same reasons. However "impatient" the word of lament may be, it affirms from the human side that the relationship is still intact. Love for God is expressed by holding God accountable for a relationship that cannot survive on the basis of infidelity. Yet the word of lament implies that the quality of relationship is of such an order that, if restored, even at this late date, it is capable of absorbing and rendering void the whole past history of infidelity.

Here, of course, the analogy between the prophetic word and the word of lament breaks down. Bold as they are, the laments do not finally posit the instance of divine infidelity. Israel is very sure of instances of human infidelity. Its outcries against apparent divine infidelity are always freighted on the hope against hope that God's fidelity will not only be affirmed again, but that somehow even this intolerable moment is held in the context of divine fidelity. The lament is not merely a charge of injustice against God. It is at the same time a desperate cry for clarification, for some way of reconciling the unaccountable reality of innocent suffering with the justice of God. The lament form as such becomes a vapid charade once the innocent sufferer concludes that God is inherently unreliable, capable of injustices as well as justice. The sufferer may charge God, out of depths of suffering, with just that wrong (cf. Job 9:22), but if he finally believed it, the lament would lose its addressee, and therefore its point. This is clear above all in Job. Even though he lays down the harshest charges against divine justice, his overriding passion is for encounter, for trial, for relationship with God. One may be certain that this is no passion for relationship with an inherently unjust God. Job's ultimate human hope is that he will know himself vindicated by God, and it is transparent that no inherently unjust God is capable of vindicating the innocent.

When one puts all this in conversation with the apparently self-contradictory demands placed on the reader by the book of Job in present form, one generalization seems immediately possible. In the complex area of divine and human justice, nothing is as it seems! At least some of the complexities of Job inhere in the very questions the book raises. The variety of impulses one detects in the book—in part stemming from various hands representing various approaches to the problem—corresponds to the many dimensions of the problem itself. The question is whether the present work is merely self-contradictory or whether the unity achieved in this tradition process has produced an address to the problem that transcends the intention of any particular author.

The crux of the present question is whether or not it is possible to detect a coherence between the following key demands made upon the reader by the present form of the book of Job:

1. The initial (1:8-2:3) and final (42:7) statement of God's approbation of Job.

2. The cold and apparently "heartless" speeches of God from the whirlwind, scorning and chiding Job for the presumptuousness of his challenges (38:2ff, 40:2, 7ff).

3. Job's protestations of innocence, passionate confidence in his ultimate vindication (climaxing in the superb manifesto of chapter 31).

4. Job's humble recantations (40:3-5; 42:2-5).

If some order can be brought out of these apparent contradictions, then perhaps the way is open to account for some of the other dilemmas posed above.

On the face of it, these contradictions are insurmountable and the best solution is to divorce the inner demands of the prologue and epilogue from the inner demands of the discourses. In addition one could play with the possibility that whoever wrote Job 31 was simply not involved in composing the words of recantation in 40:3-5; 42:2-5. There is already sufficient evidence that the speeches of the Lord have been reworked more than once, for various reasons.

But is it possible to deal with these apparent contradictions in another way, without insisting that any one author ever saw them resolved in his own mind? Is it possible, in other words, that the ultimate juxtaposition of these apparent opposites forces us to follow lines of thought that no one author may have intended? Has this composite book achieved an address of its own which may be attended to in its present baroque unity?

Stimulation to this inquiry has come from a possibility hinted at in the logic of certain Psalms of lament: namely, that the *fact* of the divine answer from the whirlwind constitutes the effected vindication of Job, irrespective of the content of the divine speeches. This possibility raises a number of questions as soon as it is entertained, above all the riddle as to why an event of vindication should be attended by such scathing words of scorn and countercharge, and why a vindicated Job should "repent in dust and ashes"(42:6). Perhaps for these reasons no commentary presses a full-scale attempt to bring the possible vindication of Job into conversation with 38:2ff.

The notion that the "answer" of God from the whirlwind constitutes, in itself, the vindication of Job is not altogether far-fetched. As Marvin Pope points out[4] the link between storm and theophany is a close one, and at least one consistent occasion for theophany is the coming of God to vindicate the cause of his people: Psalm 18:6-15 (English); 50:3-6; (83:14f); Hab 3:2-16; Zech 9:14f (1 Kings 19:1ff); Ps 68:7f, 32ff, especially in response to a passionate lament.

Artur Weiser has pressed this to the point of suggesting that a theophany or a theophanic representation is precisely the longed-for resolution of a case brought before God for the vindication of the innocent sufferer.[5] Whether the evidence permits so comprehensive a judgment or not, it is difficult to deny that in some instances, perhaps only during certain periods of cultic history, such an expectation may have obtained.

The word *^{c}anah*, "answer," may be regarded as an additional clue. Consistently in the Psalms, the innocent sufferer uses the word in what must be taken as a virtually absolute sense (i.e., not as a "reply" in words, but as the appropriate vindicating response): Psalm 3:4; 4:1; 13:3; 17:6 (cf. vv 1-5, and the implication that the "answer" is identical with a demonstration of "steadfast love," v 7); 20:1, 6, 9 (in parallel with "protect" "help" "support" "mighty victories"); 22:2 (the "answer" which is withheld corresponds to "forsakenness," the absence of "help"); 22:21 (on H. J. Kraus's supposition following MT: "Thou hast answered me" expresses the startled awareness of vindication, however experienced[6]); 27:7; 34:4 (parallel with "delivered"); 38:15; 55:2; 60:5 (parallel with "delivered" "give victory"); 65:5 ("answer with deliverance"); 69:13-16f; 81:7; 91:15; 99:6, 8; 102:2; 118:5, 21; 119:26, 145; 120:1; 138:3; 143:1, 7. In each of these instances the sense of ^{c}*anah* could be rendered "vindicate" with no loss of meaning.[7] In no case is it necessary, or even reasonable, to suppose that the "answer" might consist of speeches or rejoinders.

Suppose we follow these clues, seeing in the whirlwind an allusion to theophanic vindication and in the word ^{c}*anah* the classic vindicating response longed for and celebrated by the Psalmists. Let us lay aside for the moment the fact, apparently so damaging to this supposition, that the Lord immediately breaks into speech that is anything but vindicating, together with the fact that Job falls silent and repents in the face of it. Before we decide whether there is a way out of that dilemma, let us consider the implications of a possible vindication of Job in 38:1.

The immediate antecedent to a deed of divine vindication (if such 38:1 describes) is Job's ultimate cry in 31:35-37.

> "Oh, that I had one to hear me!
>   (Here is my signature! Let the
>   Almighty answer me!)
> Oh, that I had the indictment
>   written by my adversary!
> Surely I would carry it on my shoulder;
>   I would bind it on me as a crown;
> I would give him an account of all
>   my steps;
>   like a prince I would approach him."

The direct appeal for an "answer" is there (v. 35), but delivered with a note of defiance that goes beyond anything in the Psalter. Job *demands* vindication on non-negotiable terms. He has made the case for his humanity so powerfully that, in effect, he defies even

God to find anything wrong with it. As Pope points out, it is unclear whether the document Job is prepared to wear as a badge of honor is an indictment or an acquittal.[8] If he is talking about an indictment, then his defiance is more than Promethean. He would then be saying something to the effect that if there is a God in heaven who finds fault with such a quality of humanity, then let such a "faulty" humanity be affirmed in the face of an accusing God, with regal confidence and dignity!

The tone of defiance here and elsewhere has driven hordes of readers and exegetes into the arms of Eliphaz and his colleagues. Surely in this arrogant defiance, if nowhere else, we must find the Achilles heel of the valiant and righteous sufferer. Job was no doubt a great and good man, but...! Doesn't this defiance alone prove that Job was finally unworthy of divine blessing? Doesn't it justify wholly the scathing speeches of God, and make Job's later repentance wholly appropriate? Not, of course, if Job 38:1 represents God's own vindication of the very Job who issued this as defiant challenge. And certainly not if we are compelled to take seriously, as the present book compels us to do, God's estimate of Job in 1:8, 2:3, and 42:7! If God says "Yes!" to Job it is precisely to the Job whose entire case is magnificently summed up in chapters 29-31. What this summation requires of the reader is to envision Job as the extreme case, in every respect, of 1) the righteous human being living in perfect harmony with God (ch 29); 2) the sufferer who undergoes the uttermost in human humiliation and distress through no fault of his own (ch 30); and, 3) the human being who holds fast to his own integrity without bowing the knee to any external circumstance or to any God who may see fit to condemn him (ch 31).

The language and instances employed to portray this extreme case may well be obscure, even comical, to modern readers. Yet the hyperboles employed, as I see it, represent quite simply the highest or the most extreme description conceivable to the author. If the hyperboles sound contrived, or comical, or perhaps even base to our ears, then we need to supply our own to convey the ultimate extremes the author is struggling for. In chapter 29 the author expects us to envision what a human life would be like if its inner character corresponded perfectly to the inner character of God, or at least to the character of human life that God intends and desires. The poet asks us to envision, on that basis, what it would be like if God's approbation and blessing upon such a life were expressed without any marring circumstance. It is a picture of days when "God watched over" Job, when *by God's light* Job "walked in darkness," when "the friendship of God was on [his] tent," when "the almighty was yet with [him] " (29:2-5). It is a paradise-like time of completeness and the superabundance of every good thing (29:5b-6).

For the author's imagination, such an individual in such a relationship can only be a *regal* personage (cf. 29:25), since for him the monarch embodied the highest and fullest of possible human expressions. This is another way of saying that a righteous person in untrammeled relationship with God is supremely free, with the kind of unchallenged freedom that, in the author's day, only monarchs began to approach. But as *God's* regal human being, this matchless Job of the "autumn days" exercises his regal wisdom, freedom, and power only for the well-being of his realm. All those beneath his sway: the young, the aged, the princes, the nobles, the poor, the fatherless, the perishing, the widows, the blind, the lame, the strangers—all have cause only for respect, gratitude, and rejoicing because of his presence and action (vv 7-16). Only the unrighteous need fear him (v 17).

If we set out to improve on this picture of what a superlatively righteous and blessed human being ought to be like, we need to take care not to say *less* than this picture implies. Let the utter conformity of divine and human will be expressed with at *least* this degree of freedom, wisdom, and power. And let these things be expressed, no *less* than here, in a life devoted to the well-being of others. To read this account as a pompous, self-congratulatory, and essentially arrogant depiction of the "good old days" is to miss the point altogether. Seldom, if ever, in human literature, has anyone so nearly succeeded in the attempt to depict a human life as it would be lived in utter congruence with the divine intention. If it sounds hopelessly unrealistic and ideal, let it be said in the author's defense that he was trying to describe something no human being ever saw. It is an essay in protology, an exploration of the uncharted ground of "oughtness" in the relation between God and people.

Whatever happens to this protological Job, let it be clear that it happened to one who was truly blameless and whose relationship to God was flawless from both sides. In this respect, chapter 29 picks up and elaborates magnificently the picture of Job in 1:1-5. The question of divine and human righteousness is to be tested in the absolutely extreme hypothetical case: the case of one in whom *no cause whatever* is to be found to warrant suffering and loss. With a lesser human being, all the questions immediately become ambiguous. The author of chapter 29 proposes to examine the implications of the ultimate instance.

Similar sensitivity must be brought to the reading of chapter 30.

Again, regardless of how well the reader may feel that the author succeeds, the intention of this chapter is to describe the nadir of human humiliation and suffering, following instantly upon the zenith of human fulfillment and exaltation. The extremes are so remote from each other that the reader must continually struggle to keep in mind that it is the *regal* Job of chapter 29 who has become the utterly wretched Job of chapter 30. Freedom has turned into the enslavement that results from complete social isolation and rejection, combined with incessant pain and physical disability. Wisdom has been replaced by the special madness that comes from the total incapacity to make anyone else—even God—hear and understand. Power has been replaced by weakness that is only a breath away from death, and hardly preferable to it. Insofar as human life is intended to reflect relationship to God, then God appears as the arch conspirator against Job's well-being, the cruel one *par excellence* (30:11, 19-23). Yet in retrospect Job is aware of having done his utmost on behalf of those who had preceded him into wretchedness (30:25), while he now suffers alone, without a champion (30:26-31).

Perhaps it can be said better. Chapter 30:1-8 seems to embody a harsh and uncharitable estimate of the "scum of the earth," people upon whom one might have hoped the Job of chapter 29 would have looked with unprecedented compassion. Yet v 9f provides the key to the author's intention: conceive the "leastest" of humanity in the most distasteful and wretched terms imaginable—and then conceive *that* brood making sport of Job as one utterly *beneath* them! Job has become the ultimate instance of one despised and rejected by God and by the human community. If it can be said better, then let care be taken not to avoid the author's intention to achieve the ultimate imaginable portrayal of human lostness and misery.

Now it is time to render accounts in the matter of this extreme imaginable reversal. If such a fate befell such a man, how then would one perceive the question of divine and human righteousness? Is the universe a howling absurdity? One could forgive the Job of chapter 30 for reaching that conclusion. Is God inherently unjust, cruel, uncaring—or irrelevant—or simply not there at all? How could one think otherwise in such a case? Or is it remotely possible that there is some horrendous error in Job that makes this reversal fully appropriate, so that right-thinking people can only applaud the deity for having made the punishment so exquisitely fit the crime? Is the Job of chapter 29 so utterly despicable in the eyes of God? Can God's idea of what human life *ought* to be consist of the virtual *opposite* of such a person?

Job is not in a position to make the case for God, but at least his last word is not a lugubrious, self-pitying howl of despair. There is yet one thing Job is able to do from that level below the least, beneath the worst of human experience. He can make the case for Job, and with it the case for the truly human as he understands it.

One sees him struggling into an imaginary dock, in an imaginary courtroom, before an imaginary tribunal—imaginary, because nothing in this experience of reversal has led him to believe that there is any place for a human being to stand, any court of law, anyone to hear his case. And yet, absurdly, he begins the summation for the defense!

"Nothing else," Job implies, "makes any sense to me at all. But one thing makes sense to me, one thing is worth all the pain, all the indignity. It is the enterprise of being all the human being I know how to be, at whatever cost. I will affirm that with my last breath, though the heavens were brass and all the earth a bedlam. There is a way of being human that matters, that *counts,* even if nothing else does. And there is nothing vague or imprecise about it. Let me tell you what it is. It is my case for the defense, my *apologia pro vita mea.* I will affirm it whether anyone ever hears it or not."

Chapter 31 constitutes a third attempt on the part of the author to depict the extreme case. It is the least transparent, and perhaps the least successful of the three from the standpoint of modern readers. The form of affirmation by self-imprecation sounds bizarre and quasi-comical to modern ears, and the relatively homely ethic of human behavior that emerges is hardly a spectacular breakthrough in the literature of moral reflection. If one penetrates the obscure form of self-imprecation, however, it is possible to secure a positive list of values that can take its place among more familiar ones such as the Decalogue or the Sermon on the Mount. Its *Leitmotif* is the conception of a human center of thinking and feeling and acting that is structured from within, so that external pressures or blandishments are simply incapable of distorting it. The apparent advantages of instant sexual gratification, or deceit, or corruption, or exploitation of the less powerful, or selfishness, or indifference to the needs of others, or wealth, or superstition, or vengefulness (including the peculiar delight Germans call "*Schadenfreude*"!), or the favorable opinion of majorities bent on injustice and terror are all rejected. In their place Job affirms chastity, simple honesty, fairness based on deep respect for the other as equal, generosity born of compassion, moderation of personal use of resources, fearlessness in the face of the unknown and imponderable, refusal to let the actions of the other determine one's own responses and attitudes toward him or her, steadfast courage of conviction in the face of contrary public opinion.

Homely and incomplete? Possibly. The product of a rustic society far removed from the modern world? No doubt. Yet it has a certain recognizable ring to it at the point of basic reflection upon what it might take to achieve a human life of full freedom, dignity, and responsibility. If one undertakes to improve on the author's intention to portray the extreme case of human righteousness and integrity, care must be taken not to claim *less* for the human possibility than is here claimed.

And one should note further that the—to us—grotesque form of self-imprecation retains a certain poetic appropriateness in the present context. Obviously the terrible fates Job wishes upon himself, according to the intention of the ancient formulae, are predominately to be understood as means of asserting innocence of the crimes listed, in the most vehement terms. By implication, the positive fulfillment of the corresponding ideal actions and attitudes is asserted with equal strength. Yet it can hardly have escaped the author that all of those self-sworn fates and more have already befallen Job, in one sense or another, if we accept the author's intention in chapter 30 to depict Job as the most "accursed" of men. But the implication of this grotesque antiphony between self-imprecation and Job's actual experience is not that he has been proved guilty of each of the crimes listed. Quite the contrary. The power of chapter 31 lies precisely in the fact that Job is able to affirm his humanity from the very depths of an "accursedness" that has no bearing on or correspondence with the state of his fidelity toward God and people.

The *satan* of the prologue had staked his reputation as a prosecuting attorney on the proposition that this ultimate assertion of human integrity could not be made in the absence of discernible props and guarantees from the side of God. The question had been, from the viewpoint of the heavenly council chamber, "Can there be such a human being, such a quality of relationship within a human spirit, such an integrity,—even in the extreme case of Job, who was incomparable for blamelessness and uprightness, reverence for God and revulsion toward evil (1:8)?"[9]

Now the *satan* and God have their answer. Not only is it possible, but Job has actually brought the thing off. But with this ringing "Yes!" from the side of the human there comes an equally resounding question to him who sits enthroned in the heavenly council: "Is there a God in heaven worthy of such a human life?" In one sense the power and passion of Job's summation for the defense already imply that there *must* be. But given the contrived absence of God throughout the struggle, one must also hear the defiant challenge of

Job's final words: If there is *not* a God in heaven who corresponds to this affirmation of the human, there *ought* to be! And if there is a God in heaven prepared to face down and deny such a man, then let God come on with his accusations. At least God will be dealing with a *prince* who stands before the bar of justice without shame or embarrassment!

That brings us to 38:1. Again laying aside the content of the divine speeches, let us savor the possibility that 38:1, in itself, constitutes an unqualified and everlasting "Yes!" to the Job of chapters 29-31 as they sum up and conclude Job's entire case. The *fact* of the "answer" (see above) *is* God's act of vindication. In some respects such a vindication tells us less about Job than it does about Job's God. We have already been persuaded by 29-31, or at least I suspect the author intended that we should have, that the case for Job, the case for the ultimate human possibility, has been completely and thoroughly made. That case has now become the litmus paper by which the possibility of God is to be tested. The result of that test, on our reading, is that the sovereign Lord of the universe affirms and confirms such a humanity. There is a deep and utterly integral relationship between God and such a man that allows the very character of God to be read from this human life. Of *course* such a life is vindicated by God! Of *course* the intactness of their relationship is affirmed from the side of God as it has been affirmed in the darkness by Job as he simply refused to let go of his God-willed integrity. That is quite simply who God is. The structure of all reality hinges upon it.

But now what is to be made of those ice-cold, heartless, inquisitorial speeches of God? How can a God who has vindicated Job now thrust him immediately into the dock and confront him with sheerly unanswerable questions, one heaped upon another? And how can a Job who has withstood every test, to the point of *defying* God not to be God, now fall silent, submissive, repentant? Perhaps we have read too much into chapters 29-31. Perhaps we have simply invented *ex nihilo* the alleged vindication of 38:1. If so, the errors are compounded if we move now to interpret the speeches of the Lord and Job's repentance in that light. Perhaps the text will simply not bear the weight. If not, Stuart Currie will no doubt be shaking his head, in some book-lined corner of heaven, with brotherly but stern disapproval. But, we must now risk that eventuality.

Everyone is agreed that the speeches of God in 38-41 are calculated, at the very least, to affirm the "infinite, qualitative difference" between the wisdom of God and human wisdom, between the power of God and human power. The finite is simply and forever *not* capable of the infinite. The aggregate of all conceivable human understanding, the total concentration of all conceivable human capacities and powers are so infinitesimal by comparison with the understanding and power of God as to make the comparison ludicrous. Perhaps one needs to hear the laughter of God and the tittering of angels at the very thought of Almighty God squared off in some kind of contest with even the most exalted imaginable human being, even with Job. "Come on, Job," says God, "put up your dukes! Let's spar a few rounds. Play the man. You've won a reputation as a fighter, you have said some tough things. Now let's see how you do in a *real* contest!"

Is that something Job needs to hear? His dear friend Eliphaz had already made that point in his opening words of pastoral advice (cf. 5:9-11), and Job repeatedly postulates it as an unquestionable truism (cf. 9:3-10, 19; 12:13-25; 14:18-20; 23:6, 13-17; 26:2-14 [Job?]). What sense can it now make for God to take up that old refrain and repeat it *ad nauseam et infinitum,* making Job smaller and smaller, more and more ludicrous in the presence of infinite wisdom and power?

One problem we face in order to entertain these questions is the fact that the Lord's speeches are an altogether finite attempt on the part of very human author(s) to produce the impact of the infinite. Again we need to attempt to read their *intentions,* to give ourselves over to the imagery as if it really were capable of describing what it might be like to stand there, a naked human being, in face-to-face encounter with Almighty God. If we can bring off that highly demanding work of imagination, as the authors of these speeches are inviting us to do, we might be in a position to hear something new, something really worth listening to. By all accounts Job did (40:3-5; 42:2-5).

First of all, we are to understand that the encounter between God and Job in 38:1-42:6 was a new experience, not a familiar one revisited. We do well to put out of our minds the ordinary analogies drawn from human religious experience. What is described here is something altogether different from warm feelings of the pious heart, or the mystic's "beatific vision," or soulful intimations of transcendence. At best all such religious feelings have the distance from God that belongs to the "hearing of the ear" rather than the "seeing of the eye." In every respect Job is the "ultimate instance," typical of the rest of us only in the sense that what we experience in bits and pieces he experiences totally and in depth. This holds true not only for his legendary piety, his incomparable suffering, his superb victory of spirit, but also and *a fortiori* for his experience of the immediate presence of God. In every instance we are being asked, "What would it be like if...!"

Now we are being asked, "What would it be like if the Job of chapters 29-31 were granted his longed-for face-to-face hearing with Almighty God, if he experienced the unqualified "Yes!" of God's vindication of his embattled humanity, and, at the same instant, found himself on the wholly unfamiliar turf of direct and immediate perception of the divine person?" If he sensed himself only in the presence of a blustering cosmic bully, then his submission and repentance are merely base. Sheer muscle has won out, as it so often seems to in ordinary human affairs, over decency. But quite another factor intrudes if the cosmic giant of the divine speeches is the same Lord who heard Job's innocent cry for justice and "answered" him with a cosmic "Amen!" Then the God who is everlastingly on the side of Job's kind of humanity is disclosed as the God whose wisdom and power in the ordering of the universe utterly transcend the capacity of human beings to discern. On the points of wisdom and power, it will always be the part—and the delight!—of the creature to adore the creator in perfect wonder. In the presence of such a transcendent Lord, it is not possible for Job to speak such condescending words as "Lord, forgive my little jokes on thee and I will forgive thy great big one on me!"[10] No condescension of any sort is appropriate in the presence of the transcendent one, if it is indeed true that God's character corresponds to and eternally affirms such a humanity as Job's.

It is worth noting, as Marvin Pope does,[11] that neither the speeches of God nor the "recantations" of Job ever touch on the relational questions of divine and human righteousness which have, up until 38:2, provided the entire substance of the book. But if 38:1 in itself describes the event of vindication, then the fundamental issue of divine and human righteousness, in its most exquisite form, has already been answered with an antiphonal "Yes!" from the side of the human and the divine. If one can imagine humanity as God intends it, then its correspondence with the divine will and purpose is complete, without remainder.

What obviously *remains* is the question as to *how* this correspondence is actually woven into the divine ordering of the universe. Where and how, in God's order of things, is it made self-evident that God *knows* and *cares* and *does something* about the human situation where suffering and loss are rampant, even among the innocent? Where are the clues that a life such as Job describes in chapter 31 is anything more than a piece of absurd posturing in the void? If God is asserted to be a vindicator of Job and the humanity he represents, where is the proof for the argument?

My God! Can it be that the case for the righteousness of God must be made altogether in the darkness of human experience, with only the tantalizing hint but never the self-evident documentation of God present on the side of human justice and righteousness? Will the providential ordering of the universe by God forever remain beyond the scope of human understanding, so that it is left up to human beings to perceive and express the fact that the heart of the universe is justice upheld by love?

I take that to be what has been called "the intolerable compliment." Job discovers that he must work out his commitment to divine and human righteousness with never an echo from nature or history. It is only when Job affirms with his next to last breath that such a course is worth the investment of a lifetime, no matter what, that he hears the word of vindication. Only then does he find God unmistakably on his side as champion and next-of-kin.

If Job is genuinely assured of his unqualified vindication, and if in the same instant he is permitted to sense the overwhelming transcendence of the one who in fact orders all things according to plan, then it is altogether appropriate for him to say: "Behold, I am of small account; what shall I answer thee? I lay my hand on my mouth. I have spoken once, and I will not answer; twice, but I will proceed no further." And again: "I know that thou canst do all things, and that no purpose of thine can be thwarted....Therefore I have uttered what I did not understand, things too wonderful for me, which I did not know....I had heard about thee with the hearing of the ear, but now my eye sees thee; therefore I despise myself and repent in dust and ashes."

What is that purpose of God that cannot be thwarted? The grinding out of wholly inscrutable divine maneuvers in the universe, or the vindication of the human through people like Job in the face of all evidence to the contrary? What are those "too wonderful things" Job has uttered? That he has declared God to be unjust and uncaring, or that in his solitary tenacity for God's way in the world, against the apparent opposition of God, he has in fact been articulating in the world the very character of God? What is it that Job now sees that before now he only had rumors of? That God's wisdom and power render human beings laughable, or that God was ever and always his vindicator, his next-of-kin, even when he felt himself totally cut off and rejected? And finally, on what grounds does Job despise himself and repent in dust and ashes? Because he has asserted his own innocence and insisted on affirming his integrity even if it means challenging God? Or is it because he has now discovered that only by such affirmation, in the absence of all self-serving motives and all confirming support, can the righteousness that belongs to God become evident in the world?

To arrange cosmic affairs differently would have made God eternally vulnerable to the *satan's* snide but devastating question. Even the tiniest providential device that consistently turned up benefits for the human practice of divine righteousness would inevitably turn people into eager robots of God for fun and profit. The slightest statistical evidence that one's bread is buttered on the side of avoiding the appearance of evil would precipitate a gold rush for righteousness.

The authenticity of human righteousness and integrity can only be tested in the extreme case. That means only in the situation in which it must seem to be self-generated, wholly from within the resources of a frail and vulnerable human being. Freely, without coercion or seduction, yet undaunted by the coercion of an apparently heartless universe, or the seduction of surrender to more agreeable, self-serving patterns of existence. Only in retrospect, only from the unthinkable vantage point of the immediate presence of the vindicating and transcendent Lord, can it become perfectly and (now!) self-evidently clear that the human work of justice and righteousness was always a joint enterprise with the one who "described a circle upon the face of the waters...and by his power...stilled the seas. Lo, these are but the outskirts of his ways; and how small a whisper do we hear of him! But the thunder of his power who can understand?"

Now it becomes clear that Job's vaunted integrity was nothing more than what his design specifications called for, including the specification that his response to God and to the challenge of his humanity be truly his own and truly free. The inscrutable order of divine providence now proves to be not a *threat* to the truly human but the indispensable context in which the truly human, by God's design, can come into being at all.

When that sinks home, Job discovers that the time for disputation is over and the time for genuine humility and wonder has come. It is not just that he now seems so tiny. He is accustomed to that feeling. But that so tiny a one has been accorded so glorious and pivotal a function in the overwhelmingly transcendent order of things! Job may now have reflected again upon that verse from a Psalm that he had cited earlier in a different spirit: "What is the human that you think so much of us; ordinary human beings that you care for us?... But now you have made us a little less than *Elohim*, crowned us with glory and honor." (Cf. Job 7:17-19).

Perhaps then it is not the questions in the book of Job that prove unanswerable, but the "answer." At least Job ultimately falls silent, on this reading, only when he perceives the reality of God's vindication of the truly human in the context of a universe the wonder of whose ordering no human being will ever comprehend. Job "repents in dust and ashes" only when the answer sinks in that the question of divine and human righteousness must, by the very character of the question, be worked out in a context of reality and experience that does not force the answer. If, indeed, "times of judgment (were) kept by the almighty," as Job cries out that they should be in 24:1, then perception of the divine righteouness would become as commonplace as the perception of earthquakes. While this might establish divine righteousness as an inescapable "natural" phenomenon, universally acknowledged, it would preempt forever the possibility of human righteousness as anything more than the highest form of self-aggrandizement. Its opposite would never be evil, but only self-destructive stupidity or ignorance, wholly lacking in moral content.

Perhaps Job now perceives the possibility of genuine human righteousness in a necessarily inscrutable universe. Perhaps he now perceives that his outrage against injustice, his protest against "God," his affirmation of integrity, has corresponded all along to the righteousness of God. Perhaps now he perceives, with overwhelming clarity, that God has been his constant ally and champion in the protest, and more, that in his human protest God's own righteousness has taken visible form and been given audible words in a morally formless and silent universe. The "intolerable compliment" has been paid him. The unqualified approbation of God rings in his ears. He sees the ineffable wisdom and grandeur of the now unmistakably just and compassionate God extending infinitely beyond him in every direction. It is time to "repent in dust and ashes!" He *couldn't* have known, yet somehow he *should* have known. Repentance, in this mode, contains nothing of servility. It is simply the appropriate mode of tardy adoration.

If this is the effect achieved by the present text of Job 38:1-42:6, the way is open for a somewhat different reading of the epilogue than one usually encounters. Immediately the words of God addressed to the friends take on fresh import: "...you have not spoken of me what is right as my servant Job has!" Job's friends have chosen words carefully in order to protect the deity against the charge that the divine ordering of human affairs fails to demonstrate God's justice and compassion. Job's intemperate outbursts, on the other hand, have been motivated by the single-minded intention to affirm the fact of inexplicable suffering on the part of one who simply knows he has not deserved it. From the vantage point of such unswerving integrity, Job proclaims that neither nature nor history conspire in the direction of justice or compassion. Insofar as God is seen to be the one whose providential will is expressed in nature and history, the charge must be placed where it belongs—at the feet of God (cf. esp. 9:22). If God is just and compassionate, then that case has to be made against, not proven from, the evidence of human experience. It is not Job's part to make the case for God (cf. 13:7!). If God is to be vindicated it is up to him to hear and answer the cry of the innocent sufferer, something Job relentlessly pleads for, always holding open that possibility for God. But that must not involve—and for Job it can never involve—an "answer" that destroys his conviction of innocence, or the truth of his claim that human beings, frequently and *en masse,* suffer hurts that bear no relationship to their relative worth or righteousness. It is Job's part to make the case for the human, against God if need be, on the grounds that human righteousness can be genuine though all the universe conspire to cry "Fraud!"

"That is my kind of talk," says God to Job's friends, "at least when it comes from the lips of my servant Job, a blameless and upright man who reveres God and turns away from evil. But *you*—you 'friends'—have stifled the cry of innocent suffering in order to serve yourselves by currying favor with him whose will you presume to know. In standing against Job's cry for justice, you have withstood me!"

The extreme demand of 42:7 is that we perceive God standing with and for Job even when he cries out *to* God, *against* God, on the very grounds of God's own justice and compassion. It is *God's* cry for justice and compassion that Job articulates in frail human words. And it is *God's* justice and compassion that come to expression when Job defends his ways in chapter 31. The cause of God and the cause of the authentically human are one and inseparable. The whole of God's providential ordering of nature and history is the inscrutable proscenium arch beneath which the drama of the divine and human struggle for love and justice unfolds. If God's way for people cannot emerge on that stage, in just that surrounding darkness, then not only the human but the divine righteousness are silently submerged in the absurd.

But, if genuine righteousness can and does emerge on *that* stage, then all the imponderable reaches and mysteries of the universe become eloquent with the adoration of the just and loving God.

Eliphaz and Bildad and Zophar are left wholly without resources of their own in the face of God's judgment. Their goal had been to achieve maximum security in this life by bending every religious effort to guarantee divine approval and protection. In the light of that goal, their religious structures now lie in ruins and they face the one most dreaded and least expected eventuality: the radical disfavor of God.

At this point a note intrudes that is nowhere prepared for in all the prior disputations between Job and his friends. Only the gentlest hint of it appears in the prologue (1:5). Basically two alternatives for a positive relationship to God have been laid out in Job 3-41:

1. Unswerving religious affirmation of the justice of God which ignores or suppresses even the thought that human beings may suffer unjustly. The alternative is regarded as a blasphemy of sufficient enormity to cut one off from God and make forfeit any hope of human blessedness; and,

2. Unswerving affirmation of justice and compassion in human affairs carried through to the point that nothing in the universe that compromises them is to be tolerated. Any alternative is regarded as an abject and self-serving surrender of the human.

The switch ending of 38:1-42:7 affirms that, of the two, only the latter genuinely affirms the justice and love of God, and only in that mode can positive relationship to God be expressed.

But now a third possibility of positive relationship to God is put forward in one deceptively plain sentence (42:8): It may not be possible for the friends to achieve what Job has achieved, but they can recognize that achievement for what it is. They can ask for Job's intercession on their behalf, and they have God's promise that through such a prayer, offered by such a man, they too can participate in the relationship which Job has achieved.

It has often occurred to me that Job's righteousness never faced a more demanding test than now, when Eliphaz, Bildad, and Zophar stand before him in humiliation and supplication. Their former roles are completely reversed. It is the premier occasion in all of human letters for the dearly beloved words: "I told you so!" The temptation for Job to pronounce just those words to just these people must stand as the most exquisite and delicious temptation imaginable. But Job is God's man. By his own God-vindicated ethic he knows himself bound not to rejoice "at the ruin of him that hated me" or to exult "when evil overtook him," or to sin "by asking for his life with a curse" (31:29-30).

The words of Job's prayer are not recorded. Christians can hardly put down the impulse to supply them with words like "Father...forgive them...for they knew not..." or "Father...lay not this sin to their charge." This is not to suggest that only Christians have access to this utterly extraordinary new suggestion about how it is possible for people to stand in God's favor, having failed to achieve the lonely pinnacle of Job's righteousnes. Jews also remember texts like Isaiah 55:6-9, Psalm 103:10-12, and Isaiah 53:10-12, where the mystery of God's gracious way for those who have failed is superbly celebrated.

It is especially worth noting, however, that the divine forgiveness is achieved in Job through the intercession of God's righteous *man.* I hear in this an extraordinarily powerful link with chapters 29-31 and the vindication of 38-41 as we have interpreted it. This compels me to think less in the traditional Christian terms of the need for a "mediator," than in another direction that may prove interesting for a reassessment of that traditional doctrine.

We have attempted to make the case that Job's righteousness *is* the extraordinary way in which the justice and love of God come to expression in an inscrutable universe. Decisive for Job's ethic is that, while it is his task to hold fast to his righteousness against every conceivable assault, it is also the part of that same righteousness to take the side of those in distress, even to the point of renouncing vindictiveness (31:29f). As one detected God's righteousness through the prism of Job's human righteousness, so one now detects God's forgiveness through the prism of Job's human forgiveness. It is not then merely a human forgiveness which God accedes to out of high regard for the intercessor, a fatherly indulgence granted to less-beloved children in order to please his pet child. It is the divine forgiveness taking shape in the free decision of God's regal man to act as God's man is expected to act—an altogether extraordinary affirmation of the intimate congruence of a divine and a human will. But then, that is just the kind of man God always said Job was (1:8, 2:3).

"There is none like him on earth"—a disheartening judgment about the rest of us, in some respects! Yet people "unlike him" managed to present him to us in the book of Job with such grace and power that one can see through him to the supreme mystery of which human hearts are capable. There is a justice and a love at large in the world, fragmentarily visible in every human gesture, against all the odds, to affirm these things in relationship to each other. Yet that fragmentary human passion for justice and love is no quixotic product of the human imagination. It bears the everlasting "Amen!" of God and discloses the heart that beats behind the unsearchable grandeur and mystery of the silent universe. In the fragmentary, less than Joban capacity of ordinary human righteousness to express itself in forgiveness, the forgiveness that belongs only to God intrudes into the world.

Outside the boundaries of Jewish and Christian faith commitments, the book of Job hurls a challenge to the human community that deserves a hearing even among agnostics and atheists. By the standards for the truly human disclosed in Job, the usual grounds for human arrogance as well as human self-pity are radically undercut. It would be easier to settle for a much lower estimate of human dignity in an absurd universe if it were not for this book. Job affirms the human in the face of the absurd on a level of freedom and responsibility that even the most sanguine humanist must concede still lies out there as a frontier to be explored rather than an achievement to be boasted of. If human beings are fundamentally "innocent" in an amoral universe, then there is a *quality* of innocence discernible in Job that we have not yet begun to approach. We are compelled to stand breathless in wonder before the unfulfilled possibilities of the "merely" human. A kind of "transcendence" then re-enters, through the back door of the ruined cathedral of allegedly bankrupt religions, a transcendence capable of restoring to human beings, in some measure, their lost capacity for wonder and awe.

Yet the ultimate wonder for Job is not the vindication of his untarnished humanity. It is the awe-struck recognition that it is the one behind all wonders who vindicates him. On the strength of his human perception of the heart that beats behind the universe, he is led to discover the incomprehensible wonder of all reality beating with that same pulse, and not another. At such a moment of disclosure, even the highest imaginable humanity can bend the knee in adoration, not in servile abnegation of human dignity, but as the ultimate expression of it.

But now follows Job 42:10ff: "And the Lord restored the fortunes of Job, when he had prayed for his friends...." Surely now the moral heights achieved by Job in his superb struggle on behalf of the human are hopelessly compromised by this return to the old dogma of rewards and punishments. Or is that the only construction that can be placed on this fuguing tune of restoration (42:10-17)?

The epilogue itself contains at least one minor note that might have jarred purists who defended the doctrine of retribution as the key to the justice of God. "Then came to him all his brothers and sisters *and all who had known him before;* and they showed him sympathy and comforted him for *all the evil that the Lord had brought upon him....*" Could such a purist have endured calmly the judgment that it was indeed the Lord who had somehow brought upon Job "all the evil" that he had suffered, even upon one whom God himself has declared innocent (42:7)?

Or again, could it have escaped the purists, or have been reconcilable with their doctrine, that Eliphaz, Bildad, and Zophar were among "all who had known him before" who joined in the comforting of Job and the joyous celebration of his restoration? What sort of retributive justice is that, when sinners condemned by the direct judgment of God (42:7), not by mere inference from their descent into wretchednes̄, are allowed part in the celebration of the righteous? One suffered, though righteous, and is affirmed. Three prospered, though unrighteous, and were condemned. Yet now righteous and unrighteous, him who suffered wrongly and those who prospered in spite of wrong, are discovered dancing at the same feast in the midst of a spectacular outburst of *shalom*, God smiling all the while! Where are the just rewards and punishments of God in such a wild scene?

Of course, the casuistry of retribution theology is infinitely nuanced, and ways can be found to make even such an apparently undisciplined festival fit the scheme of divine rewards and punishments. After all, the friends have eaten humble pie before God and Job, and the doctrine of retribution always made room for repentant sinners. Moreover, the restoration of Job might stand as evidence that, however long and painfully delayed, God's reward for righteousness does ultimately befall the innocent. Even "all the evil that the Lord has brought upon him" can be taken, if one has read the prologue, as a way of describing a "test" of Job's innocence. The missing allusion here to the *satan's* role in imposing Job's suffering can be dismissed as a relatively minor literary discrepancy. Job's wretchedness could never have happened without divine permission. The test itself could be described as a kind of divine accolade, preparing the way for a triumphant vindication and the appropriate reward.

Yet the interpretation of 29-31 and 38-41 undertaken here suggests an alternative way of responding to Job 42:10-17. If Job is understood, in every respect, as the extreme case for exploring the righteousness of God and man, then the final paragraph of the epilogue deserves to be explored as an ultimate instance as well. Just as there is a protological ring to Job 1:1-5 and Job 29, so there is an eschatological ring to Job 38:1, as we have interpreted it, and Job 42:10-17. One must leave room, in reading Job 1:1-5 and Job 29 for the possibility that the relationship between God and Job in that happy time was utterly intact and genuine from both sides. Theirs is not to be understood as a mutually self-serving relationship, in which each feigns good will toward the other on the basis of private needs or the lust for future benefits. If we postulate that Job *does* feign piety for such reasons, then we take the *satan's* position in

1:10ff, and the story turns out rather against us. Yet if the *satan* was *not* correct in his estimate of Job, there can be no talk of "rewards" for righteousness in Job 1:1-5. What is described there, and in Job 29, is the extreme imaginable instance of what unmarred *shalom* between God and the human might look like if one ever saw it. One must not only vindicate Job against the charge that he has base motivations for maintaining his side of the relationship. God must also be exonerated from the indictment that all divine "blessings" are merely bribery, what B. F. Skinner might call "positive reinforcement." God gives no blessing to human beings out of the ignoble motive of coercing a desired behavioral response from creatures who might otherwise prove recalcitrant. One must leave room for the possibility that the love of God for people is genuine, expressed freely for the sake of the beloved; in other words, at *least* as genuine as Job's celebrated integrity!

On his part, Job demonstrated that everything essential to maintaining the human side of the relationship was genuine, by affirming it into the void, in the absence of any of the just and lovely tokens that signaled the presence of the loving God. Yet if 1:1-5 and 29 reflect the relationship as it is intended to be, then one must speak of a kind of deprivation of God that corresponds to Job's time of suffering. The interim of pain and lostness is capable of testing the authenticity of the divine/human relationship, in the absence of any self-gratifying or self-aggrandizing motive. But it is not capable of reflecting the dimensions of fullness and richness and shared joy for which such a relationship is intended.

If 38:1 constitutes God's vindication of Job's suffering innocence, then in a deep sense God is involved in the suffering of Job as well as his innocence. Job's anguish cannot be said to reflect God's proper intention toward Job, as the friends contended it did. Rather it is an incredible affront to the divine will, endured in silence for the sake of permitting what is indispensable for the divine/human relationship to stand exposed and illuminated, without a shadow of ulterior motivation. If chapter 31 constitutes Job's untarnished human "Yes!" to God, *de profundis,* then 38:1 constitutes the irreproachable "Yes!" of God to Job out of the same depths, the same surrounding darkness. No more than Job is God able to point to external delights and advantages that would seem to validate their mutual commitment. Instead God honors the vindicated servant by disclosing to Job, with apparent heartlessness and insensitivity, that it is precisely in the context of a humanly incomprehensible order of things that the mutual integrity of their relationship must prove itself, and now has proven itself. These are the "angry" speeches of God that correspond to the "angry" speeches of Job, each demonstrating in an apparently inverse way the radical commitment of one to the other at the irreducible point.

Yet, neither for God nor for Job can this irreducible point of mutual commitment express the lovers' intention for their relationship in all its breadth and depth. If it were *not* for the tested validity of their essential relational integrity, then no amount of "confirmation" from the side of nature or history could make it authentic. But in the presence of unimpeachable mutual integrity, the way is now fully open for every delightful surprise through which lovers ring the changes on their selfless fascination with the other.

That is the way it once was between God and Job, say Job 1:1-5 and Job 29. And thus it ever shall be, says Job 42:10-17. God has permitted himself to be provisionally absent, in every way but the indispensable one, for the sake of the integrity of God's servant Job. Now that Job's integrity stands proven beyond reproach, God claims the lover's freedom to express delight in the beloved.

Again, Job is the extreme case. If 42:10-17 strikes us as all too homely and limited a way to describe the lover's extravagance of God toward the vindicated servant, it is only a failure of imagination, not intention. Paint it on whatever canvas you will, but let it show—no *less* than here—that God's eschatological intention for the authentically human is rich and joyous beyond all imagination.

Since Job is the extreme case, no human being remembers what it was like before the fact of suffering and injustice drove Job to the ultimate point of affirming God, against God, on the grounds of God's own love and justice. Nor has any human being experienced, as Job did, the full restoration of that idyllic love affair between God and the human. Job is not "everyman" in the sense that all of us repeat within ourselves the totality of Job's former blessedness, or his God-forsakenness, or his restoration. Job is "everyman" only in the sense that each of us can recognize in ordinary human experience authentic bits and pieces of the incomparable instance of divine and human righteousness. Every fragment of human lostness in the face of pain and injustice reverberates with the sound of Job's faithful lamentation and protest. Every flash of human compassion, dignity, and integrity reflects for an instant, in the absurd darkness, Job's brilliant case for the human. Every elusive perception, in spite of everything, that God is not only just and loving but present in the darkness on the side of the truly human is a glimpse of Job's vindication and his awe-struck adoration.

But one must then also say that every fleeting moment when life overflows with richness and beauty, with unself-conscious delight in the good things of life in the context of justice and love, may also stand as a time of disclosure. Such times, breaking into the everydayness of hurt and failure, betray the purpose of the lover who remains ultimately discontent with anything less than the establishment of his *shalom* for the world, without remainder. It has been made clear in Job that the authentic human being does not need this kind of "confirmation" of relationship. Perhaps the ice-cold speeches of God from the whirlwind strangely affirm that God does not need it either, in order for the indispensable quality of the divine/human relationship to be intact. But the restoration of Job in 42:10-17, at the very least, discloses the delicious lover's secret that God, for lover's reasons, wants it. In that light, the eschatological peace that belongs so inextricably to biblical expectation for the future may not be looked forward to as the "reward" that will ultimately prove all the suffering to have been worthwhile. Rather it is to be anticipated, and proleptically enjoyed in every fragmentary way possible, as God's freely chosen design to celebrate love with God's beloved world. W. H. Auden and Gerard Manley Hopkins were familiar companions on Stuart Currie's journey toward understanding himself and his world. He would not be altogether displeased, I think, to have them make the final summary of the theme of this essay, implying at the same time their own envisionable criticisms of it.[12]

From W. H. Auden:

"Now it is over. No, we have not dreamt it. Here we really stand, down stage with red faces and no applause; no effect, however simple, no piece of business, however unimportant, came off; there was not a single aspect of our whole production, not even the huge stuffed bird of happiness, for which a kind word could, however patronizingly, be said.

Yet, at this very moment when we do at last see ourselves as we are, neither cosy nor playful, but swaying out on the ultimate wind-whipped cornice that overhangs the unabiding void—we have never stood anywhere else,—when our reasons are silenced by the heavy huge derision,—There is nothing to say. There never has been,—and our wills chuck in their hands—There is no way out. There never was,—it is at this moment that for the first time in our lives we hear, not the sounds which, as born actors, we have hitherto condescended to use as an excellent vehicle for displaying our personalities and looks, but the real Word which is our only *raison d'être*. Not that we have improved; everything, the massacres, the whippings, the lies, the twaddle, and all their carbon copies are still present, more obviously than ever; nothing has been reconstructed; our shame, our fear, our incorrigible staginess, all wish and no resolve, are still, and more intensely than ever, all we have: only now it is not in spite of them but with them that we are blessed by that Wholly Other Life from which we are separated by an essential emphatic gulf of which our contrived fissures of mirror and proscenium arch—we understand them at last—are feebly figurative signs, so that all our meanings are reversed and it is precisely in its negative image of Judgment that we can positively envisage Mercy; it is just here, among the ruins and the bones, that we may rejoice in the perfected Work which is not ours. Its great coherences stand out through our secular blur in all their overwhelmingly righteous obligation; its voice speaks through our muffling banks of artificial flowers and unflinchingly delivers its authentic molar pardon; its spaces greet us with all their grand old prospect of wonder and width; the working charm is the full bloom of the unbothered state; the sounded note is the restored relation.''

   And finally from Hopkins,
''Not, I'll not, carrion comfort, Despair, not feast on thee;
Not untwist—slack they may be—these last strands of man
In me ór, most weary, cry *I can no more*. I can;
Can something, hope, wish day come, not choose not to be.
But ah, but O thou terrible, why wouldst thou rude on me
Thy wring-world right foot rock? lay a lionlimb against me?
   scan
With darksom devouring eyes my bruisèd bones? and fan,
O in turns of tempest, me heaped there; me frantic to avoid
   thee and flee?

  Why? That my chaff might fly; my grain lie, sheer and
   clear.
Nay in all that toil, that coil, since (seems) I kissed the rod,
Hand rather, my heart lo! lapped strength, stole joy, would
   laugh, chéer.
Cheer whom though? the hero whose heaven-handling flung me,
   fóot tród
Me? or me that fought him? O which one? is it each one?
  That night, that year
Of now done darkness I wretch lay wrestling with (my God!)
   my God.''

NOTES

1. Gerhard von Rad, *Old Testament Theology*, trans D.M.G. Stalker (New York: Harper & Brothers, 1962) I, 409ff (cf. esp. 411). See also his *Wisdom in Israel* (Nashville and New York: Abingdon Press, 1972) 217f.

2. Christoph Barth, *Die Errettung vom Tode in den individuellen Klage und Dankliedern des Alten Testaments* (Zollikon: Evangelischer Verlag, 1947) 91f.

3. Walter Zimmerli, "Promise and Fulfillment," *Essays on Old Testament Hermeneutics*, ed C. Westermann, J. L. Mays (Richmond, Virginia: John Knox Press, 1963) 101ff.

4. Marvin Pope, *Job* (AB; Garden City, N.Y.: Doubleday & Co., Inc., 1965) 249f.

5. "The prerequisite and aim of most of the laments is encounter with God who is conceived to be present, an encounter which is mediated by Yahweh's theophany in the cult." Artur Weiser, *The Psalms*, trans Herbert Hartwell from the 5th (revised) German edition, 1959 (Philadelphia: The Westminster Press, 1962) 72. See also 29f, 38-41, 57f, 68, 72ff, 76, and 163 (Ps 13:3), 207f (Ps 20:6).

6. H. J. Kraus, *Psalmen I* (BKAT 15/1; Neukirchen: Neukirchener Verlag, 1960) 176, 182.

7. "Vindication" is conceived in relational terms, in accord with the discussion above. It is not a matter of God declaring the Psalmist innocent or righteous by the measure of some standard of justice external to God and human beings. The Psalmist's cry for an "answer" or for "vindication" is above all the plea to know that the relationship between himself and God is fully congruent. Vindication by God, then, is the longed-for confirmation that the quality of life affirmed by the Psalmist indeed corresponds to the quality of life God intends. Such an "answer" has the effect of confirming the wholeness of the divine/human relationship, the congruence of divine and human righteousness as relationally defined.

8. Pope, 209.

9. Just this way of perceiving the question of Job was brought home to me in a paragraph from Samuel Terrien's popularly written *Job: Poet of Existence* (Indianapolis and New York: The Bobbs-Merrill Co., Inc., 1957) 30. In this and many other respects I am overwhelmingly indebted to Dr. Terrien (above all for his superb commentary on Job in the series Commentaire de L'Ancien Testament, XVII, Editions Delachaux & Neistlè, Neuchatel [Suisse], 1963). He is not, however, to be held responsible for the approach taken in this paper. In view of my respect, bordering on awe, for what he has accomplished in the French commentary, it has taken no little courage to offer the present exegetical alternative. Note especially his powerful rejection of approaches comparable to mine on 47f of that work. My hope is that I have found an alternative that is not altogether vulnerable to the criticisms there rendered. I would argue against Terrien that neither the Old nor the New Testaments make room for a conception of divine transcendence so sublime that there is simply no link between the human struggle for justice and righteousness and the reality of God. The Old Testament uniquely forbids divorcing God's transcendent being from divine commitment to and insistence upon justice

and righteousness in human affairs—by God's definition, not man's. The New Testament word about Jesus Christ undercuts even more radically the possibility of "honoring" God by thinking to exalt God above the issues of justice and righteousness precisely as they come to focus in one who is authentically human.

10. Words attributed to Robert Frost as a suggested inscription for his tombstone.
11. Pope, LXXIVf.
12. For Auden, see "Caliban to the Audience," *W. H. Auden: Collected Poems,* ed Edward Mendelson (New York: Random House, Inc., 1976): 340. Hopkins' poem, Carrion Comfort, written in 1885, is available in various anthologies and collections of the works of Gerard Manley Hopkins (1844-1889).

The Watchers in the Twelve and at Qumran

Prescott H. Williams, Jr.

The episode of the Wakeful Ones (usually translated "Watchers") and the Women occurs in varying forms in the literature now available from Qumran. When the forms and uses of the episode in the Testaments of Reuben and Naphtali are placed alongside the Qumran versions, with their established dates and milieu, an intriguing set of possibilities emerges which may contribute to the identification of date and human community of the Testaments.

The Testaments of the Twelve Patriarchs have been the subject of modern scholarly study for many years, but no consensus concerning their dates (generally somewhere between 200 B.C.E. and 200 C.E.) has emerged. Their milieu has been identified variously as Jewish, Jewish-Christian, Essene, and many other combinations.[1] The Qumran manuscripts have been studied beside the Testaments, again without resolving the issues. I will address the issues by analyzing the two references to the episode in the Testaments, and then by analysis of references to and constructions of the myth in literature from Qumran. These will be discussed in their probable chronological order: Enoch (with passing references to Daniel 4), Jubilees, the Damascus Document (Zadokite Documents), and the Genesis Apocryphon. Throughout this survey I will identify elements which seem central to the myth as reflected in these documents, as well as the modifications or adaptations peculiar to the individual compositions. My current conclusions, particularly with reference to the placement of the Testaments in relationship to the Qumran documents, will be summarized at the end.

In the Testament of Reuben 5:5-7, the first testament of the twelve, and in Testament of Naphtali 3:1-5, the episode is adduced to support warnings against fornication. The ethical concerns of the

Testaments give a primary place to fornication among the vices to
be assiduously avoided.[2] This is particularly true of T. Reuben,
where the cognate verb and noun (*porneia*) occur 13 times in all.
The singular importance of fornication for the exhortations in T.
Reuben would be clear from the structure and contents of this
testament, even if there were fewer occurrences of these words.

Primary concern focuses on what 3:3 terms the first of eight
spirits of error which work against mankind. After listing and identifying the spirits, warnings concerning relationships with women
immediately ensue. As is usual in the Testaments, the vice warned
against or the virtue advocated is illustrated by an episode from the
life of the individual patriarch addressing his offspring just before
his death. In this case, Reuben tells of his intercourse with Bilhah,
his father's wife. Then he explicates the power of fornication,
indicates ways to avoid involvement in it, and describes the
spiritual and physical consequences of engaging in it. As is often
the case in the Testaments, Joseph's exemplary behavior is contrasted to the guilty patriarch's. Joseph's resistance to the persistent
seductive efforts of the Egyptian woman is recounted to Reuben's
offspring, and then an ethical rule is stated, "For if fornication
overcome not the mind, neither shall Beliar overcome you" (4:11).

Then follows a diatribe against women: "hurtful are
women...they act subtilly through outward guise...whom they cannot overcome by strength, him they overcome by craft. For
moreover the angel of God told me concerning them, and taught me
that women are overcome by the spirit of fornication more than
men, and they devise in their heart against men" (5:1-4).[3] In 6:1-4
the episode of the Wakeful Ones and the Women is reported, from
which this warning is drawn:

> Beware, therefore, of fornication; and if you wish to be pure in
> your mind, guard your senses against every woman. And com-
> mand them likewise not to company with men, that they (f.)
> also be pure in their mind. For constant meetings...are to them
> an irremediable disease, and to us an everlasting reproach of
> Beliar; for fornication hath neither understanding nor
> godliness in itself, and all jealousy dwelleth in the desire
> thereof.

T. Reuben continues with a prediction of future Reubenites' opposition to Levi (and Judah?), i.e., opposition to God's designated
leader(s), and concludes with an account of Reuben's two-phase

burial, in a coffin in Egypt, then in a cave at Hebron.

Chapter 5:5-7 is at the core of this closely structured testamentary narrative:

> Therefore, flee fornication, my children, and command your wives and your daughters that they adorn not their heads and their faces; because every woman who acted deceitfully in these things hath been reserved to everlasting punishment. For thus they allured the Watchers before the flood; and as they (m.) continually beheld them (f.), they fell into desire each of the other, and they conceived the act in their mind, and changed themselves into the shape of men, and appeared to them in their congress with their husbands; and the women, having in their minds desire toward their apparitions, gave birth to giants, for the Watchers appeared to them as reaching unto heaven.

The episode as employed here shows several of the central elements which will be found in other uses:

1. The Wakeful Ones are males;
2. The Wakeful Ones behold the women and react;
3. The episode is closely associated with the flood;
4. Unusual births result from the relations of the Wakeful Ones and the women.

The additional features of this particular account of the episode include:

1. Active allurement by the women.
2. The metamorphosis (?) of the Wakeful Ones.
3. The curious relationship of the parties and the associated conception of giants (the giants are conceived as a result of intercourse while the women experience great desire toward the apparitions).

This last matter brings together the later subtitle of T. Reuben, "Concerning Intentions," and its preoccupation with fornication by providing an example of intentions transmuting physical actions to produce unexpected results. The women's fantasies became the effective agency in conceiving giants.

While this version stresses the women's initiative, seductive allurements, and fantasizing, the Wakeful Ones are also described as active respondents. In fact, their first response, continually beholding the adorned women, seems to play on the designation of the Watchers (*'Egregorous*) and their initial act of "seeing" the women. Their threefold response to what they continually looked upon clearly lays responsibility on them: they conceived the act (of fornication), they changed themselves into human shape, they appeared to the women at the critical times.

The assignment of double responsibility in this version undergirds the double exhortation which it supports: that women should avoid adornments and allurements, that men should guard themselves against women. If the scales of responsibility are tipped at all, they are tipped toward the women whose initiative opened the way for the virtual fornication. The episode, therefore, supports the contentions of the author about women in ways which the description of Reuben's behavior with Bilhah does not. For according to 3:11, Bilhah "was drunk, and lay asleep uncovered, in her chamber." Reuben, not Bilhah, was the initiator of their fornication. The women in the Watchers' episode, however, conform more closely to the portrayal of the Egyptian woman of the Joseph story. In T. Reuben 4:9 her behavior is summarized: "For the Egyptian woman did many things unto him (Joseph), and called for magicians, and offered him love potions, and the purpose of his soul admitted no evil desire." This summary of Genesis 39:9-20, especially verse 10, is expanded, developed, extended, and told twice in the T. Joseph, leaving no doubt of the aggressive initiatives which Joseph resisted.

While T. Reuben clearly derogates the actions of the women and the Wakeful Ones and develops sharply etched exhortations from these actions, the consequences, the giants, are simply mentioned without the elaboration we shall encounter elsewhere. Moreover, the derogatory view of women found in T. Reuben is one with that expressed in the remainder of the Testaments. In these explicit and implicit ways T. Reuben sets the tone for the following eleven testaments, which return often to the concern about fornication and reiterate the assessment of women as temptresses.

The T. Naphtali also, though eighth in the order of the individual Testaments, may be primary. M. de Jonge, whose 1953 study of the Testaments marked a turning point in recent studies of both the text and the content of the Testaments, regarded both T. Levi and T. Naphtali as basic to the entire Testaments project.[4]

The subtitle of T. Naphtali indicates that it focuses on the nature of goodness. The contents of the testament demonstrate that this goodness is bound up with the order which God created in the world:

> For God made all things good in their order, the five senses
> in the head, and He joineth on the neck to the head....So then,
> my children, be ye orderly unto good things in the fear of God,

and do nothing disorderly in scorn or out of its due season. For if thou bid the eye to hear, it cannot; so neither in darkness can ye do the works of light. (2:8-9)

T. Naphtali 3:1-5 follows immediately upon the interpretation of the importance of the order of the commandments in 2:8-9:

Be ye not therefore eager to corrupt your doings through excess, or with empty words to deceive your souls; because if ye keep silence in purity of heart, ye shall be able to hold fast the will of God, and to cast away the will of the devil. Sun and moon and stars change not their order; so also ye shall not change the law of God in the disorderliness of your doings. Nations went astray, and forsook the Lord, and changed their order, and followed stones and stocks, following after spirits of error. But ye shall not be so, my children, recognizing in the firmament, in the earth, and in the sea, and in all created things, the Lord who made them all, that ye become not as Sodom, which changed the order of its nature. In like manner also the Watchers changed the order of their nature, whom also the Lord cursed at the flood, and for their sakes made desolate the earth, that it should be uninhabited and fruitless.

T. Naphtali 4:1 follows immediately, "These things I say, my children, for I have read in the holy writings of Enoch that ye yourselves will also depart from the Lord, walking according to the wickedness of the Gentiles, and ye will do according to the iniquity of Sodom." Despite the apparent allusion to 3:5, no particular exhortation is derived from the episode of the Wakeful Ones.

T. Naphtali's treatment of the episode seems dependent on that in T. Reuben. The transgression of the Wakeful Ones here, however, is not described as in response to women's allurements nor is it specified exactly what they did. On the other hand, the consequences are specific: cursed by the Lord at the flood, the earth made desolate.

The truncated treatment of the episode here seems both to be strictly limited by the writer's "order"[5] concerns and to imply a concern specifically referent to sexual relations. The hortatory con-

struction put upon it, however, does not focus on women, as did T.
Reuben.

These two passages (T. Reuben 5:5-7 and T. Naphtali 3:1-5) contain the only references to the Wakeful Ones in the Testaments.
Both are clearly bound up with a primary concern of the whole of
the Testaments, disorderly sexual relations. Both are essential to
the specific concerns of the individual Testaments in which they
are found. Both represent references to the earliest examples of the
evil which they describe. (Gen 6:1-4 is as early in the biblical
sources as the Testaments reach for examples and the only example
which is pre-patriarchal.) Both provide the bases for warnings.
Both present the Wakeful Ones as having done evil.

The Wakeful Ones thus join most of the fathers themselves,
except for Joseph, Naphtali, and Issachar, as having committed
errors which their offspring must scrupulously avoid. They also
join women in general, the Egyptian woman in particular, even
though, in T. Naphtali, women are only respondents.

If one considers the Testaments' use of the episode as derived
from Genesis 6, directly or indirectly, the changes made in the
entirety of the episode and the hortatory uses of it are striking. The
name of the figures, the initiative of the women, the concern for an
'order of nature,' the description of fantasy-influence, the explicit
assignment of responsibility for the flood, are noteworthy. Too, in
contrast to other uses to be analyzed below, most of the distinctive
terminology used in Genesis is missing.[6,7]

The Enoch literature, with the exception of Parables, is extensively represented in the Qumran libraries. In his 1976 publication,
The Books of Enoch, J. T. Milik identified several copies to which he
assigned dates on the basis of palaeography:

Enoch[a]—200 150 B.C.E.
Enoch[b]—ca. 150 B.C.E.
Enoch[c]—150-125 B.C.E.
Enoch[e]—100-50 B.C.E.
Enoch[g]—ca. 50 B.C.E.
Enoch[d]—(Is Enoch[d] a copy of Enoch[c]?)—last third of the first
    century B.C.E.

There is also an Enoch[f] ms which Milik assigned to 150-125 B.C.E.;
he identified its scribe as the copyist of the document named 4Q
Testament of Levi.[b8] All of these are from Cave Four and there are
copies from no other Qumran cave. The Parables are not attested at
Qumran, but the 'Book of Giants' is; some copies of it are in the
'classical' Herodian script of the Qumran scribes. Milik suggested
that the evidence indicates a diminution of interest in the Enoch
literature as the life of the Qumran community developed. He pro-

posed that early Christians substituted the Parables for the Book of Giants in an Enochic 'pentateuch.'

The extent and chronological range of these samples of the Enoch materials from Qumran document the presence and use of the older Enochic corpus during the second century B.C.E. in Palestine by the Jews at Qumran. According to Milik they point toward a pre-second century origin for them. More precisely, he dated the Visions of Enoch (chs 6-19) from the end of the third century B.C.E. This is a section of the Book of Watchers (chs 1-36) particularly important for the interests of this essay.

Milik also discussed 4Q TestLevi 8 iii 6-7, the equivalent of Greek T. Levi 14, and concluded that this Aramaic document contains the earliest allusion to the Book of Watchers. He has promised to try in a future study of the available Greek and Aramaic fragments of Testament of Levi to prove "that it is Samaritan in origin and was composed in the course of the third century, if not towards the end of the fourth." At the present, however:

> For the moment we will maintain that its attestation of the Book of Watchers (or more precisely of the Visions of Enoch, chs. 6-19) dates from towards the end of the third century. The altogether incontestable *terminus ante quem* falls in the year 164 B.C., the date of the composition of the Book of Dreams, which is closely dependent on the Book of Watchers....

This dating of the Book of Dreams derives from an allusion to the Battle of Bethsur, 164 B.C.E. Milik also noted the dependence of Jubilees 4: 21-22 on the Book of Watchers.[9]

In Enoch 1-36, the Book of Watchers, the figures prominent in the episode under study here are regularly termed ^{c}*irīn*, often times joined with *qaddishin*, a coupling to be discussed below. This noun is derived from the widely used semitic stem ^{c}y/wr, "to be awake." Because of its intransitive form, I prefer to translate it "Wakeful Ones," rather than the more active "Watchers."

The construction and use of the episode of the Wakeful Ones and the Women in Enoch 1-36 is at variance with that in the Testaments as indicated by Milik's summary:

> The religious thinker reflects here on the problem of the evil existing in the world and sees the origin of it in the union of the sons of heaven with the daughters of men. The basic theme, which he develops in his own way, is the celestial provenance of human techniques and sciences....

According to the author of En. 6ff.,...sexual appetite dominates the angels from the beginning (6:1-6 and 7:1), and the sciences they teach are all turned to wicked ends (7:1 and 8:1-3). The writer imagines two chiefs of the fallen angels, a king (*Šemîhazah*) and a sage (*ᶜAśa'el*), each presiding over about ten Watchers (and each of these ten presiding over about ten anonymous angels), thus drawing on the Babylonian model of antediluvian kings and sages....The names of the twenty principal Watchers (En. 6:7), of which the fragments of 4Q give the correct form (with the exception of the name of the fifth), are for the most part derived from astronomical, meteorological, and geographical terms.[10]

The critical passage is, as Milik indicated, 6:1-7:6, most of which is attested by 4QEnoch[b] 1 ii, which covers 5:9-6:4 and 6:7-8:1. Milik's translation:

[5⁹...] all the days [of your life]. 6¹ And it came to pass when [the children of men multiplied in those days, there were born to them daughters], beautiful and [fair. ²And the Watchers, sons of heaven, saw them and desired them]; and they said, [one to another: 'Let us go and choose for ourselves wives from the daughters of men and beget for ourselves children.' ³But Šemîhazâ who was their chief said to them: 'I fear that you will not wish to do this deed; and I alone shall be guilty of a great sin.' ⁴And they all answered] and said [to him]: 'Let us [all] swear [an oath, and all bind one another by it, that we shall not any of us turn aside from] this counsel, [until] we do [this deed⁵....] ⁸These are the chiefs of tens.

[7¹Those (two hundred) and their leaders all took for themselves] wives from all [that they chose]; and they began [to go in to them, and to defile themselves with them and (they began) to teach them] sorcery and spell-binding [and the cutting of roots; and to show them plants. ²And they became pregnant by them and bore giants, three thousands cubits high, who were born (and multiplied) on the earth according to the kind of their] childhood, [and growing up according to the kind of their adolescence,³ and] they were devouring [the labour of all the children of men and men were unable] to supply [them. ⁴But the giants conspired to slay men and to devour them. ⁵And they began to sin against all birds and beasts of the earth], and reptiles [which creep upon the face of the earth, and (creatures) in the waters and in the heaven, and the fish of the sea, and to devour the flesh of another; and they were] drinking blood. [⁶Then the earth made the accusation against the wicked concerning everything] which was done upon it.

8[1'] [C]Aśa'el taught [men to] make swords of iron and breast plates of brass, [and he showed] them (metals) which are dug out, [and how] they should work gold to fashion it apt (for uses), and concerning silver, to fashion it for bracelets, [and for (other) adornments] of [women. And] he [showed to women] concerning antimony, and concerning eye-shadow, [and concerning all precious stones, and concerning dye-stuffs].[11]

In this passage, and in a similar narrative in Enoch 15 (not attested at Qumran), the central figures are designated *irin, with qaddishin* as a pair word. In the Greek texts, these are regularly rendered by appropriate forms of *'egregoros* and *hagios*. However, references to those who left heaven to have intercourse with women regularly are designated only by *irin*. The combination *irin w^e qaddishin*, 'Watchers and Holy Ones' or, better, 'Holy Watchers,' refers to those heavenly beings who did not leave their station and engage in relations with human females. My own survey of all the occurrences in all the portions of Enoch found at Qumran bears out Milik's contention:

The author of the work made a distinction in his angelological terminology between the 'Watchers', who as a rule refer to the evil angels (fallen stars, incubi), and the 'Watchers and holy ones', who refer to the good angels, messengers of God, the guardians and guides of just men....[12]

Milik noted how this usage is reflected in Daniel 4:10, 20 where the agent of revelation is so designated, with no suggestion that he is a fallen creature. He also noted the similar usage in 1Q Genesis Apocryphon, to which reference will be made below.

Milik observed a clear distinction in Enoch between the singular, *ir* and the plural, in which, as in Daniel, the singular refers to the agent of God's disclosure to Enoch, again not a fallen angel. This seems to be Gabriel, as found in the reconstruction of Enoch 10:8-12, where the plural occurs in reference to those who will be destroyed because of their evil action:

[And to Gabriel] the Lord [said]: 'Go [to the bastards and the children of fornication, and destroy] the children of the Watchers [from among men, and send them] into a war of destruction; and length [of days they will not have.][13]

This translation is based on 4Q Enoch^b, the second earliest of the copies, and is the earliest clearly attested mention of *irin* in the corpus.

4Q Enoch[e] furnishes another example of the plural reference in 33:3-4, which Milik translated on the basis of the Aramaic fragment alone.

There are numerous other examples of the plural of ^{c}*irin* in Enoch 1-36, most of which Milik reconstructed from the parallel word, *qaddishin*. They are not references to the fallen angels.

What emerges from this testimony in the surviving portions of Enoch 1-36 at Qumran is a consistent pattern of references to the central figures in the episode narrated in 6:1-8:1 and in 5:1-12. While the uses of the narrative are not turned directly to exhortations addressed to men and women, they are employed to explain the disorder in the universe of humankind occasioned by the actions of the 'Watchers.' Their actions become the reason for devastating judgment on the 'Watchers,' their offspring, and humankind. Their actions are described as a disturbance of the divinely established order of nature, as attested in 2:1-5:5, amply attested at Qumran in 4Q Enoch[a, c].

Given the excellent chronological controls on the Qumran Enoch materials which indicate their precedence, it is clear that in Enoch the episode is more fully and completely described. The use made of it by the Testaments may be derived from some of the elements found in the Enoch material, with modifications to suit the hortatory purposes of the Testaments. The core elements previously summarized are all present, in order: 'Watchers' are regarded as males, their seeing and beholding of the fair human females is their first act, their fulfilled acts result in judgment (although not specified as the flood), and unusual births result from their cohabitation with women, destructive giants who reproduce their own kind (7:2-5).

Other elements in Enoch differ from the Testaments' construction of the episode: designating them as 'sons of heaven' (6:2); indicating that the initiative was all theirs; clear indication of repeated and actual intercourse with the women (7:1), sinning against animals (7:1, 8:1), defilement as a result of their acts (7:1), and that their teaching of skills and crafts follows their cohabiting with the women (7:1, 8:1). In addition, the number 200 for their company is given (7:1), and the earth is described as accusing them (7:6).

One of the most striking differences between the Enochic version and the Testaments' version is the description in Enoch of actual, and repeated, intercourse between Watchers and women. In the Testaments, on the other hand, the assertion seems to be only 'influence through fantasy.' Given the probable dependence of the Testaments on Enochic materials, this indicates a move away from actual intercourse, and clearly shifts responsibility to include the women. The Enoch materials really make no place for such, except as compliance may constitute responsibility, and certainly do not attribute initiative to the women, who do not learn the skills of adornment until after their cohabitation with the angels.

When these comparisons are made the Enochic version seems much closer to Genesis 6:1-4 than the version in the Testaments. The relationship is so close that Milik has decided that the Genesis account is dependent upon Enochic sources.

> The very close interdependence of En. 6-19 and Gen. 6:1-4 is perfectly obvious; the same phrases and analogous expressions are repeated in the two texts....
> The ineluctable solution, it seems to me, is that it is the text of Gen. 6:1-4, which, by its abridged and allusive formulation, deliberately refers back to our Enochic document, two or three phrases of which it quotes verbatim....If my hypothesis is correct, the work incorporated in En. 6-19 is earlier than the definitive version of the first chapters of Genesis.[14]

Given the fact that Milik reckons this material about the Watchers as from a source anterior to the extant form of Enoch 1-36, it seems that he is not asserting dependence of Genesis 6 on the extant form of Enoch, but on the sources on which it draws. How old were these sources? At least third, possibly, fourth century B.C.E., in his opinion. Our only access to them is through extant Enoch. Does this provide suffcient evidence to decide dependence? Or should we think about a much older tradition, reflected in both of these early versions? Is there mutual dependence on a presently inaccessible tradition which structured the narrative in ways now reflected in both? The 'disconnected' placement of Gen 6:1-4 in its present context, where only by implication or inference is the flood a judgment on the Watchers' act(s), suggests the possibility that Gen 6:1-4 is an addition to Genesis after its basic framework and contents were established. But when and how? It is probably too soon to attempt answers to these questions.

What is eminently clear is that the "active presence of spiritual beings in the world of men is thus in no way the first cause of evil in the earth, as the two authors of the Book of Watchers taught."[15] In this matter, both the Testaments and Enoch 1-36 agree.

In the Book of Jubilees, also attested at Qumran, there is a different construction of the Watchers' episode, for a different purpose, but at the same time the dependence of this version on earlier sources, particularly upon Enoch 6-19, is evident. The differences from the Enoch version are therefore all the more important.

Jubilees is attested at Qumran by fragments of ten manuscripts from three of the Caves: 1, 2, and 4. This is ample attestation for the use of Jubilees at Qumran by a group which shared the special calendaric concerns of Jubilees. In 1959, Milik expressed his judgment about these fragments:

> Its Hebrew style flows easily, and the text corresponds closely to that of the archetype presupposed by the (complete) Ethiopic and (incomplete) Latin versions. The insistence on a special form of the solar calendar and on fixed dates for the main festivals—both important characteristics of the Qumran sect (see below)—suggest that, in this case the work was itself written by a member of the sect; historical allusions make it probable that its composition occurred well before 100 B.C.[16]

In his 1976 work on Enoch, Milik discussed the relationship between Jubilees and the Enoch literature attested at Qumran and offered 128-125 B.C.E as the earliest date for composition of Jubilees.[17]

Because these fragments are not yet published, R. H. Charles' translation from the Ethiopic will have to suffice. The first reference to the episode is at 4:15, which dates the descent to the days of the antediluvian Jared:

> . . . in his days the angels of the Lord descended on the earth, those who are named the Watchers, that they should instruct the children of men, and that they should do judgment and uprightness on the earth.[18]

Already in this first notice a difference from Enoch's presentation is evident because the descent comes before the seeing and desiring of women and is a descent for the good purpose of instructing humans. Thereafter, 5:1 describes the ensuing involvement of the angels with women, here in accord with the Enochic version:

> And it came to pass when the children of men began to multiply on the face of the earth and daughters were born unto them, that the angels of God saw them on a certain year of this jubilee, that they were beautiful to look upon; and they took themselves wives of all whom they chose, and they bare unto them sons and they were giants.[19]

The ensuing lawlessness and corruption is described then, among men and animals, and the corruption of "their ways and their orders," which when God saw it, "He said that He would destroy man and all flesh upon the face of the earth which He had created" (5:3-4).[20]

This condensed version of the episode reflects its dependency on earlier versions. The consequences are explicit, as the following context shows in its retelling of the Noah-flood story. After the flood destruction and subsequent events, Noah speaks to his off-spring in a hortatory manner reminiscent of the pattern found throughout the Testaments.

> And in the twenty-eighth jubilee Noah began to enjoin upon his sons the ordinances and commandments, and all the judgments that he knew, and he exhorted his sons to observe righteousness, and cover the shame of their flesh, and to bless their Creator, and honour father and mother, and love their neighbour, and guard their souls from fornication and unclean-ness and all iniquity. For owing to these three things came the flood upon the earth, namely, owing to the fornication wherein the Watchers against the law of their ordinances went awhor-ing after the daughters of men, and took themselves wives of all which they chose; and they made the beginning of unclean-ness. (7:20-21)[21]

Thereafter, in 8:3-4, Jubilees describes Kainam's search for a city:

> And he found a writing which former (generations) had carved on the rock, and he read what was thereon, and he transcribed it and sinned owing to it; for it contained the teaching of the Watchers in accordance with which they used to observe the omens of the sun and moon and stars in all the signs of heaven.[22]

Seemingly his sin was involved with the calendaric matters of im-portance to the writer of Jubilees. Put together with 4:15, this sug-gests that the original teaching of the Watchers was later corrupted and led to sin.

In commenting on the relationship between this form of the myth and the Enochic form, Milik affirmed:

> The book of Jubilees presents a more archaic form of this myth: the Watchers, angels of the Lord, come down to the earth to instruct the children of men and to bring about justice and equity on the earth (4:15); it is not until later that the cor-ruption and punishment of the Watchers and their children

will occur (5:1-10). According to the author of En. 6ff., on the contrary sexual appetite dominates the angels from the beginning....[23]

Again, in this construction and use of the episode in Jubilees the core elements are present: the Wakeful Ones are males, the vision of human women's beauty is the occasion for their interest, giants are born from the union of angels and women, and the flood is God's judgment on their acts.

Unlike the Testaments' use, the initiative in the cohabitation is all with the angels, the intercourse is certainly actual, and nothing is said about the women's responses or complicity.

Jubilees 7:20-21 and its context, nevertheless, bear some striking resemblances to the use of the episode in the Testaments of Reuben and Naphtali: the scene is a gathering of offspring, the intent is warning and admonition, and at least one of the admonitions involves avoidance of what Noah himself had done by letting his nakedness be seen. And, like the Testaments and Enoch, it is evident that the acts of the Wakeful Ones are regarded as the primal instance of the disturbance of the universal order, as well as 'the beginning of uncleanness,' even though the disobedience of Adam and Eve had been reported in 3:15-29.

The manifestly didactic purposes of Jubilees in its use of the episode have provided the author with a principle of selectivity and emphasis which results in a version and use which are similar to that of the Testaments, though differing with respect to the role of the women. Like the Testaments, Jubilees reflects no distinction between good and bad angels; rather, like them, it implies that the angels, who originally descended on a teaching mission, became corrupted through their interest in and attachment to the 'beautiful' women.

Whether Milik was correct in calling this a more archaic version needs much more study. It is possible that the Jubilees version was an alternative construction of a myth which Enochic literature used for different purposes and with a much more speculative interest in angelology.

Similar to the use of the episode in Jubilees is the construction in the Damascus Document, long known from the Cairo Genizah materials and now attested in fragments as early as *ca.* 75 B.C.E. at Qumran. The dates of the fragments and the character of the contents, in comparison with the previously known copies, makes a date for composition of *ca.* 110-100 B.C.E. likely. The Qumran copies were found in Caves 4, 5, and 6; they show close relationships with the previously known manuscript A of the Damascus Document. Their distribution in three caves and the fact that they represent different sections of the document point toward the presence of the substantial entirety of the Damascus Document at Qumran. Further, the much-studied teachings within it show the proximity to, if not identity with, central concerns and teachings of the Qumran community.[24]

Since the Qumran fragments are not yet published, C. Rabin's *Zadokite Documents* provides our best text. The first reference to the episode is in 2:14, where it is based on a correction of the reading ^{c}ydy to ^{c}yry, a correction thoroughly justified by the context, which Rabin translates:

And now, children, hearken unto me, that I may uncover your eyes to see and to consider the works of God; to choose him in whom (or: that in which) He delights and to reject him whom He hates; to walk uprightly in all His ways and 'not to seek after thoughts of guilty inclination and eyes of whoredom.' For many went astray through these, and mighty men of valour stumbled through them, from old times even until now. When they walked in the stubborness of their hearts, the watchers of heaven fell; in it they were entangled because they kept not the commandments of God, as well as their sons 'whose height was like the tallness of cedars' and whose corpses were like mountains when they fell. (2:14-19)[25]

Evidently in one of the Qumran fragments, the height is given as 30 cubits (see Milik's discussion of reduction from 3000 cubits in Enoch 7:2 to 30 cubits).[26]

3:1-6 traces the history of humans who went astray as did the Watchers of heaven. It is again clear that the Watchers' action was the beginning of such straying from God's commanded order. The list of those who followed this precedent includes Noah, his sons, their families, and the sons of Jacob, with no exception made of Joseph. Abraham, Isaac, and Jacob were exceptions, who did not 'walk in it,' that is, in the stubbornness of their hearts. The 'it' is whoredom and other sexual aberrations, as the recurrent exhortations and warnings make clear. In an eschatological declaration, 4:13-18, this is evident.

And during all those years shall Belial be let loose upon Israel, as He spoke by the hand of the Prophet Isaiah son of Amoz, saying: 'Fear, and the pit, and the snare are upon thee, O inhabitant of the land.' Its explanation: the three nets of Belial, about which

Levi son of Jacob said that he 'catches in them the heart (or: the house) of Israel' and has made them appear as three kinds of righteousness. The first is whoredom, the second is wealth, the third is conveying uncleanness to the sanctuary.[27]

This passage presents a *pesher* in which Isaiah's prophetic words are interpreted in a way which assigns primacy to the trap of whoredom. The Hebrew word in these passages, *znwt,* is that which the LXX regularly rendered by cognates of *porneia.* The shared concern of the Damascus Document and the Testaments in this matter is attested in several passages in the Damascus Document, 4:19-21, 5:8-10, and 7:1-2. The episode of the Wakeful Ones and the Women is not recounted in the Damascus Document, only cited in 2:14 as the original instance of a transgression which became the besetting sin of many.

These exhortations do not derive a derogatory view of women from the episode, but rather focus on the problem this original fall initiated for the males of Israel's earlier and later history. Clear also is the assertion that this fall was the occasion for the judgment, after which the problem persisted for Noah and his offspring. But the women are unmentioned.

The final document from Qumran which employs this episode is the Genesis Apocryphon from Cave 1, a relatively complete document, unattested except by its presence at Qumran. There are two references to Watchers in the story of Lamech's reaction to Noah's unusual appearance at birth, column 2, lines 1 and 16. The distinctive character of the newborn Noah is also described in Enoch 106:1-2, which Milik translated:

And after a time I Enoch took a wife for Methuselah my son and he brought forth a son and called] his name Lamech [saying: 'Brought low, indeed, righteousness has been to this day.' And when he came to maturity, Methuselah took for him] a wife, and she [became pregnant by him and bore a boy. And when the boy was born, his flesh was whiter than snow and] redder [than the rose, and all his hair was white as the pure wool, and thick and bright. And when he opened his eyes he lighted up the] whole [house as the sun...][28]

Reference to this surprising appearance of Noah at birth is also found in 1Q19. These Qumran fragments seem to be parts of what Charles published as a "Fragment of the Book of Noah." In his puzzlement at this, Lamech, according to the Apocryphon, requested Methuselah to inquire of Enoch, because he suspected that one of the 'sons of the God of heaven' or 'the angels' was his sire. 4Q Enoch[c] preserves Enoch's reply, found in 106:13-107:2 in the fuller version. In it, Enoch recounts the episode and its meaning, in harmony with the earlier teachings of Enoch 1-36, and assures Lamech that the son is indeed his own.

The narrative in the Genesis Apocryphon presupposes this description of Noah and also reflects the inquiry directed to Enoch, which is fragmentarily recounted in the surviving portions of columns 2, 3, and 5. If column 3's small fragment is rightly placed it seems to reflect a narrative in which the Watchers' episode is dated to the days of Jared.[29]

Before looking at column 2, where the story of Lamech's reaction is retold, the matter of date should be discussed. Joseph A. Fitzmyer concluded his discussion of the Cave 1 manuscript with the comment, "The palaeographical date of this copy is to be set at the end of the first century B.C. or the first half of the first century A.D." If, as seems possible, this copy is the autograph, the first century B.C.E. could be the probable time of composition, which Fitzmyer characterized in these words:

> We stress then the independent character of this composition. Though it depends on the biblical text of Genesis and displays at times traits of targumic and midrashic composition, it is in reality a free reworking of the Genesis stories, a re-telling of the tales of the patriarchs (Lamech, Noah, Abram, etc.). It is definitely related to the intertestamental literary compositions such as *Enoch, Jubilees,* the *Testaments of the Twelve Patriarchs, etc....The Genesis Apocryphon* represents then an example of late Jewish narrative writing, strongly inspired by the canonical stories of the patriarchs, but abundantly enhanced with imaginative details (accounts of dreams, reports of plagues, descriptions of beauty, accounts of journeys, explanation of geographical terms, and modifications of the text to eliminate difficulties or apparent contradictions). It is hardly likely that this text was used in the synagogue as a targum, but it was most likely composed for a pious and edifying purpose.[30]

Is it Essene? Fitzmyer concluded:

> There is nothing in this text which clearly links it with any of the known beliefs or customs of the Essene sect. There is little Essene theology in this work, and it is difficult to see what exegetical or dogmatical meditations were at work in the composition of this text.[31]

Unlike Jubilees and the Damascus Document, didactic purposes are not prominent. The references to the Watchers fit into the general characterization because there is no specific surviving reference to their fall, even though cohabitation with women is presupposed by the suspicions of Lamech expressed in column 2, lines 1-7 and 14-18, which Fitzmyer translated as follows:

1. So then I thought in my mind that the conception was due to the Watchers or that it w[a]s due to the Holy Ones, or to the Nephil [im...;
2. and my mind wavered because of this child.
3. Then I, Lamech, became frightened and I went to Bitenosh, my wi[fe and said ''....]
4. [ ]...by the Most High, by the Great Lord, by the King of all A[ges,
5. [with] the sons of heavens, that you truthfully make everything known to me, whether [   ]
6. you must tell me [truthfully] and without lies whether this [...Swear]
7. by the King of all Ages that you are speaking to me truthfully and without lies [   ].''

Bitenosh is vehement at this accusation. She defends herself with tears and an impassioned recounting of the conception of Noah, at the conclusion of which she declares:

14. my pleasure. I swear to you by the Great Holy One, by the King of the h[eavens   ]
15. that this seed is from you; from you is this conception, and from you the planting of [this] fruit [   ];
16. and not from any stranger, nor from any of the Watchers, nor from any of the sons of hea[ven. Why is the expression]
17. of your face so changed and deformed? (Why) is your spirit so depressed? [For I]
18. am speaking to you truthfully.[32]

Whether Lamech regards this newborn child as a 'giant' is not clear, but that its visage arouses his suspicions of a birth influenced by other than himself or another human is evident. In both his report of his thoughts and in Bitenosh's earnest reply a distinction seems to be made between the Watchers and the sons of heavens, a distinction like that found in both Enoch and Daniel.

But the recounting of the story does not accuse Bitenosh of any initiative toward these beings, does not refer to her beauty, nor does it use the 'seeing and desiring' which lead to the fall of the Wakeful Ones in other versions. Nor is the matter employed in any hortatory or didactic manner.

This reference to the Watchers is very restricted and is adduced as a possible explanation of the awesome birth of Noah. No evil is suggested except the possibility of Bitenosh's involvement with a male other than Lamech. This is not too surprising given the character of the narrative in places where it is more fully preserved; such concerns do not seem to be involved in the composer's purpose(s). This retelling of the Genesis-derived narrative assumes knowledge of a form of the myth in which the consequences of the merging of angels and women did not necessarily have only evil results. And there is certainly no effort to derogate Bitenosh's character.

In summary, the form of the episode in T. Reuben and T. Naphtali, the designation of the main figures, and the association with the antediluvian time, indicate the close relationship of the Testaments' use of the episode to that in Enoch 1-36. Dependence upon Enoch 1-36 or upon its sources seems the most likely way to account for the strategic use of the episode in the scheme of the Testaments' address to Jewish males concerning its ethical concerns.

The parenetic use of the episode stands close to Jubilees 7:20-21 and Damascus Document 2:14-19, but in both cases this hortatory use does not lead to the peculiar derogatory view of women expressed throughout the Testaments. The example of the male Wakeful Ones is used rather as the basis of exhortation to Jewish males only.

The form, designations, and uses of the episode in the Testaments are least like those found in the Genesis Apocryphon, and quite unlike the loosely connected use in Genesis 6:1-4, where neither specific consequences are stated nor parenesis developed, neither for males or about females.

If, as this essay contends, the episode is basic to a central and pervasive ethical concern of the Testaments of Reuben, Naphtali, and the whole, the importance of its use in the first Testament and its recall in another 'basic' Testament magnifies its importance, and justifies regarding it as important in identifying date and milieu of the Testaments. Taken together with the absence of specifically Qumranian constructs and concerns and the absence of clear Christian ethical constructs, a case can be made for the distinctly Jewish character of the Testaments and their origin in the period anterior to and no later than 100 B.C.E.[33]

The relationship of the episode to the Testaments' concept of the order of nature (universe) established by the Creator, and the framework which this concept provides for the Testaments' ethical analysis and address, the reflections of this concept in both Enoch and Jubilees, together with the Testaments, add force to the arguments for an early Jewish context. The fact that these documents explain evil in the human world as arising from this disturbance of divinely established order, that it becomes the earliest example of evil and provides a construct for an understanding of the human dilemmas related to the power of evil, argue for recognizing a close relationship among these documents, two of which can be closely dated on the basis of Qumran documentation.

Kee has argued forcefully for a hellenized Jewish, non-Palestinian community as the community of the Testaments, *ca.* 100 B.C.E.[34] The data which he has analyzed to show the indebtedness of the Testaments to Middle Stoicism clearly support his milieu contentions, but using the same data one could argue, as I would, for an earlier date, toward the beginning, rather than the end of the second century.

A concluding question. As hellenized as the Testaments show themselves to be, is the use of this episode part of anti-hellenistic polemic? The rituals associated with the Olympic games, part of the hellenization of the provinces, in which human males engage in sexual rites with a goddess, could have provided the peculiar occasion for the use of this episode and the distinctive, anti-female parenesis developed in the Testaments.

NOTES

1. For a thorough, critical review of Testaments scholarship, see H. Dixon Slingerland, *The Testaments of the Twelve Patriarchs: A Critical History of Research.* Society of Biblical Literature Monograph Series, Number 21 (Missoula, Montana: Scholars Press, 1977).
2. Howard Clark Kee, "The Ethical Dimensions of the Testaments of the XII Patriarchs as a Clue to Provenance," *NTS* 24/2 (January, 1978), 259-270, asked, "What are the major moral concerns expressed in the relation to law in the Testaments?" and answered, "Negatively, the author deplores above all sexual promiscuity," 260.
3. Robert Sinker, "The Testaments of the Twelve Patriarchs," Alexander Roberts and James Donaldson, eds, *The Ante-Nicene Fathers* (Grand Rapids, Michigan: Wm. B. Eerdmans Publishing Company, 1951), VIII, 3-38. Sinker's 1871 translation anticipated the outcome of recent textual studies, because he preferred the text which Marinus de Jonge and his colleagues now regard as the most dependable, the manuscript referred to as *b*, i.e., Cambridge University Library MS Ff I, 24 of the 10th century A.D. This text was published, with critical apparatus as *Testamenta XII Patriarchum,* Volume 1 in the series *Pseudepigrapha Veteris Testamenti Graece,* A. M. Denis and M. de Jonge, eds (Leiden: E. J. Brill, 1964). This manuscript, which Sinker

earlier transcribed, is part of the group *aef + bdg (k)*, designated as a group by the siglum *beta*. Unless otherwise noted Sinker's translation is used in this essay with occasional brackets and inclusions to clarify genders.

4. M. de Jonge, *The Testaments of the Twelve Patriarchs: A Study of their Text, Composition and Origin* (Assen: Van Gorcum, 1953) 37-60.

5. The frequency of *taxis* in T. Naphtali, 8 times is striking in view of only one occurrence elsewhere in the Testaments, T. Levi 11:3, where Gersam is said not to have remained in his original *taxis.* Beside T. Naphtali 3:1-5's four uses of it, it occurs four other times in 2:8-9 and 8:9-10, where, following a poetic exposition of the twofold aspect of the commandments, the author insists that even the keeping of the commandments, if not in order, will lead to sin.

6. Genesis 6:1-4 involves the following 'distinctive terms': "sons of God," "daughters of men were fair," "they took to wife," "as they chose," "Nephilim," "the mighty men that were of old," and "the men of renown." (*RSV*) The intriguing possibility that this pericope, loosely connected to its present context and not distinctly assignable to the major sources of Genesis, is a 'preface' to the 'jeopardy of the matriarch' episodes in Genesis 12:10-20, 20:1-18 and 26:1-14, is worth close scrutiny.

7. Some Qumran fragments have been given designations as "Testaments," e.g., "of Levi," but examination of the published fragments so designated does not clearly support this categorization. It is not yet clear that any portion of the Testaments in the form previously known has been found at Qumran. Those Qumran fragments designated "Testament," may represent some of the many sources which the Testaments used. If so, they do not assist an inquiry into the date and milieu of the Testaments in any definitive manner.

8. J. T. Milik, ed, *The Books of Enoch: Aramaic Fragments of Qumran Cave 4,* with the collaboration of Matthew Black (Oxford: Clarendon Press, 1976). I am of the opinion that Milik regularly restored too many letters and words in lacunae. The lengths of lines shown in the plates seem to allow for as many as 12-13 fewer than Milik often restored, even given his opinion that haplography, the apparent bugaboo of Qumran copyists, is a sufficent explanation for the shortness of the Aramaic texts, 5, 244.

9. *Ibid.,* 24, 44.

10. *Ibid.,* 28-29.

11. *Ibid.,* 165-168 (The brackets are Milik's).

12. *Ibid.,* 144.

13. Explicit internal evidence of the Testaments' dependence on Enoch writings is found in T. Simeon 5:4, T. Levi 10:5, 14:1 (*beta*), 16:1 (*beta*), T. Judah 18:1 (*beta*), T. Zebulon 3:4 (*beta*), T. Dan 5:6, T. Naphtali 4:1, T. Benjamin 9:1, 10:6.

14. *Ibid.,* 31.

15. *Ibid.,* 52-53.

16. J. T. Milik, *Ten Years of Discovery in the Wilderness of Judaea.* Studies in Biblical Theology No. 26, trans J. Strugnell (London: SCM Press, 1959), 32.

17. Milik, *Enoch,* 11.

18. R. H. Charles, *The Apocrypha and Pseudepigrapha of the Old Testament in English, Volume II: Pseudepigrapha* (Oxford: Clarendon Press, 1913 and 1963) 18.

19. *Ibid.,* 20.

20. *Ibid.,* 20.

21. *Ibid.,* 24.

22. *Ibid.,* 25.

23. Milik, *Enoch,* 29; cf. 57.

24. Milik, *Ten Years,* 152; *Enoch,* 57-58.

25. Chaim Rabin, ed and trans, *The Zadokite Documents: I. The Admonition, II. The Laws,* 2d rev ed (Oxford: Clarendon Press, 1958) 8. Line markings and footnote citations have been omitted in this quotation.

26. Milik, *Enoch,* 57-58.

27. Rabin, *Zadokite,* 16.

28. Milik, *Enoch,* 207.

29. Joseph A. Fitzmyer, *The Genesis Apocryphon of Qumran Cave I: A Commentary, Biblica et Orientalia, 18A,* 2d rev ed (Rome: Pontifical Institute Press, 1971) 55.

30. *Ibid.,* 10-11, 15.

31. *Ibid.,* 12.

32. *Ibid.,* 51-53.

33. Kee, *"Ethical Dimensions,"* 269.

34. *Ibid.,* 268-270.

TEXTS and TESTAMENTS

*Patristic Texts and
Doctrinal Reflection*

Marcion Revisited:
A "Post-Harnack" Perspective

David L. Balás

The Marcion known to most present day students is Adolf von Harnack's Marcion. No other has so influenced the current understanding of one of the church's first great "heretics" than has Harnack. Much has come to light, however, which calls into question the prevailing interpretation and which may necessitate a reexamination of both Marcion's and Harnack's work. Another essay by B. Aland has already raised the signal. This study addresses the issue from another position with the hope of suggesting some needed reassessment.[1]

Harnack's interest in Marcion first bore fruit in 1870. In that year the theology faculty of the University of Dorpat, a German university in Estonia (now incorporated in the U.S.S.R.) established a competition for the following task: "Marcionis doctrina e Tertulliani adversus Marcionem libris eruatur et explicetur," and a young student named Harnack won the prize.

Fifty years later, in 1921, at the height of his scholarly achievements, Harnack published his monumental work on Marcion.[2] The first part (1-235) contains a historical and doctrinal study on Marcion and Marcionism; the second (1*-444*), consisting of XII appendices, seems to preserve every quotation and allusion of Marcion in early Christian literature. Harnack summarized and responded to the first reactions to his work in 1923 in *Neue Studien zu Marcion* and issued a revised edition in 1924.

No one since has attempted a study of comparable ambition on Marcion, though several have attempted partly to correct Harnack's picture. Of these, only E. C. Blackman[3] gave a comprehensive view, and although he corrected Harnack in many ways, he did not critically reexamine the materials as collected and interpreted by Harnack.

A restudy of Marcion appears imperative for at least two reasons. First, Harnack's handling of the evidence leaves much to be desired, and second, because knowledge about the milieu pertinent to the study of Marcion has considerably increased. New sources, such as those from Nag Hammadi, present a more complete picture of Gnosticism than that possessed by Harnack. Better editions and new studies of Marcion's main opponents, in particular Tertullian, provide more reliable documentation. Improved editions of Tertullian's *Adversus Marcionem*[4] and other writings are available in series such as Corpus Christianorum and Oxford Early Christian Texts,[5] and are supplemented by other relevant studies.[6] Finally, extensive examinations of ante-Nicene theology, as those of J. Daniélou[7] and especially the too little known Antonio Orbe,[8] provide both a more complete panorama and detailed analyses of several important texts and doctrines of Marcion.

The task of reassessing Marcion must begin with a reconsideration of Harnack. There is no question that Harnack produced a most erudite study, but it also seems quite certain that his work was strongly shaped by his personal theological judgments and interests. An obvious example is the manner in which, especially in the first part of the monograph, Marcion is repeatedly presented as a Luther before Luther; a Luther, moreover, whose image has been molded by the theology of Harnack.

Such "reading into" the past does raise two important questions. Did Harnack's theological prejudices influence only his *interpretation* of Marcion's teaching? Or did they also have a part in the way he reconstructed the evidence? My reading of the evidence suggests a negative answer to the first question and an affirmative to the second. If this be true, considerable incertitude is cast upon the reliability of the immense documentation on which Harnack's interpretation and others' subsequent studies were based.

A specific example[9] of Harnack's questionable treatment of the evidence will be instructive. In discussing the place of faith for Marcion and Paul, Harnack cited Tertullian as follows:

> Since eternal life is due to God's love alone (Tert. IV, 25: "Ex dilectione dei consequentur vitam aeternam Marcionitae"), so the only, but also necessary, condition here is faith. [Marcion, 134; trans. mine]

In so doing, Harnack commited a triple fallacy. First, he should have pointed out that he was not quoting Tertullian verbatim as the reference and quotation marks lead the unsuspecting to assume. Actually Tertullian wrote, "Ergo non ex dilectione dei tui consequetur vitam aeternam Marcionites, sicut longaevam dilector creatoris."[10] Harnack presented his reconstruction of the text on the basis of a different sentence by Tertullian. Second, Harnack interpreted *dilectione dei* as referring to God's love for us, whereas in Tertullian, in the context of a comment on Lk 10:25-28, i.e., the great commandment of the love of God and of our neighbor, *dilectione dei* referred to our love for God.

In the third place, Harnack failed to report that the point he claimed from Tertullian was *Tertullian's* conclusion and not necessarily drawn from Marcion at all. Tertullian pointed out that in the heretical Gospel, Lk 10:25 had only *vitam,* not *vitam aeternam,*[11] in order to indicate that the scribe inquired not about the eternal life which only Marcion's good God could give, but about the long life (*vita longaeva*) promised by the Creator. It is on this basis that Tertullian constructed the following reasoning:

> And again, if the consultant's question and Christ's response were concerned with that long life which is under the Creator's control, and not with eternal life which is under the control of Marcion's god, how does he obtain eternal life? Certainly not on the same terms as the long life, because the difference in the rewards demands belief in a difference in the work to be done. *And therefore your Marcionite* will not obtain eternal life as a result of loving your god, as he who loves the creator will obtain a long life.[12]

The last sentence, the point used by Harnack, is Tertullian's conclusion. There is no clear indication that it is a reference to a contrary statement by Marcion. Harnack, purposely or because of his own bias, misrepresented the evidence, a fact that raises suspicion regarding his overall treatment of the data.

Another line of questioning centers on Harnack's fundamental thesis that the starting point (*Ausgangspunkt*) of Marcion's whole criticism of previous tradition was found "in the Pauline opposition between Law and Gospel...,"[13] i.e., Marcion was primarily a biblical theologian, not a Gnostic speculator.[14]

Indeed, Marcion's emphasis on the tension between law and gospel is clear, but it was certainly not unique. Tertullian, too, affirmed a certain opposition between the law and the gospel, but with St. Paul attributed this to the new dispensation of the same God. What was startlingly new in Marcion, in contrast to all previous Christian tradition except early Gnosticism, was the explanation of this opposition by the doctrine of two opposed Gods.[15] Even as reconstructed by Harnack,[16] most of the antitheses did not contrast moral law to unmerited grace, but rather a morally and metaphysically imperfect Creator to an all-good God. The "justice" of the Creator was viewed as a very selfish and petty justice. He was blamed further for his violence and lack of foresight and for having created this ugly and despicable material universe with its insects, beasts, and sexuality. All ancient witnesses[17] and many modern scholars of Gnosticism have noted the unmistakable parallels with Gnostic dualism.[18] This is not to deny that Marcion's views differed on several points from, e.g., Valentinian gnosis. It is, nevertheless, legitimate to question Harnack's view that Marcion's position represented an entirely original "biblical" view rather than a form of Gnosticism.

In this context, Harnack's contention of the entirely un-philosophical character of Marcion's teaching must be challenged. Surely, Marcion's doctrines are marked by a certain simplicity, not to say single- and simple-mindedness that distinguish them from the elaborate speculations of other Gnostics or the metaphysical analyses of leading philosophers. John G. Gager has recently shown, however, the similarity of some of Marcion's arguments, as reported by Tertullian, to certain philosophical (notably Epicurean) proofs against providence.[19] The difference is that, whereas for Epicure the (especially physical) evils of this world excluded divine providence (the gods dwelled unconcerned in the *intermundia*) and lead, according to the Skeptics, to doubt of the existence of god(s), Marcion accepted (with the Old Testament!) the existence of a Creator, but concluded from the popular-philosophical arguments that the Creator was neither omniscient nor truly good.

Of course, Marcion's opposition to matter, body, and passions was also close to contemporary philosophy (Stoic and Neo-Pythagorean). Thus the contention that Marcion's teaching was unphilosophical at least should be qualified. Harnack's thesis is at best an overstatement.

What seems constant in all the above instances was Marcion's tendency to provide a *simple solution,* without much concern for either the complexities of the data or the consistency of the system, a tendency which may explain the popular success and enduring strength of Marcionism.

Besides the Gnostic and popular-philosophical sources, I believe Marcion's "point of departure" was deeply influenced by his and his fellow Christians' relationship to Judaism in the middle of the second century. Marcion came to Rome around 136-140 and was expelled from the Roman Church in 144.[20] These dates coincide with the period of the bloody suppression of the great Jewish revolt in 135. R. M. Grant has argued that the disillusionment of Jewish sects with the seemingly powerless and deceptive God of the Old Testament was one of the reasons for the Gnostic reduction of Yahweh to an imperfect or even hostile deity.[21]

Whether this is wholly or partially correct or not, Grant's similar hypothesis concerning Marcion seems quite possible. Grant said that Marcion "...wanted to dissociate Christianity not only from apocalyptic Judaism, but also from Judaism in general."[22] Politically and socially, the Christians, especially hellenistic Christians with no national or cultural roots in Judaism, found at this time their association with Jewish history an embarrassing and dangerous liability. Marcion may have found a way to effect this desirable separation by using Jewish self-interpretation at several main points. For instance, by accepting the anti-Christian contention of some Jews that Jesus Christ was not the Messiah promised by the Old Testament, a Messiah the Jews rightly expected to be political and warlike, Marcion made a counter claim that Christ was in fact the self-revelation of a previously entirely unknown, all-good God. Secondly, the Jewish rejection of Christian typological or spiritual exegesis of the Old Testament, which seemed to threaten Christianity's claims to historical legitimacy, was now seen as a liberating insight.[23] Finally, the shaken confidence of many Jews in the confirmed goodness, omniscience, and all-powerfulness of Yahweh (incompatible as it seemed with the historical realities of the time) was taken as an admission that the God of the Old Testament was inferior to the all-good and perfect God revealed in Jesus Christ. Paradoxically, it was precisely by having accepted Jewish scriptures and history, at least to a large extent, in their contemporary Jewish interpretation that Marcion arrived at his radical dissociation of the two Testaments![24]

If Harnack's handling of the primary data is questionable and his guiding thesis less than adequate, how then is Marcion to be understood? How are some of Marcion's doctrines to be reinterpreted? Perhaps Marcion's teaching concerning the "first principles" is a good place to begin. Most scholars have described Marcion as assuming *two unrelated* "principles," the "just God" and the "good God." Tertullian, however, presented another view of Marcion, namely, that Marcion taught that the just God or demiurge "created" the world from *uncreated matter*,[25] which implies a doctrine of *three principles*. Are they *unrelated*? Not entirely, it seems. While the "good God" was unknown to the lower principles, according to Marcion, his knowledge embraced all. But, Tertullian pointed out repeatedly, despite God's goodness, he strangely left the world entirely to the demiurge and intervened for the first time suddenly through Christ. This intervention, however, and the subsequent events (descent of Christ to Hades to liberate the sinners, final punishment by the demiurge of those who did not believe in Christ) showed that the lower principles, albeit unwillingly, served the plan of the good God. If Tertullian was right, Marcion seems to have taught, as did the commonly so-called Gnostic systems, that ultimately all principles proceeded from a first source. Is, then, the Marcionism described by the fifth-century Armenian bishop Eznik of Kolb, in which *hyle* is a personified principle, i.e., the female consort of the God of law,[26] a later assimilation of Marcion's principles to the Gnostic Aeons or an indication of their Gnostic origin and conception according to Marcion himself?

Marcion's christology and soteriology may also be in need of reconsideration. Irenaeus described Marcion's teaching on Christ's entrance into the world with these words:

> From the Father, who is above the God who made the world, Jesus came to Judaea in the time of the governor Pontius Pilate, procurator for Tiberius Caesar, and was manifested in the form of a man to those who were in Judaea;...[27]

This report is confirmed by Tertullian.[28] According to Marcion, then, Christ did not have a human birth nor a true human body, but appeared suddenly in the semblance of a human body. Marcion, nevertheless, insisted on the death of Christ and its redemptive significance.[29] Having been crucified by the Creator's powers and helpers,[30] Christ (who was by "death" separated from his human disguise) descended to Hades to liberate the souls detained by the Creator.[31]

If this was Marcion's view of Christ's humanity, what did he teach of his divinity? Harnack strongly contended that Marcion was a strict modalist who distinguished Christ from his Father only by name,[32] but the proof he offered was the later association by their opponents of Marcionists with the Sabellians.[33] A fresh analysis of the sources might well challenge Harnack's "proof."

Marcion's anthropology differed, at least in its more explicit features, from both "orthodox" Christian views and Gnostic theories.[34] In opposition to the Gnostics who generally divided mankind into three categories, the *sarkikoi,* the *psychikoi* and the *pneumatikoi,* Marcion accepted, in his own way, the teaching of the Old Testament that humanity was created in the image and likeness of God. This is attested by Tertullian who wrote:

> Here are the bones of wranglings you gnaw at. If God is good,
> you ask, and has knowledge of the future, and also has power
> to avert evil, why did he suffer the man, deceived by the devil,
> to fall away from obedience to the law, and so to die? For the
> man was the image and likeness of God, or even God's
> substance, since from it the man's soul took its origin.[35]

Marcion, in opposition to Tertullian (see esp. *AM* II, 9), conceived
the human soul as consubstantial to God the Creator, or rather,
seen in his simplistic way, a portion of God's substance.[36] This, of
course, did not guarantee salvation: the Creator God could not
grant eternal life, but only a long life, and not only his punishments
but also his rewards were confined to the nether world. Only the
good God could bestow salvation. There are some hints that Marcion viewed this salvation as a transformation to a *substantia
spiritualis,* though decisive proof is lacking as yet.[37]

Speculation concerning those saved introduces Marcion's
eschatology. From his contempt for matter and body and Marcion's
docetist christology followed his rejection of resurrection, although
he may have attributed to those ascending to the good Father a
spiritual body. What is the fate of those not saved, i.e., the just of
the Old Testament who did not trust Christ when he descended to
them in Hades[38] and those who since then did not accept the gospel
of Marcion? According to Tertullian, the Marcionite answer was
that the Creator's fire would overtake the rejected![39] The good God
did not punish directly, though, as Tertullian pointed out, he in fact
both judged and punished since he clearly foresaw the consequences of excluding sinners from the kingdom of heaven.[40]
Is this the final end? Harnack thought that Marcion taught that
the Creator would ultimately annihilate himself, thus demonstrating that in reality the inferior God was nothing but the world
itself. Here again Harnack's interpretation is not supported, so far
as I see, by convincing evidence.[41]

Marcion's notion of history likewise bore similarity to that of the
Gnostics. In an interesting and influential article, H. C. Puech symbolized the Greek, Christian, and Gnostic conceptions of time and
history by a circle, a straight line, and a broken line respectively.[42]
A. Orbe criticized this conception by pointing out that the Gnostics,
in particular the Valentinians, had a more complex view:[43] though
they rejected the orthodox conception of the identity of the Old

Testament God with the Father of Jesus Christ, they affirmed the existence of a superior providence which, though ignored or misunderstood by the *psychikoi*, was nevertheless at work throughout the history of mankind.[44] The broken line comparison, however, applies very well to Marcion who did not admit any providential work of the good God in history preceding Christ's sudden appearance.[45] As Tertullian wrote:

> Subito Christus, subito et Joannes. Sic sunt omnia apud Marcionem, quae suum et plenum habent ordinem apud creatorem.[46]

Against Gnosticism and Marcion in particular, Irenaeus worked out his theology of a continuous and progressive salvation history.[47] Even though, out of an understandable over-reaction against his opponents, he tended to exaggerate its homogeneity, Irenaeus' views were much more faithful to the earliest Christian tradition than those of Marcion.

To summarize the discussion thus far, Harnack's view of Marcion has been challenged along several lines. Harnack's methodology as well as his prejudices may well have produced a distorted picture of Marcion. While Harnack concluded that Marcion was no Gnostic, a review of Marcion's teaching, particularly through a re-examination of the sources from Marcion's great foe Tertullian, has called Harnack's position into question.

Now another major issue will be considered. What was the role of Marcion in the development of the Canon? Harnack was convinced that Marcion gave the impetus, if not the initial impulse, to the creation of a Canon in the early church.[48] Though Harnack granted that the four Gospels had already been brought together and associated with the letters of Paul by both orthodox (1 Clem, Ignatius) and heretical authors (Basilides, Valentinos), he claimed that nonetheless Marcion played the essential role in bringing the process to a logical conclusion. Was Harnack correct?

To examine Harnack's view, it is necessary once again to turn to Tertullian, for in Tertullian's *Adv Marc*, books IV and V, is to be found the primary evidence we have for reconstructing Marcion's scriptures. It appears that Marcion rejected all the Old Testament and much of the New Testament as well. *Adv Marc* IV seems to imply that Marcion's only Gospel was some form of Luke while *Adv Marc* V preserves Tertullian's commentary on Marcion's ten letters of Paul.

A preliminary issue involves the character of the text or texts that Tertullian had at hand. In opposition to Zahn and other earlier scholars, Harnack firmly asserted that Tertullian had before him Marcion's *Apostolikon* in an early Latin translation[49]. With only a little less certitude, he affirmed the same of the Gospel.[50] In opposition to Harnack, Quispel has argued that Tertullian read Marcion's version of Luke in Greek (see, e.g., the Greek terms quoted in IV, 9), and that in discussing the *Apostolikon* he used the Greek text, though he knew and sometimes consulted an early Latin text.[51] In A. J. B. Higgins' review of the question,[52] he concluded that in *Adv Marc* IV Tertullian used two translations of Luke, the Marcionite (M) and the Catholic (T), a conclusion that paralled von Soden's concerning *Adv Marc* V and the text of Paul[53]. T. P. O'Malley has recently seemed to confirm Tertullian's acquaintance with Marcionite Latin and early Latin translations, although he was more cautious in generalizing from the cases studied.[54] In his brief but excellent introduction Evans wrote that Tertullian "had before him Marcion's *Antitheses* and the Greek text of his gospel and *Apostolikon*. It is conceivable that he also had at hand a Marcionite Latin version of some part of these documents."[55] Finally, it is noteworthy that the studies of Blackman suggested a real but limited influence of the Latin text of Marcion's New Testament on that of the Old Latin.[56] It seems clear that Harnack's conclusion has not gone unchallenged.

Without denying the plausibility of Marcion's influence on the formation and fixation of the New Testament Canon, it is important to examine this influence more accurately. Concerning the collection of the Pauline letters: if a collection(s) existed as early as Ignatius, how was Marcion related to these earlier collections? Since he considered it necessary to eliminate large portions of several of Paul's epistles and to alter or expurgate individual verses, in order to fit Paul into his own mold of thought,[57] it is somewhat difficult to imagine him collecting for the first time documents he then was prepared to mutilate. Marcion himself claimed that the earliest Christian tradition had been corrupted by the first apostles Christ had chosen, and that even the writings of Paul, the apostle installed by Christ directly to rescue his true message, were in turn adulterated by the Judaizers. Thus Marcion did not initiate the notion of the Canon but attempted to reform an already-existing body of normative writings.

After the question of the Pauline letters, we have to examine the rather startling theory of John Knox concerning Marcion's influence on the formation of Luke-Acts. Knox put forward his view in *Marcion and the New Testament*[58] and reiterated it in his later "Acts and the Pauline Letter Corpus" where he wrote:

> The general thesis of the book is in my judgment still defensi-
> ble and I am persuaded of its truth: that Marcion appropriated
> and revised as 'the first Christian Scripture' the collected let-
> ters of Paul and a primitive Gospel substantially equivalent to
> what later became the first volume of Luke's work, and that
> this action stimulated, and determined the definitive form of,
> both Luke-Acts and the ecclesiastical canon of the New Testa-
> ment.[59]

In *Marcion and the New Testament,* Knox posited that "a primitive
Gospel...was somewhat shortened by Marcion or some predecessor
and rather considerably enlarged by the writer of our Gospel, who
was also the maker of Luke-Acts."[60] In his article Knox expanded
this view to include the theory that "Luke" (i.e., the author of
Luke-Acts) knew or at least knew of the letters of Paul but
deliberately made little use of them. "Acts was itself prompted, at
least in part, by what its author regards as a schismatic use of them
among pre-Marcionite, perhaps even Marcionite, Christians."[61]
Following the lead of Knox, H. P. West, Jr. has argued that "the existence of Primitive Luke as a source of Marcion, Luke and Matthew cannot be proved, but it seems at least as probable as Q as a
source of Matthew and Luke."[62]

These hypotheses show the impact Harnack's interpretation of
Marcion is still having on the reconstruction of Christian origins,
unacceptable as they are. Marcion admitted to be an innovator in
relation to earlier Christian tradition, though he considered this in-
novation to be a restoration of the earliest tradition. There were, as
seen above, most plausible reasons why Marcion did severely alter
Luke, stemming from both historical circumstances and doctrinal
presuppositions. Knox's hypothesis, in addition, has the difficulty
of putting the redaction of Luke-Acts into the second half of the second century, not only "as late as, say, A.D. 125" as he would admit,[63] a consequence which few scholars, if any, would be ready to
accept.

Thus, I tend to agree with Evans in his assessment of Marcion's
influence on the canon:

> Marcion is the first person known to have compiled a closed
> canon of Christian scriptures....But it need not follow that it
> was his influence which rescued Pauline writings from an obli-
> vion into which they would have fallen; nor need it follow,
> that except for the needs of controversy against him, the great
> church would not at some time have defined its own canon, or

that its introduction of Petrine and Johannine elements was designed as a counterweight to the influence of Marcion and St. Paul.[64]

Closely connected with the question of Marcion's influence on the formation of the Canon is that of his "Paulinism." Harnack viewed Marcion, in spite of his more or less admitted imperfections, as a rescuer of Paul who anticipated the "rediscovery" of Paul centuries later by Luther.[65] From this perspective Marcion was an exception in the otherwise theologically impoverished second-century, at least as some historians view it,[66] an age which is considered by some even to have neglected the specifically Pauline elements in the Christian message.[67]

It is clear from the preceding sections that, with many other historians, I do not share this view.[68] There is, of course, no reason why imperfections, weaknesses, gaps, and inconsistencies should not be admitted in second-century theology: the task of historical research is to point them out in detail. The summary negative judgments, however, mentioned above are due mostly to theological prejudices which should be critically reexamined from both a theological and a historical point of view.[69]

As for Marcion's Paulinism, it is of a very ambiguous sort, to say the least. He accepted indeed some points of Paul's message and theology, but he rejected many others no less essential for Paul himself. As a consequence, even the elements retained were often misunderstood and/or distorted.

Though Marcion did not rescue Paul, one could admit that he did give a special impetus for his study. Irenaeus, Tertullian, Origen, and a whole series of Christian writers of the early church are witnesses to the fact that "Catholic Christians" did not consider Paul as an alien with whom they were uncomfortable,[70] but as one of their own whom they, as a matter of fact, accepted much more completely than Marcion.[71] Marcion's one-sided over-emphases have, however, often resulted in an over-emphasis in the opposite direction (e.g., stressing one-sidedly the continuity between the Old Testament law and prophets and the New Testament).[72]

As the brief reexamination of the evidence on the preceding pages has shown, Harnack's Marcion is in need of a serious revision. Far from being the theological hero depicted by Harnack, Marcion was, in my judgment, a typical "heretic." I am using this term here in an historical sense, not only in the sense that the Roman church and subsequently the universal church rejected his distinctive views, but primarily in the sense that he made a one-sided choice discontinuous with that mainstream of the total Christian tradition which both rejected and transcended him.[73]

NOTES

1. The substance of this essay was presented in April, 1974, at a meeting of the Seminar on the Development of Catholic Christianity in Fort Worth, Texas. After completion of the essay, the related article by B. Aland, "Marcion: Versuch einer neuen Interpretation," *ZTK* 70 (1973) 420-47, became accessible to me. Whereas her results strongly converge with mine as to the urgent need for reinterpretation, my essay retains its validity as a statement of an important question still before us.

2. Adolf von Harnack, *Marcion: Das Evangelium vom fremden Gott. Eine Monographie zur Geschichte der Grundlegung der katholischen Kirche* (TU 45, 2d ed; Leipzig: J. C. Hinrichs, 1924, repr Darmstadt: Wissenschaftliche Buchgesellschaft, 1960). This reprint contains also Harnack's *Neue Studien zu Marcion* (TU 44/4; Leipzig: J. C. Hinrichs, 1923). In the following notes, Harnack's work will be referred to as *Marcion*. (For background on Harnack's method and intent, cf., preface, VI, and G. W. Glick, *The Reality of Christianity; A Study of Adolf von Harnack as Historian and Theologian* [New York: Harper and Row, 1967] 112-121).

3. E. C. Blackman, *Marcion and His Influence* (London: S. P. C. K., 1948).

4. *Quinti Septimi Florentis Tertulliani Opera,* I-II (Corpus Christianorum, Series Latina, I-II; Turnholt: Brepols, 1954).

5. Tertullian, *Adversus Marcionem,* ed and tran Ernest Evans, 2 vols; Oxford Early Christian Texts (Oxford: Clarendon, 1972); hereafter referred to as *AM.*

6. E.g., G. Quispel, *De Bronnen van Tertullianus' Adversus Marcionem* (Leiden: Burgersdijk en Niemans, 1943); J. W. P. Borleffs' rev. in *VC* 1 (1947) 192-198; T. P. O'Malley, *Tertullian and the Bible: Language - Imagery - Exegesis* (Nijmegen: Dekker and van de Vegt, 1967); C. P. Hammond's rev. in *JTS* 20 (1969) 309-11.

7. J. Daniélou, *The Theology of Jewish Christianity* (London: Darton, Longman and Todd, 1964) and *idem, Gospel Message and Hellenistic Culture* (London: Darton, Longman and Todd, 1973).

8. A. Orbe, "Homo nuper factus," *Gregorianum* 46 (1965) 481-544; "La definicion del hombre en la teologia del s. II°," *Gregorianum* 48 (1967) 522-76; and *Estudios Valentinianos* III (Roma: Gregoriana, 1961) 190f.

9. This example was also examined by Quispel, *De Bronnen:* 89; see Borleffs, *VC* 1 (1947) 197.

10. *AM* IV, 25, 16.

11. *AM* IV, 25, 14.

12. *AM* IV, 25, 16; trans Evans, 405.

13. *Marcion,* 30.

14. *Marcion, passim,* e.g., 142: "Das wahre Christentum ist daher objektiv biblische Theologie und nichts anderes."

15. Cf. Irenaeus, *Adv Haer* I, 27, 2-3; *AM* I, *passim.*

16. *Marcion,* 89-92.

17. Justin, Irenaeus, Tertullian, Hippolytus.

18. E.g., R. M. Grant, *Gnosticism and Early Christianity,* 2d ed (New York:

Harper, 1966) 121-28: U. Bianchi, "Marcion, theologien biblique ou docteur gnostique," *VC* 21 (1967) 141-49.

19. J. G. Gager, "Marcion and Philosophy," *VC* 26 (1972) 53-59, esp. 55-58 where he compares *AM* II, 5, 1-2 with Epicurean fragments.
20. *Marcion*, 25-27.
21. Grant, *Gnosticism and Early Christianity*, 27-38.
22. *Ibid.*, 122.
23. Gager, "Marcion and Philosophy," 58, also indicated probable parallelisms with Epicurean views.
24. This partial agreement between Marcion and Jewish critics of Christianity was repeatedly noted by Tertullian (e.g., *AM* III, 23, 1).
25. *AM* I, 15, 4.
26. Cf. "Eznik's Résumé of Marcion's Doctrine," ed R. M. Grant, *Gnosticism: A Source Book of Heretical Writings from the Early Christian Period* (New York: Harper and Brothers, 1961) 101-04.
27. Iren, *Adv Haer* I, 27, 2; trans Grant, *Sourcebook*, 45.
28. E. g., *AM* I, 19, 2; this was indeed the *beginning* of Marcion's gospel: cf. *AM* IV, 7, 1; *Marcion*, 183*f.
29. *Marcion*, 132.
30. *AM*, III, 23, 5.
31. Iren, *Adv Haer* I, 27, 3.
32. *Marcion*, 123.
33. *Marcion*, 391*.
34. A. Orbe, "La definicion del hombre"; Bianchi, "Marcion," 142, 144.
35. *AM* II, 5, 1; trans Evans, 97.
36. *Ibid.*: "...immo et substantian suam...."
37. *AM* III, 9, 4 may be Tertullian's inference and not Marcion's teaching. The texts mentioned in *Marcion*, 139, n. 2 are not decisive.
38. Iren, *Adv Haer* I, 27, 3; *AM* V, 11.
39. *AM* I, 28, 1.
40. *AM* I, 27, 1ff.; *Marcion*, 138.
41. *Marcion*, 140-141.
42. H. C. Puech, "La gnose et le temps," *Eranos Jahrbuch* 20 (1951) 60.
43. A. Orbe, *Estudios Valentinianos*, 190f.
44. With Orbe cf. H. I. Marrou, "La théologie de l'histoire dans la gnose valentinienne," *Le origini dello Gnosticismo*, ed U. Bianchi (Leiden: E. J. Brill, 1970) 215-25.
45. The rejection of the typological exegesis of the OT reinforced this conception.
46. *AM* IV, 11, 4.
47. A. Orbe, "Homo nuper factus," 481-544.
48. *Marcion*, 441*-444*.
49. *Ibid.*, 47*-56*.
50. *Ibid.*, 178*-181*.
51. Borleffs *VC* 1 (1947) 196-98.
52. A. J. B. Higgins, "The Latin Text of Luke in Marcion and Tertullian," *VC* (1951) 1-42.
53. H. von Soden, "Der lateinische Paulustext bei Marcion und Tertullian," *Festgabe für Adolf Jülicher zum 70. Gerburtstag* (Tübingen: J. C. B. Mohr, 1927) 229-81.
54. O'Malley, 62-63.
55. Evans, *AM* Intr. XX.
56. Blackman, *Marcion*, 60.

57. *AM* V, *passim; Marcion,* 35-73, 40*-176*.
58. J. Knox, *Marcion and the New Testament* (Chicago: The University of Chicago Press, 1942).
59. J. Knox, "Acts and the Pauline Letter Corpus," *Studies in Luke-Acts* (Nashville: Abingdon, 1966) 287, n. 8.
60. Knox, *Marcion,* 10.
61. Knox, "Acts," 285.
62. H. P. West, Jr., "A Primitive Version of Luke in the Composition of Matthew," *NTS* 14 (1967) 95.
63. Knox, "Acts," 286.
64. Evans, *AM* Intr. XVI.
65. *Marcion, passim;* Blackman, *Marcion,* 110-11 (with reservations).
66. E.g., T. F. Torrance, *The Doctrine of Grace in the Apostolic Fathers* (Edinburgh: Oliver and Boyd, 1948).
67. H. F. West, "Paulus und die Häretiker," *Christentum und Gnosis,* ed W. Eltester (Berlin: A. Töpelmann, 1969) 116-28.
68. E.g., Evans (above n. 64) and A. C. Outler, "The Sense of Tradition in the Ante-Nicene Church," *The Heritage of Christian Thought,* ed R. E. Cushman (New York: Harper and Row, 1965) 29.
69. Cf. the just remarks of R. M. Grant, *The Apostolic Fathers, Vol. I: An Introduction* (New York: Nelson, 1964) 6-8.
70. As Harnack claimed: *Marcion,* 142, n. 2.
71. Cf. esp. K. H. Schelkle, *Paulus: Lehrer der Väter* (Düsseldorf: Patmos, 1956); M. F. Wiles, *The Divine Apostle: The Interpretation of St. Paul's Epistles in the Early Church* (Cambridge: University Press, 1967).
72. Wiles, *The Divine Apostle,* 132-39.
73. Against W. Bauer, *Orthodoxy and Heresy in Earliest Christianity* (Philadelphia: Fortress Press, 1971) 212-28, I basically agree with H. E. W. Turner, *The Pattern of Christian Truth* (London: Mowbray and Co., 1954) 117-24.

"Prophets and Apostles": The Conjunction of the Two Terms before Irenaeus

Denis M. Farkasfalvy

In the last decades of the second century the theological use of the formula "prophets and apostles" is widely attested. It became customary to refer to the totality of Christian revelation as that handed down through "the prophets" (Old Testament) and "the apostles" (New Testament). This usage is most frequent in Tertullian and Irenaeus[1] who in connection with these terms developed a whole "theology of revelation." The *Muratorian Fragment*, the earliest known description of the Canon of the New Testament, used it in a quasi-technical sense when explaining why *The Shepherd* of Hermas could not be inserted among the sacred books of Christianity:

> It should be read, yet it cannot be publicized in the Church to the people, neither among the Prophets for their number is complete, nor among the Apostles with the end of times (being at hand).[2]

The rough Latinity of the Fragment raises a few problems of interpretation, which are, for our purpose, of lesser importance. What is certain in the text is the conviction that biblical books, in order to belong to the Canon, must fall into one of two categories: "prophets" or "apostles." The former group could not grow because their "number is complete" (*completo numero*); the latter was closed because we live in the last phase of salvation-history. We see, therefore, that a triple periodization of history was supposed, and the conviction was expressed that the biblical books represented revelation handed down in the first two periods of that history. The main concern of this study is not so much the concept of revelation as a historical process, nor the idea of dividing this history into basic time periods, but the designation of the two groups who mediated revelation as "prophets and apostles."

The importance of this topic becomes evident when one realizes that the vocabulary and the theology of the Canon as established by Irenaeus and Tertullian became standard for Christian preaching and theological reflection for at least the following thousand years. Still in the twelfth century the totality of scriptures was routinely referred to as "prophets and apostles."[3] The consequences are well known. Up to recent times Christian preachers, theologians, and spiritual writers treated the Old Testament as a collection of prophetic writings and the New Testament as works of more or less immediate apostolic origin. In other words, the exegetical and theological implications of the formula "prophets and apostles" survived until the present day.

For the history of the Canon as well as for an accurate evaluation of Irenaeus' anti-Gnostic synthesis, it is important to see how the combination of these two terms emerged and became part of Christian theological usage from New Testament times up to the middle of the second century.

We will begin by considering texts where "prophets and apostles" are connected by the theme of martyrdom. Probably the oldest Christian text relevant to our topic is 1 Thess 2:13-15. The context refers to the ministry of the word. The Thessalonians accepted Paul's preaching not as *logon anthrōpōn* but *alēthōs logon theou*. They became imitators of Paul and the churches of Judea. Consequently, they started also sharing in the sufferings of that church, for they were similarly maltreated by their own countrymen. "You suffered the same things from your own countrymen as they did from the Jews who killed both the Lord Jesus and the prophets, and drove us out" (vss 14-15). Paul listed Jesus, the prophets and "us," i.e., the Christian missionaries (Paul, Silvanus, Timothy) called "apostles of Christ" in verse 6. He certainly referred to the persecution specifically provoked by their preaching to the Gentiles: they hinder "us from speaking to the Gentiles that they may be saved" (vs 16). But the ultimate reason of comparison lies deeper. It is found in the hostility that God's word encountered time and again in people reluctant to believe. In the way Jesus, the prophets and the apostles were treated by their contemporaries, Paul saw a historic pattern. This suggests that in Paul's thought "prophets and apostles" were linked together not only by their similar destiny of persecution but also by the similarity of their roles as authentic witnesses of God's word. Behind the historical continuity of persecution, we detect the historical continuity of revelation: God sends messengers in succession but they all receive the same ill treatment. So the theme of continued martyrdom involves that of salvation-history. These ideas were not Paul's original creation. Anticipated in the Old Testament, they found developed expression in the Synoptic tradition.[4] It is therefore no surprise that we find the formula "prophets and apostles" in Luke and precisely in the context of martyrdom and salvation-history.

In considering Lk 11:49 it is tempting to dispose of Luke's phrase "I will send them prophets and apostles" as secondary in comparison to the Matthaean parallel: "Therefore I send you prophets and wise men and scribes" (Mt 23:34). We know that Luke had particular interest in the apostles as a special group chosen by Jesus and given the name *apostoloi* (Lk 6:13). So it might appear plausible that the expression "prophets and apostles" in 11:49 is the result of Luke's editorial adjustment of a traditional passage attested in its original form by Matthew. Some interpreters add that the future of the verb in Luke ("I will send") shows that Luke projected the future sending of the apostles. This, however, is contradicted by those who think that Luke was speaking of Old Testament prophets and New Testament apostles and attached no special significance to the tense of the verb.[5] In either case, Luke is regarded as creating a highly artificial connection between the two groups, which is, however, understandable in view of his alleged theology of history and *Frühkatholizismus*. Moreover, Luke seemed to be aware that the passage could not be convincingly fitted into a discourse of Jesus. Consequently, unlike Matthew, he did not put it into the mouth of Jesus but made of it a quotation from "God's Wisdom."[6]

There may be, however, another explanation for the appearance of this important phrase in Luke. In Jeremiah we find three times a phrase that is conceivably the source of Luke's quotation. In Jer 7:25 we read: "I sent to them all my servants, the prophets again and again with urgency and persistence."[7] Almost the same text appears in Jer 25:4 and Jer 35:15. Behind the phrase "with urgency and persistence" the Hebrew text has the idiomatic expression *haskkēm weshālōach*, the conjunction of two infinitive absolutes. Apparently the Septuagint had difficulty translating it. Although the Hebrew text of Jer 7:25 agrees word for word with Jer 25:4, for the former we read in the Septuagint *orthrou kai apesteila* while for the latter we have *orthrou apostellōn*. In both cases the resulting Greek sentence is not only awkward but obscure and would need some adjustment in order to be interpreted. Lk 11:49 might contain such an adjusted quotation of Jeremiah's text. Jeremiah's *shālōach* has the same consonantal form as *shālûach* the Hebrew equivalent for *apostolos*.[8] Furthermore, it is of significance that Matthew's parallel text is combined with Jesus' lament over Jerusalem in which we have: "killing the prophets and stoning those who are sent [*apestalmenous*] to you" (Mt 23:37). In Luke the corresponding verse is in 13:34, two chapters apart from 11:49. Our conclusion can go in two different directions. On one hand, the Matthaean parallel is not lacking the phrase "prophets and apostles" except that it appears in a slightly different form and three verses later. On the other hand, there are sufficient stylistic reasons for Matthew to prefer "prophets and scribes and wise men" to "prophets and apostles" since in his composition the latter text must appear three verses later, as Jesus starts his lament over Jerusalem.

So there is enough reason to doubt the assumption that "prophets and apostles" in Lk 11:49 is a secondary composition of Luke, motivated by theological bias. It would be much more advisable to say that both Lk 11:49 and Mt 23:37 (with its parallel Lk 13:34) contain derivates of a Semitic usage associating "prophets and apostles" as terms of Hebrew parallelism. Of course "apostle" in such pre-Christian usage coincides with "authorised envoy" or "delegate" according to the Rabbinic meaning of the word shālûach/shālîach and has no direct reference to the twelve disciples of Jesus. Yet, Luke's "theological bias" probably played a role when he chose *apostoloi* for 11:49 so that the Christian reader might think not only of Old Testament prophets but also New Testament apostles. The latter are implied in the text by allusion and connotation but are not indicated directly.

Our conclusion contains nothing surprising. Echoing Jeremiah's formula *hashkēm weshālōach* the Synoptic tradition made the statement that God sent his "prophets and delegates" but they were all maltreated and killed. What is special in Lk 11:49 is that (a) he was aware that this theme was founded on scriptural texts ("Wisdom says"[9]) and (b) that by his choice of wording he related it to the recent experiences of the church, the maltreatment of the apostles of Jesus Christ. Lk 11:49 can be regarded, therefore, as parallel to 1 Thess 2:13-15, not by its direct significance but by its implication in the Christian context of the word *apostolos*. This passage in Luke reveals how the Pauline parallel between Old Testament prophets and New Testament apostles was built on the basis of earlier terminology associating "prophets and apostles" as almost synonymous terms. We can agree, therefore, with Hans von Campenhausen who saw in Lk 11:49 not two different groups but the same persons. "Prophets and apostles" means prophets who are delegates of God in the same sense as in Lk 13:34 (and Mt 23:37) where the participle *apestalmenous* and the noun *prophētas* designate the same individuals.[10]

In Rev 18:20 "prophets" and "apostles" are combined in reverse order and attached to a third noun "saints" (*hagioi*). The three members of the phrase could be grouped as "the saints: both apostles and prophets," but it is also possible to understand the sentence as a triplet: "saints and apostles and prophets."[11] The order "apostles and prophets" seems to indicate that both groups consisted of holy men of the New Testament. This conclusion is confirmed by the general use of the term "prophet" in Revelation, customarily meaning a New Testament prophet, as the writer himself[12] or the two witnesses also called "two prophets" in chapter 11 (Rev 11:10). Following an article by J. Munck,[13] Oscar Cullmann has advanced impressive arguments for the thesis that the "two prophets" represent the apostles Peter and Paul and so the passage Rev 11:3-13 would be our earliest document about their martyrdom in Rome.[14] If this is correct, then chapter 11 contains a clear case for overlapping usage of the terms "apostles" and "prophets." The Book of Revelation exhibits clear awareness of the special significance of the term "apostle" used in a restricted sense for the Twelve Apostles of Jesus,[15] but it pays very little or no attention to the historic figures of the Old Testament prophets as predecessors or forerunners of the apostles. We therefore conclude that both "the apostles and the prophets" of Rev 18:20 represent the persecuted saints of the Christian church. Two separate groups, at least certainly not two disjointed groups, are not indicated. The expression simply appears as a comprehensive formula to describe the saints of the Christian past and present, whose main common characteristic is the fact that they were victims of persecution by godless and diabolic forces.

The connection of "prophets and apostles" based on their common fate of martyrdom obtains no prominence in later Christian literature. Although we find occasional references to the example of the holy prophets as models of faith and endurance in suffering, even this theme loses importance.

In the New Testament, other references to the suffering of the prophets come from a strongly Jewish Christian background: Jas 6:10 and Heb 11:32. The theme appears also in First Clement,[16] and the epistle of Barnabas[17] but later references are scarce. This is understandable from the social and political changes that took place in the first decades of the second century. The Christian communities were much less worried about persecution by Jews than about persecution by Roman authorities. This preoccupation with a new hostile power, seen as the embodiment of the evil forces, is already quite obvious in Revelation. In fact, "the prophets" mentioned in Rev 18:20 are not those of the Old Testament but actual members of the Christian church, on whose account God exacts punishment from the "great city" Babylon, meaning Rome. Later when the formula "prophets and apostles" was understood more and more univocally as a reference to the two Testaments, and references to New Testament prophets became scarce, it became quite natural that "prophets and apostles" were not connected on account of their common fate of persecution either in the sense of 1 Thess 2:3-15 (and Lk 11:49) or in the sense of Rev 18:20.[18]

There are other early Christian texts (1 Cor 12: 28-29; Eph 2:20; 3:5; 4:11; Did 11:2-5) in which "prophets" and "apostles" are listed along with other persons endowed with spiritual gifts destined to the service and edification of the church. There is sufficient evidence in these texts to exclude the possibility that either "prophets" would mean those of the Old Testament or that "apostles" would be identified with the twelve disciples of Jesus. Nonetheless, in the writings of Clement of Alexandria, Tertullian and Irenaeus, these texts are applied to prophets of the Old Covenant and to the original apostles of Jesus showing that, in some way, they contributed to the development of the second century's theology on "prophets and apostles."[19]

In 1 Cor 12:28-29 the order of the two groups is reversed and with emphasis: "And God has appointed in the church *first* apostles, *second* prophets, *third* teachers..." (italics mine). "Apostles" and "prophets" are here part of a longer list of charismatic church functionaries, although the most important ones. By *apostles* Paul means the traveling missionaries of the early church, including himself, the "great apostles" of Jerusalem and most probably also many other seemingly less important personalities like those mentioned in Romans or his own associates in apostolic work like Timothy. With some disagreement on details, both Lucien Cerfaux and Hans von Campenhausen concluded that Paul's use of the term reflected an early Christian usage (*Sprachgebrauch*) susceptible of flexibility rather than a technical terminology based on rigidly established concepts.[20] Paul was quite clear about the first-ranking importance of the service of the apostles. Their ministry was crucial for the church: they provided opportunity for the word of God to spread and elicit the response of faith. Rom 10:14-15 is justly regarded as a text explaining the crucial importance of the "apostles." "But how are men to call upon him whom they have not believed? And how are they to believe in him of whom they have never heard? And how are they to hear without a preacher? And how can men preach unless they are sent?"[21] This last word (*apostalōsin*) shows that Paul saw not only behind his own apostleship, but behind the missionary activities of the church as such, a divine mission guaranteeing the spread of the gospel "to all the earth" (vs 18) and assuring that the word heralded by them might qualify as "the word [*hrēmatos*] of Christ" (contra RSV vs 17 "preaching of Christ"; cf. also variant reading: "word of God"). In the text the semantic ties between *apostolos* and the verb *apostellō* are vividly felt. So we must keep before our eyes the verbal root of *sending* and classify the "apostles" of the early church according to the dignity of the one from whom they received their immediate sending and authorization. In this sense there is a specific meaning for *apostolos:* "an apostle—not from men nor through man, but through Jesus Christ and God the Father who raised him from the dead" (Gal 1:1).[22]

The ministry of prophecy was distinguished from that of the apostles. The prophet "speaks to men for their upbuilding and encouragement and consolation" (1 Cor 14:3). Such service supposes faith (1 Cor 14:22), it is a gift of the Spirit, and is given for "building up the church" (1 Cor 14:12).

On the other hand, prophets were also distinguished from teachers. While prophets receive and communicate "revelation" (*apocalypsis*) and "knowledge" (*gnōsis*), teachers give "instruction" (*didaskalia*). This distinction should not be pressed. Both prophets and teachers are destined to continue the work of the apostles (they build upon the foundation of faith elicited by the apostolic preaching) and both gifts were opposed by Paul to the gift of tongues.

In spite of all these distinctions, in general Paul's categories of the different "gifts" should not be considered mutually exclusive or even adequately distinguished and separable. Through his very act of writing to the churches, Paul took on himself the role of "prophets" and "teachers" by imparting revelation and knowledge. Meanwhile, of course, he claimed for himself the highest ranking title of apostleship as "apostle of Jesus Christ." Since he understood his apostolic vocation according to the pattern of prophetic election, he demonstrated that in his thinking, "prophecy" and "apostolate" were analogous concepts. The Pauline expression "apostles and prophets," therefore, does not necessarily designate disjointed groups.

In Ephesians there are three passages of special importance, Eph 2:20, 3:5, and 4:11. Of these three passages, Eph 4:11 appears to be the closest to 1 Cor 12:28. It lists "apostles and prophets" together with other charismatics (evangelists, pastors, teachers) and com-

pares the church with the human body. There is, however, an
important point of discrepancy: in Eph 4:1-17 no mention is made
of the difference between the ministries nor of the diversity of the
members of the body.

The other two passages blur more obviously the distinction that
Paul had established between "apostles and prophets" in First
Corinthians. In Eph 2:20 we read about the church built on the
foundation (*themelion*) of apostles and prophets.[23] The phrase really
combines the "founding" function of the apostles and the "upbuilding" ministry of the prophets without distinguishing specific
functions for the two groups. Eph 3:5 puts emphasis on prophetic
functions while describing a ministry of receiving revelation.
Nonetheless, the author declared that the revelation of the mystery
of Christ unknown "has now been revealed to his holy apostles and
prophets by the Spirit." (3:5)[24]

The merging of "apostleship" and "prophecy" is apparent also in
the Didache. "Apostles" and "prophets" designate different
groups, the first being traveling missionaries, the second, local
charismatic ministers. With regard to "apostles" there is emphasis
on the concept of delegation: "Welcome every apostle on arriving,
as if he were the Lord" (Did 11:3). The prophets receive their status
from their inspiration: "they speak in the Spirit" (Did 11:7). Yet the
distinction is not complete. If an apostle is proven inauthentic, the
Didache calls him "a false prophet" (Did 11:5). This suggests that a
genuine apostle could be regarded as a "true prophet." But there is
more involved than just this implication. A traveling apostle might
be interested in "settling" in a community with more or less
permanence, and the Didache gives some rules for such a case (Did
12:1).[25] The following section clearly speaks of prophets who had
settled in the community. This settling of some apostles and the
mobility of some local prophets makes the distinction between
"prophets and apostles" rather tenuous. Further, in chapter 11, the
Didache speaks of "itinerant teachers" to be received just like the
apostles, "as the Lord himself" (Did 11:2), a phrase applied later to
the apostles. Thus, in the same way as in Ephesians, the distinction
between these categories is superficial and blurred.[26]

According to all indications, church functionaries are not called
"apostles" and "prophets" in later texts. The book of Revelation
and the Didache are the latest documents which refer to "apostles
and prophets" as related groups of church ministries. *The Shepherd*
of Hermas refers to "apostles and teachers" but does not combine
apostles with prophets.[27] The Montanist crisis focused on the

survival of New Testament prophecy but failed to connect it with the word or concept of apostleship. It seems that in the second century, to use the terminology of Did 15, the *leitourgia* of bishops and deacons took over that of "apostles and prophets." For instance, in the second half of the century a phrase is found in *The Martyrdom of Polycarp,* designating Polycarp "an apostolic and prophetic teacher of the Catholic Church in Smyrna."[28] The order of the two adjectives is by no means accidental, following the pattern of "apostles and prophets" established with emphasis in First Corinthians and reproduced in Ephesians, Revelation, and the Didache. The passage shows the complete merging of the triple ministries carefully distinguished in First Corinthians (apostles, prophets, teachers) but fused in later texts. Here they are absorbed by the role of the monarchical bishop. In fact, the phrase describing Polycarp is a compendium of the ideal church leader as it emerged in the second half of the second century. This ideal celebrated the traditional charismatic roles of apostles, prophets, and teachers, consolidated them in the monepiscopate, and crowned them with the glory of martyrdom.

For explaining the use of the term "prophets and apostles" in Irenaeus' theology of the Canon, most important are the texts that employ a historical scheme of revelation. In the New Testament there is only one explicit passage (2 Pet 3:2) but the epistle to the Romans (especially Rom 1:1-2, together with 1 Pet 1:10-12) must be first considered as background and foundation. Further, the salvation-history scheme built around prophets and apostles, is often found in Ignatius and Justin, with some important fragmentary references in other writings.[29]

In Rom 1:1-2 the crucial words of the passage are: *apostolos aphōrismenos eis euaggelion theou, ho proeppēggeilato dia tōn prophētōn autou en graphais hagiais.* Paul presented his own self-understanding as an apostle in reference to his *euaggelion* which in turn he understood as fore-announced by the prophets in holy scriptures. Correspondence between the role of the apostles and that of the prophets is shown in the use of *euaggelion* and *proepēggeilato.* Also the reference to "holy scriptures" is important. Most probably it is a global reference to all sacred writings inherited from Judaism and not only to those specifically called "Prophets" in the Jewish classification of scriptures. If we accept Rom 15:4 (*hosa proegraphē*) and Rom 16:26 (*graphōn prophetikōn*) as authentic, the probability is heightened. Rom 3:21 equally corroborates that, in Paul's view, all scriptures (see the comprehensive formula "the law and the prophets" used here) testified to God's salvific act in Christ: the manifestation of God's justice independently from the law (*chōris nomou*).

In the epistle to the Romans the articulation and unity of God's salvation plan are demonstrated in a comprehensive scheme. To this end three points are made: a) both pagans and Jews are in need of salvation, b) both groups are treated with justice when offered access to justification, and yet c) the validity of all Old Testament events and institutions is maintained and defended. Paul achieved this argumentation by a periodization of history and by assigning true but relative (temporary) validity to the Old Testament data according to their own respective time period. In this structure the prophets and their writings serve not so much by witnessing to their own particular periods of time but much more by anticipating and foretelling the final period of fulfilled promises and, in this way, exhibiting the transient character of the period to which they belong. The apostle's preaching matched what the prophet fore-announced. Announcing his *euaggelion* and showing that the prophets had fore-announced it, the apostle made salvation-history understandable for both Jews and Greeks. Thus Romans antici-pates the main points of the later anti-Gnostic position of the catholic church:

a) the same one God provides for Jews and Greeks alike;[30]

b) the totality of the Old Testament Scriptures are the church's rightful possession without compromising on the principle of justification without the law;

c) by linking the *euaggelion* of the apostle with the writings of the prophet a theological method is provided which leads to a com-prehensive and unified history of salvation and justifies the use of the combined witnesses of prophetic writings and apostolic preaching.

As these considerations show, the appearance of *apostolos* and "prophets in the holy scriptures" at the opening of Romans is by no means accidental or negligible. On the combination of these two terms a theological program is based.

Another passage which presents a theology of salvation-history similar to the one found in Romans is 1 Pet 1:10-12. Instead of using the word "apostle" it refers to the carriers of the Christian message as *euaggelisamenoi*. The preachers of the gospel and the prophets treat the same basic topic: "the sufferings of Christ and the subse-

quent glory" (vs 11), a topic not to be taken in a narrowly historicized sense, for the rest of the epistle[31] leaves little doubt that the
"prophets" referred to in these verses must be understood in a
general sense as in Romans.[32] In fact, the epistle makes just as
copious use of the Psalms and the Book of Proverbs as of prophetic
books.[33]

It is generally recognized that in 2 Pet 3:2 prophets of the Old
Testament and apostles of the New Testament are put into
parallelism. The author wrote as *Symeōn Petros*, apostle of Jesus
Christ and therefore eyewitness of the Transfiguration. His being
an apostle provided guarantee to his teaching on the question of the
parousia, a doctrine under attack by the "scoffers" (3:3). In this
description of the Transfiguration, he presented his own reception
of the voice from heaven as direct exposure to the divine glory. He
stood by as Jesus "received honor and glory from God the Father
and the voice was borne to him by the Majestic Glory, 'This is my
beloved Son, with whom I am well pleased' " (1:17-18). Right after
the description of the Transfiguration, the author connected the
role of the apostolic eyewitness with that of the prophets by stating:
"and we have the prophetic word made more sure" (1:19). The rest
of the chapter is about "the prophetic word" shining as a lamp in
the darkness but being in need of an inspired interpretation since it
was itself produced under the inspiration of the Holy Spirit. The
prophētikon logon of vs 19 is specified as *prophēteia graphēs* of vs 20,
and the text leaves no doubt about its broad meaning by adding the
adjective *pasa.*

In the first section of the epistle the parallelism between apostles
and prophets is therefore built around the concept of revelation.
Both the apostles, who by "divine power" have been granted "all
things that pertain to life and godliness" (1:3), and the prophets
"moved by the Holy Spirit" (vs 21) are presented as privileged
recipients of revelation. Their role is similar not only in that they
provide light but also in that they need careful and divinely guided
interpretation. In fact, this same epistle that states in 1:20 the need
for guidance in interpreting the prophetic writings also insists in
3:15-17 on the need of enlightened interpretation for the letters of
"our beloved brother Paul."

There is one more aspect that connects "prophets and apostles"
here. In 3:1 the author of Second Peter referred to a previous letter
(most probably First Peter) and wrote that "in both of them I have
aroused your sincere mind by way of reminder [*hypomnēsis*]." Then
the author continued citing the purpose "that you should

remember the predictions of the holy prophets [*tōn proeirēmenōn hrēmatōn hypo tōn hagiōn prophētōn*] and the commandment of the Lord and Savior through your apostles" (3:2). In this passage both the instructions of the apostles and the teaching of the prophets are said to be matter of remembrance. Moreover, apostles are presented in strict dependence from Christ: it is his commandment that they transmit.

That the author of Second Peter belonged to a post-apostolic age has been demonstrated sufficiently. In the mind of the author, the apostolic teaching together with the prophecies of the Old Testament constituted material for remembrance because it belonged to a normative past.[34] The pseudepigraphic writing itself comes about on this presupposition. It serves this very purpose. The verbs in 1:12 (*hypomimnēskein*) and in 1:15 (*mnēmēn poieisthai*) attest to this preoccupation about the memory of the past. The references to the Pauline epistles and to First Peter plus the pseudepigraphic claim show the author's awareness that the teaching of the apostles was remembered not only (not even primarily?) by reminders given *viva voce* but also (most importantly?) by means of written records. So the juxtaposition of "prophets and apostles" in Second Peter was done in a context that shows that both groups (not only the prophets) exercised their "reminding" function because they were remembered through written records that had emanated from earlier activities.

2 Pet 1:20-21 may be regarded as a rather complete theological statement on inspiration. Moreover, 2 Pet 3:2, standing as it does in the context of the epistle (cf. particularly 1:12-21 and 3:1-16), appears to sketch a theology of the Canon, or, as I prefer to call it, a theology of the "pre-Canon" or "proto-Canon," from which the anti-Gnostic Church Fathers developed their theology of the Canon.

We also find two passages in the letter of Ignatius to the Philadelphians, in which "prophets and apostles" are mentioned within the framework of salvation-history. The first is in chapter 5 where Ignatius expressed his trust in the Philadelphians' prayers:

> Your prayers to God will make me perfect so that I may gain that fate which I have mercifully been allotted, by taking refuge in the gospel as in Jesus' flesh and in the Apostles as in the presbytery of the Church. And the Prophets, let us love them too, because they anticipated the gospel in their preaching....[Phld 5:1-2][35]

Cyril Richardson thought that "gospel" and "apostles" referred to the double division of the Christian writings, a claim disputed by

John Knox and H. von Campenhausen who attributed the invention of this division to Marcion.[36] While the claim that Marcion originated this terminology may be questioned, other objections can be raised against Richardson's interpretation. Ignatius consistently compared the apostles with the presbytery and in the parallel texts there is certainly no question of apostolic *writings*.[37] At the same time, "gospel" was for Ignatius a comprehensive term, meaning the full Christ event from Incarnation to Resurrection. Yet, following the traditional terminology, observable in the New Testament (see what we said above about Rom 1:1-2), "gospel" was closely related to the role of the apostles, as the content of their preaching and the object of their vocation, representing the totality of their message. The text of Ignatius basically means then that the role of the apostles was to communicate the gospel just as it was the role of the presbytery to present and transmit "the flesh of Jesus." Such an interpretation supposes a liturgical setting for Ignatius' imagery as he depicted the presbytery, with the bishop and the deacons, as representatives of heavenly realities.[38] In other words, the presbytery was presented as in Eucharistic assembly and symbolically identified with the band of the apostles in their gospel-giving (= Christ-giving) function.[39]

The mention of the prophets might appear as an afterthought. Indeed, the completeness of the liturgical image of the previous sentence hardly permitted any other way of introducing them. But their appearance in the text follows logically. According to Ignatius, the Christians received the gospel not only from the apostles but also from the prophets who anticipated it. Here, as at several other places, Ignatius affirmed in a defensive tone the legitimacy of the use of Old Testament prophecies in support of the gospel.[40] He then continued the text quoted above:

> ...they anticipated the gospel in their preaching and hoped for and awaited Him and were saved by believing on Him. Thus they were in Jesus Christ's unity. Saints they were, and we should love and admire them, seeing that Jesus Christ vouched for them and they form a real part of the gospel of our common hope. [Phld 5:2][41]

While elsewhere Ignatius repeatedly cautioned against Judaizing tendencies,[42] here he reaffirmed the doctrine of Romans and First Peter about the link between the gospel and the prophets of the Old Testament. New was the warm personal relation that he, on the one hand, stated between the gospel (= Christ) and the prophets and, on other hand, demanded from the Christians with regard to the prophets

("we should love and admire them"). These statements only reinforce his claim that the prophets formed part of the "unity" of Jesus
Christ. In fact, Ignatius stressed not so much the successive stages
and continuity of salvation-history as the unity formed around
Christ by all the former protagonists and present-day participants
of that history. This thrust of Ignatius' thinking appears with even
greater clarity in our second text, a passage to the Philadelphians:

> Priests are a fine thing, but better still is the High Priest who
> was entrusted with the Holy of Holies. He alone was entrusted
> with God's secrets. He is the door to the Father. Through it
> there enter Abraham, Isaac and Jacob, the prophets and the
> apostles and the Church. All these find their place in God's
> unity. But there is something special about the gospel—I mean
> the coming of the Saviour, our Lord Jesus Christ, his passion
> and resurrection. The beloved prophets announced his com-
> ing; but the gospel is the crowning achievement forever. [Phld
> 9:1-2][43]

Here the list of leading figures of salvation-history was expanded:
to prophets and apostles, patriarchs were attached at one end and
the church at the other. The result was a complete panoramic view
of "God's unity" formed by all those united with Christ. *The
primacy of the gospel* was again reaffirmed in the sense that it was
synonymous with the total Christ event. The "gospel" therefore
appears as the organizing, unifying principle of salvation-history,
constituting also the link between the prophets and the apostles.[44]

In the letter of Polycarp to the Philippians there is another
passage which formulates the attitude of the subapostolic age with
exceptional clarity and simplicity. After a series of instructions per-
taining chiefly to morality and church order, Polycarp wrote as sort
of a summarizing conclusion:

> So then let us "serve him with fear and all reverence" (cf. Ps
> 2:11) as he (Christ) has commanded and the apostles who
> preached the gospel to us (*hoi euaggelisamenoi hēmas apostoloi*)
> and the prophets who foretold the coming of our Lord. [6:3][45]

Prophets and apostles are combined here with reference to Christ
who himself stands at the peak of the list as the legislator of Christian life. The apostles' chief function was the spreading of the
gospel while the prophets are characterized as preannouncing
(*prokēruxantes*) the coming of Christ. Thus, Polycarp justified his
instruction by presenting the same "tryptichon" (prophets and

apostles combined through Christ) detected in Rom 1:1-2, 2 Pet 3:2, and in Ignatius' Phld 5:2 While in those texts the "tryptichon" was embedded in the context, here it stands with stark simplicity as a general ground for moral and ecclesial precepts. The formula of Polycarp appears as the practical application of a principle: "prophets and apostles" arranged in dependence on Christ and his commandments serve as norm of teaching in the church.

In the development of the Canon, Justin's work is generally recognized as an important milestone. Knox went as far as stating that through Justin, "What had been simply the Jewish Bible had become as truly and completely Christian as the Gospels."[46] Although this is a strong exaggeration—not even for Paul was the Old Testament "simply the Jewish Bible," nor after Justin was the Christianization of the same writings a completed process—there is no doubt that Justin carried the program of the Christian expropriation of the Jewish sacred writings further than any of his predecessors or contemporaries. After Romans, his Logos theory was the second major attempt to give a comprehensive and synthetic account of God's all-inclusive salvation plan, unified through the identity of its main protagonist, the Logos who influenced both the prophets of the Old Testament and the great ancient philosophers of the Greeks. Such a concept of revelation which from its inception overstepped the boundaries of the Jewish people was certainly broader than that of Paul. It brought into focus, and fully exploited by using a philosophical framework, the claim of universality inherent but not explicit in the first proclamation of Christianity. Justin's system was the first truly Gentile presentation of the faith of Christ by a man who embraced the cultural values of the Greco-Roman world and found in Christ the confirmation and completion of its most noble philosophical heritage.

Justin's background modified the use and understanding of the traditional formula "prophets and apostles." In his *First Apology*, he literally reversed the theme of the "common fate" of prophets and apostles. The Jews, he wrote, had the prophecies but failed to understand them. Therefore they rejected and maltreated Christ. The apostles, however, found a *different* reception among the Gentiles: as soon as they testified about Christ "and gave over to them the prophecies," the Gentiles "were filled with joy and faith, turned away from their idols and dedicated themselves to the unbegotten God through Christ."[47] Justin saw that although the prophets chronologically preceded the apostles, from a Gentile point of view, they reached the converted Christians only through the apostles. For the Gentiles both the preaching of the gospel and the transmission of the Old Testament prophecies take place at the same time and through the same agents, the apostles. Consequently, while Ignatius stressed the primacy of the "gospel" (meaning the total Christ), in Justin the role of the apostles received primacy. This explains why in Justin the order is "apostles and prophets," although he certainly meant two groups that chronologically succeeded each other in the reverse order.[48]

Justin looked at the prophets as the "second-hand" possession of the Christians, received through the ministry of the apostles. He valued the prophets for furnishing proof-texts that authenticated the apostolic preaching by revealing that the facts about Christ were part of a pre-conceived and fore-announced divine plan.

Justin's position was both anti-Jewish and anti-Marcionite. His claim that the apostles transmitted to the Gentiles the true meaning of the prophecies underlies his argumentation with Trypho. At the same time he clung to the Jewish heritage against Marcion who wanted to deprive the Christian message of the support of prophetic anticipations. For him the error of Marcion had two detestable consequences: it destroyed monotheism and it denied that Christ was predicted by the prophets as the Son of the Creator. In contrast Justin affirmed:

> ...and we believe in the voice of God uttered through the apostles of Christ and announced to us through the prophets.[49]

In one other passage, Justin mentioned together the apostles and the prophets. In *First Apology* 67:3, Justin described writings attributed to the prophets and apostles read during liturgical assemblies:

> And on the day called Sunday there is a meeting in one place of those who live in cities or in the country, and the memoirs of the apostles or the writings of the prophets are read as long as time permits.[50]

Apparently "the writings of the prophets" mean in this text the whole Old Testament,[51] which according to the Christian usage reduces "Law and Prophets" to "Prophets" only.[52] The "memoirs of the apostles" are identified with "the gospels" in the previous chapter of the same work. Justin was not concerned with the individual composition to which he referred, nor with the particular apostles to whom these gospels were attributed. That "apostles" meant for Justin the lifetime companions of Jesus appears from a passage in the *First Apology*.[53] Yet it would be certainly false to speculate that Justin attributed the written gospels to some collective authorization of the Twelve Apostles as it was imagined in the *Muratorian Fragment* about the Gospel of John.[54] We would be also misunderstanding Justin if we faulted him for a historical error in assigning the gospels to the apostles of Jesus as their literary authors. What we have in this text is a simple report of the state of affairs as he found them in the middle of the second century: reference to prophets and apostles involved at that time besides the Old Testament writings also written records of the apostolic preaching. The liturgical use of the written gospels alternately or along with texts of the Old Testament corresponded to the traditional usage of referring to the norms of Christian teaching as "prophets and apostles." Justin's text expresses this correspondence without making specific statement about the literary authors of the compositions he called gospels or affirming that the "memoirs of the apostles" were the only documents carrying apostolic teaching. Doubtlessly, the word "memoirs" (*apomnēmoneumata*) poorly corresponds to the literary genre of "gospels." Yet, it would be another mistake to blame Justin for misrepresenting the kind of literature that gospels constitute. As early as Second Peter, reference to "apostles" was made in the context of "remembrance" or "reminding." Justin used a word apt to convey for the Hellenistic reader that gospels were written memories of apostolic preaching. What was new in Justin's text was a slowly but surely developing fact in the life of the church during the second century: the normative role of apostolic teaching is attributed more and more largely to written records that represent their teaching.

What then can be concluded from this survey? The combination of terms "prophets and apostles" is found within the framework of a continuous historical development that reflects the prehistory of the Canon. This development can be sketched in the following successive stages.

At first the two terms were closely related and almost synonymous. They were used in parallel constructions and applied to God's messengers preaching God's word as both spokesmen and delegates. This usage had a base in the Old Testament, in particular in Jeremiah, and was closely connected with the Hebrew *shāliach/shālûach* translated into Greek as *apostolos* or *apestalmenos*. That the term *shālach* was used in connection with the divine mission of Old Testament prophets[55] explains to a large extent the convergence of the terms *prophētēs* and *apostolos* in this early stage. Mt 23:37, Lk 11:49, and Lk 13:34 reflect this usage.

In the second phase the term "apostles sent by Christ" expressed a new reality that appeared at the beginning of the Christian movement. This new reality gave new specific meaning to the words *shālīach/apostolos.*[56] The apostles of Christ were connected with the Old Testament prophets as their common fates of rejection and persecution were recognized. In First Thessalonians a "tryptichon" is based on this comparison: prophets—Christ—apostles. (Lk 11:49 probably reflects this same Pauline theme.) By stating the similarity of their destinies, Paul implied similarity of function between apostleship and prophecy: they transmitted the word of God, unacceptable to the disobedient people. Also, in Revelation the theme of martyrdom connects the terms "prophets and apostles," but here probably New Testament prophets were meant. The author of Revelation knew the specific group of the "Twelve Apostles" and their fundamental role for the church. Yet by calling the apostles "prophets" the author also showed the persistent fusion of the two concepts. In later literature this connection of "prophets and apostles" on account of persecution became scarce and insignificant, probably because later persecutions did not support the analogy.

A third phase is marked by Paul's epistle to the Romans where there appears clear awareness that the preaching of the gospel by the apostles corresponds to the fore-announcing of the Messiah by the prophets of old. Paul considered "the law and the prophets" as basically prophecy and thus contributed to the Christian reduction of this double term to the single term "prophets."[57] At the same time he claimed that Christian usage of the Old Testament texts was not only legitimate but was the only interpretation satisfying the divinely given meaning of the texts. Indeed, Rom 15:4, whose Pauline authenticity is supported by Rom 1:1-2 and 3:21-22, declares a Christian claim to all Jewish scriptures. 1 Pet 1:10-12 reveals a similar understanding of salvation-history, sees in Christ the common content of "prophets" and gospel, and attributes the prophecies to the Spirit of Christ, the same Spirit who coming from heaven effected the preaching of the gospel. This passage even claims that the prophets knew that their prophecies were destined for the use of the future believers of Christ. Indeed, the passage expropriates for the church not only the prophecies but the prophets themselves, for they are pictured as sharers of the same spirit and consciously serving the future Christian community.

Contemporary to the texts just cited, we also have record of Pauline usage of the terms "apostles and prophets" as referring to church functionaries. While in First Corinthians an attempt was made to distinguish clearly between these functions (and also the role of "teaching"), later writings, like Ephesians and the Didache, blurred the concepts considerably and certainly did not see in "apostles and prophets" two disjointed groups. The disappearance of terms for designating church ministries happened rather rapidly. In any case, the references to "apostles and prophets" were interpreted as references to the two Testaments not only by Tertullian and Irenaeus but probably already by Marcion.

Second Peter, Ignatius and Polycarp are witnesses of a fourth phase where there existed a proto-Canon consisting of "prophets and apostles." In both theory and practice, they referred to the prophets of the Old Testament (i.e., the Old Testament scriptures) and the gospel delivered by the apostles as the norm of faith and morals in Christian doctrine. Their authority was derived from that of Christ: the apostles received from him their message and mission, and the prophets anticipated him through prophetic inspiration. In Ignatius, prophets and apostles appear as an actual part of the church in virtue of sacramental and liturgical symbolism, rather than as representatives of previous historical periods. The "apostles" are not specified by number or name and their anonymity is even more apparent as they are compared to the presbytery surrounding the bishop in the liturgical celebrations. Ignatius made no explicit reference to written records of the apostolic preaching. In his vision it was first of all the actual ecclesial structure that effectively represented the apostles and provided the continued presence of the gospel they had preached. In Second Peter, however, both Paul and Peter are mentioned as authors of written records which were actually used in the church although with difficulty and controversies. The pseudepigraphic activity of the author indicates the growing conviction that written apostolic documents were needed to assure the permanent memory of the apostolic teaching and resolve the controversies. The author also relied heavily on the function of church authorities to avoid divergent interpretations of the apostolic tradition. The "proto-Canon" of "prophets and apostles" was insufficient because of the incomplete documentation of apostolic teaching. This position is consistent with a state of affairs in which oral tradition still played a prevalent role while the collection of ancient documents was furthered alongside the creation of pseudepigraphs. Polycarp's references to Paul's preaching and writing, together with his general statement about "prophets and apostles" as norms of doctrine, represent this very same situation.

Finally, in Justin we see the proto-Canon put to use in constructing a systematic presentation of the Christian faith. His interest in the Old Testament as prophecy was part of a doctrinal position. He used the texts of the prophets to prove the credibility of the Gospels as part of a preconceived divine plan, and to outline a comprehensive prehistory for Christianity that included even philosophers. The memory of the teaching of the "apostles" was available in the church's liturgical assemblies and was read along with the texts of the "prophets." This gives the impression of complete parallelism between Old Testament and New Testament writings. However, for Justin "apostles" did not coincide with the normative function of a set of documents, and certainly "the memoirs of the apostles" did not exhaust the apostolic tradition as he knew it. Yet, Justin's texts point to a continued development by which the term "apostles" increasingly means written books and the terms "prophets and apostles" progressively achieve parity. They signify not just two periods of the same salvation-history, not only two consecutive sets of agents of the same God, but two sets of sacred writings originating from them as preachers of the divine word.

The findings of this essay point to a prehistory of the Christian Canon of scriptures. They must be read, however, in the context of what has taken place in the last decades of the second century, when the theology of the Christian Canon took shape with reference to the writings of "prophets and apostles." It appears that in his anti-Gnostic defense, Irenaeus was able to find all the material he needed, in the writings of his predecessors. His scheme of salvation-history, his teaching about the same Spirit working in all of its phases, his insistence on the oneness of God providing for all people of all ages, his teaching about the revelatory presence of the Logos throughout the course of human history—all these assertions can be found in the material we have analyzed. The bishop of Lyons collected, arranged, and organized them for his anti-Gnostic purpose. As far as the Canon is concerned, the specific novelty of Irenaeus' system consisted of the substantial identification of "apostolic teaching" with the teaching available in what he called "apostolic writings." This identification was far from being complete. In his understanding, church structures, the sacraments, and the Holy Spirit are considered as "apostolic heritage"; so Irenaeus never reduced apostolic tradition totally to a set of writings. Yet, when specific doctrinal positions were examined, he evaluated the evidence of apostolic teaching by returning to those writings which the church at large considered of apostolic origin. It was not the norm of apostolicity that was new in Irenaeus or his contemporaries—without that norm, no pseudepigraphs would have been ever composed! What was new was the way in which this norm was made practical in the church as the well-defined list of available documents whose apostolic authority was assured.

The transition from proto-Canon to Canon needs further research. The concepts of apostolicity, canon, inspiration, and the use of the terms "prophets and apostles" have not been researched adequately, for instance, in the works of Tertullian. There are also other late second-century sources like the *Epistula Apostolorum* and the *Muratorian Fragment* that can enlighten us if they are analyzed with the "proto-Canon" in mind.[58]

The role of Marcion also needs reevaluation in the light of what has been said above. Since the norm of "prophets and apostles" was generally accepted in the church in the first decades of the second century, Marcion's reduction of "prophets and apostles" to one Gospel with one apostle must certainly appear as a break with the tradition, rather than as one of the viable options still open at his time. As a matter of fact, Marcion's attempt to reduce the question of normativity to the question of normative writings and then to select a few writings from the many documents held in esteem by the church was contrary to the traditional position on both accounts. His influence on the formation of the canon is certainly important but not so much that we should credit him with the invention of the idea of an exclusive list of books to be held as normative in the church. It is rather by accelerating a process *already in course* that he exercised his influence: the process by which apostolic teaching was channeled and concentrated in written documents. Rather than being a conservative mind searching for what authentic material was left from the past, Marcion precipitated a development and went "overboard": first by turning the question of apostolic authenticity into the exclusive question of authentic writings and then by finding the answer in a selective Paulinism.

NOTES

1. About Irenaeus see D. Farkasfalvy, "Theology of Scripture in St. Irenaeus," *R Ben* 78 (1968) 323, n. 7 and 328-29. On Tertullian there is no comprehensive study. Some important texts are quoted by Y. Congar, "Inspiration des écritures canoniques et apostolicité del Église," *Recherches des sciences philosophiques et théologiques* 45 (1961) 32-42. Most striking is *Adv Marcionem* IV, 24, 8-9 (CCL I, 609): "Tam enim apostolus Moyses quam apostoli prophetae, aequanda erit auctoritas utriusque officii ab uno eodem domino apostolorum et prophetarum."

2. Lines 77-78; M. Meinertz, *Einleitung in das neue Testament* (Paderborn: F. Schöningh, 1950) 323. The Latin text is as follows:
   ...legi eum quidem oportet,
   se publicare vero in ecclesia populo
   neque inter prophetas, completo numero,
   neque inter apostolos in finem temporum, potest.
   In my translation "completo numero" and "in finem temporum" are

taken as parallel members. "In finem" is either equivalent to "in fine" (with the rather frequent confusion of the accusative and the ablative) or is the direct translation of the Greek "eis telos" which can signify both "until the end" or "at the end." The latter is definitely preferred. Excluding Hermas from the Canon "until the end of the ages" is hardly the point. The admission of writings in the future as opposed to the present time is not a question considered. Thus, unacceptable is A. C. Sundberg's translation: "while it ought to be read, to the end of the ages, it cannot be read publicly in the church to the people...." Sundberg's thesis that the Muratorian Canon is from the fourth century is not convincing. The expression "nuperrime, temporibus nostris" is irreconcilable with the meaning "about 150 years ago." Since this expression is embedded in a sentence giving biographical details about Hermas and his brother, Pius, as bishop of Rome, it cannot be interpreted as referring to theological phases of history but must be taken in a chronological sense. Cf. A. C. Sundberg, "Canon Muratori: A Fourth-Century List," *HTR* 66 (1973) 1-41.

3. Y. Congar, "Inspiration," 41-42. I have studied the use of this same terminology by Bernard of Clairvaux in D. Farkasfalvy, *L'inspiration de l' Ecriture Sainte dans la théologie de saint Bernard* (Rome: Herder, 1964) 106-136.

4. For instance, cf. the Parable of the Wicked Husbandmen. (Mk 12:1-12 and par.) The close parallel between this text and First Thessalonians would indicate that the tradition belonged to a primitive layer. Scholarship is, however, divided on the issue.

5. M. J. Lagrange, *Évangile selon saint Luc* (Paris: Gabalda, 1948) 346: "Mt. a mieux conservé le texte de la citation par l'envoi de prophètes, de sages et de scribes, tandis que Lc. a mis des prophètes et des apôtres pour désigner les envoyés du Nouveau Testament, de sort qu'il se serait plus préoccupé de l'interpréter de l'évangile un passage auquel il conservait son charactère de citation que Mt. qui mettait les paroles dans la bouche de Jésus."

6. E. Haenchen, "Matthäus 23," *ZTK* 48 (1951) 52, quoting Bultmann, Merx, Mellhausen, Harnack, Loisy, Reitzenstein and Schniewind, said it was a common supposition ("Man nimmt heut meist an") to claim that Luke was quoting from some lost book of Jewish wisdom. He added: "This widely spread opinion, however, does not excuse us from doing our own research."

7. John Bright, *Jeremiah* (AB; Garden City, N.Y.: Doubleday, 1965) 54.

8. I follow here K. H. Rengstorf (*TWNT* I, 429) with modifications proposed by H. von Campenhausen, "Der urchristliche Apostelbegriff," *ST* 1 (1947) 103.

9. We must, of course, explain why a quotation from Jeremiah is attributed to God's Wisdom. It seems to me satisfactory to refer to Prov 9:1-3: "Wisdom has built her house...She has sent out her maids...." This text is thematically close to the Parable of the Wedding Feast. (Lk 14:16-24) The latter also describes the repetitious sending of servants, stated in the quotation from Jeremiah. Tertullian, when commenting on the Parable of the Wedding Feast, quoted in a most natural way Jer 7:25: "Et emisi omnes ad vos famulos meos prophetas—hic erit spiritus sanctus, admonitor convivarum." (*Adv Marcionem* IV, 31, CCL I, 630)

10. H. von Campenhausen, "Der urchristliche Apostelbegriff," 102: "(...es handelt sich um die 'Gesandten,' die Gott selbst im Laufe der Heilsgeschichte bis zuletzt in die Welt und zu seinem ungetreuen Volke geschickt hat [vgl. Lk 20:9-19]: aber um die von Lukas sonst vorausgesetzten zwölf Apostel oder überhaupt um irgendwelche christliche Apostel im engeren, technischen Sinne handelt es sich offensichtlich nicht. Vielmehr handelt es sich um dieselben Personen, die Lukas an einer anderen Stelle mit einer partizipialen Umschreibung *apestalmenous* nennt (13, 34)."

11. Such is the understanding of the *RSV*, the *New American Bible:* "you saints, apostles and prophets," and the French *Bible de Jérusalem:* "et vous, saints, apôtres et prophètes."

12. Cf. Rev 22:6, 9-10, 18-19.

13. J. Munck, *Petrus and Paulus in der Offenbarung Johannis: Ein Beitrag zur Auslegung der Apokalypse.* Theologiske Skifter, 1 København: Rosenkilde og Bagger, 1950).

14. O. Cullmann, *Petrus, Jünger—Apostel—Märtyrer* (Zürich: Zwingli Verlag, 1952) 99-101.

15. Cf. Rev 21:14. J. M. Ford, *Revelation* (AB; Garden City, NY: Doubleday, 1975) 333, has written that the phrase "looks suspiciously like an interpolation," but has provided no convincing argument.

16. 1 Clem 17:1. *Early Christian Fathers,* ed Cyril Richardson (New York: Macmillan, 1970) 52.

17. *Ancient Christian Writers,* 6, ed and trans J. Kleist (Westminster: Newman, 1948) 43: "Surely then, the Son of God came in the flesh to fill to the brim the measure of the sins of those who had persecuted His Prophets to death."(5:11)

18. In a completely new perspective, later centuries list the saints of Christianity as "Apostles—Prophets—Martyrs" as in the hymn *Te Deum* (fourth or fifth century): "Te gloriosus Apostolorum chorus, Te Prophetarum laudabilis numerus, Te martyrum candidatus laudat exercitus." The list is inspired by a concern for organized cult of the saints, yet the establishment of these three categories is certainly influenced by scriptural texts, especially Rev 18:20.

19. For Eph 4:11 see Clement of Alexandria, *Stromata* IV, 132, 1 (GCS 2, 306-7); for Eph 2:20 Tertullian, *Adv Marcionem* V, 17, 16 (CCL I, 716) and IV, 39, 6 (CCL I, 651-52).

20. L. Cerfaux, "Pour l'histoire du titre *Apostolos* dans le Nouveau Testament," *Recherches de science religieuses* 48 (1960) 76-92; H. von Campenhausen, "Der urchristliche Apostelbegriff," 102-3.

21. In Catholic liturgy this text was used widely throughout the Middle Ages for both the mass and the Divine Office on the feasts of the holy apostles.

22. H. von Campenhausen, "Der urchristliche Apostelbegriff," 103: "Der christliche *apostolos* gewinnt wie jeder *shālîach* seine Besonderheit und seine neue Bedeutung einfach aus der Besonderheit seines Auftrags und gemäss der Bedeutung dessen, der ihm den Auftrag erteilt, ihn als seinen *apostolos* bevollmächtigt hat."

23. There has been much debate concerning whether the "prophets" mentioned in Eph 2:20 belong to the Old or the New Testament. M. Barth, *Ephesians 1-3* (AB; Garden City N.Y., 1974) 315, surveys ancient and modern authors and concludes that a "time-honored interpretation" of the text holds that the "prophets" are related to the Old

Testament. Tertullian, *Adv Marcionem* V, 17, 16 (CCL I, 716), mentioned that Marcion wanted to delete the term "prophets" from 2:20 so as to avoid references to the Old Testament: "...superaedificati super fundamentum apostolorum. [Eph 2:20] Abstulit haereticus: et prophetarum oblitus dominum posuisse in ecclesia sicut apostolos ita et prophetas [cf. I Cor 12:28-29], si non timuit, ne et super ueterum prophetarum fundamentum aedificatio nostra constaret in Christo, cum ipse apostolus ubique nos de prophetis exstruere non cesset."

24. The exact interpretation of these passages can hardly be isolated from the question of authenticity. I find these texts better explained when denying Pauline authorship. It seems that the blurred distinction of "prophets and apostles" not only corresponds to a later ecclesiastical situation but also to a retrospective assessment of Paul's apostolic ministry in which the charismatic gifts distinguished by him overlapped and mixed.

25. I consider chapter 12 as referring to the itinerant preachers, i.e., those ministers who are called "apostles" in chapter 11. The expression, "Anyone coming in the name of the Lord" in 12:1 and the phrase "every apostle must be welcomed as the Lord" in 11:4, convincingly show the continuity of the subject.

26. The fact that in 15:1 the bishops and the deacons are said to fulfill the *leitourgia* of the prophets and teachers lends further support to the thesis that the distinction of the ministries is blurred in the Didache. For the refutation of Harnack's thesis of a dual system of offices in the early Church, see H. Conzelmann, *A Commentary on the First Epistle to the Corinthians* (Philadelphia: Fortress Press, 1975, in German 1969) 215.

27. *Similitudes* IX. xvi. 5; IX. xxv. 2. Also *Visions* III. v. 1. This combination also appears in 2 Tim 1:11.

28. 16:2 (Richardson, 155).

29. We should notice both the continuity and the development. There is evidence for the pre-Marcionite character of the main theological concepts involved and so for showing that the great anti-Gnostic writers drew their material from a tradition that antedates the Marcionite controversy.

30. See especially Rom 3:29. Interestingly the idea of the one same God governing the Old and New Testaments receives emphasis in Rom 1:1-2 by the sequence *euaggelion theou, ho proepēggeilato dia tōn prophētōn autou en graphais hagiais.*

31. 2:21, 3:18; 4:1 and especially 4:13: "But rejoice in so far as you share Christ's sufferings, that you may also rejoice and be glad when his glory is revealed." Also: "a witness of the sufferings of Christ as well as a partaker in the glory that is to be revealed." (5:1)

32. Rom 1:4 also makes reference to *pneuma hagiōsunēs* but does not establish the connection between prophecy and apostolate by means of the common Spirit. It is important to remark that for Irenaeus' anti-Gnostic synthesis one of the main ideas was the sameness of the Spirit working in both the prophets and the apostles. Thus this thought of Irenaeus appears in its rudimentary form already in First Peter.

33. Explicit quotations are drawn from at least Lev, Is, Ps, and Prov (cf. 1 Pet 1:16, 24-25; 2:6-8; 3:10-12; 4:18; 5:5).

34. K. H. Schelkle emphasized this particular aspect of Second Peter in his commentary: *Die Petrusbriefe, Der Judasbrief* (Herders

theologisches Kommentar zum Neuen Testament XIII, 2; Freiburg: Herder, 1970) 242.

35. Richardson, 109.
36. J. Knox, *Marcion and the New Testament* (Chicago: The University of Chicago, 1942). H. von Campenhausen, *Die Entstehung der christlichen Bibel* (Tübingen: J. C. B. Mohr, 1968).
37. Trall 2:2; 3:1; Smyrn 8:1.
38. From 4:1 on, the context is explicitly about the Eucharistic assembly with emphasis on the oneness of the Eucharist: "just as there is one bishop along with the presbytery and the deacons." (Richardson, 108) This is the usual setting for Ignatius who sees no *temporal* succession for the chain Christ—apostles—hierarchy but sees them all in the eternal present of heaven, actualized in the liturgy.
39. That for Ignatius *euaggelion* is identical with Christ is also the conclusion reached by G. Friedrich, *TWNT* II, 734.
40. J. Klevinhaus, *Die theologische Stellung der apostolischen Väter zur alttestamentlichen Offenbarung* (Gütersloh: C. Bertelsmann, 1948) 86-112. For our specific concern, it is not necessary to enter the debate on the exact meaning of Smryn 5:1 and Phld 8:2. However, both texts have important implications for the relationship of the two Testaments. In Smryn 5:1 the meaning of *euaggelion* and in Phld 8:2 the word *archeia* is unclear. Cf. I. Frank, *Der Sinn der Kanonbildung* (Freiburg: Herder, 1971) 38-42.
41. Richardson, 109.
42. Magn 8-10; Phld 6:1; probably also 8:2.
43. Richardson, 110-11.
44. Ignatius also saw the Holy Spirit as the link connecting the prophets to Christ: "How, then, can we live without him (Christ) even when *the prophets who were his disciples by the Spirit,* awaited him as their teacher?" Magn 9:2 (Richardson, 96; italics mine).
45. Richardson, 134. This passage is immediately followed by Polycarp's invectives against "false brothers." It is not certain that he had Marcion and his followers in mind. In that context, however, he gave a precious formula of normativity: "let us turn back to the word delivered to us from the beginning." (7:2) There can be little doubt that he meant the word delivered "by the apostles who preached us the gospel," as stated a few sentences earlier. Thus, Polycarp saw in the apostles and their doctrine a guarantee of authenticity. It is probably correct to see in his *hoi hēmas euaggelisamenoi apostoloi* a reference to the *first* preaching of the gospel, meaning, therefore, by *hēmas* not the present-day members of the community but the original recipients of the apostolic preaching. This is in accord with the way Polycarp referred to Paul's activities among the Philippians in 3:1.
46. J. Knox, *Marcion and the New Testament,* 29.
47. *First Apology* 49 (Richardson, 273).
48. See *Dialogue* 119:6; *First Apology* 67:3.
49. *Dialogue* 119:6.
50. *First Apology* 67:3 (Richardson, 287).
51. Cf. J. Knox, *Marcion and the New Testament,* 29, n. 14.
52. "Prophets" standing for the longer formula "Law and Prophets" appears as Christian usage, based on theological presuppositions. However, the esteem of Moses as an eminently prophetic figure

would certainly make the short formula possible within a purely Jewish context.

53. *First Apology* 50:12 (Richardson, 274).

54. The Muratorian Canon contains legendary details about the origins of the Fourth Gospel: although the Gospel was composed by the apostle John alone, it was approved by all the apostles. This story appears as an outgrowth of 1 John 1:3-4. Isidor Frank considered this story a sure sign that the concept of apostolicity combined with the normative supremacy of the Fourth Gospel and its christology, was the main shaping force of the New Testament Canon: *Der Sinn der Kanonbildung,* 183-84.

55. In LXX Jeremiah the term *apostellein* applied to a prophet means the prophet's authorization. This is most obvious in negative sentences ("I did not send them"): Jer 34:14 (Mt 27:15), 36:9 (Mt 29:9), 50:2 (Mt 43:2)

56. H. von Campenhausen, "Der urchristliche Apostelbegriff," 103: "Es gibt keine christlichen Apostel im engeren und im weiteren Sinne, sondern es gibt nur einen allgemeinen Gebrauch von *shāliach/apostolos* der auch im frühchristlichen Schrifttum und im kirchlichen Bereich begegnet, und es gibt die neue Wirklichkeit eines Apostels Jesu Christi."

57. I find most revealing the double use of *nomos* in Rom 3:21: "the law and the prophets" testify that justification is to be offered "apart from the law." This sentence, while using the expression "law and prophets" in designating the Old Testament, discards the Old Testament as *law* (norm of conduct) and admits its validity only as testimony to the salvation brought by Christ. In other words it both discards the legal binding force of the law and admits its value as prophecy.

58. The dating of the *Epistula Apostolorum* is uncertain but most probably it belongs to the second half of the second century. It used the formula "prophets and Apostles" to describe the norm of Christian teaching, yet apparently it did not admit any other apostolic writings than itself. For itself, it claimed the authority of all the apostles just as the Muratorian Canon claimed such authority for the Fourth Gospel. For a detailed discussion, see I. Frank, *Der Sinn der Kanonbildung,* 178-89. Other late second-century occurrences of "prophets and apostles" are found in the *Letter to Diognetus* 11:5-7 (Richardson, 223) and in Second Clement 14:2: *ta biblia kai hoi apostoloi* (Richardson, 199). On the other hand, starting with the Fourth Gospel, a whole set of works in early Christian literature avoids the word *apostolos* in its special Christian sense. Such is, for example, the *Plea* of Athenagoras and the whole work of Tatian.

The Covenant Idea in the Second Century

Everett Ferguson

Delbert Hillers concludes his survey on *Covenant: The History of a Biblical Idea* with these words:

> The Essenes had a covenant, but it was not new; the Christians had something new but it was not a covenant. That is to say, to call what Jesus brought a covenant is like calling conversion circumcision, or like saying that one keeps the Passover with the unleavened bread of sincerity and truth. For Christians the coming of the substance made shadows out of a rich array of OT events, persons, and ideas, among them covenant....The reality brings the image to an end.[1]

The covenant was a central category in Israel's faith. There have been a number of important studies of the covenant idea in the Bible,[2] and there have been studies of the covenant as articulated in the Middle Ages and Reformation.[3] Thus far, however, I have found no monograph on this important theological idea dealing with patristic literature. Stuart Currie, demonstrating his mastery of second-century Christian literature, explored the use and significance of *koinōnia* in the early church and pointed out the close association of this term with the concept of covenant in Paul's writings and elsewhere.[4] Thus, it seems fitting in a volume dedicated to Stuart Currie to undertake a consideration of the way the concept of covenant functioned in the writings of second and early third-century authors.

My intention is to present as complete a set of texts bearing on this subject as possible and then draw some conclusions. The study is ordered by three developments related to the discussion of "covenant" in the early church. First, "covenant" was an important topic in the dialogue and debate between Christians and Jews. Second, questions concerning "covenant" were also kept alive in the controversies of the "orthodox" with "heretics" who rejected or disparaged the Jewish heritage of the church. Third, the

establishment of a two-part Canon in the church extended theological reflection on the function of the "old covenant." As Hans von
Campenhausen discussed the "pre-history of the New Testament
canon,"[5] much of this material may be considered a pre-history of
"Old and New Testaments" as a title of the Christian scriptures.

As preparation for this study, however, brief note must be taken
of the biblical (particularly the New Testament) use of the term
"covenant" as the background out of which the developments of
the second and third centuries emerged.

The Hebrew word translated "covenant," *berîth*, referred to a
mutual relationship. It was used in a wide variety of human con-
tracts and agreements and was chosen to describe the gracious relationships which God established with chosen individuals and the
nation of Israel. The Greek translation of the Old Testament might
have been expected to render *berîth* by *synthēkē* ("treaty" or "compact"). The translators, however, presumably thought *synthēkē*
implied too much of mutual agreement and thus chose instead
diathēkē ("disposition" and "testament") in order to emphasize, it
seems, God's initiative and superiority.

The New Testament clearly used *diathēkē* in the Hellenistic sense
of "last will" in Gal 3:15 and Heb 9:16. A larger number of the
occurrences of the term are in quotations from or references to the
covenants of the Old Testament (Lk 1:72; Acts 3:25; 7:8; Rom 9:4;
Eph 2:12; Heb 9:4, 18-20; Rev 11:19). Otherwise the word *diathēkē*
appears in three contexts.[6] (1) It occurs in the accounts of the Lord's
supper (Matt 26:28; Mark 14:24; Lk 22:20; 1 Cor 11:25) in order to
explain the significance of Jesus' death, viz., his blood sealing a
new covenant (with allusion to Ex 24:5ff and Jer 31:31ff). (2) It was
used by Paul in explaining the relationship between the Mosaic and
Christian dispensations (2 Cor 3:6, 14) and between the fleshy and
spiritual Israel as recipients of the promises to Abraham (Gal 3:17;
4:24). (3) It is especially frequent in the Epistle to the Hebrews
which combines the themes of covenant blood and a new covenant
people in order to demonstrate the superiority of the Christian
dispensation over the Jewish because Jesus is the mediator of a
better covenant offering better promises (Heb 7:22; 8:6; 9:15; 10:29;
12:24; 13:20) in fulfillment of Jer 31:31-34 (Heb 8:8-10; 10:16).

The earliest use of *diathēkē* in Christian literature outside the
New Testament is in 1 Clement when Clement used the word in
two quotations from the Septuagint.[7] It is characteristic of Clement
that in both passages the Old Testament was used for moral exhortation. Perhaps significantly both passages are about unfaithfulness
to the covenant. While Clement used the texts as warnings to Christians, the texts could just as well be turned against Jews.[8]

The first extra-canonical Christian author for whom the covenant was an important category was Barnabas. In chapter 4 Barnabas punctuated his eschatological message with this anti-Jewish polemic:

> Be not like some, heaping up your sins, by saying that the covenant is theirs and ours. It is ours. They lost it forever when Moses had barely received it. For Scripture says: "Moses was on the mountain fasting forty days and forty nights, and he received the covenant from the Lord, stone tablets written by the finger of the hand of the Lord." But they turned to idols and lost it. For the Lord says, "Moses, Moses, Go down quickly, because your people whom you brought out of Egypt broke the law." And Moses understood and threw the two tablets from his hands. And their covenant was broken in order that the covenant of Jesus the Beloved might be sealed in our heart by the hope of his faith. [Barn 4:6-8; trans mine]

This passage reflects the language of an actual intramural discussion among Christians (Jewish Christians?) about their heritage. The passage, based on Deut 32:9-17 (cf. Ex 24:18; 31:18; 34:28; and 32:7, 9),[9] about Moses breaking the tablets containing the ten commandments was important to Barnabas, for he returned to it in his major discussion of the covenant in chapter 14. In the latter passage he included, apparently as if part of the biblical text, the statement, "And the tablets of the covenant of the Lord were broken" (14:3). Since the breaking of the stone tablets symbolized for Barnabas the breaking of the covenant, the text provided scriptural proof that the Jews had lost their right to the covenant from the beginning.

While discussing things characteristic of Judaism—after sacrifices, circumcision, food laws, washings, and before the sabbath and the temple—Barnabas raised the question of the covenant in 13:1: "Let us see if this people [i.e., Christians] or the first people receive the inheritance, and if the covenant is ours or theirs." Barnabas then introduced two narratives from the Old Testament where a younger son was favored over an older: Jacob over Esau (Gen 25:21-23) and Ephraim over Manasseh (Gen 48:9-19). Concerning the latter, he concluded, "You see whom he has appointed [the younger son] to be the first [people] and the heir of the covenant" (13:6). Not only did Isaac and Jacob (who bestowed the blessings) have knowledge (*gnōsis*) of who would be God's people, but so also did Abraham, to whom God promised that he would be the father of the nations [Gentiles] who believed in God (14:7). That made all three patriarchs witnesses to the claim that a later people

(Gentile Christians) would have the favor of God.

Barnabas then considered in chapter 14 whether the covenant which God swore to the fathers ever was given to the older [first] people.[10] It was given, Barnabas admitted, but they were not worthy to receive it (14:1). In this context came the proof from Moses referred to above (14:1-3) followed by the important corollary:

> Moses received it, but they were not worthy. How do *we* receive it? Learn. Moses as a servant received it, but the Lord himself has given it to us to be the people of the inheritance, because he suffered on our behalf....We receive it through the one who inherits the covenant, the Lord Jesus. He was prepared for this very purpose in order that when he appeared and ransomed us out of darkness...he might establish in us a covenant by his word. [14:4-5; trans mine]

That Christ should ransom and prepare a holy people for himself was a matter of prophecy. Is 42:6-7 was quoted as if addressed to Christ: "I gave you for a covenant of the people, for a light of the nations" (14:7). Barnabas' other quotations (Is 49:6f; 61:1f) share the universalism of salvation found in 42:6-7 and are so used by later Christian authors.

The concern with the identity of the people of the covenant was shown also in Barnabas' conclusion to the discussion of the eschatological promises: "If then this does not happen at present, he has told us the time when it will: when we ourselves are perfected to be the heirs of the covenant of the Lord" (6:19). The sign of the Jewish covenant, circumcision, prompted Barnabas to recall other peoples who were circumcised—Syrians, Arabs, and Egyptians—and to comment sarcastically, "They therefore are of their covenant" (9:6).

To summarize, for Barnabas Jesus was both the giver of the covenant and the covenant itself. The covenant of Jesus and the covenant of Moses are essentially identical in their meaning. Barnabas did not speak of a new covenant, but of a new people (5:7). The covenant had not changed, but the recipients were different.[11] "Whose is the covenant?" was another way of asking "Who are God's people?"[12] *Diathēkē*, therefore, carried the Old Testament meaning of a relationship. This understanding of covenant accounts for the full appropriation of the Jewish scriptural heritage by Barnabas, yet at the same time his full rejection of Jewish religious practices and institutions. This Old Testament understanding of relationship with a people was not lost in the second century but it was altered subtly by the Hellenistic idea of "testament" as may be seen in the repeated association of "inheritance" with "covenant."

One further topic deserves comment: the prevailing scholarly view that Barnabas viewed the covenant as timeless. For example, "*Diathēkē* is for Barnabas simply the expression of the same divine saving will from the beginning and for all time."[13] Without entering into a serious debate with such a statement,[14] I consider it important to point out some signs of historical consciousness in Barnabas. For instance, he did not deny that the Jewish ritual was actually in operation for a long time. He also recognized the historical fact of Moses but contrasted the servant Moses' giving the covenant with the Lord Jesus' giving the covenant. Finally, Barnabas clearly had an eschatological frame of reference, hardly a "timeless" notion. Nevertheless, Barnabas' approach left too many unresolved questions for him to be copied exactly by later thinkers.

With Justin Martyr, Barnabas' intramural contest was moved into the arena of the church's actual combat with Judaism.[15] The understanding of the covenant was crucial in this competition. Justin's view of salvation-history was in the tradition of Paul and Luke, although without explicit use of their writing.[16] For Justin the covenant was an important category for interpreting God's saving plan as it related to Jews and Christians.

The importance of covenant for Justin is seen in his discussion of circumcision. Justin's Jewish opponent, Trypho, identified the covenant with circumcision, its seal (Gen 17:7,13). Trypho reproached Christians for not observing various Jewish practices. Concerning circumcision he said, "But you, rashly despising this covenant, do not care for the consequent duties" (*Dialogue with Trypho* 10:4). Justin's reply begins in chapter 11, which introduces the doctrinal debate proper, thus showing the importance of the covenant concept. Justin employed several arguments based on the Old Testament itself for the invalidity of the Mosaic law: the prophecies of a new covenant point to the cessation of the law through the coming of Christ; the prophets declared that God did not really desire observance of the ritual law but a spiritual obedience; worthies such as Noah, Job, Abraham and other patriarchs were justified without keeping the law. Justin affirmed in *Dialogue* 11 that Christians trusted in "no other God" than the one "who led your fathers out of Egypt," perhaps with his eye on the Gnostics and Marcion.[17] But Christians did not trust "through Moses or through the law." "I have read," Justin wrote, "that there shall be a final law, and a covenant, the best of all." He continued,

For the law given on Horeb is already old and is yours alone; but this one is for all universally. Now, law placed against law has put an end to that which is before it, and a covenant which

comes after in like manner has annulled the previous one; and
an eternal and final law—namely, Christ—has been given to us,
and the covenant is trustworthy. [trans mine]

This new covenant was a matter of prophecy; Justin cited Is 51:4-5
and Jer 31:31-32. God had "proclaimed a new covenant" and "this
for a light to the nations" (cf. Is 42:6; 49:6). Jesus Christ "is the new
law and the new covenant," and the "true spiritual Israel...are we
who have been led to God through this crucified Christ." In
chapter 12 Justin continued by quoting Is 55:3ff about "an eternal
covenant" and charging, "This same law you have despised, and
his holy covenant you have slighted."

In Justin, unlike Barnabas, was used the explicit language of an
old and new covenant.[18] This, moreover, was discussed in terms of
the law embodying the covenant, so that the content of the covenant (again unlike Barnabas) comes to the fore. The combination of
"law" and "covenant" was frequent in the *Dialogue*. Christ
established "a new law and a new covenant" (34:1).[19] "There is
now another covenant and another law has gone forth from Zion"
(24:1—see excursus at the end on Is 2:1-4). After his initial consideration of the proper understanding of the covenant, Justin
discussed (with numerous digressions) washings, fasting, circumcision, food laws, sabbath, and sacrifice. The Christian had no need
of these things, for their spiritual counterparts have been established (here we are in the perspective of Barnabas except that Justin
did not reject the literal meaning as historically valid for a time):
circumcision of heart, "perpetual sabbath," "sacrifices of praise
and thanksgiving," baptism accompanied with "the Holy Spirit,"
etc. These spiritual interpretations were found by Justin in the Old
Testament scriptures themselves. Although the old covenant was
rejected, the scriptures were not. These words "are contained in
your scriptures, or rather not yours but ours" (29:2).[20] Since he held
that God gave something which was temporary, Justin was
obligated to give a reason for these abrogated rituals. His explanation was that they were imposed because of the transgressions and
hardness of heart of the Jews (18:2; cf. 27:2). The laws were to keep
them from idolatry (67:8) and by their very number to keep God
ever before them (46:5).[21] A somewhat more positive statement of
purpose is found in 44:2:

Some commandments were laid down in reference to the worship of God and practice of righteousness; but some commandments and actions were likewise mentioned either in reference
to the mystery of Christ, or on account of the hardness of your
people's heart. [trans mine]

This statement approximates the threefold classification of law as moral, ceremonial, and judicial.[22]

The old covenant, therefore, was limited to the Jews and temporary:

> As, then, circumcision began from Abraham, and the sabbath and sacrifices and offerings and feasts from Moses, and it has been proved that they were enjoined on account of the hardness of your people's heart, so it was necessary in accordance with the Father's will that they should cease in...Christ the Son of God, who was proclaimed to all the world as about to come as the eternal law and the new covenant. [43:1]

Justin sketched a fourfold periodization: before the law, under the law, under Christ, and eschatological glory at Christ's second coming.[23] The covenant (as Barnabas too had said) and the new law was Christ. "The new covenant which God formerly announced was then present, Christ himself" (51:3).[24] Therefore, this covenant was considered eternal (final) and universal.

> God promised that there would be another covenant, not like that commandment and without fear, trembling, and lightnings...and showing that God knows the command and work that is eternal and suited to every race. [67:10; trans mine]

"Through the wonderful foreknowledge of God...that we might be found more understanding and God-fearing than you through the calling of the new and eternal covenant, that is of Christ" (118:3). The prophecies about a "covenant...and light to the nations" (Is 42:6) referred not to proselytes but to Christ and all those enlightened by him (122:3). "What is the inheritance of Christ? Is it not the Gentiles? What is the covenant of God? Is it not Christ?" (122:6). And he is not to be limited to one race:

> If the law were able to enlighten the nations and those who possess it, what need is there of a new covenant? But since God announced beforehand that he would send a new covenant and an eternal law and commandment, we will not understand this of the old law and its proselytes but of Christ and his proselytes, namely us Gentiles whom he has enlightened. [122:5; trans mine]

These passages show that "people" and "relationships" were still important aspects of the covenant for Justin despite his frequent identification of covenant with law. The covenant which was Christ was for the "true spiritual Israel" (11:5). This association of covenant with Christ also implied the continued association of covenant with God's promises.

When the surviving literature of the Gnostics and the Jewish Christian groups is examined, it appears that the covenant was not a significant category for them. In the Gnostic *Gospel of Truth* Jesus was presented as the revealer of "the living Book of the Living" (the *Gospel of Truth* itself? a metaphor for salvation?) and that Book compared to a testament before and after being opened. Then the author wrote, "This is why Jesus appeared: he opened that Book. He was nailed to a tree, he fastened the testamentary disposition from the Father to the Cross. O such magnanimity!" (19:35-20:28).[25] The language was influenced by Col 2:14, but instead of nailing to the cross what was "against us" Jesus nailed a testament that was for believers and so validated the wonderful gift of life.

Without using the word "covenant," Ptolemy, the Valentinian, in his *Letter to Flora,* did a piece of source criticism on the Pentateuch. A part, he concluded, came from God, a part from Moses, and a part from the elders. That part which came from God himself was further subdivided into three parts: the pure law of God, free from evil (the decalogue), which Christ came to perfect and fulfill; laws concerning retribution for wrongdoing (an eye for an eye), which Christ took away completely; and the "typical" ceremonies (sacrifice, circumcision, sabbath, fasting, etc.) which the Savior transformed from physical into spiritual realities. The God who gave the law was the Creator. Ptolemy offered this view as a middle ground between the view that the law came from the Perfect Father (which he thought impossible) and the view that it was given by the devil (perhaps held by later Marcionites and a view which Ptolemy considered not "just" to hold).[26] Ptolemy gave a theoretical basis for what the church did in practice, but this did not make it any more acceptable (in fact less so). His separation of the Creator God from the Father of the Savior ruined anything he had to say in the eyes of the orthodox.

The orthodox Christian position, as the orthodox Jewish position, maintained against the Gnostics the unity and wholeness of scripture. Gnostics, however, were not the only ones to make a theoretical as well as a practical distinction in the contents of the old law. Certain Jewish Christians did the same. In this way it was possible to maintain a loyalty to the Mosaic covenant and yet treat its documents in their existing form as less than sacrosanct. The Ebionites formulated a theory of "false pericopes" introduced into the scriptures.[27]

> For the scriptures have had joined to them many falsehoods against God on this account. The prophet Moses having by the order of God delivered the law, with the explanations, to certain chosen men, some seventy in number, in order that they also might instruct such of the people as chose, after a little the written law had added to it certain falsehoods contrary to the law of God....[Ps Clem, *Hom* II. xxxviii][28]

> If, therefore, some of the scriptures are true and some false, with good reason our Master said, "Be good money-changers," inasmuch as in the scriptures there are some true sayings and some spurious.[II. li] [This was not a doctrine to be proclaimed in public lest it perplex the unlearned multitude. cf. II. xxxix]

The false sayings could be identified, according to the Ebionites, by those passages which had an inferior view of God or attributed sins to the Old Testament fathers. One feature of the law in particular that was rejected by the Ebionites was the entire sacrificial cultus (*Hom* III.xlv; *Recogn* I.xxxvi-xxxix). Moses and Christ really taught the same doctrine: "For, there being one teaching by both, God accepts him who has believed either of these. But believing a teacher is for the sake of doing the things spoken by God" (*Hom* VIII. vi).

> Neither, therefore, are the Hebrews condemned on account of their ignorances of Jesus...if doing the things commanded by Moses, they do not hate him whom they do not know. Neither are those from among the Gentiles condemned, who know not Moses...provided that these also, doing the things spoken by Jesus, do not hate him whom they do not know. [*Hom* VIII. vii]

There seems to be a view of a covenant for the Jew through Moses and a covenant for the Gentiles through Jesus, parallel but essentially the same in content. Although the word covenant was not used, the idea is another variation on the covenant theme.

A radical distinction within the contents of the Old Testament, but without assigning any of it to a source other than God, could also be made within orthodox circles. The third-century Syriac *Didascalia* warned constantly about the dangers of the Deuterosis (the second legislation):[29]

> For the first Law is that which the Lord God spoke before the people had made the calf and served idols, which consists of the Ten Words and the Judgements. But after they had served idols [the golden calf episode], he justly laid upon them the bonds, as they were worthy. But do not thou therefore lay

them upon thee; for our Saviour came for no other cause but to fulfill the Law, and to set us loose from the bonds of the Second Legislation.[30]

There is an extended discussion of this concern in chapter XXVI. "The Law therefore is indissoluble; the Second Legislation is temporary, and is dissoluble."[31] Among those things abolished were the distinctions of meats, sacrifices, circumcisions, washings. These were a burden imposed because of idolatry and making the calf. "[Christ] came, that he might affirm the Law and abolish the Second Legislation."[32] Although the sabbath was included in the Ten Words, the *Didascalia* treated it as part of the Second Legislation superceded by the Lord's day.[33] So, such efforts at making distinctions within the Old Testament were troubled by a lack of consistency.

A different approach to the problems posed by Gnostic and Jewish Christianity that did not accept the premises of either was needed. The anti-Gnostic fathers achieved this. Where the sense of proximity or alienation with reference to the Old Testament was strongest, covenant was not an important word. Covenant became important when Christians wanted to maintain both a significant continuity and a significant discontinuity.

Against the attacks of Marcion and the Gnostics,[34] the only hope of salvaging the old Bible was to acknowledge different eras.[35] The covenant scheme of the interpretation of holy history became the foundation of Irenaeus' theological method. He employed it not in anti-Jewish polemic but in anti-Gnostic polemic. He used the covenant not to explain why Christians did not keep the law but to affirm that the law was from the same God as the gospel. God gave the law as a stage in his preparation and education for Christ. According to Justin, Christianity replaced, not just fulfilled, Judaism; the law disappeared as darkness before light. According to Irenaeus, the law retired as a pedagogue was effaced before the teacher.[36]

The letter of introduction from Irenaeus' home church of Lyons described him as "zealous for the covenant of Christ" (Eusebius, *HE* V. iv. 2). Irenaeus was a "covenant" theologian.[37] He held the divine dispensations together in continuity because they came from "one and the same God."

Irenaeus made an understanding of the covenants part of the foundation scheme of the faith which learned teachers imparted: "they reveal why several covenants came to mankind and teach what is the character of each of the covenants'' (*Against Heresies* I.x.3).[38] He himself laid out ''four general covenants given to mankind'' (III.xi.8). Unfortunately the old Latin version and the later Greek texts of Irenaeus differ as to what these covenants were. According to the Greek:

> One was from the flood of Noah with the rainbow; the second was from Abraham with the sign of circumcision; the third was the giving of the law by Moses; the fourth was the covenant of the Gospel through our Lord Jesus Christ. [trans mine]

According to the Latin,

> One was before the flood, under Adam; the second, then, after the flood, under Noah; the third, the law, under Moses; and the fourth, then, that which renews man and sums up all things in itself by means of the Gospel. [trans mine]

The Greek has in its favor that the Bible uses the word covenant in connection with the four named (see below from Irenaeus' *Proof of the Apostolic Preaching*). The Latin translates *diathēkē* by *testamentum,* the usual translation in the western languages, a fact which has given a legal and formal cast to the understanding of the covenant. Such an understanding does not seem appropriate to Irenaeus, who rather maintained the interpretation of the covenant found in Justin.

More commonly Irenaeus wrote of two covenants, for that of Moses and that of Christ were the major·concern for his polemical situation. Interpreting Matt 13:52, Irenaeus gave to the two covenants the designations law and gospel, so familiar·to us:

> Now those things new and old which are brought forth from his treasure certainly mean two covenants. The old would be that previous giving of the law; and the new points out that manner of life according to the gospel. [(IV.ix.1); trans mine]

Irenaeus then cited Old Testament passages about a new song and a new covenant and New Testament passages about the greatness of Christ and his legislation. He continued:

> For the new covenant has been known and preached by the prophets...that men by believing in Christ might always make progress and grow to the attainment of salvation through the covenants. For there is one salvation and one God. [(IV.ix.3); trans mine]

This passage summarizes some of the characteristic emphases of Irenaeus: two successive covenants, one for Jews and the other for all; the old law replaced by the gospel of liberty; the different covenants suited to the stage of human development contributing to human maturity; the whole sequence, as the prophecies demonstrated, presided over by one God.

That there would be two covenants, Irenaeus held, was foreshadowed in Abraham. He was the forerunner of Christian faith, having received justification before circumcision by means of a faith which sprang up once more among humankind through the coming of the Lord. "Circumcision and the law of works obtained during the intermediate time." Of this too Abraham was the source, for he received the covenant of circumcision (IV.xxv.1).

The contrast which Irenaeus saw between the old and the new was that between bondage (law) and liberty (gospel), based perhaps on Gal 4:21ff. "The new covenant of liberty" was a favorite description—III.xii.14; IV.xxxiii.14; IV.xxxiv.3; IV.xvi.5—contrasting with "laws of bondage." The gospel was not just a new law for Irenaeus but a new spiritual relation of humanity to God.[39] The old covenant was superceded. In one passage Irenaeus wrote that the law ended with John the Baptist, for Jerusalem had an end of legislation when the new covenant was manifested (IV.iv.2). In the *Proof of the Apostolic Preaching,* Irenaeus made more of the termination of the old covenant, treating the history of salvation and referring to the covenants with Noah (ch 22), Abraham (ch 24), David (ch 64), and Jeremiah's prophecy of a new covenant (ch 90). "These promises were to be inherited by the calling from the Gentiles, in whom also the new covenant was opened" (ch 91).[40] The heirs of the new covenant supplant Israel and have no need of the law (93-96; cf. 87 and 89).

Nevertheless, "both the Mosaic law and the grace of the new covenant were adapted to the times and given for the benefit of the human race by one and the same God" (III.xii.11).[41] So, Irenaeus promised to discuss "the cause of the differences in the covenants and their unity and harmony" (III.xii.12). The necessity for dealing differently with humanity in an earlier era was because humanity was in its childhood (IV. xxxviii.1). So the laws of Moses were "for the instruction or for the punishment" of the people (IV.xvi.5). To a people prone to idolatry God called them

> by secondary things to what is primary, by types to the reality, by temporal things to what is eternal, by carnal things to the spiritual, by earthly things to the heavenly....By means of types they learned to fear God and to persevere in his service. (IV.xiv.3)

Whereas Justin had emphasized the hardness of heart of the Jews, Irenaeus (without omitting the punitive aspect) emphasized the immaturity of mankind and so the educative aspect of typology.[42]

There were two covenants and two people, but only one God.[43] As the old covenant came from the same God, Irenaeus could argue that it contained in its fundamentals the same laws as the new.

> In the law therefore and in the gospel the first and greatest commandment is to love God with the whole heart, and then like to it, to love one's neighbor as oneself. So is shown one and the same author of the law and the gospel. The precepts of the best life, since they are the same in both covenants, demonstrate the same God. He has prescribed particular laws which are adapted to each covenant, but the highest and best laws, without which there is no salvation, he has exhorted us to the same in both covenants. (IV.xii.3)

This argument was of obvious importance against the Gnostic separation of Jesus from the Creator. Irenaeus' terminology of law and gospel seems still to refer to covenants of which these were the chief characteristics, but his language closely approximates the identification of these terms with the books containing each.

Irenaeus' major connected treatment of the covenant idea is found in IV.xxxii-xxxiv where he claimed to present the reasoning of a certain "old man, disciple of the apostles, showing that the two testaments were both from one and the same God." The one God is the creator God. If the scriptures are read in company with the presbyters of the church, Irenaeus argued, it will be seen that every word is consistent. "For all the apostles taught that there were two covenants for the two peoples but one and the same God who ordered both for the good of the man to whom the covenants were given" (IV.xxxii.2). The former covenant was not given without purpose:

> It subdues those to whom it was given to the service of God for their good...exhibited a type of heavenly things...prefigured the things which are now in the church...and contained a prophecy of future things. [trans mine]

This valuable statement of the purposes of the old covenant anticipated later classifications of the levels of interpretation of the Old Testament. Chapter xxxiii then showed how this understanding refuted various heresies. There was an extensive appeal to the prophets, including reference to those who spoke "of a new covenant to be given by God to men, not like that given to the fathers on mount Horeb." This "new covenant of liberty" would be for God's chosen people acquired through Christ to show forth God's praise (IV.xxxiii.14). Christ by his advent fulfilled the new covenant foretold by the law. The prophets would not have had the power to predict all of the things concerning Christ, including the new covenant, if they had received their inspiration from another than the God revealed by Christ. This line of argument demonstrates a major apologetical reason why the church could not give up the Old Testament: the argument from prophecy. Such an argument could work two ways: not only proving Christ (as in Justin), but (as used by Irenaeus here) also proving that the Old Testament scriptures belonged to the one God. With Irenaeus the various covenants were integrated as progressive and ordered phases in a total, organic history of salvation.[44]

The word "covenant" has thus far been found mainly in Christian works dealing with Judaism and Gnosticism. Tertullian also used it principally in his *Against the Jews* and *Against Marcion*. The former treatise began with the Christian interpretation of the two peoples. Then Tertullian developed the idea (ch 2-3) of a general and primordial unwritten law from Adam to Moses. Moses' law was viewed as a change and intended to be temporary,[45] as shown by the prophecy of a new covenant (Jer 31:31f) and a new law (Is 2:2-3).[46] Tertullian considered especially circumcision, sabbath, and sacrifice (as well as the law) as being superceded. The word "covenant" is not prominent but is included in the summary passage in chapter 6:

> First we must inquire whether there be expected a giver of the new law, and an heir of the new testament, and a priest of the new sacrifices, and a purger of the new circumcision, and an observer of the eternal sabbath, to suppress the old law, and institute the new testament, and offer the new sacrifices, and repress the ancient ceremonies, and suppress the old circumcision together with its own sabbath, and announce the new kingdom which is not corruptible.[47]

The new covenant as a new law has been encountered already, and Tertullian's balancing of old law and new testament in this quotation is a reminder that the concept of a new law was completely at home with Tertullian.[48] The legal understanding of *testamentum* (a last will)[49] perhaps facilitated this. Tertullian's preference seems to have been to express *diathēkē* by *instrumentum* (an authorization, hence a legal document), but he recognized that more usual usage was to call it *testamentum* (*Adv Marc* IV.i below).[50] Tertullian often wrote, moreover, of two dispensations, old and new, in order to express the covenant idea.[51] Repeatedly he emphasized that the law was temporary, ending with John the Baptist (Luke 16:16).[52]

Tertullian followed the path marked by his predecessors in his polemic against Marcion. His own standpoint was succinctly stated when he summarized the nature of Paul's controversy with his opponents: "The whole essence of the discussion was that while the same God, the God of the law, was being preached in Christ, his law was under criticism" (*Adv Marc* I.xxi).[53] This view was set over against Marcion's *Antitheses* which "strained into making such a division between the Law and the Gospel as thereby to make two separate gods, opposite to each other, one belonging to one instrument (or, as it is more usual to say, testament), one to the other" (IV.i; cf. IV.vi and *Prescription of Heretics* 30). Books IV and V of *Against Marcion*, devoted to a refutation of Marcion's interpretation of the scriptures as set forth in his *Antitheses*, demonstrate Tertullian's use of covenant. The gospel did not indicate that a new God was being revealed, for the Old Testament prophesied a new covenant (Jer 31:31ff). "Thus he indicates that the original testament was temporary, since he declares it changeable, at the same time as he promises an eternal testament for the future" (Is 55:3). So the prophet, according to Tertullian, was declaring that "other laws and other words and new ordainings of testaments would come from the Creator" (IV.i; cf. IV.xxii). Therefore, Marcion derived no advantage from the supposed diversity between the law and the gospel, since the Creator predicted this "by that promise of a new law and a new word and a new testament" (IV.ix). Tertullian proposed a figurative interpretation whereby the law signified spiritual truths by material ordinances.[54] He developed an Irenaeus-like relationship between the covenants in IV.xi:

> We admit this separation, by way of reformation, of enlargement, of progress, as fruit is separated from seed, since fruit comes out of seed. So also the gospel is separated from the law, because it is an advance from out of the law, another thing than the law, though not an alien thing, different, though not opposed.

The word "covenant" (testament) occurs in Book V in quotations from Paul's epistles with "dispensation" coming to the fore as Tertullian's own term. On Gal 4:24 Tertullian argued that he need only to prove that the Creator intended to break down the law in order to show that Paul's words were not in opposition to the Creator (V.iv). On 2 Cor 3:6ff he affirmed that "if...the brightness of the

New Testament, which remains in glory, is greater than the glory of
the Old Testament, which was to be done away, this too is in agreement with my faith, which sets the gospel above the law." On the
other hand, "the giving of superiority is possible only where there
has existed something to give superiority over" (V.xi), proving the
two were connected.

Tertullian also used the covenant idea in intramural polemics,
but this was only occasional and mainly because "covenant" was
becoming a title for scripture.[55] It was a logical step for Tertullian to
use "covenant" as a designation for the documents [56] which contained and witnessed to the covenant. Since Marcion's *Antitheses*
purposely arrayed passages from the "New" over against the
"Old" Testament, Tertullian in *Against Marcion* IV.i appears to
have referred to the respective bodies of writing as "testament."
This understanding is made explicit later in the chapter: "I do not
deny a difference in records [*documenta*] of things spoken [in the
two dispensations (*disposititione*)]." Book IV.vi also may be compared: the *Antitheses* have "the one purpose of setting up opposition
between the Old Testament and the New." This terminology was
Tertullian's but may it not have been a reality for Marcion? Von
Campenhausen has argued strongly that the two-part Bible was a
creation of the later second century in reaction to Marcion. Though
the actual text of the *Antitheses* has been lost, its methodology as
reflected by Tertullian's refutation seems to presuppose something
very much on its way to a two-part Bible. Tertullian, to be sure,
used the terminology of his day, namely, "covenant," to refer to
the books of the New Testament. "The documents of the gospel
[*evangelicum instrumentum*] have the apostles for authors" (*Adv
Marc* IV. ii). "For the new testament[57] is made very concise, and is
disentangled from the intricate burdens of the law" (IV.i).

The use, however, of "covenant" as a title for the books of the
two parts of the Christian Bible appears relatively recent in Tertullian's time (ca. 160-225). Melito of Sardis (d. ca. 190) reported
that he went to Palestine to "learn accurately the books of the old
covenant" (Eusebius, *HE* IV.xxvi.14). An anonymous anti-
Montanist writer (ca. 192) wrote of "the word of the new covenant
of the gospel" (*HE* V.xvi.3). That the author had in mind the total
message and not only a collection of books, however, is evident
later in the passage, because his list of prophets of the old covenant
and the new included persons of the early second century not mentioned in the New Testament books. He apparently had an era in
mind (V.xvii.2-3). Irenaeus' *Against Heresies* is the first surviving
Christian document to construct a "formal proof from Scripture"[58]
using the New Testament as the Old Testament had previously

been used. There is no clear indication, however, that he knew the name "New Covenant" as a collective designation of the new Christian Canon.

Clement of Alexandria, Irenaeus' near contemporary, did seem to use the terms of old and new covenants as designations of the canonical books. "Covenant" meant or referred to written documents in *Miscellanies* V. vi. 38, "In both covenants mention is made of the righteous," and V.xiii.85, "It is preached and spoken by the old and new covenant." Moses was described as laying down the law in the old covenant (III.vi.54; cf. IV.xxi,134), and Matt 5:27, 28 was quoted as "the voice of the Lord in the new covenant" (III.xi.71). Clement in *Excerpts from Theodotus* 24 wrote that the "holy Spirit worked continuously according to the old covenant." For Origen "old and new covenants" were designations for two parts of the Bible, although somewhat strange as book titles to his philological training: "the divine scriptures of the so-called old and new covenant" (*De princ* IV.i.1; the same qualification in *Comm Joh* V.8 and for Old Testament in *De or* XXII.1).

"Law" and "Gospel" were both designations of written documents as well as descriptions of an unwritten reality. The rather constant association of these terms with the old and new covenant respectively[59] prepared for the acceptance of the latter terminology as the designations of the two parts of the Bible, a usage established by the beginning of the third century.

The theology with its development of covenant themes attained in the struggle with Jews and heretics was used for the edification and spiritual development of the community and the individual Christian. Melito of Sardis, as his predecessors generally, did not employ the word "covenant" in writings directed to the church. His homily *On the Passover,* however, offered an original illustration to explain the relationship between the Jewish scriptures and Christian faith and practice. This illustration certainly places him in the tradition of the covenant interpretation of salvation-history found in Justin and Irenaeus (cf. Eusebius, *HE* IV.xxvi.14 cited above). Melito had much to say about the law as old, temporal, and a type, and about the gospel as new, eternal, and grace (ch 3, 4, 7, 58). The law issued in the gospel. Their relationship was more fully worked out in chapters 34-45 in the comparison of a model to a finished product. Material or earthly things require a pattern or model, whether of wax, clay, or wood. The reality surpasses its model; the model had its place for a time, but after the thing itself comes into existence the model has no more value. The Lord's salvation and truth were prefigured among the Jews in this way. "The people, therefore, became the model for the church, and the law a parabolic sketch. But the gospel became the explanation of the law and its fulfillment." The type had value prior to its realization. "The law was fulfilled when the gospel was brought to light, and the people lost their significance when the church came on the scene, and the type was destroyed when the Lord appeared."[60]

The writer of the Pseudo-Cyprian sermon *Adversus Iudaeos* used the traditional themes associated with the covenant in Christian thought with the intention of "de-Judaizing" the church.[61] The sermon declared its theme as the transfer under the new covenant of the inheritance (the fusion of the testamentary with the relational idea of covenant) to the Gentiles. The heirs of Christ are able to understand the spiritual nature of his covenant. The old people have been disinherited because of their crimes, and God has written a new covenant (testament), witnessed by heaven and earth. The new covenant invites the Gentiles to enter the eternal inheritance which Israel rejected. "Christ tore up your old covenant and wrote a new one by which he called Gentiles to the possession of your privileges" (ch 31). Chapter 43 refers to the new covenant on the mount of transfiguration to be revealed after the resurrection. The appeal is to a spiritual understanding.

Spiritual understanding is also the hallmark of Clement of Alexandria's writings, albeit of a different type from that of the Latin author of the *Adversus Iudaeos*. The term "covenant" entered Clement's vocabulary fully apart from a polemical context. The occurrences of the word are too numerous to treat exhaustively here. Clement's writings present a many-sided theology of the relationship of the covenants.

The language of the "old and new covenant" came naturally to Clement. The covenants were among the good things of which God was the cause (*Strom* I.v.28). Corollary with the idea of the two covenants was the idea of two peoples: "Formerly the older people had an old covenant, and the law disciplined the people with fear...but to the fresh and new people has also been given a new covenant" (*Paed* I.vii.59).[62] Since the same Word was the instructor in both, one can find many of the teachings of the "new covenant written in the old letter" (*Paed* I.vii.59). Clement believed there were pious men before the giving of the law (*Strom* I.ix.44; cf. VI.vi.47, "those who lived rightly before the law").[63] Thus Clement posited a periodization: before the law, under the law, and under Christ (*Strom* I.xxi.135; II.xix.100).[64] He associated covenants with five figures: Adam, Noah, Abraham, Moses, Christ (*Ecl* 51f).[65] So thoroughly was Clement embued with the idea of covenant that he even described philosophy as "given to the Greeks as a covenant peculiar to them" (*Strom* VI.viii.67).[66]

The new covenant brought by Christ in fulfillment of Jer 31:31ff made both the Jewish law and Greek philosophy old:

> He made a new covenant with us; for what belonged to the Greeks and Jews is old. But we who worship Him in a new way, in the third form, are Christians. For clearly, as I think, he showed that the one and only God was known by the Greeks in a Gentile way, by the Jews Judaically, and in a new and spiritual way by us.

> And further, that the same God that furnished both the Covenants was the giver of Greek philosophy to the Greeks....[*Strom* VI.v.41f][67]

Since the different covenants came from the same Lord, they were in harmony: "The ecclesiastical rule is the concord and harmony of the law and the prophets in the covenant delivered at the coming of the Lord" (*Strom* VI.xv.125). Thus, Clement summed up the results of the anti-heretical polemic: " 'The just shall live by faith' which is according to the covenant and the commandments. Since these—the old and the new— are two in name and time, given by economy in accordance with the degree of development and advancement, but are one in power, they are administered through the Son by one God" (*Strom* II.vi.29; trans mine). Here is Irenaeus' distinction in time under one God of covenants adapted to the state of mankind's maturity. Christ is the real mediator of all the covenants, for

> the covenant of salvation, reaching down to us from the foundation of the world, through different generations and times, is one, though conceived as different in respect of gift. For it follows that there is one unchangeable gift of salvation given by one God, through one Lord, benefitting in many ways. [*Strom* VI.xiii.106]

Indeed, on the basis of Gen 17:4 Clement claimed that the Lord was himself the covenant (*Strom* I.xxix.182). Clement went further than his immediate predecessors in affirming that the different covenants were in reality one: the universal church collects the righteous "into the unity of the one faith, which results from the distinctive covenants, or rather the one covenant in different times by the will of the one God through one Lord" (*Strom* VII.xvii.107). This viewpoint prepared for the distinctive Alexandrian way of

using the Old Testament as a Christian book. Accordingly, the
"gnostic" Christian "advances in the gospel, using the law not only
as a step but comprehending it as the Lord who gave the covenants
delivered it to the apostles" (*Strom* IV.xxi.130; cf. later in the
chapter: "Faith in Christ and the knowledge of the gospel is the exegesis and fulfilling of the law...." 134).

Clement offered some of the fullest and most varied statements
on the purposes which the law served. It was a preparatory
discipline (*Strom* II.viii.37) which by fear taught the beginning of
wisdom, enjoined human beings to avoid bad things, showed what
sin was, taught what was salutary, and trained in the good (*Strom*
II.vii.32-35). Clement's theology resembles some Reformation
theology in its description of the uses of the law: it "trains in piety,
prescribes what is to be done, and restrains each one from sins, imposing penalties even on lesser sins" (*Strom* I.xxvii.171). In
Miscellanies II.xviii he discussed the reason for a number of Old
Testament regulations under the theme "teaching wisdom by
abstinence from sensible images and by inviting to the Maker and
Father of the universe" (78). In addition to this educative aspect
there were also typical and prophetic purposes: "The sense of the
law is to be taken in three ways—either as exhibiting a symbol, or
laying down a precept for right conduct, or as uttering a prophecy"
(*Strom* I.xxviii.179). The symbols in the Old Testament had three
purposes: to arouse curiosity so people would study in order to
discover words of salvation; to hide the true meaning from those
who were not worthy; and to make it possible to speak of the incomprehensible God (*Strom* VI.xv.126ff).

Origen is an appropriate figure with whom to close this essay.
There is no attempt to offer a complete review of Origen, but only
to note how some of the themes already uncovered relate to his
writings. As mentioned above, Origen qualified "covenant" as a
title of the scriptures by "so-called." He did this even for the
general use of the word: "We must also realize that we have
received the so-called covenants of God on conditions, set forth in
the agreements which we have made with him" (*Exh ad mart* 12).
This passage keeps the biblical sense of "covenant" as "an agreement." Origen seemed to lack the testamentary emphasis frequently encountered in other writings from this period. The beginning of
the law was in the time of Moses, "while the beginning of our
legislation and second covenant" was in the time of Jesus (*C Cels*
II.1xxv).[68] From Origen's lofty standpoint the old burning issue of
the relation of the Christian writings to the Jewish scriptures was on
the same level with other discrepancies within the various books of
each collection.

> There is too a third peacemaker, the man who shows that what
> to others seems the discord of the Scriptures is no discord, and
> who makes their harmony and peace evident, be it of the old
> with the New; or the Law with the Prophets, or of one passage
> from the Gospel with another; or of the Gospels with the
> Apostolic writings; or of one Apostolic writing with another.[69]

Origen invoked Paul's authority for the spiritual exegesis of the
Old Testament; Paul taught the Galatians how to allegorize lest the
church "run risk in using a strange covenant."[70] So Christians
when they read the Old Testament do not become disciples of the
Jews. A controlling idea in Origen's *Commentary on John* was the
unity of scripture. There was no difference between the Old and
New Testament for exegetical purposes (I.119ff). In fact, in Book II
Origen seems to debate with ecclesiastical typologists. He denied
that historical events were the primary means of revelation. The
prophets spoke by the Logos of direct spiritual reality. Moses'
breaking the tablets of stone "signifies that the power of the law
resides not in its letter but in its spirit" (*Comm Rom* II.14). With the
allegorical method of discovering new meanings in the old
writings, temporal distinctions disappear: "I do not call this law an
Old Testament if I understand it spiritually. The law becomes an
Old Testament only for those who want to understand it carnally"
(*In Num hom* IX.4).[71] From one direction Origen sounds like
Barnabas; from another he approaches the view of Augustine,
which has improved in translation: "In the Old Testament the New
is concealed; in the New the Old is revealed."[72]

These brief comments concerning Origen bring this review to its
end. Several conclusions seem justified on the basis of this study:
   (1) Covenant was part of the Old Testament-Jewish heritage of
the church. Like other Old Testament categories it was subsumed
in Jesus Christ (the Covenant), becoming less important as a
category in itself to second-century Christians.
   (2) The covenant idea had its significance in structuring holy
history against Jewish claims for and the Gnostic repudiation of the
law. The polemical and theological setting of the remarks of these
early Christian authors slants the material as it relates to the Old
Testament scriptures. A study of the respective authors' actual use
of the Old Testament would perhaps modify some of the
statements above. Nevertheless, a covenantal, "dispensational,"
"history of salvation" view was one of the fundamental

hermeneutical principles employed by many early Christian writers. Although I have not attempted to do so, I think that we could find this covenant scheme fundamental in catechesis and liturgy.[73]

(3) This covenantal structure may fairly be claimed to be rooted in the early kerygma and to be based on the first developments of it by Paul and Luke.

(4) The covenant concept is closely related to the theme of "God's people."

(5) Both Hebraic (relationship) and Hellenistic (testament) components persisted in early Christian texts about *diathēkē*.

(6) The association with "law" and "gospel" prepared for the adoption of the term "covenant" as a title for the scriptures.

Excursus on Is 2:2-4 [= Mic 4:1-4][74]

Is 2:2-4 has served as an important Old Testament prophecy for the beginning of the church and proclamation of the new covenant on Pentecost in Acts 2, this in spite of the absence of a direct quote of the text in the New Testament (with the possible exception of an allusion in John 4:22, which does not bear on this particular point).

Origen indicated that the text was familiar to all Christians: "For who of all believers does not know the words of Isaiah?" quoting 2:2-4 and Mic 4:1-3.[75] He used it himself in his treatise *Against Celsus* (V.xxxiii), giving a sort of homily on the phrases, from which are these excerpts:

> For the law came forth from the dwellers in Zion and settled among us as a spiritual law. Moreover, the word of the Lord came forth from that very Jerusalem that it might be disseminated through all places and might judge in the midst of the heathen....We have become children of peace for the sake of Jesus, who is our leader, instead of those whom our fathers followed, among whom we were as strangers to the covenant.[76]

Clement of Alexandria quoted "For out of Zion shall go forth the law, and the word of the Lord from Jerusalem" in his *Exhortation* chapter 1, but made no interpretation or application of it. Melito alluded to the text in a declaration based on the contrast of the two covenants: "For indeed the law issued in the gospel [*logos*]—the old in the new, both coming forth together from Zion and Jerusalem; and the commandment issued in grace, and the type in the finished product [the truth]."[77]

Justin and Irenaeus both explicitly connected the text with the new covenant. Justin alluded to it in *Dialogue* 24, "There is now another covenant, and another law has gone forth from Zion." In his *First Apology* (39), he quoted the text and declared it fulfilled in the fact that from Jerusalem there went out into the world twelve men who preached the word of God. Justin emphasized also the aspect of peace in the passage, calling attention to the peaceful ways of Christians. Justin quoted the Micah version of the prophecy in full with reference to the conversion of the Gentiles in *Dialogue* 109 (so presumably the allusion in 110 is to this quotation). Irenaeus included an extended discussion of Is 2 in *Against Heresies* IV.xxxiv.4. In refutation of the Jewish claim that the new covenant consisted in the rebuilding of the temple after the Exile, Irenaeus declared that no new covenant was given but the people lived under the Mosaic law until the coming of the Lord. "But from the Lord's advent, the new covenant which brings peace, and the law which gives life, has gone forth," and he then quoted Is 2:3-4. "The law of liberty, that is the word of God, preached by the apostles (who went forth from Jerusalem) throughout all the earth" brought in a reign of peace among the Gentiles. He too stressed that Christians did not fight but turned the other cheek. Irenaeus again quoted Is 2:3 in *Proof of the Apostolic Preaching* 86 to confirm the universality of the word of God ("which is also for us [Gentiles] the law") preached by the apostles. The use of "law of the Lord" in Isaiah seems to be a contributing factor in the frequent conjunction of law and covenant in the authors examined.

Tertullian made very extensive use of the text. His *Against the Jews* 3 quoted the entire text of Is 2:2-4 as referring to the fulfillment of the new covenant prophecy of Jer 31:31-32. The "house of Jacob" was the new people, and the word of the Lord that judged among the nations applied to the Gentile church.[78] Those who no more learn to fight are Christians, who instead of taking vengeance practice clemency and instead of war take up peaceful pursuits. The passage was quoted three times in *Against Marcion.* In III.xxi the "house of God" is "Christ, the universal temple of God." "The gospel" is "the way of the new law and new word in Christ, no longer in Moses." Once more there is emphasis on pursuing peace. In IV.1 Tertullian declared that it was not the Jewish race alone but the Gentiles "who by the new law of the gospel and the new word of the apostles are being judged." Because of this the dispositions of those once cruel and fierce become productive of good fruit. Finally in V.4 there is a briefer allusion to Is 2:3 as indicating that "old things might pass away and new things might arise."

NOTES

1. Delbert Hillers, *Covenant: The History of a Biblical Idea* (Baltimore: Johns Hopkins Press, 1969) 188.
2. G. E. Mendehall, "Covenant," *IDB;* D. J. McCarthy, *Treaty and Covenant* (Rome: Pontifical Biblical Institute, 1963); *idem, Old Testament Covenant* (Richmond: John Knox Press, 1972); G. W. Buchanan, *The Consequences of the Covenant* (Leiden: E. J. Brill; Supplements to Novum Testamentum, 1970); H. Pohlmann, "Diatheke," *Reallexikon für Antike und Christentum* (ed Th. Klauser; Stuttgart: Hiersemann) 3 (1957) 982-990 includes Barnabas; K. Baltzer, *Das Bundesformular* (Neukirchen, Kreis Moers: Neukirchener Verlag, 1964), includes the Apostolic Fathers but does not deal with the question of this essay; J. Behm, *Der Begriff Diathēkē im Neuen Testament* (Leipzig: A. Deichert, 1912) includes an appendix on Justin, 102-106; and relevant articles in *TDNT* and *TDOT.*
3. E.g., J. S. Preus, *From Shadow to Promise: Old Testament Interpretation from Augustine to the Young Luther* (Cambridge: Belknap Press of Harvard University Press, 1969); Kenneth Hagen, *A Theology of Testament in the Young Luther: The Lectures on Hebrews* (Leiden: E. J. Brill, 1974); E. H. Emerson, "Calvin and Covenant Theology," *Church History* (June, 1956) 136-144; L. J. Trinterud, "The Origins of Puritanism," *Church History* (March, 1951) 37-57.
4. S. D. Currie, *Koinonia in Christian Literature to 200 A. D.* (Ann Arbor: University Microfilms, 1962).
5. H. von Campenhausen, *The Formation of the Christian Bible* (Philadelphia: Fortress Press, 1972) ch 4; cf. 262-68 where the terminology of "old and new covenant" as a title for the two parts of the Christian Bible is discussed.
6. Colin Brown, ed, *The New International Dictionary of New Testament Theology* (Grand Rapids: Zondervan, 1975) 365-76.
7. 15:4 citing Ps 77 [78]:36-37 and 35:7 citing Ps 49 [50]:16.
8. As was Ps 49, quoted in its entirety by Justin, *Dial* 22. Ps 49 became a part of the anti-sacrificial, polemic; Pierre Prigent and Robert Kraft, *Épître de Barnabé* (Sources chrétiennes n. 172; Paris: Editions du Cerf, 1971) 82f. Ps 77:36f is followed by the declaration of forgiveness and so was not so suitable for the anti-Judaic argument.
9. The author of 1 Clem 53 also quoted from this episode but for an entirely different purpose. He included the sequel where Moses prayed for the forgiveness of the people and commended the willingness to be blotted out for the sake of the people.
10. Studied by Pierre Prigent, *L'épître de Barnabé I—XVI et ses sources* (Paris: Librairie Lecoffre, 1961) 60-65.
11. Pohlmann, col 987-90.
12. See Marcel Simon, *Verus Israel* (Paris: Editions E. de Boccard, 1964) 102-05 for the relation of the new people to the new covenant. Barnabas would indicate that the question of people was prior. He gave one answer—different people but the same covenant—but later thinkers decided that a new people required a new covenant. Cf. Simon, 203-08 on the rejection of Israel in Christian authors.
13. Pohlmann, col 989; cf. Klaus Wengst, *Tradition und Theologie des Barnabas Briefes* (Arbeiten zur Kirchengeschichte; Berlin, New York: de Gruyter, 1971) 75ff.

14. In relation to the later Alexandrian reading of the Old Testament one might liken Barnabas to an advance scout who goes well beyond the ground occupied by the main party.

15. Simon, 166ff, opposed Harnack's view that the *Dialogue with Trypho* was a literary exercise, and without going to the extreme of Lukyn Williams, *Adversus Judaeos, a Bird's Eye View of Christian Apologiae until the Renaissance* (Cambridge: The University Press, 1935), saw a real contact between Jews and Christians. He pointed out that even when used for other purposes the arguments arose initially in an anti-Jewish context. He added that in general the writings "Against the Jews" are by themselves insufficient to determine whether real Jewish-Christian relations were being addressed, for certain themes and methods of argument remained constant.

16. Auguste Luneau, *L'Histoire de salut chez les Pères de l'Eglise* (Paris: Beauchesne, 1964) 89-92; von Campenhausen, 169 and 178; Theodore Stylianopoulos, *Justin Martyr and the Mosaic Law* (SBL Dissertation Series, 20; Missoula: Scholars Press, 1975) 104ff and 116ff.

17. Von Campenhausen, 94f sees *Dial* 10-29 originally as a self-contained treatise directed against Gnostics and Marcion. In this view he follows P. Prigent, *Justin et l'ancien testament* (Paris: Librarie Lecoffre, 1964) 235-85 which studies *Dial* 10-29 in relation to primitive Christian testimonia. Stylianopoulos, 31, 75, 157ff sees Justin's historical periodization as first arrived at in opposition to Marcion and Gnostics and then applied to the anti-Judaic polemic.

18. Cf. Mk 14:24; 1 Cor 11:25; 2 Cor 3:6, 14; Heb 8:6-10; 9:15; cf. Gal 4:24.

19. Cf. "new law of our Lord Jesus Christ," *Barn* 2; "we have a law," Athenagoras, *Plea* 32. The new covenant as a new law finds full expression in Tertullian. On the idea see Simon, 100-05.

20. Origen acknowledged that the scriptures were common to Jews and Christians (*C Cels* II.lviii) but claimed that Christians understood them better (II.lxxvi).

21. The purpose of particular regulations are given in different places: circumcision (16:2), food laws (20:1); sacrifices (22:11); sabbath (21:1).

22. Stylianopoulos, 51-68 described Justin's classification as ethics, prophecy, and historical dispensation.

23. Luneau, 34, 45ff, 95ff; cf. von Campenhausen, 97.

24. For Jesus as himself the covenant, cf. J. Daniélou, *The Theology of Jewish Christianity* (London: Darton, Longman, & Todd; Chicago: Henry Regnery, 1964) 163-66.

25. Kendrick Grobel, *The Gospel of Truth* (Nashville, New York: Abingdon, 1960) 58-67.

26. Epiphanius, *Adv haer* XXXIII. 3-7 in Robert Grant, *Second-century Christianity* (London: S.P.C.K., 1946) 30-37.

27. Hans Joachim Schoeps, *Theologie und Geschichte des Judenchristentums* (Tübingen: J.C.B. Mohr, 1949) 147ff.

28. Trans from the Pseudo Clementines in Thomas Smith, ed and trans, *Ante-Nicene Fathers* (Grand Rapids: Eerdmans reprint, 1951) VIII 236; cf. Hom XVIII.xix-xx on the "false pericopes" as in scripture to test us.

29. Simon, 111-18.

30. *Didas* II (R. H. Connolly, *Didascalia Apostolorum* [Oxford: Clarendon, 1929] 14).

31. Connolly, 218.
32. Connolly, 224.
33. Connolly, 236-38.
34. See Ptolemy's criticism discussed above and compare Irenaeus' description of Marcion as "the only one who has dared openly to mutilate the scriptures" (*Adv haer* I.xxvii.2).
35. Von Campenhausen, 166.
36. See Luneau, 90.
37. J. Lawson, *The Biblical Theology of St. Irenaeus* (London: Epworth, 1948) 235-38 treats the relation of Old and New Testaments but not particularly of the covenants as such. A. Benoit, *Saint Irénée: Introduction à l'étude de sa théologie* (Paris: Presses universitaires de France, 1960) 74-102 more adequately looks at Irenaeus' relation to the Old Testament but without reference to the covenant idea.
38. I employ the numbering in Massuet (and the Sources Chrétiennes edition) followed in the *Ante-Nicene Fathers.*
39. F. R. M. Hitchcock, *Irenaeus of Lugdunum: A Study of his Teaching* (Cambridge: University Press, 1914) ch 11.
40. *Irenaeus, Proof of the Apostolic Preaching* (trans and annotated by Joseph P. Smith; Westminster, Md.: Newman, 1952) 103.
41. See Luneau, 96-101 on the "Divine Pedagogy" in Irenaeus.
42. *Adv haer* IV.xiv.3; IV.xvi.1 and 5; IV.xxvi.1. Paul's solution in Gal 3:24 has had a long history in Christian theology; Clement of Alexandria picked up the word pedagogue—Simon, 96-99.
43. Hitchcock, chapter 11.
44. Luneau, 103.
45. Cf. his "disciple" Cyprian, *Test* III:99, who quoted Rom 2:12 to distinguish a time before the law of Moses and after the law.
46. J. Daniélou, *The Origins of Latin Christianity* (Philadelphia: Westminster, 1977) 267f, points to Justin's influence on Tertullian here.
47. Translation by S. Thelwall in *Ante-Nicene Fathers* (Grand Rapids: Eerdmans reprint, 1951) III 157.
48. Cf. *Adv Iud* 9, "Two testaments of the old law and the new law," and *Adv Marc* IV.1, "new law of the gospel." See the list of references in J. Quasten, *Patrology,* II (Utrecht: Spectrum, 1953) 322.
49. The meaning of covenant or agreement is present in *De pud* XI. 3, "For Christian discipline dates from the renewing of the testament and...from the Lord's passion," and in XII.10 about the conditions of the "latest testament."
50. *Instrumentum* is used of the scriptures in *Apol* XXI.1; *Res carn* XXI.1; XXXIII.1; XXXIX.8; XL.1; *Adv Herm* XIX; XX; *Adv Marc* IV.vi.7; *De praesc haer* XXXVIII. 8. On Tertullian's usage see René Braun, *Deus Christianorum* (Paris : Presses universitaires de France, 1962) 463-73.
51. *Apol* XXI; *Adv Marc* III. 20; V. 4; IV. 1 and 6; *Virg vel* 1.
52. *Adv Mar* IV. 33; *De pud* VI; *Adv Prax* 31; cf. *Adv Iud* 2f; 6f; 8; *De or* 1; *Ad ux* I.2; *De monog* 7; 14; *Adv Marc* I. 19ff; IV.1; IV.11; V.2; 4; 13.
53. Cf. V.ii. Quotations from *Against Marcion* are based on Ernest Evans, *Tertullian Adversus Marcionem,* Oxford Early Christian Texts (Oxford: Clarendon, 1972).
54. *Adv Marc* II. 19; V.11. Other uses for the law suggested by Tertullian were these: to cause the people to think about God at all times (*Adv*

       Marc II.xix); to fit the needs of the time (II.xviii); and to give an advance announcement of Christ (III.ii).

55. *Adv Prax* 15 and *De Ieiun* 14. *De praesc haer* 37 is the regular legal use of *testamentum.*

56. W. C. van Unnik, "*Hē kainē Diathēkē*—A Problem in the Early History of the Canon," *Texte und Untersuchungen* 79 [*Studia Patristica* 4] (Berlin: Akademie-Verlag, 1961) 212-27; von Campenhausen, 264-68.

57. Evans did not capitalize the term here, as he did when he understood Tertullian to refer to the scriptures of the New Testament. The decision does not appear to me to be clearcut. *Testamentum* is a title for Scripture in *De pud* I. 5 and VI. 5; *Adv Prax* 15 ("old scripture and new testament").

58. Von Campenhausen, 185.

59. Cf. Tertullian, *Adv Marc* III.14, "Two testaments of law and gospel."

60. The translation is that of Gerald F. Hawthorne, "A New English Translation of Melito's Paschal Homily," *Current Issues in Biblical and Patristic Interpretation* (Grand Rapids: Eerdmans, 1975) 158f.

61. Dirk van Damme, *Pseudo-Cyprian Adversus Iudaeos: Gegen die Judenchristen,* Paradosis 22 (Freiburg: Universität Verlag, 1969) 21-24, 27-30.

62. Translations from Clement follow the *Ante-Nicene Fathers* (Grand Rapids: Eerdmans reprint, 1951), II.

63. For the pious before the law, a kind of "Christianity before Christ," a view most fully formulated by Eusebius, see Simon, 105-11.

64. Luneau, 112.

65. The same in Origen, *Comm Matt* 15:32 on the parable of the workers in the vineyard, called at five different times (Matt 20). Aphrahat, *Hom* XI.11 has the same five. See Jacob Neusner, *Aphrahat and Judaism,* Studia Post-Biblica, 19 (Leiden: Brill, 1971). Cf. Pseudo-Cyprian, *Adv Iudaeos* and the discussion of Irenaeus above.

66. But note *Ecl* 43 as recognizing there was no proper covenant with the heathen.

67. The first two sentences may be part of Clement's quotation from the early second-century apologetic work, *The Preaching of Peter,* but I have assumed that the quotation stops earlier.

68. Cf. *In Ex hom* 11.2, "Christ on the cross caused the fountains of the new covenant to flow."

69. R. B. Tollinton, *Selections from the Commentaries and Homilies of Origen* (London: S.P.C.K., 1929) 48, citing *Comm Matt* 2 (= *Philocalia* 6).

70. Tollinton, 72, citing *In Ex hom* V.1.

71. "When one begins to understand the law spiritually then he passes from Old Testament to new"—*In Ex hom* 7.3.

72. *Quaest in Hept* 2, q. 73; cf. *C adv leg et proph* 1.17.35 and *Enarr in Ps* 56.9 (57.7 in NPNF).

73. For catechesis Irenaeus, *Proof of the Apostolic Preaching* and see H. Musurillo, "History and Symbol: A Study of Form in Early Christian Literature," *Theological Studies* 18 (1957) 357-86; for liturgy see Melito's sermon and the eucharistic prayer in *Ap Const* VIII.xii.

74. See the interesting suggestions about the use of this text in early Christian authors by Jean Daniélou, *Primitive Christian Symbols* (Baltimore: Helicon, 1964) 89-101.

75. Origen, *Ep to Africanus* 15. Cyprian, *Test* I:10 quoted both along with

Matt 17:5 under the heading, "That a new law was to be given." He quoted it again in II.18.

76. Trans in *Ante-Nicene Fathers* (Grand Rapids: Eerdmans reprint, 1951) IV 558.

77. *On the Passover* 7 (Hawthorne, 151).

78. Cf. *De Anima* 50:4; cf. Pseudo-Cyprian, *Adv Iudaeos* 3 and 9; and Ps Cyprian *De mont Sina et Sion* 4. The relation of Tertullian's writings and other passages dealing with the text from Isaiah are discussed in J. Daniélou, *Origins of Latin Christianity* (Philadelphia: Westminster, 1977), 47-49.

Anselm Concerning the Human Role in Salvation

George S. Heyer, Jr.

The *Cur Deus Homo* is, by general agreement, Anselm's master-piece. It does not suit the taste of every palate, but it is an enduring theological monument, and any student of the person and work of Jesus Christ must reckon with it. One familiar objection is that it yields a purely objective, even abstract, doctrine of the atonement. Christ's work *for* the human race takes place *apart* from the human race, a sort of transaction in heaven between Father and Son. As a result, it is difficult to see how persons of flesh and blood con-cretely share in the benefits of this work. What place is there for human response?

A quick but far too short reply would be that in the *Cur Deus Homo* Anselm simply was not interested in the question; our appropriation of Christ's benefits did not there concern him. Whatever the truth of this answer, a great deal more needs to be said, and that, in fact, is the task of the ensuing essay. We shall begin with a glance at Anselm's philosophical realism, for it casts light upon the issue. It is the unvarying background against which all his theology (and not merely this portion of it) must be understood. We shall then examine a number of passages, both within and beyond the *Cur Deus Homo,* in which Anselm addressed the subject of the way of salvation that human beings ought to pursue in this life.

In the Medieval philosophical debate over the problem of univer-sals, Anselm stood firmly with the realists. In a passage rare for its sarcasm, he derided his nominalist opponents as "those dialecti-cians of our own time (or, rather, the heretics of dialectic), who think that universal substances are only the 'breath of the voice', and who cannot understand that color is something different from body, or wisdom from the soul...." They, he added, "are to be blown right out of the discussion of spiritual questions." And he continued:

> For instance, how can someone who does not yet understand
> how several men are one man in species comprehend how in
> that most mysterious and lofty nature several persons, each
> one of whom is perfect God, are one God? Or how can
> someone whose mind is so dark that he cannot distinguish
> between his own horse and its color, distinguish between the
> one God and his several relations? Finally, he who cannot
> understand that anything except the individual is man will
> only be able to understand 'man' as referring to a human per-
> son. For every individual man is a person. How, then, will he
> be able to understand that manhood, but not a person, was
> taken by the Word—in other words, that another nature, not
> another person, was taken?[1]

This trenchant statement of the realist position obviously has
large implications for the doctrine of Christ's person and work.
Jesus was not two persons. He was instead a single divine person,
the Word of God, possessing at once two natures, one divine and
one human. For a realist it is quite enough that God assume a
human nature without, as well, a human person, for it is the nature
which has suffered corruption as a consequence of Adam's and
Eve's sin. Ever since the fall individual humans have shared (as
persons, of course) in this damaged nature and thus themselves
been tangled in the coils of sin. It is the work of the God-Man to
restore human nature. How he does so Anselm was at pains to
explain in the *Cur Deus Homo,* but that argument will not be
rehearsed here. It will suffice to make the point that, failing the
restoration of human nature, no individual person can possibly
hope for one's own salvation. Here stands the essential (both literally and figuratively) beginning of the entire process, and it is this
beginning which Anselm strove to understand in the *Cur Deus
Homo.*

Yet even in that work Anselm took a few peeks down the road—if
only because Boso was such a relentless interlocutor! The chief of
these is found in the long sixteenth chapter of Book II, where
Anselm told his parable of the "magnanimous ruler." Its purpose
was to show how the efficacy of Christ's work extends both forward and backward in time to embrace those who were not
immediately present. Suppose, the parable runs, there once was a
king who ruled over a city in which the entire population, save for
one person, had sinned against him and therefore deserved to die.
The single innocent citizen, however, is able and willing to perform
for his ruler some great service that will reconcile the guilty. Not all
can be present on the day when the service is to be rendered, but
the king agrees that even the absent shall receive absolution as

well, provided they seek it through the deed of the innocent man and thereby ratify the agreement made on that crucial day. What form shall this search take? Here the parable must be set within the context of the chapter. Anselm was trying to answer one of Boso's more detailed questions—how Mary's purity could precede the death of Christ—and Anselm appealed to faith, Mary's faith in the future sacrifice of her Son. It is through faith that she is pure and through faith that she shares in the reconciliation which Christ will later secure with his death.

There is no doubt that Anselm placed this stress upon faith. With respect to Mary he reiterated the point several times in the chapter and once mentioned the "many others" cleansed by faith. Not quite so clear from the *Cur Deus Homo* itself is what, precisely, he meant by faith. Elsewhere, however, he devoted two long passages to the subject, one in the *Monologion* and one in the *De Concordia*.[2] In the former,[3] he held together both faith *in* God (*credere*, or *tendere, in deum*) and right belief. He who confesses the one without the other does not truly strive for God. Then Anselm added a distinction between living faith and dead faith. The former is strong and active through love. It is stirred up to do good works, "for that which loves the highest justice can condemn nothing just, can tolerate nothing unjust."[4] Dead faith, by contrast, lacks life-giving love and is idle. It is properly called "dead" not merely because love is absent but also because it *ought* to have this love. The case parallels that of a blind man. He is called blind not so much because he has lost his sight but more because, though he should have sight, he does not have it. Finally, dead faith believes what ought to be believed, but unlike live faith it does not also believe *in* what ought to be believed.

In *De Concordia*,[5] Anselm repeated much that earlier he had written in the *Monologion*. Here, however, he specified as the touchstone of true faith not love but rather rightness of will. Even if a person believes rightly and understands rightly, his faith is dead unless he also wills rightly (*recte vult*). He must preserve justice, defined by Anselm as rightness of the will maintained for its own sake. No one, Anselm declared, is saved without this justice. In the person whose will is unrighteous, the work of Christ accomplishes nothing. But through faith, true faith, that person may receive a right will and may regain the pristine justice lost in the fall.

If this summary suggests something of the fullness of Anselm's doctrine of faith, it by no means exhausts all that he had to say concerning the way in which a person appropriates the fruits of Christ's death.

Returning to the *Cur Deus Homo,* to the same sixteenth chapter of

Book II, one finds another less explicit theme present there that requires examination. It is the theme of the sacraments. Sacramental practice in the Church of Anselm's day had led to progressive emphasis upon the importance of the eucharist (with its attendant sacrament, penance) and a corresponding decline in the significance of baptism. Anselm's doctrine of the work of Christ reflects this shift.[6] The language he used in the parable of the "magnanimous ruler" includes terms such as "fault," "pardon," "make satisfaction," and "remit," all of which conjure up penitential-eucharistic practice. More broadly, Anselm's interpretation of Christ's work stresses not so much its universal scope or the rescue of human beings from death and the demonic (which would be typical if the doctrine were linked to baptism), but rather Christ's fulfillment of justice through self-immolation and the corresponding incorporation of believers into Christ through their participation in the eucharist.

In Anselm hints are found of the older view of baptism, that a person thereby throws off bondage to Satan and dies and rises with Christ,[7] but these are exceptions to the main theme. Again and again Anselm appealed to baptism as that way by which persons are cleansed from original sin and, indeed, from all prior sins. In the case of infants, of course, it is a question of original sin alone. Furthermore, the infant who dies after being baptized is saved apart from free will and its right exercise—that willing maintenance of justice for its own sake. Before baptism the lack of justice in the infant constituted original sin, and the inability to have justice was imputed as yet additional sin, because it was linked to Adam's and Eve's fall. Upon being baptized, however, the infant is not only delivered from original sin but is also no longer held accountable for the inability to have justice. The cause of this inability, which now has nothing to do with Adam and Eve, lies solely in the quite natural fact that no infant is old enough to exercise free will and hence maintain justice on its own behalf. Consequently, the infant who dies after being baptized is saved by the justice of Christ, who gave himself for the infant, and by the justice of the child's Mother, the Church, which believes on the infant's behalf.[8] Thus the rule still holds that no one is saved without justice.

Such an instance of salvation entirely by grace is, however, an exception. Upon reaching the age of reason, persons are not saved without justice of their own, nor without the free will that preserves it. Like the baptized infant, the baptized adult is also relieved of original sin. But the adult enjoys as well a further, slightly different advantage: the inability to understand justice and the inner corruption that constituted punishment for sin are no longer counted against that person. It is perfectly true that the brute passions and the corruption persist beyond baptism. Yet now sin springs alone from the will, for personal sins do appear after baptism has disposed of original sin. At this point the eucharist enters. It is this sacrament by which, along with penance, the Christian gains forgiveness of personal sins. Moreover, through this sacrament the believer participates more and more in the sinless humanity of Christ, that renewed human nature cleansed by the sacrifice of his death. The eucharist is indeed that sacrament of incorporation. Anselm heavily stressed the example of Christ, who remained obedient all his life and, preeminently, in his death. The believer is called to imitate the labor and sufferings of Christ and, by participation in the eucharist, to mirror his death, thus gaining a share in the merits of Christ and in his justice.[9] There can be no doubt that incorporation into Christ means above all the appropriation of his justice. The divine justice is satisfied by the sacrifice Christ offers. His work bears away injustice (original sin) and restores to human beings the just will lost in the fall. The very example of Christ is, as Anselm wrote, "an example of dying for the sake of justice,"[10] to teach humans "not to draw back from justice on account of injuries or insults or sufferings or death...."[11]

So it is that the eucharist becomes a means by which the original just order which God created is restored, and more than restored. For, Anselm contended, restoration exceeded creation,[12] and; in putting the matter thus, he echoed the prayer offered at the mixing of the chalice in the mass: "O God, who didst wonderfully create and yet more wonderfully renew the dignity of the substance of man...."[13] The superiority of restoration rests upon the fact that a human as a sinner deserves only to lose life, whereas before creation a person was nothing at all and deserved nothing at all.[14] Anselm further heightened the miracle of redemption by arguing that it exceeded the revival of a dead body. The body loses its life of necessity and does not sin by dying, for it is under no obligation to maintain its life. The rational creature, on the other hand, is obliged to maintain that original justice which it abandoned; it is therefore a surpassing wonder that it regains this righteousness.

For all his talk of miracle, however, Anselm did make room for a mild—and very Augustinian—synergism. Never, of course, did he suggest that the bestowal of righteousness was anything but the gift of God, a gift which, as we have seen, is even more miraculous in its restoration than in its initial endowment. Thus Anselm guarded the primacy of grace and rejects Pelagianism. Nonetheless, he strives to understand the harmony between grace and free will.

The case of the infant who dies after baptism is no help, for, as we have noted, the infant is saved purely by grace. Instead, it is a question of that free will without which a person who gains the age of reason cannot merit salvation, just as it is a question of that grace without which no person is saved. The harmony between them centers upon the very definition of free will—the power to maintain justice for its own sake. Since a person can have this justice only by grace, there must exist no conflict between grace and the power to preserve justice.[15]

> And although [God] does not give [this righteousness] to all, since "he has mercy on whom he will and he hardens whom he will," he still gives nothing on account of previous merit, since "who first gives" to God "and is rewarded?" If, however, the will, in maintaining by free choice what it has received, deserves either an increase in the justice received or strength for the good will or any reward whatever, all these are the fruit of the first grace and "grace for grace." So, everything must be imputed to grace, "for it is neither of the one who wills," because of what he wills, "nor of the runner," because of what he runs, "but it is of a merciful God." For it is said to all save God alone: "What do you have that you have not received? If you have received it, what is that in which you glory, as if you did not receive it?"[16]

When he raised the question of how grace aids the free will to preserve justice, Anselm remarked that he could not give an exhaustive answer, because grace operates in such a variety of ways. He made the common distinction between prevenient grace, whereby a person gains a right will, and subsequent grace, by which that will is maintained. Unless the free will abandons justice, this subsequent grace is never lacking and aids the will to withstand temptation either by lessening or removing the temptation or else by strengthening the will's resistance. While it is true that a person can fail to receive, can reject, or can lose grace, it is also true that neither grace alone nor free will alone works salvation. Salvation is engendered, Anselm wrote, by the two together in much the same way that natural generation takes place by the activity of both a father and a mother.[17]

Another metaphor Anselm developed at length was that of the field and the seed. The Christian is the field into which the seed of God's Word is dropped. Or, to refine the image, as Anselm did, the seed is a thought that is useful to salvation and that is perceived through the Word. "Not only the meaning of the Word, but every meaning or understanding of rightness that the human mind conceives—whether by hearing or by reading or by reason or in any other way—is the seed of right willing."[18] Without this seed, this mental conception, faith cannot arise. Yet the conception does not, by itself, generate faith; rightness of will must first be added to the idea, so that the mind *believes* what it hears. A person "hears" because there are preachers of Christ's Word, and there are preachers because they are sent, and the fact that they are sent is grace. So, working back, Anselm concluded that, since preaching, hearing, and understanding all stem from this gracious sending, they too are grace—grace for grace.

> Truly, the sending, the preaching, the hearing, the understanding are nothing, unless the will wills what the mind understands. This the will cannot do unless it has received rightness. For it rightly wills when it wills what it ought. Therefore, what the mind conceives by hearing the Word is the seed of him who preaches, and rightness is the "increase" that God gives, without which "neither he who sows nor he who waters is anything, but he who gives the increase—God."[19]

Hearing and conceiving mean nothing without rightness added to the will; but if it receives this rightness (and it does so purely by prevenient grace) the will springs to life. The "plant" thus born demands, however, careful cultivation.[20] And with that we reach the heart of Anselm's synergism—his doctrine of merit.

Of course it is true that, in good Augustinian fashion, Anselm consistently traced all benefits to the original, prevenient grace of God. All else is grace for grace. Nevertheless, Anselm espoused a clear doctrine of merit. In fact, when the question arises why a person is not immediately perfected in baptism and translated at once to the goal of incorruption, the first answer is that, in that event, the person would be saved without merit. No one can merit salvation without faith and hope, which, however, are directed toward things not seen. But the person who has gained incorruption has gained blessedness and, seeing it, lives neither by faith and hope nor by merit.

> Therefore, so that we may more gloriously obtain through the merit of faith and hope the blessedness which we desire, we remain, as long as we are in this life, in that which already is not imputed as sin [i.e., the punishment for sin], even though it resulted on account of sin.[21]

Anyhow, by strenuous cultivation of the seed that grows in him, the Christian acquires merit. The planting and the labor belong to the individual, while the increase and the effect come from God. And even though a person's own part is accomplished solely with the aid of God, nevertheless God rewards the person for it.[22]

When Anselm wrote of merit apart from this elaborate metaphor of the field and the seed, he consistently ascribed it to rightness of the will, that justice maintained for its own sake. In order to understand his meaning, one must note the dual affection he discerned in the will: it wills rightness on the one hand; it wills well-being on the other.[23] All merits, both good and bad, stem from these affections. Anselm seemed to regard the will for well-being as, at best, morally neutral; it is evil only when it consents to the flesh in the struggle with the spirit. The will for rightness, however, causes no evil and

> is the mother of all good merit. For this helps the spirit in lusting "against the flesh" and it delights "in the law of God after the inner man," that is, after that very same spirit. If, nevertheless, evil seems sometimes to follow from this [rightness], it does not proceed from it but from something else. Certainly the apostles were through righteousness "a good odor" "to God." But that which was to some "the odor of death unto death" did not stem from the justice of the apostles but from the wickedness of malevolent men.[24]

We are back again to Anselm's central point that salvation comes by justice alone. Certainly, it comes with merit, but merit is granted only because of that rightness of will which is justice. And this, in turn, is a gift of sheer grace. Very typical are these words, which Anselm wrote to his great friend, Gilbert Crispin, Abbot of Westminster: "May God almighty, who has appointed you guardian of others, so aid and guard you by his grace that, on account of your justice and theirs, he may reward you with eternal blessedness."[25]

Grace and free will, baptism and eucharist, faith and merit, each plays its part in the restoration and maintenance of justice, which is the chief adornment of the human race. In this process the individual has an indispensable role to play. Whatever the impression gleaned from the *Cur Deus Homo* alone, reconciliation is not done *to* a person without reference to personal participation. Its achievement requires the person's concentrated effort, and, having gained righteousness, the individual is able to look forward to that blessedness which God has held in store from all eternity. It is Christ who will judge each person. Human effort to steal likeness to God offended especially the Word, God's perfect image. And as this Word became man, so also nothing is juster than that he be the one to punish or to spare.[26] Although the vision of the Judge frequently appalled him,[27] Anselm found ultimate comfort in this thought:

> He who so ordered things that he should belong to our nature by maternal generation, and that we should be his Mother's children through our restoration to life, himself invites us to confess ourselves his brethren. Therefore, our Judge is our Brother. The Savior of the world is our Brother. In short, our God was made our Brother through Mary.[28]

Thus, by the judgment of Christ, the believer enters upon that reward which is given to those who are "just without any injustice."[29]

NOTES

1. *A Scholastic Miscellany: Anselm to Ockham,* ed and trans Eugene R. Fairweather (London: SCM Press Ltd., 1956) 99.
2. In this discussion of faith consideration of special questions, such as Anselm's view of the relationship between faith and understanding, is omitted.
3. *Monologion* 76-78. *S Anselmi Opera Omnia,* ed Franciscus Salesius Schmitt, 6 vols (Edinburgh: Thomas Nelson and Sons, 1946-1961) I, 83-85.
4. *Opera* I, 84, 11, 21-22.
5. *De Concordia* III, 2 (*Opera* II, 264-65).
6. The first person to call attention to this point was George Huntston Williams in two works: "The Sacramental Presuppositions of Anselm's *Cur Deus Homo,*" *Church History* XXVI, 3 (September, 1957) 245-274; *Anselm: Communion and Atonement* (St. Louis: Concordia Publishing House, 1960).
7. Cf. *e.g., Oratio* 10, 11. 192-93 (*Opera* III, 40) and *Epistola de Sacrificio Azimi et Fermantati* (*Opera* II, 228, 11. 1-5), where, following Romans 6:3-4a, baptism is hailed as a figure of Christ's death. But Anselm does *not* proceed to cite Romans 6:4b, where Paul speaks of the life that follows death.
8. *De Conceptu Virginali et de Originali Peccato* 29 (*Opera* II, 172, 1. 16-173, 1. 3).
9. Williams, *Anselm* 51-54.
10. *A Scholastic Miscellany,* 180.
11. *Ibid.,* 160. Cf. *Meditatio* 3, 11. 93-99 (*Opera* III, 87).
12. *Cur Deus Homo* II, 16 (*Opera* II, 117, 11. 6-7).
13. Cited in *A Scholastic Miscellany,* 166, n. 50. See Williams, *Anselm* 49.
14. *Cur Deus Homo* II, 16 (*Opera* II, 117, 11. 7-13).
15. *De Concordia* III, 2-3 (*Opera* II, 264, 1. 15-265, 1. 23).
16. *Ibid.,* III, 3 (*Opera* II, 266, 1. 24-267, 1. 5). Down even to the citations of John 1:16 and 1 Cor. 4:7, this passage might have come straight out of Augustine.
17. *Ibid.,* III, 4 and 5 (*Opera* II, 267, 1. 7-268, 1. 12; 269, 11. 2-8; 270, 11. 2-9).

18. *Ibid.,* III, 6 (*Opera* II, 270, 11. 25-27).
19. *Ibid.* (*Opera* II, 271, 11. 13-19).
20. *Ibid.* (*Opera* II, 270, 1. 11-271, 1. 19).
21. *Ibid.,* III, 9 (*Opera* II, 276, 11. 16-18).
22. *Epistola* 186, 11. 28-30 (*Opera* IV, 72).
23. *De Concordia* III, 11 (*Opera* II, 280, 11. 10-12; 281, 11. 6-7).
24. *Ibid.,* III, 12 (*Opera* II, 284, 1. 25-285, 1. 3).
25. *Epistola* 106, 11. 21-23 (*Opera* III, 239). Anselm also believed in ac-
    quisition of the merits of saints both living and dead. Cf. *e.g., Oratio*
    13, 11. 53-56 (*Opera* III, 51-52); *Epistola* 45, 11. 20-30 (*Opera* III,
    158-59); *Espistola* 50, 11. 23-27 (*Opera* III, 164.)
26. *Epistola de Incarnatione Verbi* 10 (*Opera* II, 28, 11. 4-10).
27. Cf. *e.g., Meditatio* 2, 11. 10-11 (*Opera* III, 80).
28. *Oratio* 7, 11. 137-41 (*Opera* III, 23). The translation is that of
    Fairweather, *A Scholastic Miscellany,* 205.
29. *De Concordia* III, 4 (*Opera* II, 268, 11. 15-21). In at least one place—not
    a theological work, but rather the rapturous prayer just cited
    above—Anselm suggests that the atonement touches nonrational
    creatures. All things subject to human power and use, he says (and he
    includes heaven, earth, day, night, stars, and floods!), have received
    back, through Christ, their lost glory. In the beginning they were
    made for the benefit of, and use by, the worshippers of God. Through
    sin they fell into the hands of idol-worshippers, but now they have
    been restored and they rejoice once again. See *Oratio* 7, 11. 64-75
    (*Opera* III, 20-21).

1 Corinthians 15:24-28 and the Future of Jesus Christ

John F. Jansen

Then comes the end, when he delivers the kingdom to God the Father after destroying every rule and every authority and power. For he must reign until he has put all his enemies under his feet. The last enemy to be destroyed is death. 'For God has put all things in subjection under his feet.' But when it says, 'All things are put in subjection under him,' it is plain that he is excepted who put all things under him. When all things are subjected to him, then the Son himself will also be subjected to him who put all things under him, that God may be all in all. (1 Cor 15:24-28)[1]

The entire passage (vv 20-28) in which the preceding verses appear has been a *crux interpretum* for exegesis. This essay, however, examines a question not raised directly by the text but one raised in the history of dogma with appeal to the text. Is the incarnation a permanent or a temporary reality? Is the humanity of Jesus Christ eternal or provisional?

Further, this essay examines three theologians for their interpretations of the text: Marcellus of Ancyra from the patristic age; John Calvin from the reformation period; Arnold A. van Ruler from the present time. These three may appear to be a strange company, for Marcellus was condemned as a heretic while the other two were theologians in the reformed tradition. This selection was not arbitrary, however, for one critical appraisal of van Ruler[2] points a warning finger at Marcellus, and Calvin is claimed in support by van Ruler himself in interpreting the Pauline text.

Without attempting to examine the numerous exegetical questions posed by this Pauline text,[3] a few observations are appropriate before proceeding to the history of dogma. The chapter begins with the common faith of the church which the Corinthians have received, in which they stand, and by which they are saved, if indeed they hold it fast.

Why did some of Paul's readers deny the future resurrection of the dead? Apparently there was in Corinth an enthusiasm so confident of present arrival that it needed no future. "Already you are filled! Already you have become rich!" (4:8). The presumptions of such enthusiasm are clearly discernible in the Corinthian correspondence (especially in 1 Cor 12-14 and in 2 Cor 11-12). The apostle countered such a *theologia gloriae* with the message of the cross and with the "not yet" of apocalyptic eschatology.

In 1 Corinthians 15 Paul's concern was not so much with individual eschatology as with the cosmic significance and scope of Christ's resurrection. The risen Lord is the second Adam. He must reign until all the opposing powers have been subdued. Christ's victory began with his exaltation as the risen Lord, but death is the last enemy—and death has not yet been destroyed. Death itself must be swallowed up in victory. Corinth needed the "not yet" of apocalyptic eschatology.

Of no concern here are the questions posed by vv 20-23 about "each in his own order." We are concerned with that *telos* when Christ, having completed his victory, delivers the kingdom to the Father. How did Paul understand "kingdom"? Apart from the passage, the epistle always speaks of the kingdom *of God.* The kingdom of God is not in talk but in power (4:20; cf. Rom 14:7). The unrighteous will not inherit the kingdom of God (6:9; cf. Gal 5:21). The kingdom of God is future because flesh and blood cannot inherit it (15:50). And always the kingdom of God is a summons to present response (cf. 1 Thess 2:12; 2 Thess 1:5; Col 4:11).

Did Paul write elsewhere of the kingdom *of Christ?* In Col 1:13 we read that the Father has delivered us from the dominion of darkness and already transferred us "to the kingdom of his beloved Son." (In the more disputed epistles, Eph 5:5 parallels the warnings of 1 Cor 6:9 and Gal 5:21 that no idolater has inheritance in the kingdom—but here it is "the kingdom of Christ and of God."[4] The Pastorals have the most explicit pointers to the kingdom of Christ [2 Tim 4:1, 4:18], although 1 Tim 6:15f ascribes honor and eternal dominion to God as "the King of kings and the Lord of lords.") Only in the 1 Corinthians 15 passage does one read that the Son will deliver the kingdom to the Father. Nevertheless, reminders that the Son is subjected to the Father are frequent, the best example being 1 Cor 3:23, which declares that "Christ is God's." Paul's christology is always theology—"to the glory of God the Father" (Phil 2:11).

How did Paul distinguish the kingdom of Christ from the kingdom of God? Some see a sharp contrast, holding that the kingdom of Christ is temporary while that of God is eternal.[5] Paul's concern, however, was less to separate the two than to attest to the completeness of Christ's redemptive work by appeal to two quotations from the Psalms. In any case, the verb "to reign" (*basileuein*) helps to interpret the noun "kingdom" (*basileia*). "Death reigned from Adam to Moses" (Rom 5:21). Indeed, "death reigned through that one man" (Rom 5:17) so that "grace might reign through righteousness to eternal life through Jesus Christ our Lord" (Rom 5:12). As the second Adam, Christ has been raised to reign until all enemies have been subdued. Paul was not the only New Testament writer to link the royal psalm (110) with that psalm (8) which celebrates God's purpose for humankind (cf. Mt 21:16, 22:44; Heb 2:6f, 5:6).

When the last enemy has been destroyed, God will be "all in all." Twelve times in vv 20-28 and ten times in vv 24-28 we meet the word "all"—moving from the "all" who are Christ's to the cosmic "all things" of the final glory. Paul pointed to the goal of history, the glory of God, when God shall be "all in all." This is not pantheism. There is no need to render *pasin* as masculine (as does the RSV rendering, "everything to every one"). Both *panta* and *pasin* may be read as neuter ("all in all"). Such expressions, frequently liturgical, are characteristic of Paul. In 12:6 the same phrase occurs, *ta panta eis pasin* (and here *kyrios* may be compared with *huios* in 15:24). The doxology in Rom 11:36, "For from him and through him are all things," and the "all in all" ascribed to Christ in Col 3:11 may be noted.

Some have seen in 1 Cor 15:24-28 a cessation of Christ's lordship.[6] But does the early Christian confession that "Jesus is Lord" (Rom 10:9) envision a time when he will not be Lord? Whatever the verdict as to the authorship of Ephesians, its confession that God "has made him sit at his right hand in the heavenly places, far above all rule and authority and dominion, and above every name that is named, *not only in this age but also in that which is to come*" (Eph 1:29f, italics mine) is congruous with the Pauline confession that Jesus Christ is Lord. To suggest an end to the humanity and lordship of Jesus Christ is contrary to the Pauline hope expressed in 1 Thess 4:17 ("so shall we *always* be with the *Lord;*" italics mine).

In short, Paul's focus of interest was on what Jesus Christ *did* and *does* and *will do.* In some later interpretations the focus was shifted to ask who Jesus Christ *was* and *is* and *will be,*[7] which introduces the next phase of this investigation.

A statement by Aloys Grillmeier serves as point of departure:

"We know the temptation which 1 Corinthians 15:24-28 has been to theologians: the Arians found in it their thesis of the inferiority of the Son to the Father, and Marcellus of Ancyra...wanted to derive from it the abolition of the Incarnation and the separation of the Logos from the flesh, so that in the return of the Logos to the Father the latter became all in all."[8] That Arians and their arch opponent could appeal to the same text is ironic indeed.

No one was more opposed to Arianism than was the bishop of Ancyra. It is not surprising that Marcellus, like Athanasius, could be deposed and exiled, reinstated and deposed again, in view of the turbulent ecclesiastical politics of the fourth century. Ultimately Athanasius was vindicated while Marcellus was condemned and posthumously declared a heretic by the Second Council of Constantinople in 381.

For a long time Marcellus was viewed only through the eyes of his adversaries, such as Eusebius, whose several books against Marcellus preserved 127 fragments from Marcellus' writing, and through Epiphanius, whose refutation of heresies preserved two more pieces, including the letter to Julius of Rome. Modern scholarship, especially since Rettburg (1794), has sought to let Marcellus speak for himself.[9] Although many still label him as heretic, others, like Theodor Zahn,[10] have seen him as a biblicist who found disfavor because he rejected the philosophical language of dogma by insisting on scripture alone. Still others, like Friedrich Loofs and Wolfgang Gericke,[11] have approached him through the history of tradition and have seen in his work an attempt to overcome the impasse of his time by returning to earlier patristic tradition. Recent research has enlarged considerably sources for his theology beyond the fragments. For example, Martin Tetz[12] has argued persuasively that Marcellus was the author of several pseudo-Athanasian writings. "Important additions have been made to the *Corpus Marcellianum,* and research into it and interpretation of it is in full swing."[13]

Marcellus began with an uncompromising "monotheism." God is one. It is impossible for three *hypostases* ever to unite in one Monad unless previously the triad had its origin in the One (fr. 65). While the word *homoousios* did not appear in the fragments, Marcellus sided with the Nicene formula because everything he had said about God's being was *homoousios*. Distinctions such as Father, Son, and Holy Spirit belong to the "dispensations" or "economies" (*oikonomiai*) of salvation history. Only the One is properly called "Lord and God" (*despotēs kai theos*). The term "almighty" (*pantokratōr*) appeared in such phrases as "Almighty God" (fr. 19), "Almighty Lord" (fr. 31), or "Almighty God, the

Lord" (fr. 117). Even when he wrote Julius to affirm the Roman symbol he did not say "God the Father Almighty" but rather "God Almighty" (fr. 129). The word "Father" appeared when Marcellus wrote of the Logos and the dispensations of the Logos. The Logos is "the Logos of God" (fr. 1, 6, etc.) and "The Logos of the Father," and quite often the two names are combined (fr. 44, 117). When he described the Logos as proceeding, he used "from the Father" rather than "from God" (fr. 36, 60, 129, esp. 121), placing the stress on the full deity of the Logos. The Logos proceeds *as* God. There is one God, and beside him there is no other.

While Marcellus did not use the phrase "first dispensation," its use is a natural inference from his repeated references to the "second dispensation" (fr. 73) or "dispensation according to the flesh" (fr. 4, 17, 19, 43, 70, 100, 117). The "first" dispensation reaches from the creation to the incarnation. In his interpretation of the creation story, "Father" and "Logos" are the "we" who made man "in our image and likeness," but always it is "God" who made man (fr. 80). Before creation all that can be said about God is that God is One. To say that the Logos is "in the Father" is already to point to God's revelation of himself in creation. And when it comes to the Spirit, the same force of *homoousios* pertains, for God is Spirit, as the Logos is Spirit and is inseparable from Spirit (cf. fr. 68 on Jn 20:22). Whether or not Marcellus posited a "third" dispensation of the Spirit is debatable—at any rate, this would not follow the second but would parallel the second from the time of Christ's exaltation and gift of the Spirit.

Be that as it may, for Marcellus the Logos is eternal. As his letter to Julius indicated (fr. 129), Marcellus wanted at all cost to safeguard the eternity of the Logos and to refute those who saw the Logos-Son as "another God" (cf. also fr. 82), or as a "second God" (fr. 40). The Logos is eternal. The Logos is *dynamis* residing in God and *energeia* proceeding from God without ever ceasing to be *dynamis* in God (fr. 52). Before creation the Logos was *dynamis* in God, but when Almighty God determined to create all things in heaven and on earth, his Logos as active *energeia* proceeded to effect God's will (fr. 60). For Marcellus the eternal Wisdom of Prov 8:21 ("when he established the heavens I was there," fr. 59, 60) corresponded to the creative work of the Logos expressed in Jn 1:3 ("all things were made by him," fr. 52, etc.). Through the Logos as active *energeia,* God is active throughout the whole of the first dispensation from creation to incarnation. Throughout this dispensation the Logos "was nothing other than the Logos" (fr. 48).

Only in the dispensation according to the flesh (fr. 70), the second dispensation when the Logos assumed our flesh through the virgin,

is it appropriate to give the Logos those "new and later" names that
declare his coming in the flesh: "first born of the new creation" and
"first born of the dead" (fr. 2), "Son of God" and "Son of man" (fr.
41), "Jesus," "Christ," "Life," "Way," "Day," "Resurrection,"
"Door," "Bread" (fr. 43). If the evangelist gives him "some new
and later name," this "fits from his new and later dispensation
according to the flesh" (fr. 43). Similarly, when Col 1:15 speaks of
Christ as "the image of the invisible God," this applies only to the
incarnate Logos because an image must be visible (fr. 92, 93, 94,
96).

Of interest is the use of Proverbs 8. As with the Johannine prologue, Marcellus attributed to the eternal and preexistent Logos
those phrases that speak of Wisdom as God's creative *energeia*. But
such phrases as 8:22 (LXX, "the Lord created me at the beginning
of his ways for his works") were understood as applying to the time
of the incarnation (fr. 10, etc.). "At the beginning of his ways"
referred to the time when the Logos assumed our flesh, and "for his
works" pointed to the words of Christ in Jn 5:17, "My Father is
working still, and I am working" and in Jn 17:4, "I have completed
the work which thou gavest me" (fr. 15).

For Marcellus christology found its expression in soteriology.
Christ never calls himself "Son of God" but always "Son of man"
to prepare us for sonship with God through fellowship with himself
(fr. 117). We, who formerly were deceived by the devil, may now
through the Logos rule and overcome that devil who once over-
came us. It was for us and for our salvation that the Logos assumed
our humanity "in the form of a servant" (fr. 117). This brief sketch
indicates how Marcellus countered every Arian suggestion that
there was a time when the Logos was not. True, the incarnate Son
did not exist before he was born of the virgin, but the incarnation
was but "the form of a servant" of that Logos who himself was and
is eternal deity.

This leads to Marcellus' interpretation of the kingship of Christ
and his interpretation of 1 Cor 15:24-28. That kingship had a beginning in the second dispensation. Such texts as Ps 2:6 (LXX, "I have
been appointed king by him on Zion, his holy mountain") attest to
the beginning of his reign (fr. 113). If the Logos as the incarnate Son
obtained a kingdom "less than 400 years ago" (fr. 115, 116), why
should we think it strange (*paradoxon*) if he also delivers up that
kingship which was entrusted to him "for a little while" (fr. 115)?

"Less than 400 years ago" he became king by assuming our
humanity. Just as there was a beginning, so there will be an end
when he has defeated all his enemies. What then will happen to his
humanity, his flesh? Will he keep this flesh in the coming ages—or

only until the time of judgment (fr. 116)? For Marcellus it was clearly the latter. The humanity will continue until the time of judgment for "they shall look on him whom they pierced," and it was his flesh they pierced. But then, when all enemies have been subdued, the Logos will return to unite himself wholly in God. *"Then he will be what he was before"* (cf. also fr. 41). When Paul writes Christ must reign *until* all enemies have been subjected, "clearly the holy apostle says that this will be the end of the kingdom of our Lord Christ" (fr. 113). Indeed, "The Apostle here discloses a great mystery to us when he says that the kingdom of Christ will have an end, when he has put all things under his feet" (fr. 114).

The kingship and the humanity are inseparable. Marcellus reminded his readers that Christ assumed flesh for their sake, not for his own sake. The incarnation made possible a restored humanity able to triumph over the devil who once had led them astray. For the Logos himself the flesh is "the form of a servant" (fr. 117). Indeed, Marcellus cited Jn 6:61f, "Does this offend you? What if you should see the Son of man going where he was before? The Spirit makes alive, the flesh is useless" (fr. 117, 118). The flesh served us, not himself. It was a temporary accommodation to our need. Along with Ps 110:1 and 1 Cor 15:24-28, Marcellus turned to Acts 3:21 which speaks of the times of restoration, and to Rom 8:21 which speaks of a restored creation free from its bondage (*apo tēs douleias*) to decay. But when the creation itself is free from bondage, can we suppose that the flesh which the Logos assumed as "the form of a servant" (*morphēn doulou*) will continue to be united to him (fr. 117)?

To the argument that the flesh is worthy to be united to the Logos permanently because Christ's flesh became immortal through the resurrection, Marcellus replied (fr. 120) that God is greater than the resurrection. Nor is everything immortal worthy of God. After all, principalities and powers may be immortal but they certainly are not worthy of God.

When asked what happens to the flesh of the Logos, Marcellus warned not to dogmatize on that which has not been learned from scripture. "Therefore do not ask me what I have not learned from the divine scriptures." Better to be content with the apostle's reminder that "now we see through a mirror dimly, but then face to face" (fr. 121).

Since Marcellus' christology found its expression in soteriology, what did the end of Christ's kingdom mean soteriologically? To study this question, one must supplement the fragments with those later writings which research now includes in the corpus of Marcellus' writings. For example, in *De incarnatione et contra*

Arianos, note the manner in which the Pauline text is used:

> For we are those who are subjected in him to the Father, and
> we are those who rule in him until he has set our enemies
> under our feet; for because of our enemies the ruler of the
> heavens became like us and received the human throne of
> David, his father according to the flesh, to rebuild it and
> restore it, so that when it was restored we might all rule in him
> and he might hand over the restored human rule to the Father,
> so that God might be all in all, ruling through him as through
> the Logos-God, after he had ruled through him as the Man-
> Redeemer.[14]

Here Marcellus equated "the flesh" of Christ with the church. "For
so long as his members have not yet all been subjected, he, as their
head, has not yet been subjected to the Father, but awaits his own
members."[15] This identification of the humanity of Christ with the
church as the body of Christ tended to push the question of the continued existence of Christ's humanity into the background. "For
now 'the body of Christ' exists for all eternity," but this "body" no
longer rules, for God alone rules.[16] This solution was problematic at
best—for it implied that the "fruits" no longer needed the "first
fruit" who was the incarnate Christ. The incarnation as such is
temporary because ultimately the Logos will return to the Monad
of deity to "be what he was before."

One question remains. How should the letter to Julius (fr. 129) in
which Marcellus affirmed the eternity of Christ's reign be
understood? "In accordance with the divine scriptures I believe
that there is one God and the only begotten Son-Logos of the one
(God) who always existed with the Father...and whose kingdom is
without end, according to the apostolic testimony." Here Marcellus
equated Son and Logos in a manner he did not do in those
fragments preserved by Eusebius. Not evident was his earlier clear
distinction between the eternal Logos and the incarnate Logos-Son.
In the earlier fragments he never quoted Lk 1:33 ("and of his
kingdom there will be no end"), a text much used against him. Did
Marcellus disguise his true position for prudential reasons? Recent
research does not support this charge. In *De incarnatione et contra
Arianos,* Lk 1:33 was cited, as also Dan 7:14 ("his dominion is an
everlasting dominion which shall not pass away, and his kingdom
one that shall not be destroyed"), while Marcellus still cited 1 Cor:
15:25 and Ps 110:1, noting "but the apostle says that his kingdom
has an end."[17]

Here we must leave him. Although accused by Eusebius of being
a Sabellian, Marcellus himself disavowed Sabellius as one "who,

having fallen from the true faith, did not accurately know either God or his holy Logos" (fr. 44). If Marcellus did not resolve the christological problem of his day, neither did those who vehemently opposed him.[18] Marcellus sought to be true to scripture, not to propound a novel christology. In the half century of strife that followed Nicea, when Arianism appeared to be winning the day, however, he so championed the unity of God and the eternity of the Logos that he separated too sharply the incarnate Son from the eternal Logos. Henry Melvill Gwatkin went too far in holding that for Marcellus "the incarnation became a mere theophany."[19] Johannes Quasten (following Zahn) suggested more appropriately that Marcellus was "more reactionary than revolutionary."[20]

It is becoming increasingly clear that Marcellus served as a catalyst for later formulations.[21] He sought to express the truth that the history of God's condescension to his creation is not only a history for us but also a history within God himself. In Hendrikus Berkhof's words, Marcellus saw

> that the Logos as well as the Spirit is God himself in a special activity. He saw that Scripture is not interested in the God of an abstract eternity, but in the God who acts in time and history. That inspired him to his bold concept of God's trinitarian extension in history. So he made a radical attempt to historicize the theological categories. His tragedy was that he was not radical enough. He limited the trinitarian extension to the present *oikonomia.* He felt urged to dehistoricize God's being in the eschaton.[22]

Indeed. That is why 1 Cor 15:24-28 became a stumbling block for him. He understood it to mean that the end would simply be like the beginning. The humanity of Jesus Christ would cease because the Logos "will be what he was before" (fr. 41).

That is why the Creed of Constantinople condemned Marcellus and affirmed the future of Jesus Christ who "will come again with glory to judge the living and the dead. His kingdom shall have no end." For Christian faith the incarnation is more than "the form of a servant." It is the abiding and crowning seal of God's fellowship with us. In the "flesh" of Jesus Christ we see the glory of God.

John Calvin, the second theologian of interest in this essay, never referred to Marcellus. His christology and trinitarian theology were informed not by Marcellus but by the Cappadocians and by Augustine. Indeed, Calvin's answer to Servetus would be his answer to Marcellus when it comes to the titles of Christ: "those who deny that Christ was the Son of God except in so far as he became man are wicked slanderers" (*Inst* 2.14.7).[23] Nonetheless, some of Calvin's interpreters hold that his exposition of 1 Cor 15:24-28 implied a cessation of Christ's humanity at the end of history.[24] If this is the case, Calvin would be closer to Marcellus than has been assumed. Thus the passages in Calvin that bear on this question are worthy of consideration.

In Calvin's commentary on the Pauline text (1546), he began with a reminder that "Paul put a bridle on man's impatience, by asserting that the time would not be ripe for our new life until the coming of Christ." Paul warns against an enthusiasm of premature arrival because "we must wait for that end, because it is not appropriate for us to receive the crown in the middle of the race." The passage stresses "that Christ will not deliver up the Kingdom before the end." Paul stresses the "until" of Ps 110:1 more than the psalmist because "he has made use of the evidence of this Psalm merely for the purpose of proving that the day for delivering up the Kingdom has not yet arrived, because Christ still has to deal with His enemies." The apostle's interpretation of Ps 8:7 stresses "that the Father has handed everything over to the Son, but so as to keep the chief authority in his own hands." After all, God appointed Christ "Lord and supreme King so that He may be the Father's Viceregent, so to speak, in the governing of the world."

Until the end Christ is "the intermediary between us and the Father, so that He may bring us to Him in the end." As for 1 Cor 15:28, "It is as if he (Paul) said, 'Let us calmly wait until Christ is victorious over all His enemies and bring us, *along with Himself*, under the sovereignty of God, so that the Kingdom of God may be brought to complete fullness in us.'" (Italics mine.) What, then, is the meaning of Christ delivering the kingdom to the Father? Calvin answered this question in his commentary as follows:

> Of course we acknowledge that God is the Ruler, but His rule is actualized in the man Christ (*sed in facie hominis Christi*). But Christ will then hand back the Kingdom which He has received, so that we may cleave completely to God. This does not mean that He will abdicate from the Kingdom in this way, but will transfer it in some way or other (*quodammodo*) from His glorious divinity, because then there will open up for us a way of approach, from which we are now kept back by our weakness. In this way, therefore, Christ will be subjected to the Father, because, *when the veil has been removed, we will see God plainly*, reigning in His majesty, and *the humanity of Christ will no longer be in between us to hold us back from a nearer vision of God*. (Italics mine.)

From the commentary we turn to the crucial passage in the *Inst* (2.14.3) which begins with an affirmation of the unity of the mediator's person. Calvin used Johannine texts to show that these refer "neither of deity nor of humanity alone, but of both at once." In the same way, "we ought also to understand what we read in Paul: after the judgment 'Christ will deliver the Kingdom to his God and Father' (1 Cor 15:24). Surely the Kingdom of the Son of God had no beginning and will have no end." For a time the splendor of majesty lay concealed under the lowness of flesh (cf. Phil 2:7), until "he was at last crowned with glory and honor" (Heb 2:9), and he was "exalted to the highest lordship" (Phil 2:9f). "So then will he yield to the Father his name and crown of glory, and whatever he has received from the Father, that 'God may be all in all' (1 Cor 15:28)." Now the Father governs us through the lordship of Christ. "Yet this is but for a time, *until we enjoy the direct vision of the Godhead.*" (Italics mine.) Now Christ is the mediator, human and divine. "Until he comes forth as judge of the world Christ will therefore reign, joining us to the Father as the measure of our weakness permits. But when as partakers in heavenly glory we shall see God as he is, Christ, having then discharged the office of Mediator, will cease to be the ambassador of his Father, and will be satisfied with that glory which he enjoyed before the creation of the world." Calvin added:

> And the name 'Lord' exclusively belongs to the person of Christ only in so far as it represents a degree midway between God and us. Paul's statement accords with this: 'One God...from whom are all things...and one Lord...through whom are all things' (1 Cor 8:6). That is, to him was lordship committed by the Father, until such time as we should see his divine majesty face to face. Then he returns the lordship to his Father so that—far from diminishing his own majesty—it may shine all the more brightly. Then, also, God shall cease to be the Head of Christ, for Christ's own deity will shine of itself, *although as yet it is covered by a veil.* (2.14.3; italics mine.)

In these passages Calvin stressed the completion of Christ's mediatorial work. But also notable is Calvin's image of a "veil." The present mediatorial lordship is still a hidden glory that will be transcended when the eternal Son shares fully that glory which he had before the world was. But what does it mean if the kingdom is transferred "in some way or other" from his humanity to his divinity? Does this imply that the humanity ceases? Does the "veil of his flesh" imply a provisional humanity?

Before attempting to answer, there are other passages that may

help us to interpret the two cited. In his eighth sermon on Ephesians (1:19-23), Calvin asked whether the phrase "not only in this
age but in that which is to come" did not contradict 1 Cor 15:24. He
concluded that this was only an apparent contradiction because for
God to reign through Jesus Christ did not mean that God was idle.
Humankind would not know God if Christ had not become our
brother. We need new eyes. In the last day, when we have been
transfigured into God's glory, we shall see him as he is.

> Thus you see how these two passages agree very well, for
> Christ will render up the kingdom to God his Father. And
> why? For we shall then see his heavenly majesty which we are
> not able to conceive at present because we are carnal. Also we
> shall perceive that whereas Jesus Christ has appeared to us a
> mortal man, he has been so glorified *in his human nature* that in
> very deed he is God, of one and the same substance with his
> Father....[25] (Italics mine.)

In this Calvin was like Luther who often referred to 1 Cor 15:24-28
in contrasting the kingdom of grace and the kingdom of glory. "It is
not that the two kingdoms are different from each other, but they
are ruled over in different ways—now in faith 'dimly' (1 Cor 13:12)
through the humanity of Christ, then visibly and in the revelation
of Christ's divine nature."[26] But notice. "Not that He will get rid of
the humanity, but that He will clearly show also His divinity hidden there, which we now see confusedly and in the riddle of His
humanity."[27]

In his commentary on the Pauline text, Calvin had asked whether
this delivering up of the kingdom conflicts with 2 Pet 1:11 ("an
entrance into the eternal kingdom of our Lord and Savior Jesus
Christ"). In his commentary on 2 Peter he wrote, "He calls it the
kingdom of Christ because we only reach heaven by His guidance
and favour." Since nothing is said about the kingdom of Christ
being eternal, however, the question of Christ's humanity is not
clarified.

Commenting on the close of Romans 8 Calvin said, "Although
Paul is speaking hyperbolic language, he in fact asserts that no
length of time can separate us from the grace of the Lord." Christ is
the bond and will always be the bond.

Perhaps the best context for Calvin's interpretation of 1 Cor
15:24-28 is found in *Inst* 1.13.26. There within the discussion of
God the Creator, Calvin turned to the text to refute those who
denied the eternal deity of the Son. There, as in 2.14.3, he
contrasted "the perfection of splendor that appears in heaven"
with "that measure of glory which was seen in him when he was

clothed with flesh.'' Of special interest is his comment on 1 Cor 15:28: ''And certainly for this reason Christ descended to us, to bear us up to the Father, and *at the same time to bear us up to himself,* in as much as he is one with the Father'' (italics mine).

As noted above, some scholars understand Calvin's interpretation of the Pauline text to imply or to assert an end to the humanity of Christ or at least to suggest that for Calvin the humanity will become superfluous. Not enough attention has been paid to what E. David Willis calls ''the catholic christology of Calvin,'' referring to the so-called ''extra-Calvinisticum''[28] which teaches that the eternal Son of God, even after the incarnation, was united to the human nature to form one person but was not restricted to the flesh. This has implications for Calvin's use of the word ''mediator'' which is not limited to Christ's flesh. ''Even if man had remained free from all stain, his condition would have been too lowly for him to reach God without a Mediator'' (*Inst* 2.14.1). How much more is it then true for fallen man. Quoting 1 Tim 2:5 (''one mediator between God and man, the man Jesus Christ''), Calvin said that Paul ''could have said 'God'; or he could at least have omitted the word 'man' just as he did the word 'God' '' (2.12.1). To say ''the man Jesus Christ'' serves to underscore the gracious character of God's approach to us in Christ. Elsewhere Calvin said that Christ ''began to perform the office of Mediator not only after the fall of Adam but insofar as he is the Eternal Son of God'' because ''already from the beginning of creation he was truly Mediator because he was always the Head of the Church and held primacy even over the angels and was firstborn of all creatures.''[29]

If Christ effects a mediation not only of reconciliation but of sustenance, this has implications for that future described in 1 Cor 15:24-28. Willis has written:

> It is noteworthy that Calvin never says, even in describing the meaning of this final state, that Christ will *relinquish* his humanity: he says only that Christ will transfer his reign from his humanity to his divinity. One may think this entails the virtual surrender of the humanity, since the humanity of Christ has then no further soteriological function, and since Calvin has all along judged the nature of Christ's Person by the soteriological criterion. But Calvin himself does not choose to follow this logic, any more than he chooses to say that our humanity, including our spiritual bodies, will be abandoned at the end. Indeed, our being in proper order again is the antithesis of losing our humanity: restored and perfected humanity is the condition for right relation to God. Man will remain man; he will not become God.[30]

To take the "extra-Calvinisticum" seriously is to question the conclusion of Jürgen Moltmann[31] that Calvin's christology was so functionally understood that the crucified Christ became superfluous in the realm of a redeemed existence immediate to God. At most we could say that logically there might be an eschatological inference which Calvin himself did not draw. Nor should the metaphor "veil" be pressed overmuch.[32] Was Calvin not thinking of the manner in which Christ's divinity was veiled in his humanity during the days of his ministry? Will that "veil" not become transparent when we see the glorified Christ face to face? Withal, "Jesus Christ is the same yesterday, today, and for ever" (Heb 13:8). Commenting on this text, Calvin said the writer "is not speaking there simply of Christ's everlasting divinity but of his power, a power perpetually available to believers" (Inst 2.10.4).

Accordingly, it is not surprising that later Calvinist theologians have sought to be more explicit as to the future of Christ's humanity. Olevianus, basing his view on the eternity of the covenant of grace, held that "the two natures are united for all eternity."[33] The Dutch theologian, Herman Bavinck, concluded his discussion of the work of Christ in his exaltation with reference to 1 Cor 15:24-28. Recalling the position of Marcellus, and recognizing that there has been difference of opinion within the reformed tradition, he suggested that, while the mediation of redemption will cease because it has been accomplished, there will always remain a mediation of union.[34] Bavinck vigorously disavowed any notion that one day the Son would lay aside his humanity.

At least one Calvinist theologian, however, not only understood Calvin's exposition of 1 Cor 15:24-28 as pointing to an end of the incarnation, but made this a firm thesis in his own theological work, namely, Arnold A. van Ruler, professor at the University of Utrecht from 1947 until his death in 1970.

Not widely known to English and American readers except for the English translation of his 1955 book in German, *The Christian Church and the Old Testament,* Moltmann has recently called attention to his christology.[35] A provocative and vigorous thinker, van Ruler's published volumes comprise thirty-seven books, including his magnum opus, *De Vervulling van de Wet,* an extensive doctoral dissertation whose theological themes find continuing expression in his other writings. Publication was completed recently of *Theologisch Werk,* a six-volume collection of his published and unpublished articles and addresses.[36]

Van Ruler was a churchman. As a pastor he played a leading role in the revision of the church order of his Netherlands Reformed Church. Some five volumes and a goodly number of articles indicated his concern for the doctrinal significance of church polity,[37] but also stressed that the church is never an end in itself. The church exists for the kingdom. Its mission cannot be narrowed to the salvation of individuals; it must include an active intercession for and participation in the world. From his first volume on, van Ruler sought to forge a theology of culture based on a theocratic vision of the kingdom of God. Systematic theology "stands or falls with the degree of christianizing (*kerstening*). It presupposes 'a corpus christianum' around that 'corpus Christi' which is the church."[38] Indeed, "The 'corpus christianum' is more important so far as goal is concerned than the 'Corpus Christi.'"[39] He loved to speak of "christianizing" the social order, insisting that while one must distinguish the gospel from ideology, one cannot avoid cultural responsibilities.[40] The broken signs of a "corpus christianum" bear witness to the fact that God's creation was not a fiasco.

Van Ruler sought a fresh perspective on the relation of law and gospel by grounding his theology on the kingdom of God. Apart from a theocratic vision of the kingdom, in which God's glory is reflected in the whole of creation, the purpose of God is limited and distorted. This purpose is not simply redemption. Doxology is more than soteriology. The old reformed doctrine of the covenant of works was reclaimed by van Ruler, because it points to a reality more fundamental than the covenant of grace.[41] He insisted that the gospel means the fulfilling and effecting of the law, not its abrogation. The law expresses God's will in and for creation. Redemption is God's gracious remedy for the guilt of sin, the means to the goal of history which is a restored creation. He often said that the law was eternal while the gospel was provisional and temporary. "The law is therefore more eschatological than the gospel."[42]

Van Ruler criticized the christocentrism of Barth. He urged a trinitarian rather than a christocentric theology. He disavowed the tendency to interpret the first and third articles of the creed by the second. Too often, he said, theologians have sought in the "solus Christus" a hermeneutical attempt to read all of scripture as though it were simply a witness to Christ. Does the Old Testament point primarily or even essentially to Christ? Is its unifying center the messianic hope? Is it not rather the kingdom of God? Are not Israel and the messiah but the means and instruments to that grand design? He entertained the thought that "the OT alone is the canon and the New has just been added at the end as an explanatory glossary,'' though recognizing that its interpretation and validation are true and therefore ''canonical.''[43]

All this is said to show that redemption is for creation, not vice versa. That is why van Ruler disavowed the tendency to make of the incarnation the controlling clue for our understanding of God and his kingdom. God's creation did not have to be completed or improved. It was good at the beginning. In the same vein van Ruler was unhappy with the tendency to speak of Jesus Christ as the true or universal man. Jesus Christ is not an ''idiogram'' or symbol.[44] He is not the universal but rather the unique man, the mediator born of Mary for our redemption. Van Ruler did not like such phrases as ''Christ the meaning of history''; he preferred to say that humankind, the creation, ultimately the kingdom of God is the meaning of history.[45]

This leads to his eschatology. History, the whole of created history, finds its telos in the eschaton. ''Without an eschaton there is no history but also, without history there is no eschaton.''[46] The eschaton is not Christ but is rather a restored creation in the kingdom of God. Doxology is more than soteriology. The eschatological hope is the horizontal fulfillment of *this* world, a hope that sends us back into this world and into our own history with courage and social passion. The ''new world in which righteousness dwells'' is not a *creatio ex nihilo;* it is this world restored and transformed. Piety must cling to the theocratic vision instead of succumbing to a pietism so absorbed in Christ and in our own salvation that it becomes a flight from this world.

This brief sketch provides an approach to van Ruler's interpretation of 1 Cor 15:24-28, a passage he saw as tremendously important. ''This delivering (*paradidonai*) of the kingdom by the Son to the Father at the end (1 Cor 15:24) corresponds to the appointing (*diatithesthai*) of the kingdom by the Father to the Son at the beginning (Lk 22:29).''[47] The kingdom of Christ is not an interim kingdom (*Zwischenreich*); it *is* the kingdom of God in a particular and temporary form—not the final form. Christ's reign is mediatorial, and its redemptive character is best described by such words as ''exaltation, hiddenness, expectation'' (*verheffing, verborgenheid, verwachting*). Christ's resurrection and ascension attest to his exaltation and to his vindication by God, but the kingdom is not yet manifest. Christ is still ''lonely'' on his throne, for he still must reign in the midst of his enemies. He still reigns in grace and mercy, not yet in glory. The king is still the priest who carries on his work of redemption. As yet our life is hid in God (Col 3:3). Pointing to this hiddenness and expectation of Christ's reign, van Ruler quoted Pascal's words: ''Jésus sera en agonie jusqu'á la fin du monde.''[48]

According to van Ruler, in 1 Cor 15:24-28 the apostle wrote of deep mysteries which, even though they surpass understanding, must not be neglected. "In the final analysis, Christ and his work are not the end itself but are only the means. The one great and radiant end of all things is the kingdom of God himself and all of created reality in its final and redeemed form."[49] Jesus Christ is not the goal but the means whereby God attains his goal. In other words, the incarnation was an "emergency measure" (*noot-maatregel*). "If I may put it briefly and sharply, Jesus Christ is an emergency measure that God postponed as long as possible (cf. Mt 21:33-46)."[50]

Even more expressive is the term that constantly recurs in van Ruler's writing—"intermezzo." Special revelation is an intermezzo. Israel is an intermezzo, as is also the church. Most of all, the incarnation is an intermezzo, a messianic intermezzo. For that matter, "heaven," insofar as it expresses the present hiddenness of the kingdom, is an intermezzo because sin is an intermezzo. The present work of the Spirit is an intermezzo because it too is provisional and leads to something greater. Humankind needs the Spirit's outpouring and indwelling, just as it needs the continuing mediation of Christ. But one day the eternal light of the kingdom of glory will rise over the whole creation and then "the illumination of the Spirit (in his outpouring and indwelling) will be extinguished."[51]

If Christ's reign is his mediatorial and redemptive work, if the incarnation is for redemption and for nothing else, what is the meaning of Christ's delivering up his reign at the end? The answer has been suggested already in the word "intermezzo." "This is the ultimate and the highest that the messiah can do—that he ceases to be the messiah."[52] One day the hiddenness of the kingdom in his flesh will be over. Then the intermezzo will give way to the final glory when God is "all in all." This is not pantheism, for the distinction between the Creator and the creature will always remain; but all mediation between God and the world will be over because it is no longer needed. "God will dwell 'with men' (Rev 21:3). Between God and the naked existence of created reality there will no longer be anything. There will be inscribed on the bells of horses, 'Holy to the Lord' (Zech 14:20). So God will be 'all in all' (1 Cor 15:28)."[53] The synthesis of redemption with creation "will only be reached in the eschaton when the incarnation becomes undone and the indwelling (of the Spirit) ceases. Then all particularity (*bijzonderheid*) of God both in Christ and in the Spirit falls away. The triune God then is all in all."[54]

Does the Bible teach this cessation of the incarnation? Van Ruler responded:

I could answer with another question. Is there a single theologoumenon, a single dogma, or at least a single precise definition of dogma in the Bible? I could also answer with the question, How do you propose to understand in dogmatic terms the tremendous place of 1 Cor. 15:24-28? For that matter, if the Holy Spirit takes the things of Christ from him and brings them over in us, is that not already a beginning, a prefiguration of the fact that substitution (*plaatsvervanging*) will be given up, and doesn't that imply that the incarnation also will be given up? Did the incarnation ever serve any purpose save that of substitution?[55]

Of course, van Ruler knew that the Scriptures link Christ with creation as well as with redemption. He knew that reformed theology has spoken of Christ as the "mediator of creation." With reference to such passages as the Johannine prologue and Colossians 1, he said that the evangelists and apostles became overly "lyrical" in their praise of Christ, while "a dogmatician is more composed and sometimes has the feeling that things are run together too much in this lyric, especially when he reads Col. 1:15."[56] In another place he suggested that when it comes to creation, pneumatology is more helpful than christology. "I have the impression that what we often have tried to say of the Son—mutatis mutandis—can and should be said of the Spirit. And then it is not necessary to speak of mediation. One can simply speak of immanence."[57] Van Ruler preferred to reserve the word "mediator" for the substitutionary redemptive work. In any case, "the world was not created by Jesus of Nazareth."[58]

In assessing van Ruler's theology of the kingdom and, in particular, the implications he draws from 1 Cor 15:24-28, one can appreciate his vigorous affirmation of the goodness of creation with all that entails for Christian participation in the world. He avoided the weakness of a liberalism that underestimates the seriousness of sin, and the individualism and self-centeredness of a conservative pietism that often forgets that salvation is for service. Politics no less than church-going is "a holy business."[59] In all this he gave new voice to Calvin's conviction that this world, despite the ravages of sin, is the theater of God's glory. He rightly insisted that the kingdom of God is larger than the church, that doxology has larger horizons than redemption.

To construe such phrases as "emergency measure" and "intermezzo" as though van Ruler ever minimized the crucial significance of Jesus Christ would be incorrect. The coming of Christ, his cross and resurrection, his ascension and continuing work, his return and final victory constitute the manner in which

God accomplishes and completes his purpose. Only through Jesus Christ can history find its eschatological fulfillment. We should not confuse van Ruler's "intermezzo" with that of Marcellus.[60] Van Ruler began and ended with a firmer trinitarian theology than did Marcellus. Whereas Marcellus sought to explain the temporary character of the incarnation by appealing to the Johannine text that "the flesh profits nothing," van Ruler exalted the "form of a servant." The present hiddenness of the kingdom in the incarnate Christ represents "all the gentleness and patience, the grace and the mercy, the descent and the lowliness, the humanity and the actual communion of God, in short—the mystery of redemption."[61] Van Ruler stressed the "intermezzo" in order to affirm the Christian conviction that one day Christ's redemptive work will be fully achieved.

Nor is it quite accurate to say that for van Ruler the end is no more than the beginning.[62] He insisted that the end is more than the beginning because the consummation has a "plus" so that "it is not enough to say that the proton returns in the eschaton."[63]

Although Moltmann criticized van Ruler (and Calvin) for understanding Christ's redemptive work "radically in Anselm's terms" as substitution and satisfaction, van Ruler held that Anselm's view of the atonement should not be made into "a shibboleth of orthodoxy," however much it may be affirmed as "valuable and significant, indeed, in my view as indispensable."[64] He liked to portray the systematic theologian as busy arranging pictures and images, knowing full well that the redemptive work of Christ is too rich and manifold ever to be confined to a single image.[65]

Nonetheless, despite such qualifications, these criticisms touch some fundamental issues. Although van Ruler spoke of a "plus" which makes consummation more than creation, he had difficulty explicating this "plus." Is the law as "the form of creation" more eschatological than the gospel? Does the grace of Christ do no more than checkmate and overcome the guilt of sin? Does not "grace abound all the more?" Was not van Ruler so afraid of reducing christology to a christo-monism, so afraid of making Christ into an "ideogram," that he failed to take into account sufficiently the Pauline stress on Christ as the second Adam, the new man, *whose image we shall bear?*[66] How can we bear the image of the man of heaven if he disappears?

Will communion with God ever cease to be communion with *Christ?* Berkhof has written: "We shall not come to God without Christ, nor via Christ, but rather together with Christ as 'the first born of many brethren' and so around him as the central figure."[67]

The "via Christ" applies to the present mediation of redemption, and that will be completed. The "with Christ" will apply to the realm of glory as much as it applies to the present realm of grace.

While van Ruler interpreted the phrase that God will be "all in all" in the imagery of Rev 21:3 ("Behold, the dwelling of God is with men. He will dwell with them...and God himself will be with them"), he failed to link this with the imagery of the city in Rev 21:22, a city that needs no temple "for its temple is the Lord God the Almighty *and the Lamb*" (italics mine) where "the glory of God is its light, and its lamp is the Lamb."[68] In the Seer's vision that Lamb is forever the incarnate Lord who was slain and is now alive forever. To be sure, the exegete will not try to read the Johannine apocalypse into the Pauline passage, but van Ruler rightly insisted that the dogmatician's task is not confined to that of the exegete.

In short, provocative and stimulating as his interpretation of 1 Cor 15:24-28 may be, I do not find van Ruler's argument persuasive or his christological conclusion satisfying.

This study has shown the import of Grillmeier's words quoted above that "1 Corinthians 15:24-28 has been a temptation to theologians."[69] The text itself does not raise the question of the future of Christ's humanity. The New Testament never suggests that the incarnation is an intermezzo. It affirms rather that "all the promises of God find their Yes in him. That is why we utter the Amen through him, to the glory of God" (2 Cor 1:20). The glory of God—surely the climax of 1 Cor 15:24-28—includes Jesus Christ and finds its fullest expression in his willing subjection rather than in his disappearance.

Behind some attempts to suggest an end to the humanity of Jesus there may lurk a notion about the unchangeability and impassibility of God. That God is unchangeable in his troth and faithfulness needs no argument. But Christian theology has always had to be on guard against docetic tendencies. Dogmatic formulations have not been free of such tendencies when it comes to the "two natures" of Jesus Christ. Likewise eschatology is in danger of an ultimate docetism. Can the future of God ever be sundered from the future of Jesus? "Jesus Christ is the same yesterday, today, and for ever" (Heb 13:8). That is not christological impassibility. That "yesterday" refers to the historic coming, death, resurrection, ascension of Jesus Christ. That "today" points us to the present lordship and intercession of Jesus Christ. And that "for ever" (*eis tous aionas*) is not exhausted in the last day of this age (Mt 28:20, *heōs tēs suntelias tou aiōnos*).

Faith's vision points to a time when God will be "all in all." But how? And what does this mean for us? An unpublished letter of James Denney put it in striking fashion: "I had rather be found in Christ than lost in God."[70]

NOTES

1. I use the RSV except for the final three words, "all in all." See the discussion on page 175.
2. G. Berkouwer, *The Return of Christ* (Grand Rapids: Wm. B. Eerdmans, 1972) 431.
3. In addition to the commentaries, cf. Ulrich Luz, *Das Gesichtsverständnis des Paulus* (München: Kaiser Verlag, 1968) 332-58; Gerhard Barth, "Erwägungen zu 1. Korinther 15:20-28," *EvT*, 1970. For the interpretation of the passage in patristic literature, cf. E. Schendel, *Herrschaft und Unterwerfung Christi, 1. Korinther 15, 24-28 in Exegese und Theologie der Väter bis zum Ausgang des 4. Jahrhunderts* (Tübingen: J.C.B. Mohr, 1971).
4. That this is an unusual expression is evidenced by the textual variants. P 46 gives the usual Pauline expression, "kingdom of God." G and Ambrosiaster reverse the order of the text to read "the kingdom of God and of Christ," while 1739 has "the kingdom of God's messiah" and 1836 reads "the kingdom of God's Son."
5. E.g., O. Cullmann, "The Kingship of Christ and the Church in the New Testament," *The Early Church,* ed A. J. B. Higgins (Philadelphia: Westminster Press, 1956).
6. Cullmann, 111. "For just as the *Regnum Christi* has a beginning, so too it has an end." Cf. also his *Christology of the New Testament* (Philadelphia: Westminster Press, 1959) 225. Cullmann considered the millennial reign of Revelation 20 compatible with 1 Corinthians 15. On the other hand, R. H. Charles, *Eschatology* (1899, now New York: Schocken, 1963) 448, distinguished different stages in Paul's thought. He wrote, "What the Apostle speaks of here is a Messianic reign of temporary duration from Christ's exaltation to the final judgment. In his later epistles the Apostle conceives this reign as unending."
7. Schendel, 23, makes a similar point: "Es wird weder in 1 Kor. 15, 24ff noch in Phil. 2, 7 primär davon gesprochen was Christus *war* sondern was er *tat.*"
8. A. Grillmeier, *Christ in Christian Tradition,* 2d rev ed (Atlanta: John Knox Press, 1975) 1. 399. His sentence includes Evagrius and the Origenists as those wanting to derive from the text the abolition of Christ's humanity.
9. Cf. the critical edition by E. Klostermann, *Eusebius Werke, Vierte Band, Gegen Marcell, über die kirchliche Theologie, Die Fragmente Marcells,* 2 Auflage (Berlin: Akademie Verlag, 1972). The fragments relating to our discussion will follow Klostermann's numbering. Wolfgang Gericke, *Marcell von Ancyra* (Halle: Akademischer Verlag, 1940) offered a German translation rather severely criticized by Felix Scheidweiler, "Marcell von Ancyra," *ZNW* 46 (1955) 202ff. I have translated the fragments in an unpublished article on Marcellus.
10. T. Zahn, *Marcellus von Ancyra* (Gotha: F. A. Perthes, 1867), a work still foundational for later research.

11. Gericke, *Marcell.*
12. Martin Tetz, "Zur Theologie des Markell von Ankyra I: Eine Markellische Schrift, 'De incarnatione et contra Arianos,' " *ZKG,* 1964; "Zur Theologie des Markell von Ankyra II: 'Epistula ad Antiochenos (Sermo maior),' " *ZKG,* 1968; "Zur Theologie des Markell von Ankyra III: Die pseudathanasianische Epistula ad Liberium, ein Markellisches Bekenntnis," *ZKG,* 1972. In the first article, p. 250, Tetz points in particular to the fact that in the authentic writings of Athanasius one never finds 1 Cor 15:24-28 cited, while in *De incarnatione et contra Arianos,* ch 20, this text, so important for Marcellus, has a prominent place. Klostermann's critical edition of the fragments notes this possibility of enlarged sources which Tetz proposes. Schendel makes use of these enlarged sources when discussing Marcellus' interpretation of the Pauline text. An excellent recent summary which accepts the larger corpus of Marcellus is found in the second edition of Grillmeier.
13. Grillmeier, 274.
14. *De incarnatione et contra Arianos.* Translation by Grillmeier, 293. While I did not have access to the whole text, the Greek text of ch 20 appears in Schendel, 122.
15. *Ibid.* Translation by Grillmeier, 293.
16. Grillmeier, 294. Cf. also the long section on Marcellus in Reinhard M. Hübner, *Die Einheit des Leibes Christi bei Gregor von Nyssa* (Leiden: E. J. Brill, 1974).
17. Cf. Schendel, 122 n. 34.
18. Eusebius of Caesarea may entitle his second work against Marcellus *Peri tēs ekklesiastikēs theologias,* but his christology is unsatisfactory. Cf. H. Berkhof, *Die Theologie des Eusebius von Caesarea* (Amsterdam: Uitgeversmattschappij Holland, 1939). Cyril of Jerusalem, *Catechetical Lectures,* exhorts his readers: "And shouldest thou ever hear any say that the kingdom of Christ shall have an end, abhor the heresy; it is another head of the dragon, lately sprung up in Galatia. A certain one has dared to affirm, that after the end of the world Christ shall reign no longer; he also dared to say, that the Word having come forth from the Father shall be absorbed into the Father, and shall be no more; uttering such blasphemies to his own perdition." (*Nicene and Post-Nicene Fathers,* second series, vol 7 (1893) XV. 27. But did Marcellus ever say that the Logos "shall be no more"? Cyril's attempt to interpret the "until" of 1 Cor 15:25 does not deal with the context of the passage, content only to note other places in Paul where "until" does not suggest termination. Again, in *De Trinitate,* Hilary of Poitiers does not mention Marcellus by name but doubtless refers to him when, having refuted Photinus, he adds: "it is a deeply rooted evil even at the present day. Galatia has nourished many who have made this impious confession of God" (*Fathers of the Church,* VII, 3.226). Elsewhere Hilary seems to know a book of Marcellus entitled *De subiectione domini Christi,* but Eusebius knows nothing of such a title, else he would certainly have made use of the title.
19. H. M. Gwatkin, *Studies of Arianism* (Cambridge: Deighton, Bell, and Co., 1882) 82.
20. J. Quasten, *Patrology* III (Westminster: Newman Press, 1960) 199. While he does not quote Zahn, compare Zahn, 217: "Wenn sie

beweisst, dass Marcell eine mehr reactionäre als revolutionäre Erscheinung ist...."

21. In presenting a paper on Marcellus at a meeting of the Southwest Seminar on the Development of Early Catholic Christianity, a fruitful discussion and critique helped me with further bibliographical suggestions as well as with new insights. Dr. Albert Outler commented on Marcellus' importance in precipitating the controversies that led the church between 325 and 381 to clarify the importance of the cosmic significance of the incarnation. This led the creed of 381 to make explicit the *palin* of the second article, as well as to develop the third article of the creed. Christologically that creed made explicit: "and will come *again with glory* to judge the living and the dead. *His kingdom shall have no end."* (Italics mine.)

22. H. Berkhof, *The Doctrine of the Holy Spirit* (Richmond: John Knox Press, 1964) 120.

23. Quotations from the 1559 *Institutes of the Christian Religion* are from the translation of Ford Battles, ed John T. McNeill, in The Library of Christian Classics (Philadelphia: Westminster Press, 1960). Quotations from the commentaries are from the new edition edited by David and Thomas Torrance, published by Oliver and Boyd, and in this country (Grand Rapids: Wm. B. Eerdmans Co., 1960f).

24. Those who affirm that for Calvin the humanity of Christ will cease include: E. Emmen, *De Christologie van Calvijn* (Amsterdam: H. J. Paris, 1935) 109; F. W. A. Korff, *Christologie,* I (Nijkerk: C.F. Callenbach, 1940) 250f; A. A. van Ruler, *De Vervulling van de Wet* (see below). Those who see this implied but who leave the question somewhat open include: H. Quistorp, *Calvin's Doctrine of the Last Things* (London: Lutterworth, 1955) 170; J. Moltmann, *The Crucified God* (New York: Harper & Row, 1974) 258f. Those who deny this is Calvin's position include: G. Berkouwer, *The Return of Christ,* 431f; E. David Willis, *Calvin's Catholic Christology* (Leiden: E. J. Brill, 1966) 99.

25. J. Calvin, *Sermons on the Epistle to the Ephesians* (Edinburgh: Banner of Truth Trust, 1973) 114f. (The French reads: "que tellement il a este glorifié en sa nature humaine, que vrayement il est Dieu, d'une mesme essence avec son Pere"). The sermons, first translated in 1577 by Arthur Golding, were preached 1558-59.

26. Luther, *Lectures on Galatians* (1519), in *Luther's Works* (St. Louis: Concordia, 1964), 27.171.

27. Luther, *Lecture on Psalm 121,* in *Luther's Works* (St. Louis: Concordia, 1976) 11. 548. In vol. 28 are included 17 sermons Luther preached on 1 Corinthians 15. As compared with Calvin's metaphor of a veil, Luther spoke of "beholding the sun through a cloud," 124.

28. Willis shows that the so-called "extra-Calvinisticum," so prominent in the Reformed-Lutheran polemics, was not new with Calvin.

29. *Responsum ad Fratres Polonos,* quoted in Willis, 70.

30. Willis, 99.

31. Moltmann, 257f.

32. "Veil" need not suggest any docetic overtones. Cf. Wesley's Christmas hymn with its "Veiled in flesh the Godhead see; hail th' incarnate Deity."

33. H. Heppe, *Reformed Dogmatics* (London: Allen and Unwin Ltd., 1950) 431.

34. H. Bavinck, *Gereformeerde Dogmatiek,* III (Kampen: Kok, 1910) 459f.
35. Moltmann, 259f. He refers mainly to van Ruler's German publication, *Gestaltwerdung Christi in der Welt,* 1959.
36. For this study I have made use of the following: *De Vervulling van de wet* (Nijkerk: G. F. Callenbach, 1947); *The Christian Church and the Old Testament* (Grand Rapids: Wm. B. Eerdmans, 1971); *De Dood Wordt Overwonnen* (Nijkerk: G. F. Callenbach, 1963); *Theologisch Werk* (Nijkerk: G. F. Callenbach, Deel I appearing in 1969, II and III in 1971, IV and V in 1972, VI in 1973). References to the articles in these six volumes indicate volume and pagination without titles of the various articles.
37. Of these I have read *Bijzonder en Algemeen Ambt* (Nijkerk: G. F. Callenbach, 1952). Chapter 1, "Office and Kingdom," strikes van Ruler's constant theme that God is not locked into the sacraments or into Christians, nor even in Christ. "The messiah is his gift and deed, but he gives and does more" (19f).
38. *Theol Werk* V 200f.
39. *Theol Werk* II 98; cf. also III 155.
40. Cf. "Evangelie en ideologie" in *Theol Werk* II.
41. *Theol Werk* VI 77, "The covenant of works is more fundamental than the covenant of grace." In greater detail, cf. *Vervulling,* 276.
42. *Theol Werk* I 137; cf. also II 96, and *Vervulling,* 271.
43. *The Christian Church and the Old Testament,* 94; cf. also *Theol Werk* I 162, where he sees the thesis that Jesus Christ is the real content of the OT as a dangerous as well as an untenable position.
44. *Theol Werk* I 179; II 167.
45. Cf. *Theol Werk* VI, ch. 5, "De mens de zin van de geschiedenis" (1963). In his earlier *Vervulling,* 73, he had not hesitated to use the phrase, "Christ the meaning of history."
46. *Theol Werk* II 225; cf. I 219, IV 105.
47. *Vervulling,* 90.
48. *Vervulling,* 72, 104; *Theol Werk* III 89.
49. *De Dood Wordt Overwonnen,* 65.
50. *The Christian Church and the Old Testament,* 69. Cf. *Theol Werk* I 165, where the redemptive work of Christ "is therefore only a moment, an emergency measure, in the one counsel and the one work of God." Cf. also I 174; III 140.
51. *Vervulling,* 149. (Without attempting a full concordance of the word "intermezzo" and especially the "messianic intermezzo," cf. *Vervulling,* 36, 107, 144, 171, 196, 250, 281, 354, 435, 499, 517, 529; *Theol Werk* I 139; IV 82, 192; VI 16, 25, 126, 186.
52. *Vervulling,* 107.
53. *Ibid.,* 93.
54. *Theol Werk* VI 40.
55. *Theol Werk* I 172f.
56. *Theol Werk* I 159. H. Berkhof, *Christelijk Geloof* (Nijkerk: G. F. Callenbach, 1973) 171, points to this quotation critically.
57. *Theol Werk* VI 38.
58. *Theol Werk* I 160; II 67. Both references are directed against Barth.
59. Cf. the article, "Politiek is een heilige zaak," *Theol Werk* IV 119f.
60. Cf. Berkouwer, 431, "Without equating van Ruler's ideas with those of Marcellus, I think it is quite obvious that the problem of an in-

termezzo occupies a crucial place in both views. The church traditionally has proceeded in another direction.''

61. *Vervulling,* 95.
62. Cf. Moltmann, 261, asks, ''But can the consummation be understood as being quite untouched by the history out of which it emerges?'' He assumes that for van Ruler there is no ''plus'' in the eschaton.
63. *Theol Werk* I 170f; cf. also II 227; VI 70, ''The eschaton is the creation plus history.''
64. *Theol Werk* IV 85.
65. Cf. *Theol Werk* I 218. This occurs in an address entitled ''Eschatologische notitites.'' The same volume includes an address entitled ''Methode en mogelijkheden van de dogmatiek, vergeleken met die van exegese.''
66. In 1 Cor 15:49, with Nestle-Aland, we read the future *phoresomen,* rather than the subjunctive *phoresōmen,* despite textual evidence for the latter, because the future stands in contrast to the aorist *ephoresamen* (''we have borne the image of the man of dust'').
67. Berkhof, 558.
68. In *Vervulling,* 149, 151, van Ruler makes a passing reference to Rev 14:4 where the redeemed are the first fruits ''for God and the Lamb,'' but he does not reflect on the image ''Lamb'' as this is part of the final vision. Similarly, I have not found any reference to Eph 1:20f (''above every name that is named, not only in this age but also in that which is to come'').
69. Cf. above, note 8.
70. I owe this quotation to Professor George Hendry of Princeton Theological Seminary. He paraphrased it in an address to the World Alliance of Reformed Churches (Presbyterian and Congregational) on Sept. 1, 1976, and afterwards gave me its more exact wording.

TEXTS
and
TESTAMENTS

The Formation of Canon and the
Discipline of Interpretation

Listening to the Parables of Jesus: An Exploration of the Uses of Process Theology in Biblical Interpretation

William A. Beardslee

The force and simplicity of the parables of Jesus always have enabled them to speak directly to ordinary people, and this special character still does. Yet the simplicity and directness of the parables have not enabled them to tell the same story to every audience. People have heard them in very different ways at different times. Scholars have provided insight into the reasons for the variation in understanding the parables, thereby suggesting what the possibilities of listening are in a given state of culture. This variety in hearing and the reasons for it are the concern of this essay.

What kind of world do the parables disclose? How far do they reinforce the vision of the world which the hearer brings to them, or how far do they undermine or overturn the vision of the world of the hearer? If they do challenge the hearer's world, do they offer an alternative vision, or does that have to come from elsewhere than the parables themselves? These are the sort of questions which will be addressed. A particular aspect of the vision of the world found in the parables which will be considered is the relation between gift and demand in it.

To explore and reflect on the different ways the church has listened to the parables, the interpretation of one well-known parable will serve as illustration. Four different modes of interpretation characteristic of, though not limited to, different historical periods in the church's history demonstrate not only the variety in listening to the "sample" parable chosen for this study, but also the progressive reduction of the world within which the hearer's response to the parable is expected to take place. Reduction or loss of world means the erosion of a sense of a coherent environment within which a human response to the word of God in the parable can take place. In the light of the reduction of world so characteristic of the more recent interpretations of the parables, this essay will inquire whether a perspective governed by process theology has the possibility both of overcoming the oppositions so often affirmed between contrasting interpretations of the parables and of opening a path toward a legitimate affirmation of "world," of an environment which is responsive to the hearer's response. What is at stake is the doctrine of creation, which has been badly eroded in much recent New Testament scholarship. To sharpen the differences and clarify the manner of listening employed in each mode in order to reach this goal is the aim of this essay, and a consideration of some of the history of the interpretation of the parable of the Good Samaritan will be the means.

Allegorical interpretation has a tradition many centuries old in the church. It still persists and, in fact, is more highly regarded today than it was a half a century ago. The great function of the classic allegorical interpretation of the parables was to integrate them into the life of a religious community, the church.

Consider the parable of the Good Samaritan (Lk 10:30-35):

> A man was going down from Jerusalem to Jericho, and he fell among robbers, who stripped him and beat him, and departed, leaving him half dead. Now by chance a priest was going down that road; and when he saw him he passed by on the other side. So likewise a Levite, when he came to the place and saw him, passed by on the other side. But a Samaritan, as he journeyed, came to where he was; and when he saw him, he had compassion, and went to him and bound up his wounds, pouring oil and wine; then he set him on his own beast and brought him to an inn, and took care of him. And the next day he took out two denarii and gave them to the innkeeper, saying, "Take care of him; and whatever more you spend, I will repay you when I come back."

Luke places the parable in a framework in which it answers the question, Who is my neighbor? and in which the concluding point is, Go and do the same thing yourself.

For the moment the setting will be bypassed, to hear how the parable sounds when it is taken allegorically. This is Augustine's interpretation:

> *A certain man went down from Jerusalem to Jericho:* Adam himself is meant; *Jerusalem* is the heavenly city of peace, from whose blessedness Adam fell; *Jericho* means the moon, and signifies our mortality, because it is born, waxes, wanes, and

dies. *Thieves* are the devil and his angels. *Who stripped him,* namely of his immortality; *and beat him,* by persuading him to sin; *and left him half-dead,* because in so far as man can understand and know God, he lives, but in so far as he is wasted and oppressed by sin, he is dead; he is therefore called *half-dead.* The *priest* and *Levite* who saw him and passed by, signify the priesthood and ministry of the Old Testament, which could profit nothing for salvation. *Samaritan* means Guardian, and therefore the Lord Himself is signified by this name. The *binding of the wounds* is the restraint of sin. *Oil* is the comfort of good hope; *wine* the exhortation to work with fervent spirit. The *beast* is the flesh in which He (Christ) deigned to come to us. The being *set upon the beast* is belief in the incarnation of Christ. The *inn* is the Church, where travellers are refreshed on their return from pilgrimage to their heavenly country. The *morrow* is after the resurrection of the Lord. The *two pence* are either the two precepts of love, or the promise of this life and of that which is to come. The *innkeeper* is the Apostle (Paul). The supererogatory payment is either his counsel of celibacy, or the fact that he worked with his own hands lest he should be a burden to any of the weaker brethren when the Gospel was new, though it was lawful for him "to live by the Gospel."[1]

Of this lengthy interpretation, it is initially important to note one thing. Adam is you and I. The listener comes into the parable as the man lying in the ditch, in Augustine's interpretation of the parable. There he finds the point of contact in life for the elaborate theological interpretation that he offers. Secondarily, of course, one must follow the example of Christ and act like a Samaritan; but this is a second hearing of the parable as Augustine listens to it.

To criticize this kind of interpretation is easy, and people have been doing so for seventy-five years or more. Clearly the story has nothing to do with Paul's views on celibacy or working for a living. But emerging today once more is a period in which one can appreciate the purpose of the older allegorical interpretation, oriented to the life and faith of the church. The elaborate set of correspondences between the parable story and the larger story of the Christian faith seemed natural to the allegorical interpreter, who lived in a coherent world, a *cosmos.* The parable gave the listener access to this cosmos as did other versions of the Christian story. A concentration on the often very arbitrary details misses the point. The basic stance of allegorical interpretation is the confidence that the different versions of the story of faith cast light on one another, so that one can interpret back and forth within this network of meanings.

In this setting, the work of the parable upon the listeners is to help them find their place. The story shows where the individual belongs. In this case, the initial reading of the story focuses on Adam and Christ, but the hearer who knows this way of listening to the parables knows that the story comes home when heard from Adam's point of view. That does not exclude the possibility of other readings; identification with the priest and the Levite suggests a peril to be avoided or a sense of sin to be confessed; and since Christ is example as well as redeemer, the hortatory, imperative interpretation so familiar in other ways of listening to the parable is not excluded. But the indicative reading, a description of how things are, a declaration of God's grace, is more fundamental than the imperative in this allegorical interpretation of the parable.

Putting it differently, one notes that all story-telling balances the experience of belonging in an orderly sequence with the experience of risk and movement as choices are made within the sequence of action. Allegorical interpretation, when set as it was within the context of an established faith, tended to put the emphasis on the first of these two dimensions of story-telling—that of experiencing the sense of belonging in a sequence of events. Yet this reading of the parables did not give up the dimension of risk and openness. In contrast to some modern interpretations of the Christian faith, however, the allegorical interpretation of a parable, as in this example, did set the hearer in an ongoing story where decision and action were believed to have dependable results. Choices had appropriate consequences. The eschatological element in the allegorical interpretation of the parables served to insure this dependability amid the risk and confusion of life, and thereby better identify the place of the hearer.

In shifting from the allegorical interpretation of the parables to the ethical interpretation, the name of Adolf Jülicher, whose interpretation of the parable of the Good-Samaritan will be examined, is important. It should be noted that the turn away from allegory was not purely the result of studies of literary form such as those of Jülicher; this turn was already underway in other writers of the time, even as the faith in a coherent world interpreted by the Christian story was receding. Jülicher made clear on literary grounds what was already coming to be sensed by readers with less exact knowledge of literary style. Thus while the decline of allegorical interpretation was associated with the rise of literary analysis, crucial also was the collapse of the traditional Christian vision of which allegory was the vehicle. For Jülicher, as for many in that period, the replacement for the older Christian story was a strong confidence in the absoluteness of moral claims.

As for the Good Samaritan, our chosen example, Jülicher brushed aside all the elaborate churchly and doctrinal elements which figurative and other allegorical interpreters had seen in it. For him, the parable was an example story or illustration—an illustration precisely of how to act. Indeed, it was Jülicher who brought this parable, along with three others in Luke, into this category and made the classification current in New Testament interpretation. The distinction, still drawn, is that a parable is a metaphor which offers an analogy of how one should respond—the Kingdom is like a treasure hidden in a field, which a man found, for instance. The example story or illustration is not metaphorical but directly supplies an example of how to act, which one is to follow literally.

Jülicher described allegory as improper (*uneigentlich*) speech that did not say what it meant and contrasted it with the proper (*eigentlich*) speech of the actual parables, which meant what they said and not something else.[2] He summed up his view of the Good Samaritan in this way: the parable (or, more properly, example story) was genuinely from Jesus, but setting it in the framework of the question about "who is my neighbor" was Luke's work. Removed from Luke's setting, the meaning is: "the self-sacrificing exercise of love creates the highest value in the eyes of both God and humans, and no position of advantage of office or birth can substitute for it. The merciful person, even if a Samaritan, deserves salvation rather than the Jewish temple official who is the slave of egotism (cf. Rom 2:14ff)."[3] If this sounds a bit bare and general, Jülicher was well aware of how much more directly the story said it. But general principles impressed Jülicher. Of example stories as a class he concluded: "they illustrate a religious idea in its inescapable universal validity, in the form of an especially favorable chosen example."[4]

In his opposition to allegory, Jülicher developed the well-known "one-point" interpretation of the parable. He insisted that there is in a parable only one legitimate comparison to be drawn between the story and the intended religious application. Later interpreters have been favorable to this emphasis until recent times when scholars have once more begun to examine the many-sidedness of the symbolic language of the parables.[5] But long before wide criticism of the one-point theory, several writers on the parables criticized Jülicher for his plan of looking—as he did regularly, and as the illustration has shown—for a general moral or religious truth as the one point of a parable.[6] Many readers of the parables felt that something more than general truth was intended. Probably part of the criticism of Jülicher on this point arose from the correct perception that his interpretation of the parables involved a marked shift from the "indicative" setting of the hearer in a coherent world to the "imperative" of a general truth that tells people what they should do.

If it is correct to qualify Jülicher's position so as to find more than general truths in the parables, and to deny that a dramatic narrative can ever be successfully reduced to a static proposition, why was such a keen and able critic as Jülicher so well satisfied with this way of listening to the parables? Two aspects of his approach help us understand the appeal of his position.

In the first place, Jülicher was engaged in establishing a less christological interpretation of the parables. The example here showed how, in allegorical interpretation, the parable easily became the vehicle for a message about the Christ. Jülicher discerned that the christological affirmations of most of the parables were minimal if not altogether lacking. The parables, he saw, spoke to the human without making christological claims as such. Jülicher attempted to release the parables from a dogmatic rigidity by substituting a moral claim for a christological claim.

Jülicher was right in his effort to release the parables from christological exclusiveness, both historically and, we may venture to judge, in terms of the theological situation to which he spoke. Despite various attempts made since his time to reaffirm an explicit christological claim in the parables, those who interpret them today say, like Jülicher, that the language of the parables is not the only bearer of the reality to which it testifies. At the same time, the relation between the "message of Jesus" with its possible indirect christology and the "message about Jesus" is only indicated and not resolved by this insight.

A second aspect of Jülicher's view must be noted: general principles may not be very impressive to us, but they were to him and to many in his time. Cited above was Jülicher's phrase, "a religious idea in its inescapable universal validity." For the listeners of his time, the Kantian assertion of the absoluteness of the ethical demand, and its presence as an avenue of access to the ultimate, to God, still held power. If the move from the cosmos of the allegorical interpretation to the general moral truths of Jülicher reflected a shrinking world, a further shrinking is signaled in moving to the contemporary scene in which it is difficult to apprehend the seriousness of the universal moral or religious claim as Jülicher and many of his time perceived it. In his time there was still a sense in which a "moral truth" or "religious truth" embodied an indicative element. It was a statement about how things are as well as imperative. This aspect of Jülicher's hearing of the parables, which may easily be missed by readers today, made them exciting to the hearers of his time.

In coming to the existential interpretation, a type of reading of the parables which is still current and vital is encountered. In this view, the listener is not in a structured world of moral claims, but in a world which is simply given, without any inherent meaningful structure. There are, indeed, structures of existence that recur, but these structures of existence only offer the field within which meaning is found in the act of decision.

Such a view strongly emphasizes the "imperative" over against the "indicative." Responding to the parable means risk and decision. Decision is taken with neither the sense of a surrounding dependable world assumed by the allegorical interpretation nor even the support of the "inescapable universal validity" of a religious (or moral) idea.

Rudolf Bultmann is the scholar many remember as at the center of existential interpretation. The "imperative" of the call to response was absolutely central to Bultmann, particularly from his interpretation of the parables. He looked elsewhere in the New Testament, especially to Paul and John, for a clear statement of that which is prior to the imperative, the indicative of grace. Following an old Lutheran theme, Bultmann considered the Gospels in general and the parables in particular too close to the imperative of law to be a firm base for the gospel.

Bultmann's interpretation has the great strength of moving away from Jülicher's notion of general truths toward a powerful focus on the confrontation of the individual and the actual concrete moment of existence. The moment which real listening to the parable evokes is a unique moment on which rests the weight of the hearer's destiny.

This powerful insight is gained at the cost of virtually eliminating the sense of drama in life, the fateful movement of life through a series of events which successively shape the possibilities that follow. To Bultmann such a dramatic vision of existence threatened the wholeness of the confrontation of the moment. To picture life as a process tending in a certain direction deprives the moment of its unique weight, and gives the person making the decision some leverage and control against the moment that, rightly, requires a total commitment. The root of this tension between dramatic sequence and existential moment lay in Bultmann's interpretation of sequences as what he thought of as natural events, cause-and-effect sequences. He did not think that one could participate in ongoing life "dramatically," but only in the moment, "existentially." The consequence of this judgment is particularly clear in his treatment of eschatology. He rejected any image of hope for future fulfillment because he believed that any vision of fulfillment would give the believer a leverage with which to manipulate the moment instead of giving oneself wholeheartedly to it.

Bultmann commented only briefly on the parable of the Good Samaritan. He followed Jülicher in taking it as an example story or illustration. He went so far as to say that these example stories "have no figurative element at all."[7] Like Jülicher he thought that the parable had been put in its present setting by Luke and that the point of the parable was the contrast (addressed to Jews) between the unloving Jews and the loving Samaritan. He saw the parable as a polemic against any notion of ethnic superiority. About this general point he said: "the Jew as such has no claim before God. Consistently with this Jesus proclaims a call to decision and repentance. Consistently, too, Jesus can elsewhere picture a Samaritan as putting the true Jew to shame (Luke 10:29-37)."[8] More specifically Bultmann interpreted the parable of the Good Samaritan as follows: "Such a man, who in contrast to those learned in the Law really understands what is demanded of him in the given situation, is depicted in the story of the good Samaritan. Luke reports it, pertinently for content if somewhat awkwardly from the point of view of style, as told by Jesus in answer to the evasive question "Who is my neighbor?"[9]

Bultmann wrote these words more than fifty years ago. In the meantime, a host of very good books on the parables have been published. To my mind, the key works were those of C. H. Dodd and Joachim Jeremias.[10] Focusing on the question of the relation of the parables to Jesus' action and message as a whole, both perceived that the parables offered the best avenue in the quest for the historical Jesus. Time has confirmed their judgment in this respect: nearly all the serious subsequent efforts to speak of the intention of Jesus concentrate on the parables. It is tempting to explore all the numerous solid interpretations of the parables that have been offered, but this is not possible.

Instead, a survey of the current development in interpretation, in which there is a strong concentration on language and its effects, will be undertaken. The linguistic interpretation will be discussed as a mode that succeeds the existential approach, even though many components of the existential interpretation are being carried forward into the various types of linguistic interpretation. To avoid the narrowness of the term "linguistic," perhaps one should speak of a period of "literary and linguistic" interpretation. Varied as the studies are, they include an effort to pay close attention to how language works, to how it achieves its effects, and to how the parables can be set more fully in the context of recent studies of language. These include a variety of emphases such as the concern for literary analysis by some American critics, continuing linguistic analysis, and the contributions of French structuralism.

As samples, contributions by John Dominic Crossan and Robert W. Funk will be considered. This choice means passing over other equally important work such as that of Dan O. Via, Jr. and Daniel Patte,[11] but the choice of Funk and Crossan serves well to relate the recent mode of parable interpretation to the earlier styles sketched above.

As noted, both Jülicher and Bultmann were keen students of the form of the parables. Neither of them, however, saw any problem in the notion that along with metaphorical parables like the Sower or the Hidden Treasure, there should be among the parables of Jesus also illustrations or example stories like the Good Samaritan in which the point is made not metaphorically but directly. Some of the linguistic interpreters have questioned this assumption and have argued that the parable is by its nature metaphorical; therefore there are no example stories among the parables of Jesus. Thus, to hear the story of the Good Samaritan as it was meant to be heard, it must be heard as a metaphor, a true parable, and not as an example of proper behavior.

Both Crossan and Funk agree in this judgment. Crossan studied this parable and all the "example stories" or illustrations, and concluded that the Good Samaritan was not, as originally told by Jesus, an example of behavior to be followed at all (even though, of course, Luke understood it in that way). Rather, he concluded, it was a parable and must have a metaphorical point. Crossan followed most interpreters in saying that the point of the story was bound up with the unexpected goodness of the Samaritan. He summarized: "The original parabolic point was the reversal caused by the advent of the Kingdom in and through the challenge to utter the unutterable and to admit thereby that other world which was at that very moment placing their own under radical judgement."[12]

Crossan's analysis of the force of the language of the parable was based on the critical judgment that the church and the Gospel writers did not understand the original radical force of the parables. Instead, they tamed them, making them less extreme and more bearable—in this case converting an authentic parable about a surprising manifestation of goodness into a mere example of good behavior. Jülicher and Bultmann had already held that Luke modified the parable. Crossan was thus not following a new course. But he rigorously separated the Gospel of Luke's version of the parable from the original version of Jesus with the assumption that the uniform tendency of the Gospel writers was to take the edge off Jesus' parables, to domesticate them, so to speak, in the church.

Such a view enabled Crossan to maintain that the parables, as Jesus used them, were not only metaphorical, but that they had the specific metaphorical function of leading to the point where the hearer's vision of the world is shattered.

The world in which the hearer lives must be broken for the hearer to have the possibility, the momentary opportunity, to glimpse the ultimate, the mystery of God. Crossan described this basic process of coming to insight in the following way: the seeming naturalness of a parable compels a hearer's assent and leads into involvement in the story, only then to shock the hearer with the discovery that to give assent to the story necessitates abandoning the vision of the world the hearer originally brought to the event. Radical judgment and the possibility of redemption can suddenly but momentarily be glimpsed.

This historical analysis behind this way of listening to the Good Samaritan is basically the same as Jülicher's. Crossan separated the parable from the framework in which Luke had set it and made some acute observations about how the points of emphasis were to be located in the parable. At bottom, however, he simply listened to it differently from Jülicher, being convinced that a parable must be surprising metaphor and not merely an example of something good.

Robert W. Funk's analysis of the Good Samaritan arrived at much the same result as Crossan's although he worked out the details differently.[13] Funk, as Crossan, considered the parable of the Good Samaritan metaphorical and not an example story. His approach to understanding the metaphor has a very simple—and important—basis: with whom, asked Funk, is the listener to identify? His answer: not with the Samaritan, but with the man who is lying in the ditch. The question is not "Can I be a Samaritan?" but "Am I willing to let myself be served by a Samaritan?" Thus the parable tells a story of a person at the end of the rope; all who are truly victims, truly disinherited, have no choice but to give themselves up to mercy. If the hearer, concluded Funk, as Jew, understands what it means to be the victim in the ditch in this story, the hearer also understands what the Kingdom is. The meaning of the parable cannot be made more explicit, because it is nonliteral; it lacks specific application. In this, Funk has rejected Jülicher's interpretation of the parables as expressing general truths. About parables generally, Funk wrote,

The parable does not, therefore, involve a transfer of information or ideas about an established world from one head to another. In this parable reality is aborning; the parable opens onto an unfinished world because that world is in course of conception. This means that both narrator and auditor *risk* the parable; they both participate the narrative and venture its outcome. He or they do not tell the story; it *tells* them.[14]

Funk's simple but important point that one great clue to the meaning of a narrative lies in asking how an individual identifies with the characters is extremely helpful in clarifying how people hear the parables. The point of the story is missed if one does not or cannot identify with the man in the ditch. It is equally clear to me, however, that one is also to identify with the Samaritan. Why limit identification to only one character in the story? Funk believes that in any hearing of the story one makes a primary identification with one character who is taken to give the central perspective. Part of the richness of the narrative form itself, however, is that it invites multiple perspectives: what is it like to be the man in the ditch, the Samaritan, the priest or Levite? From any of these identifications proceeds a primary hearing of the story. The same is true of the central Christian story, the story of the crucifixion; a study of various liturgies and theologies would show the force of hearing the story in terms of various primary identifications with the different characters in the narrative.

Funk's emphasis on hearing the parable of the Good Samaritan through an identification with the man lying in the ditch ironically brings us full circle back to Augustine's allegorical interpretation which had the same thrust; this despite Funk's vigorous rejection of allegory.[15] Both interpretations have in common the primary emphasis on "indicative," on the surprise of grace that comes into the situation before one expects it and in a way not anticipated. The other obvious identification, with the Samaritan, naturally puts the emphasis on "imperative," explicit in Luke's interpretation: go and do the same thing yourself.

There is, of course, a difference between Augustine and Funk. From the allegorical interpretation through the ethical and existential to the linguistic, can be seen a progressive "loss of world," a progressive loss of the sense of a coherent environment within which the receptiveness of faith and the act of decision were understood to take place. The allegorists knew that the world was created by God and redeemed by Christ, and within this context they heard the parable. Those who employed the ethical interpretation had lost much of this sense of stability, but they still had a world of dependable moral principles. The existentialists saw the world as constituted only by the act of repeated, individual decision. The linguistic interpreters whose works have been sketched

here are still largely existentialists in their theological approach to
the parables; if there is a shift, it is toward an even stronger
negativity toward structure, toward the notion of a world on which
one can depend, as a vehicle for the ultimate.

What is surely inherent in this history of interpretation, this
history of reduction of world, is the sharp challenge to cultural
security confronting the church. The parables are shocking,
disconcerting, to those who are at home in their world in the sense
of the given cultural structures. But there is a difference between
the shattering of cultural security and what I call a "reduction of
world." For the shrinking world which the more recent interpreters offer as the context within which one listens to the parable
is a world in which neither the "other" in the sense of the neighbor
nor the "Other" as God is visible. All the more necessary and
challenging is the need to listen yet more attentively to the
parables, to rediscover an authentic wider context, a framework of
interaction between humans and God, a world hidden within or
behind the way the parables are heard.

Simple as they are, the parables nonetheless are rich and complex
enough to speak powerfully through a whole series of sharply
different interpretations. To think that we can discard these earlier
views to find at last the one true interpretation would be foolish.
Instead, I raise some questions and make some suggestions toward
a more comprehensive interpretation.

In the first place, as a more language-oriented interpretation of
the parables is developed, it is important to reexamine the presuppositions that we bring to the analysis of language. In my view,
linguistic analysis is much more neutral, and not necessarily
freighted with the existentialist, Heideggerian views that Crossan
and Funk have joined to it. To put it more positively: the Heideggerian vision of the poetic creation of the world through language is
a powerful general framework for approaching the detailed
linguistic analysis of religious speech, in this case the parable. But
the very concentration on language as world-creating event may
close the interpreter to other dimensions of the actual events which
take place in hearing the parable, notably the interchange between
language and the constraints imposed by non-linguistic reality.

If the act of listening is thought of as a part of the repeated act of
self-creation, and especially as a response to the text which arouses
in us a bundle of concrete possibilities or proposals, possibilities
which are suggested by the text as related to the tradition in which
the text is heard, a model emerges which allows us to take seriously
a variety of readings of the text and to develop a framework for
evaluating and relating the various possibilities. Putting the

emphasis on the reader's or hearer's act of self-creation allows us to leave a place for the full work of figurative analysis, but reminds us that the linguistic effect is in interaction with a host of non-linguistic factors. Above all, by positing an element of freedom in each act of self-creation, however routine and repetitive most such moments may be, the harsh break between scientific analysis, conceived as casually determined, and humanistic analysis, which strives to avoid determinism, can be avoided. Further, since the concrete possibilities suggested by a text are combinations of subjects abstracted from previous experience with hypothetical predicates, this model provides a fruitful way of relating the empirical and the imaginative.

Such a model sees that historical reconstruction, important as it is, is a special, abstract kind of listening. The emphasis is on the present quest for meaning. The reason for listening to a text is that it may open possibilities for the listener, possibilities which have not yet been experienced or which need to be recalled and reexperienced.

The sensitive insights of the schools of interpretation sketched here are invaluable. Each successive type of interpretation has brought forth a valid and authentic way of hearing the parables. Yet one cannot fail to see that each type was able to make available from the parables an interpretation that was already congenial within the acknowledged possibilities of that culture. Serious listening to a scriptural or other important text must take place within contemporary culture, but one hopes that the culture will not decide in advance what can be heard in the text. The reason for listening to such texts is that they may renew a vision of what is possible, re-structure the vision of the culture. The Whiteheadian or process model here suggested as a mode of interpretation does not, I believe, impose a process reading on the parables, but, on the contrary, has the capacity to be more open to the unexpected, the culturally rejected, possibilities that may be heard in the text.

For instance, the gains in understanding in the positions sketched above have been won at the price of a progressive loss of an element which did not seem valid to the cultures which shaped the readings, namely, the sense of a coherent world as a field for human solidarity. This becomes even more striking as one moves from the earlier to the later readings.[16] The more open model for listening suggested here could bring this element back for serious consideration.

We move from a proposal about how to think of the process of interpretation to a proposal about the theological content. Funk's emphatic rejection of allegory, noted above, has its center in a point well illustrated by the particular parable we have been studying: he has argued that allegory must be rejected because it tends to transform the parables into stories about God. This position reflects a modern view that the realm of speech is the human realm and that God is beyond speech. To me this does not sound like Jesus and the Gospels. At the same time I see the very good reasons for the move Funk made. The God of whom he was afraid is the God allegorically represented by the authoritative figures in the parables, particularly the father who appears in a number of them (though, of course, not here). Such a God is a threat to human freedom. To learn both from the New Testament and from process theology to grasp a different view of God—God as the persuader rather than as the absolute ruler—opens the way for a more comprehensive theory of metaphor in which metaphors can really point to God and tell us something about God's reality.

Some of the most imaginative New Testament interpreters, and Funk and Crossan are among them, have been so strongly taken with the poetic, metaphorical character of language that they have given up the possibility of speaking non-metaphorically about the substance of the parable. Funk has argued that a specific meaning cannot be given to the parable of the Good Samaritan. Such an insistence on the total irreducibility of metaphor, however, must be rejected. True, symbolic language has a richness that can never be reduced to propositional statements (using the term propositional in its usual sense). Yet the interchange between dense, symbolic speech and carefully constructed abstract speech has long been a principal way of enlarging our world and of testing the vision of faith for its coherence with the whole of our experience. The task of enlarging our vision of the world by keeping these two forms of speech in dialogue with each other is still crucial.

The parable of the Good Samaritan is a fine illustration of the problem. Bultmann said it had "no figurative element at all," since it was an example story.[17] Crossan and Funk tried to identify it as something other than an example story, so that it might have a figurative element. Would it not be wiser to say that, even as an example story, the Good Samaritan does indeed have a powerful figurative, symbolic element, calling up the world of risk and of love, throwing open the unfinished and unlimited nature of the claim which living together in a social world lays upon us? Even though God is not figured at all in this story, God's love is in the background, the ambience of the world depicted by the story. While true parables have a much stronger metaphorical element, we have been misled, from Jülicher onward, in thinking that example stories are non-metaphorical. Funk rightly saw that "Christian" benevolent righteousness easily becomes self-righteousness. He did well to point out that only the person who is able to accept is really able to give. This is no new point, of course; recall Deut 5:15: "You shall remember that you were a servant in the land of Egypt." But is this the exclusive point of the story? Dan O. Via, Jr., who argued that there really are example stories among the parables of Jesus, has much the better of it.[18] What becomes clear is that the hearer who listens attentively and struggles with the parables can hear it both ways.

This leads to a further point. Is it really true, as Funk says, that the truly disinherited have no choice but to give themselves up to mercy? I do not hear the outsiders from society speaking this way in North American Black theology or in Latin American theology of liberation. The disinherited find in listening to the parables a dignity and hope which enable them to act![19] It is true that the message of Jesus as set forth in the parable of the Good Samaritan calls for a very difficult kind of action, that of putting oneself in the place of the other, which is often very difficult to hear in times of conflict. But one of the reasons for the deep power of this story is its effectiveness both at the level of receptivity and at the level of the call to action. As such it fully represents the complexity of the interplay between the divine and the human as represented throughout the Gospels.

So far we have not explicitly touched on the question, whether the parables can be taken "just as they are in themselves," or how far they require a setting in the message of the Gospels as a whole for full understanding. Such a question, if really pursued, would lead again to the question of christology: how or to what extent do the parables require the figure of Christ? Here we can only indicate some directions for the exploration of this question. Surely it is the case that there is no escape from the interpretive circle between the concrete text and the larger context. The larger context does not have to be that of the Gospels; the parables of Jesus can, for instance, be set in the context of a modern collection of parables such as that edited by Howard Schwartz.[20] If so, the impact on interpretation is to highlight the reading of the parables of Jesus in terms of multiple perspectives and ambiguous meanings. Most New Testament interpreters would probably defend the "Jesus" context as the proper one for listening to the parables for historical reasons. Jesus' message of the Kingdom of God and his action on behalf of the Kingdom were the context that, so to speak, provoked the parables. The approach suggested here also favors testing a spontaneous reading of the parables against the best understanding of their original function, not simply to give priority to the first meaning, but because the New Testament setting has repeatedly shown its paradigmatic power and its ability to renew the vision of a later age. Thus, though the parables say little directly, or even indirectly, about their speaker, our understanding of them and response to them is clarified and deepened as the world they evoke is related to the world evoked by Jesus' other words and actions. If this context is problematic, so much so that some interpreters allow little beyond the parables to guide us about Jesus, nevertheless a reader of the New Testament will hear the parables in this context and try to establish it as adequately as possible.

Recent writers, many of whom have followed the same line as Crossan and Funk, have heard the parables primarily as "indicative" rather than "imperative." They have done so precisely for the reason that the finding of a place, the vision of a world in which we can place ourselves, has become so problematical in our time. Approaching the matter through the hermeneutic of a vision of language creating a fragile, temporary place for the human, they have in fact been questing in the depths of the "primal" insights that lie buried behind the rigid and concealing structures built through the centuries by Western culture including Christian theology. Their quest for liberation from the rigidity of traditional forms has taken place through a discarding of baggage, a simplifying, precisely a reduction of world, in the faith that the minimal and transitory world revealed by the shock of recognition of the parable will be truer than the much more visible forms offered by tradition. Not all, but many of the sharply defined linguistic studies operate from a faith similar to this.

That such a stance is liberating can be seen from the widespread resonance that it evokes. I do not follow a different path in order to adhere more fixedly to tradition, but because I find that recourse to the "primal," the pre-rational and pre-cultural resources of the spirit, does not fully release the movement toward hope and the new. The aim is to work toward an interpretive stance which is more consciously open toward the emerging new word and not only to that which is in the depths of the spirit and prior to cultural formulation. Such a quest is more fully in touch with the future-oriented renewing power that shows itself in the New Testament. I do not, in addition, share the negative view of a structured world that is presupposed by so many recent interpreters. Seeing that for all the weight of the past, the present does always embody momentary elements of freedom to reshape and reuse the past, one may believe that the most creative stance is not that of searching back for the primal reality, but the stance of hope, of sensitizing oneselves to the world that may come to be. Such a stance will find it natural to value positively both the receptiveness that discovers or allows the world to be broken and remade in the vision of faith and the human activity without which hope cannot be realized. Such a stance should be a productive one for listening to the parables, and one that may allow them to be foundational in the vision of the world that is coming to be. In this sense Funk is correct that "reality is aborning" in listening to the parables. The goal is how to discover a listening which can effect a connection between the moments of experience such that action and hope may result from listening. In the specific case of the parable of the Good Samaritan, as noted above, such a stance listens attentively to what it says about human solidarity.[21]

NOTES

1. Augustine, *Quaestiones Evangeliorum,* II, 19, as cited and abridged by C. H. Dodd, *The Parables of the Kingdom,* 3d ed (New York: Charles Scribner's Sons, 1936) 11-12.
2. Adolf Jülicher, *Die Gleichnisreden Jesu* (Leipzig: J. C. B. Mohr, 1899), I, 49.
3. *Ibid.,* II, 596.
4. *Ibid.,* 585.
5. John Dominic Crossan, *In Parables: The Challenge of the Historical Jesus* (New York: Harper & Row, 1973); Norman Perrin, *Jesus and the Language of the Kingdom: Symbol and Metaphor in New Testament Interpretation* (London: SCM Press, 1976); Dan O. Via, Jr., *The Parables: Their Literary and Existential Dimension* (Philadelphia: Fortress, 1967); cf. the articles in John Dominic Crossan, ed *Semeia 9: Polyvalent Narration* (1977).
6. Dodd, *Parables,* 24-25; Joachim Jeremias, *The Parables of Jesus,* trans S. H. Hooke; rev ed (New York: Charles Scribner's Sons, 1964; German 6th ed 1962) 18-19.
7. Rudolf Bultmann, *The History of the Synoptic Tradition,* trans John Marsh (New York: Harper & Row, 1963; German 3d ed 1958) 178.
8. Rudolf Bultmann, *Jesus and the Word,* trans Louise Pettibone Smith and Erminie Huntress Lantero (New York: Charles Scribner's Sons, 1958; German 1926) 45.
9. *Ibid.,* 96.
10. Dodd, *Parables;* Jeremias, *Parables.*
11. Via, *The Parables;* Daniel Patte, *Semiology and Parables: Exploration of the Possibilities Offered by Structuralism for Exegesis* (Pittsburgh: Pickwick, 1976).
12. Crossan, *In Parables,* 66.
13. Robert W. Funk, "The Good Samaritan as Metaphor," *Semeia* 2 (1974) 74-81.
14. *Ibid.,* 76.
15. Robert W. Funk, *Language, Hermeneutic, and Word of God* (New York: Harper & Row, 1966) 214, n 67: "It is for this reason that the parables should not be allegorized (allegory: reduction to a congeries of ideas or concepts, for which the narrative elements are ciphers), but it is also

the reason why the parables cannot be reduced to a leading idea...or understood to teach 'spiritual truths.' Rationalization in any form maims the parabolic image."

16. The sense of social responsibility in the parables is emphasized by Charles E. Carlston, *The Parables of the Triple Tradition* (Philadelphia: Fortress, 1975).

17. See note 7.

18. Dan O. Via, Jr., "Parable and Example Story: A Literary-Structural Approach," *Semeia* 1 (1974) 105-33.

19. See James H. Cone, *A Black Theology of Liberation* (Philadelphia: Lippincott, 1970) 222; José Porfirio Miranda, *Marx and the Bible: A Critique of the Philosophy of Oppression,* trans John Eagleson (Maryknoll, New York: Orbis, 1974) 70.

20. Howard Schwartz, *Imperial Messages: One Hundred Modern Parables* (New York: Avon, 1976).

21. My exploration of the possibilities of process thought for biblical interpretation has been greatly stimulated and clarified by taking part in a discussion group at Claremont, California in the Spring of 1977, the members of which were John B. Cobb, Jr., David J. Lull, Russell Pregeant, Theodore J. Weeden, Sr., and Barry A. Woodbridge. For a survey of work relating process thought to biblical studies, see John B. Cobb, Jr., with David J. Lull and Barry A. Woodbridge, "Process Thought and New Testament Exegesis," *Journal of the American Academy of Religion* 47 (1979) 21-30.

Peter and Paul:
A Constitutive Relationship
for Catholic Christianity

William R. Farmer

Ever since the days of Ferdinand Christian Baur, students of church history have been particularly conscious of an unresolved question. What was the relationship between Peter and Paul? Baur wanted to prove that the impression of apostolic harmony and cooperation left by the New Testament upon the minds of its readers was unhistorical.[1]. To a considerable degree he succeeded. Baur's method was to attack the credibility of Acts, just as his younger associate, David Frederick Strauss, attacked the credibility of the Gospels.[2]

Taken together the combined effect of the work of Strauss and Baur was devastating. The reaction was certain and lethal. By common agreement between church and state, no student of Baur was allowed to succeed him and the short-term fate of the Tübingen school was sealed.

In spite of the reaction against Baur, however, many of the critical results of the Tübingen school have stood the test of time. Often without proper acknowledgment, Baur's views have been adopted unobtrusively into the mainstream of twentieth-century criticism. Slowly but surely, in less radical ways, the historical critical approach pursued by Baur and his associates has won its way.

Was Baur right in leaving the impression that in place of apostolic agreement and harmony the early church was characterized by its

---

This essay was prepared for the McMaster University research project on Normative Self-Definition in Judaism and Christianity, a project supported by the Social Sciences and Humanities Research Council of Canada.

exact opposite: apostolic conflict and strife? Granting that Baur was basically correct in his recognition that the special tendencies of Acts undercut any attempt to base church history primarily or uncritically upon this account of Christian beginnings, did he do justice to the New Testament evidence as a whole and in depth? I think not. While assuming for the purpose of this essay Baur's view that Acts is a secondary source written a generation or more after Paul wrote his letters, I propose to set forth in terms faithful to Baur's historical method an argument for the view that beneath and behind and surrounding the party strife in Corinth and the open conflict between Peter and Paul in Antioch was a fundamental theological understanding and agreement shared by these apostles that made cooperation between them possible despite whatever may have led them to oppose or disagree with one another.[3] In so doing, I propose to accept Paul's letters as the primary source materials available for understanding not only his thought, but also his life.[4] I also propose to accept the text of Paul's letters, especially the text of Galatians 1-2 as it has been preserved.[5]

After a period of preaching the faith he had once ravaged, Paul went to Jerusalem to visit Peter. This visit lasted fifteen days and except for James the brother of Jesus, Paul did not see any of the other apostles (Gal 1:18-20). Fourteen years later Paul went up to Jerusalem for another visit. The purpose of this visit was to lay before those who preceded him as apostles the gospel he had been preaching during the intervening years: lest he run or had run in vain (Gal 2:1-2). Present on this occasion were Peter, James, and John, whom many perceived to be pillars of the church. Now, however, primarily in the light of the success of Paul's evangelistic efforts among the Gentiles, the need for a new organizational structure was recognized, and the practical result of the meeting was a decision to reorganize the evangelistic efforts of the church Paul had once persecuted. Those evangelistic efforts were to be formally divided, with Peter, James and John to head the mission to the circumcized and Paul and Barnabas to head the mission to the uncircumcized (Gal 2:7-9).[6] Thus, within seventeen years Paul had risen from the status of only one of many to whom Jesus had appeared to a place of co-equality with the person to whom Jesus *first* appeared, a person who had been a close disciple of Jesus and was recognized as holding membership in a triumvirate within the apostolic council in Jerusalem. This was an astonishing achievement. Just as Paul had once risen above many of his own age within Judaism so zealous was he for the traditions of the fathers (Gal 1:13-14), so, after his conversion, over a period of time, Paul rose to a corresponding place of preeminence among those engaged in the mission to the Gentiles. He obtained the recognition he sought for the gospel he preached. The desired understanding was formally sealed. The Jerusalem apostles gave to Paul and to his close associate Barnabas the right hand of fellowship.

How was this astonishing achievement accomplished? Was it merely a well-deserved reward for fourteen years of successful work in Asia Minor and Greece? Hardly! The full success of this work was itself a cause of concern which necessitated Paul's trip to Jerusalem.

Indeed, consider for a moment the achievement of arranging the conference in the first place. There can be little doubt that in certain quarters in Jerusalem there was opposition to any agreement to meet with Paul. For the very agreement to meet with him accorded him recognition that made it more difficult for his enemies to thwart him. There is evidence that people suspicious of the gospel Paul preached were surreptitiously brought into the conference room (Gal 2:4-5). This is a clear sign of the tensions that were created in some circles by the decision of the "pillars of the church" to meet with Paul.

How then was this meeting arranged? In the final analysis it appears to me that the only person Paul could have counted on to arrange for James and John to be in Jerusalem at an agreed-upon time and to agree to take part in the discussions of his gospel and to participate in the far-reaching decisions that needed to be made was Peter. Important conferences seldom are easily set up. This is especially true when great distances and important personalities are involved. All principals have their own private schedules and agendas that must be adjusted and coordinated if a meeting is to take place. Someone must want the meeting and must be able to persuade one or more of the others of the importance of the meeting.

It is conceivable that James or others in Jerusalem wanted the meeting and that Paul was, so to speak, being summoned to headquarters. Paul explicitly rules out this possibility. He went up to Jerusalem guided by God (Gal 2:2). The initiative in the first instance had not come from man. The conference, as Paul perceived it, was desired by God. But in human terms, through whom did God initiate the request for the conference? If it had come to Paul from Peter or anyone else in Jerusalem, how could Paul have been so certain that it had not originated with man? If God had originated the conference through a request for the conference made by Paul, then Paul would have had an immediate awareness of the origin of the conference in God's purpose as that divine purpose had been made known to him. It appears, then, that it was Paul, prompted by his belief that it was in accord with the purpose of God, who requested the meeting and was able to justify the need for it.

Paul's purpose in going to Jerusalem was to defend the gospel he preached. This gospel of Jesus Christ, or gospel of God as Paul sometimes called it (Rom 1:1; 2 Cor 11:7; 1 Thess 2:8), is the gospel which eventually was adopted in various modified forms (e.g., Matthew, Mark, Luke, John, Acts, Ephesians, I Peter, etc.) as the gospel of the Christian church. That is, competing gospels, especially those requiring circumcision, eventually were discarded or withered away. How then was it possible for Paul's gospel to win the day in a church which once tolerated opposition to it?

The evidence that persons opposed to Paul's gospel were let into the meeting in Jerusalem must not be forgotten. Later, when the circumcision party from James arrived in Antioch,[7] Peter, who had been led by his recognition of the validity of the gospel Paul preached (a gospel which justified both Jews and Gentiles by faith and not by works of the law) to take up the practice of eating with Gentile Christians, i.e., uncircumcized Christians, withdrew from table-fellowship with Gentile Christians, *out of fear of the circumcision party* (Gal 2:11-13). So there certainly was a time when opposition to Paul's gospel, or what is tantamount to the same, opposition to some of the practical consequences of that gospel, was tolerated in the church. When Peter and the rest of the Jewish Christians who had joined in the table-fellowship with the Gentile Christians withdrew from that fellowship, and when even Barnabas was carried away with this dissimulation, Paul was deeply conscious of the peril in which he and the gospel he preached stood (Gal 2:14-16). Another gospel, which might not in his eyes be a gospel at all, but nonetheless was an understanding of the faith opposed to Paul's gospel, was certainly being tolerated when all this happened.

That Paul's gospel won the day is certain in that Paul's letters (including Galatians with Paul's account of the Antioch incident) were given great prominence in the church's Canon. The question remains: how?

It is clear from what Paul wrote in recollecting the incident involving Peter at Antioch that the question at issue was not theological *per se*, but concerned actions that were inconsistent with an agreed-upon theology. To be specific, Paul won out in part because he was able to pinpoint and expose the inconsistency of Peter's withdrawal from a table-fellowship Peter had formerly endorsed with his presence and by arguing that it was the former practice of eating with Gentiles that was called for by the gospel. By withdrawing, Peter was denying the truth of that gospel and was making the death of Christ of no avail. It is apparent from the way Paul argued that both he and Peter understood the basic premise of the gospel, i.e., that both Jews and Gentiles are justified by their faith in Jesus Christ. Paul succeeded partly by exposing Peter's hypocrisy and demonstrating that Peter's actions were contradictory to a fundamental theological tenet shared by Peter and Paul.

When was this theological agreement reached and what was its import? It appears to have been reached prior to the conference with the apostles at Jerusalem, because that conference itself presupposed that someone besides Paul and his close associates, i.e., Barnabas and Titus, understood and was willing to endorse the fundamental theological position from which Paul worked. Who could that person have been but Peter? This is a rhetorical question, but it is one that proceeds from a factual basis. There is no evidence concerning either John or James that would lead us to think that either of them knew Paul well enough to open the door to such a high level conference. Paul did not even see John when he was in Jerusalem during his fifteen-day visit with Peter (Gal 1:19). He did see James (Gal 1:19), but in view of the ensuing difficulty at Antioch occasioned by the coming of the circumcision party from James (Gal 2:12), it seems unlikely that James was the one most likely to have taken the initiative in contacting the others. It seems intrinsically more probable that since Peter was the one Paul mainly went to see during his fifteen-day visit (Gal 1:18), Peter therefore was also the one who knew Paul's intentions best and so was in the best position to consider the merits of a conference with Paul.

Barnabas and other associates of Paul may have played some intermediary role in preparing the way for this conference, but in the final analysis it probably was Paul's effective contact with Peter that was most helpful. Yet it is not enough to think that Peter was only mildly agreeable to the meeting. Paul would have needed his active support, for it is questionable whether Paul had the power simply by himself to open doors at the highest levels of Christian leadership in Jerusalem. Someone at or near the summit needed to assist him, and Peter seems Paul's most likely ally at that level.

Now we may appreciate as perhaps never before the import of Paul's fifteen-day visit with Peter in Jerusalem three years after his conversion. I conjecture that an apostolic concurrence between Peter and Paul over the fundamental faith upon which the Christian church rested emerged during that fifteen-day stay. This faith was not to be identified with either Peter *or* Paul but rather with Peter *and* Paul, inclusive of both, neither limited to nor absolutely identical with either.

Paul acknowledged that he also met with James, who may well have been involved to some extent in the discussions with Peter (Gal 1:19). Since Paul made it clear that Peter was the primary person he went to visit, it seems to me that James probably entered the picture at Peter's initiative. In view of subsequent events (Gal 2:12), it may be doubted that James ever really understood or fully agreed with Paul. Nonetheless Peter probably did his best as a supporter of Paul to gain the cooperation and acceptance of the Jerusalem church for Paul's mission.

There is no way to know what the apostles discussed in detail. A number of matters appear likely, however. The matter of Jesus' post-resurrection appearances, for instance. Paul might well have sought to satisfy himself that Jesus' appearance to him was of the same order as the appearances to Peter and James. It is notable that some three years elapsed between Paul's conversion and the time of his initial visit with Peter (Gal 1:18). Thus, Paul had had ample time to preach and to begin to formulate what he came later to call "my gospel." Peter may well have inquired concerning Paul's faith. Paul himself perceived this faith to be the same faith preached in the churches of Christ in Judea, but he insisted later that he himself had not come into direct contact with the Judean churches. Before his visit to Peter, Paul was only known by reputation in Judea as "preaching the faith he once tried to destroy" (Gal 1:23).[8]

To suppose that Paul's faith was something other than a form of the apostolic faith shared in one way or another by Peter and the other apostles is unnecessary. Indeed, since Jesus was opposed by some Pharisees for eating with persons who were transgressing the law living like Gentiles, i.e., "tax-collectors and sinners," it is not difficult to reconstruct the reasons Paul had opposed the church.[9] As a Pharisee Paul might have been as opposed to the church as had been many Pharisees to Jesus, just because the members of this post-resurrection community persisted in table-fellowship practices similar to those initiated by Jesus. Moreover, in places like southern Syria, including the regions near Damascus, it is likely that after Paul's conversion, he had very soon to deal with God-fearing Gentiles who had already drawn near the covenant God of Israel and who would have been keenly interested in a form of the faith where the "non-observant" (specifically the noncircumcized) were fully accepted.

I conjecture that Paul's initial opposition to the church was excited in part by what he perceived to be a religiously "illicit" mixture of Gentiles and Jews as well as by the report of righteous

Jewish Christians accepting into their fellowship Jews whose reputation for nonobservance of the law had become a cause for scandal within the Jewish communities concerned. When, after his conversion, Paul preached the faith that he had formerly persecuted, he preached a faith which allowed for and encouraged the inclusion of uncircumcized Gentiles, something which on Isaianic terms was proleptically entailed in Jesus' practice of accepting into his table-fellowship "non-observant" Jews. Indeed one reason Paul was constrained to confront Peter in Antioch was precisely because he recognized that Peter's compromise on the matter of table-fellowship was not a compromise of the *bene esse* but of the *esse* of the fellowship of Jesus Christ.

I conjecture also that during the three-year period before Paul's visit with Peter his preaching had already opened his eyes to the possibility of and the need for evangelizing the Gentiles in accordance with some conscious intent to actualize a deep-felt conviction that Christ's death abrogated the necessity for those who are "in Christ" to keep the law. This provides grounds for concluding that Paul's discussions with Peter would certainly have covered the theological factors in such a development. Whether or not he discussed with Peter Jesus' attitude toward the law, Paul certainly discussed with Peter Peter's own attitude. Since Peter had been a disciple of Jesus, the two questions are virtually inseparable.

That Peter and Paul did establish a trusting relationship grounded in a deep faith in God and mutual respect for one another seems the simplest explanation for subsequent events. It helps explain how Paul fourteen years later could lay claim on Peter's sympathetic concern for his welfare and the welfare of the evangelistic work to which he had given so much of himself. It also helps explain how Paul could, when necessary, speak the truth in love to Peter and rebuke his inconsistent actions (Gal 2:14-16).

To what extent these two apostles agreed on their christology or on details of their faith is more problematic. But complete agreement on these matters would have been less mutually beneficial than deep personal trust and fundamental theological agreement. From Paul's own statement, this fundamental theological mutuality was rooted in a common trust in God's justifying grace in Jesus Christ and in the corollary of this faith, i.e., a recognition that one cannot be justified by works of the law (Gal 2:16). Nowhere does the recognition that one is justified by trust in God's unmerited grace and not by fulfilling the works of the law come to expression more clearly than in certain recorded words and actions of Jesus preserved in our Gospels.[10] Therefore, it is intrinsically probable that the considerably developed and richly diverse apostolic faith of Peter and Paul was rooted in, and inextricably bound up with, the faith which Jesus shared with his disciples.

Once it is assumed that Peter and Paul concurred in how this faith was to be made effective for the Gentiles, all else falls into place. Paul's subsequent spectacular fourteen-year mission in Asia Minor and Greece was a vindication of what must have been at first a minority position in Jerusalem, endorsed primarily by Peter and James. In any case, I am constrained to assume at least that Peter concurred in the gospel Paul preached and that Peter and Paul mutually supported one another from the day Paul left Jerusalem after his fifteen-day visit.[11] It is important, however, to recognize that Peter and Paul each could have had followers and supporters for whom this apostolic concurrence and mutuality was not normative.[12]

It follows from this interpretation of the relationship between Peter and Paul that the inner dynamic of the social and theological forces that formed the early church was not in the first place the inevitable conflicts that arose. Rather at work was a social and legal expediency in opening the original apostolic fellowship to Gentiles. This gospel took form as Jesus' particular eschatological message of monotheistic sovereign love was transformed, by the apostolic response to the death and resurrection of Jesus, into a dynamic (both personal and social) and intellectually integrating faith and fellowship open to all people. Essential to this development was the belief and conviction that the spirit that reunited the disciples and family of Jesus after his death was the same spirit they had come to know and cherish in their fellowship with Jesus and with one another before his death. Paul could call this the spirit of love, or the spirit of God, or the spirit of Jesus, or the spirit of Christ (Rom 8:9; 1 Cor 2:11; Phil 1:19). In any case it had a special character. This special character was constituted by the divine love the disciples had experienced in their relationship with Jesus and with one another before his death and which they reexperienced after his resurrection in the communities that met in his name and recalled his words and deeds. This divine love certainly entailed personal and social reconciliation and mutual acceptance based upon the forgiving love of God.

It was this same spirit of love now mystically identified as the spirit of Jesus Christ which transformed Paul and brought him into the community of faith. It seems to me to be likely that Paul became convinced that he shared this same spirit with Peter and those others who preceded Paul as apostles. This seems to provide the historian of Christian doctrine the central key to the mystery of that essential apostolicity upon which the church rests, namely, that Peter and Paul were in fact united in the same spirit of Jesus. Therefore, whatever difficulties Peter and Paul experienced were experienced within a particular spiritual context, one in which each would have felt the constraint of the spirit to find mutually acceptable ways in which to expedite the gospel. Each knew himself to be vindicated before God, made acceptable to God, through faith in Jesus Christ. In that faith there was a reconciling power against which the gates of hell could not prevail.

The significance of the relationship established in the spirit of Christ between Paul and Peter had immediate consequences for the spreading of the gospel. Their common commitment also influenced the development of the community of faith for centuries to come.

From an examination of the shape and content of the New Testament Canon, one discerns the extent of apostolic influence of Peter and Paul, for instance, on the formation of the Christian Bible. The New Testament Canon is dominated by two collections of closely related writings. One is a collection of Gospels. The other is a collection of Paul's letters. Paul's letters, including his own and those attributed to him, are not only given pride of place in the arrangement of the apostolic letters, but actually constitute by far the greater portion of this category of New Testament writings. Between the Gospels and the letters is a document that fittingly holds together the two collections and goes far in explaining how and why these two collections are found in the same Canon.

An insightful passage from Goodspeed's treatise on the Canon is instructive on this point:

> These two great collections, the gospels and the Pauline letters, were bound together by what now came to be known as the Acts of the Apostles. It had probably not gone by that name before. It is not a very accurate description of what it contains. But the rise of Acts of John and Acts of Paul between 160 and 180, and their own fixed purpose of emphasizing apostolic relations, probably suggested to the makers of the new collection the renaming of the second volume of Luke's history of the Acts of All the Apostles, as the Muratorian writer calls it. This book, which now emerges from a long period of relative obscurity, supplied a vital link in the new scripture. It filled out still further the rather shadowy figures of the apostles, and showed the relation of Paul to the primitive Christian movement. It thus served to weld together the two collections, to

show that Paul was in a real sense an apostle, and thus to make
the collection of his letters valid apostolic evidence. It is this
bringing forward of Acts to serve as the core of the new scripture that most clearly shows that it was something more than a
spontaneous, unconscious process. The gospels and the
Pauline letters indeed lay before the makers of the Canon
ready to their hands, already established in the esteem and affections of the churches, but the new role of Acts cannot be
thus explained. It had occupied no such position as they.[13]

Goodspeed was right in pointing out that Acts serves to weld
together the Gospels and Paul's letters, showing that Paul was in a
real sense an apostle, thus making the collection of his letters valid
apostolic evidence. We would like to go further and contend that
Acts is not only a "vital link" that joins together the Gospels and
Paul's letters, but it is the central span in a well-balanced threefold
division of the New Testament. Acts effectively supplies a needed
transition between the four Gospels with their multiple testimony
to Jesus and his disciples and the multiple testimony and instruction offered to the young church represented by the writings of
Paul and other apostolic witnesses. What precedes the Acts of the
Apostles nicely balances what follows it in the New Testament.

Moreover, Acts not only serves to show that Paul was in a real
sense an apostle, it shows in an evenhanded way how it was possible to perceive both Peter and Paul as leading and preeminent
apostles of the same church. As the career of Peter is featured in the
first half of Acts, so the career of Paul is featured in the second.
Acts makes it clear that there were other apostles besides Peter and
Paul, while at the same time emphasizing that these two were by
far the most important.[14]

At first sight it might appear that the great prominence of Paul's
letters among the writings that follow Acts in the New Testament
destroys the coordinate significance of Peter and Paul in favor of
the apostle to the Gentiles. Such is not the case, however, for
Peter's place of special prominence among Jesus' disciples as noted
in the Gospels preserves the balance.

If these observations have any validity, it should follow that the
story of the development of the Christian Canon in some respects is .
the story of how the early and decisive apostolic concurrence and
mutuality between Peter and Paul became normative for the
leadership of those churches that eventually formed and accepted
the authority of that Canon.

Seen from this point of view, the essential elements which
shaped the development of the New Testament Canon were

present in principle in the apostolic agreement reached by Peter and Paul (probably including consultation with James) during Paul's momentous meeting with Peter just three years after Paul's conversion.[15] Though not a single book of the New Testament had been written, the basic ingredients which decisively influenced the formation of the Canon were brought together. What were these?

First, there was the apostolic memory of Jesus' words and acts. Peter and James were representative custodians of the collective memory. Second, there were the resurrection appearances of Jesus, a common bond which existed between Peter, James, and Paul since Jesus had appeared to each following his death and resurrection. Peter had participated in Jesus' public ministry. James had known Jesus as a close relative. Paul, if he knew of Jesus during his public ministry, presumably shared the concerns about Jesus that the Gospels associate with the Pharisees. Whatever diversity there may have been in the way each of these three apostles experienced post-resurrection appearances of Jesus, the tradition upon which Paul built wherever he went was to the effect that Jesus had appeared to the twelve, then to a much larger number, and eventually to all the apostles. The only persons Paul specifically mentioned by name besides himself were the two apostles he saw during his fifteen-day stay in Jerusalem, namely, Peter and James (1 Cor 15:3-8).

So the post-resurrection appearances of Jesus and the concomitant belief in him as the Risen Christ who had gained victory over death were powerfully present as an essential element in the apostolic concurrence between Peter and Paul. As most Gentiles placed great weight upon Paul's direct testimony of having seen Jesus, it was not easily appreciated that Paul himself was dependent upon others who by virtue of their previous personal acquaintance could recognize the resurrected Jesus and give credible testimony to his identity. This is an important point, Paul's apparent lack of stress on it notwithstanding.[16]

The apostolic memory of the crucified Jesus is inextricably bound up with the confident belief among those in the early church that he had been resurrected and that he had effectively manifested himself to persons who had never known him before his death. We can even say that without the apostolic memory of Jesus and his appearance after death to some of his disciples, there never would have been a church for Paul to persecute. Moreover, without that experience of persecuting the church, the appearance of Jesus to Paul would have been something of a different order from the appearance of Jesus to Paul that plays such an important role in the New Testament.[17] Without Paul's conviction that the Son of God whom God had revealed to him was none other than the Jesus who had appeared to Peter and James as well as others, his Gentile converts could well have separated themselves from everything that rooted the church in Judaism. Paul probably held this conviction unreservedly before he went to Jerusalem for his first visit with Peter. But any reservations he might have had were resolved, we may assume, by his direct contact with Peter and James. This visit afforded him an opportunity to satisfy himself as to what some of those who had been apostles before him and who had been with Jesus had to say about these matters.

From more than one source we know that there was a tradition that James held a preeminent place in the earliest Jerusalem-centered Christian church (Acts 15:13; 1 Cor 15:7; Gal 2:9, 12). In the New Testament, however, another apostle generally is presented as the leader of this earliest church. Pride of place among those apostles before Paul clearly went to Peter in the church that developed out of the apostolic colleagueship of Peter and Paul. Paul himself was quite explicit on the point. Jesus, according to Paul, appeared first to Cephas, and, finally, as to one born out of due time, Jesus appeared to Paul (1 Cor 15: 5, 8). In this way the appearances of Jesus to Peter and Paul signaled the beginning and end of a decisive period in the history of the New Testament church. An apostle who had not known Jesus as a flesh and blood person was on an equal footing with one who had been an actual disciple. Jesus appeared to each without discriminating against either. Had this not happened there could have been no church as we know it. Paul saw himself and represented himself as consummating an authoritative series of post-resurrection appearances of Jesus. When was this tradition fixed in Paul's mind? It seems reasonable to surmise that it was fixed by the time Paul left Peter and James at the end of his fifteen-day visit. Presumably Paul passed this tradition on to all his churches during his subsequent fourteen years of missionary work in Asia Minor and Greece.

Since James joined Peter and John, his colleagues in the Jerusalem triumvirate, in extending the right hand of fellowship to Paul and Barnabas under circumstances where the gospel Paul preached among the Gentiles was at issue, we must presume that James did not allow whatever private reservations, if any, he may have personally harbored on this point to intrude.

The tradition of a post-resurrection appearance of Jesus to James is preserved only in one of Paul's letters (1 Cor 15:7). The letter of James itself does not even mention the resurrection. Likewise in contrast with most of the letters attributed to Paul including Colossians, Ephesians, and all the deutero-Pauline letters and Peter

(1 and 2 Peter), the epistle of James in keeping with 1, 2, and 3 John, Jude, Hebrews and Revelations, makes no claim to apostolic status. Indeed, it is a remarkable fact that of all the apostles, only Peter and Paul are represented in the New Testament by letters in which the authors are designated as apostles.

James is mentioned only three times in Acts. When Peter takes leave of those to whom he appears at the door of the house of Mary mother of John Mark in Acts 12:17, he is represented as saying: "Report this (how the Lord had miraculously brought him out of prison) to James and the members of the church." Peter appeared to recognize a special leadership status for James in the Jerusalem church. Later in chapter 15, James supported Peter's recommendation that the work of Paul and Barnabas be recognized as an authentic work of the Holy Spirit. Finally, in Acts 21:18 Paul was represented during his last visit to Jerusalem as visiting James and being told by James that in the interests of the church Paul should make it clear that, however lenient he was with Gentile converts, he himself was fully observant of the law.

The paucity of these references in Acts is hardly commensurate with the important place that James seemed to have held in the Jerusalem triumvirate. We know from Paul that there was a "circumcision" party that was identified with James, and that this party had sufficient power even outside Jerusalem to cause a very serious break or disruption in the Christian community as far away as Antioch (Gal 2:12). Out of fear of this party, Peter withdrew from table-fellowship with Gentile Christians, a fellowship into which he had been led by his faith in the grace of God in Jesus Christ. Thus, the power and influence of James at that time was very great indeed.

The role of John as presented in the New Testament is also intriguing. Paul gave John a place of special importance as the third member of the Jerusalem triumvirate (Gal 1:9). In Acts, however, though mentioned repeatedly as accompanying Peter in the early chapters (cf. Acts 3:1, 11, 4:13, 19, 8:14), John has no important role to play.

The manner in which both James and John are presented in Acts suggests that the New Testament was shaped by a tradition in which the apostle Peter stood far above his Jerusalem colleagues. The only person in Acts who had a status commensurate with that of Peter's was Paul. Acts is not adequate for reconstructing the actual roles of all the apostles. The fact that James and John are not featured in Acts along with Peter and Paul does reflect the growing importance of Peter and Paul for the church that made Acts the central span in the New Testament bridge from Jesus to the

Heavenly Jerusalem.[18]

The tradition that both Peter and Paul were martyred in Rome, if it can be depended on, may afford a further clue to the unraveling of the mystery of the peculiar prominence given to Peter and Paul in the New Testament. But obviously something more than this is needed to explain the special place they have in the church's Canon. We need to know how and why these two apostles, who when last seen together are in a situation of the deepest kind of confrontation, could emerge in the total New Testament Canon as irenic pillars of the apostolic faith, standing together in a unified witness to the gospel of Jesus Christ.

It is not enough to show that this confrontation took place within the context of a wide and deep theological unity that had long held these two apostles together. Peter's implied defection (Gal 2:12-13) was of the most serious nature and witnessed to a very dangerous potential disruption of apostolic mutuality and concurrence. How was this portentous disruption averted or overcome in the church which formed the New Testament? Was this primarily the creative achievement of unknown and unheralded theologians of the second-century church? Or was this primarily due to developments that took place during the apostolic period itself?[19] I think that the New Testament evidence taken as a whole supports the latter conjecture, though without precluding the former as a supplementary explanation.

We have seen that the potential cleavage or disagreement between Peter and Paul was not theological *per se*. What was it then? The New Testament itself indicates that it had to do with what fundamentally can be called a christological problem. Paul made this clear by pointing out that Peter by withdrawing from table-fellowship was nullifying or making of no avail the death of Christ. Paul's contention was that the death of Christ had brought an end to the law. The law was no longer binding upon those who believed in Christ.

There is no way to be certain what Peter thought on this point. It is unlikely, however, that he wanted to do anything that would in effect diminish in the eyes of others the importance of the death of Jesus. Presumably Peter was conscience-stricken if and when he realized he had acted hypocritically in withdrawing from table-fellowship. I conjecture that this historical confrontation with Paul was for Peter a growth experience in which his vision and understanding of the practical consequences of faith in Jesus Christ were enlarged and deepened. This would make it possible for some change in Peter's thinking. Of course, it is conceivable that Peter was quite unaffected by what happened on this occasion and that he insisted on the appropriateness of his actions at every point. The picture that finally emerged in the New Testament, however, supports the conjecture that Peter did repent, for it is a picture where Peter and Paul are represented as being in basic agreement on the fundamental points at issue, i.e., whether and to what extent it was necessary to observe the law and whether it was appropriate to have table-fellowship between Jewish and Gentile Christians.

On these fundamental questions the New Testament may represent a colossal tour-de-force where historical fact has been twisted beyond recognition. It is at least equally possible, however, and, I think, highly more likely that in fact Peter experienced something of a conversion in his understanding of the full consequences of faith in Jesus Christ. A number of passages in the New Testament can be interpreted to support the view that Peter in fact did undergo such a conversion.[20] Thus the omission in Acts of any reference to the problem between Peter and Paul at Antioch (and the general picture of apostolic harmony given) is to be understood as generally promoting the much deeper relationship of concurrence, mutuality, and cooperation that actually undergirded the sometimes stressed relationship between these two apostles.

The eventual and unreserved conversion and commitment of Peter to a more radical and basically Pauline position of the question of the admission and status of Gentiles within the church, taken together with Paul's fundamental reliance upon the pre-Pauline apostolic memory of Jesus which Peter and James had been able to authenticate,[21] completed and filled out the development of apostolic mutuality and concurrence that I propose was and remained basic to the church that produced the New Testament Canon. Such an apostolic concurrence and mutuality, if in fact it did exist, would provide substantial historical and theological support for the admittedly tendentious overall picture in Acts of essential harmony and cooperation between the church's two chief apostles.

If, in fact, Peter and Paul were both martyred in Rome, their unified apostolic witness at the administrative center of the empire would certainly have given further impetus to the development of a New Testament Canon which reflected the decisive importance of an early theological agreement and eventual christological concurrence between these two apostles.

NOTES

1. F. C. Baur, *Lehrbuch der christlichen Dogmengeschichte* (repr of 1867 ed; Darmstadt: Wissenschaftlich Buchgesellschaft, 1968).

2. D. F. Strauss, *Das Leben Jesu* (Tübingen: C. F. Osiander, 1838).

3. Bishop Joseph B. Lightfoot, *St. Paul's Epistle to the Galatians* (London: Macmillian 1865) 357-59.

4. Cf. John Knox, *Chapters in a Life of Paul* (New York: Abingdon, 1946). The hypothesis concerning the chronology of Paul's career which was developed in this book originally was stated a decade earlier in two articles by Knox which appeared in the *Journal of Religion,* XVI, 341-49 and *The Journal of Biblical Literature,* LVIII, 15-29.

5. For the sake of this project this is fair enough, since this is what Baur did. I am not unmindful of the fact that Paul's letters have almost certainly been glossed as well as edited. It is possible that some of my reconstruction would need modification in the light of further study of this important subject. The latest and most detailed study of the question of possible glosses in the text of Galatians is J. C. O'Neill, *The Recovery of Paul's Letters to the Galatians* (London: S.P.C.K., 1972).

6. What Paul wrote in Gal 2:7-9 makes it clear that he perceived Peter as his counterpart in the mission to the Jews. Just as Paul had been entrusted with the gospel to the uncircumcized, so Peter had been entrusted with the gospel to the circumcized. It is just as clear that the agreement reached at the Jerusalem conference affected the status of others as well as that of Peter and Paul, for that agreement was for Paul *and* Barnabas to have responsibility for the mission to the Gentiles and for "James, Cephas and John" to carry responsibility for the mission to the circumcized. This means that the leadership of these two missions was a shared leadership, and certainly not to be exercised by either Paul among the Gentiles or Peter among the circumcized without some collegial consultation and support from the others who were principal parties to this agreement, namely, Barnabas on the one hand and James and John on the other. This makes it even clearer how threatening was Peter's withdrawing from table-fellowship with Gentile Christians at Antioch, since even Barnabas who had been a principal in the Jerusalem agreement was carried away by Peter's hypocritical behavior. Paul was thus isolated and threatened at a most vulnerable point. A close associate Paul had brought with him to the conference at Jerusalem had sided against him in a serious dispute over proper conduct. How was the agreement reached in Jerusalem to be carried out in Antioch and other places where Jewish and Gentile Christians were closely associated? For Barnabas to disagree with Paul on this issue was to divide the apostolic leadership of the Gentile mission. Paul had no alternative but react energetically and decisively. Otherwise what had been gained in Jerusalem would have been lost in Antioch.

7. Is it possible that the incident at Antioch preceded the Jerusalem conference? Paul introduced the incident at Antioch differently from the way he introduced his references to his first visit to Jerusalem, his departure from Jerusalem, and his return fourteen years later. This makes it possible to consider taking the reference to the incident at Antioch in a nonsequential sense. Paul could have referred to the dispute of Antioch not to report a chronology of events, but because the logic of his argument required it. Apart, however, from a need to harmonize what is written in Acts with what Paul wrote in his letters, would this possibility seem probable? Is this inter-

pretation required to understand what Paul has written? Does it improve the sense of what Paul has written?

8. Here I refer to Gal 1:22-24 which O'Neill regards as a later gloss. The text as it stands, it seems to me, can be interpreted in a very straightforward way once it is recognized, as apparently O'Neill does not, that this is a report, and that it emanated from an area outside Judea where Paul had been preaching. O'Neill's objection that the use of the word "faith" as found here would not have been appropriate for Paul is considerably weakened if in fact, as I believe, these words represent Paul's reference to a report of what others were actually saying about Paul at the time. We have absolutely no way of knowing how soon the word "faith" could have been used in the church as equivalent for "gospel" apart from the New Testament itself. This text as it stands suggests the possibility that what Paul came to refer to as the "gospel" may earlier and by others have been referred to simply as the "faith." Nor need we think that Paul could not have used the word "faith" in the sense of "faith in Christ," cf. Gal 3:23, and the comments of Ernest De Witt Burton, *The Epistle to the Galatians* (ICC: New York: Charles Scribner's Sons, 1920) 198. O'Neill, *The Recovery*, 25, has argued that this passage in Galatians as well as 6:10 and Rom 1:5 where "faith" is employed in a similar way are of doubtful authenticity.

9. Cf. William R. Farmer, "Who Were the Taxcollectors and Sinners in the Synoptic Gospel Tradition?" in forthcoming *Festschrift* for Donald Miller.

10. William R. Farmer, "The Dynamic of Christianity—The Question of Development Between Jesus and Paul," *Religion and Life,* Winter 1969-1970, 570-77. Cf. Anton Fridrichsen, "Jesus, St. John and St. Paul," *The Root of the Vine* (New York: Philosophical Library, 1953) 38-62; especially 46.

11. This concurrence and support from Peter did not and could not guarantee Paul or his churches immunity from the harrassment of Judaizers who may or may not have claimed for their position the authority of the Jerusalem church. Thus, Paul's concern in Gal 2:2 that he might be running or *had* run in vain in no way calls into question the possibility of an earlier agreement between Peter and Paul that I am conjecturing. In fact, if an earlier agreement was still in place, it would help account for the fact that Paul was able to get a meeting with the Jerusalem triumvirate and that a twofold division of the church's mission was agreed upon during the conference. The fact that Peter and Paul emerged from the conference in positions of mutual preeminence is *prima facie* evidence in favor of the conjecture that they had a decisive role in organizing the conference and setting its agenda. Nor need this interpretation prejudice the question whether at any time either before or subsequent to the incident in Antioch, Peter was in Corinth, nor the question whether the "party spirit" in Corinth was at any time or in any way inspired by Peter.

12. Cf. C. K. Barrett on Peter being used at Corinth. "Cephas and Corinth," *Abraham Unser Vater,* Festschrift für Otto Michel, ed Otto Betz, Martin Hengel, Peter Schmidt (Leiden: E. J. Brill, 1963). See also Barrett's essay: "Paul and the 'Pillar' Apostles," *Studia Paulina* in hon. J. de Zwaan, ed J. N. Sevenster and W. C. van Unnik (Haarlem: Erven F. Bohn, 1953) 1-19; T. W. Manson, "The Corinthian Corre-

spondence," *Studies in the Gospels and Epistles* (Manchester: The University Press, 1962) 190-209; O. Cullmann, *Petrus: Jünger-Apostle-Märtyrer,* 2d ed (Zürich: Zwingli-Verlag, 1960).

13. Edgar J. Goodspeed, *The Formation of the New Testament* (Chicago: The University of Chicago Press, 1926) 74-75. See also John Knox, *Marcion and the New Testament* (Chicago: University of Chicago Press, 1942).

14. Through literary skill the author of Acts managed to give comparatively equal attention to the apostolic careers of Peter and Paul and to be faithful to the history of the early church as Paul perceived it. Paul himself was accustomed to parallel his own apostolate with that of Peter. Cf. Anton Fridrichsen, "The Apostle and His Message," *Uppsala Universitets Årsskrift,* 1947:3, 6.

15. Or more probably three years plus the time Paul was in Arabia.

16. Cf. Richard R. Niebuhr, *Resurrection and Historical Reason: A Study of Theological Method* (New York: Scribner, 1957).

17. To make Paul or Paul's theological position absolute and regard everything else in the New Testament that does not measure up to this as either deficient or defective, would be to reduce the New Testament to an insufficient unanimity. The way of perceiving things that is presented in this essay offers an option which may do even Paul more justice.

18. The attaching of John's name to a Gospel, three letters, and the Apocalypse may signify that this apostle also exercised an influence in the formation of the church that formed the New Testament Canon second only to that of Peter and Paul.

19. John Knox, *The Early Church and the Coming Great Church* (New York: Abingdon Press, 1955) raised this question in my mind. Knox saw no great defection or decline in the first or second century. What I propose here may be seen as supplementary to Knox's views.

20. William R. Farmer, "Jesus and the Gospels—A Form Critical and Theological Essay," *Perkins Journal,* Winter 1975, 24-31.

21. This does not at all mean that the gospel Paul preached was dependent upon the apostolic certification of Peter, or any of the Jerusalem apostles. Paul's gospel was supported by Peter as being faithful to the apostolic experience as Peter knew and represented it. So there is "concurrence" rather than "certification." But the concurrence of Peter and Paul, for reasons I have given, means more to the church than Paul alone. The apostolic memory concerning Jesus was not independent of the actual Jesus. In thinking theologically and christologically about the Christian faith, we need both Paul *and* that which he himself could not supply—i.e., the memory of those apostles who had also been disciples of Jesus. The New Testament provides us the witness of both in abundance.

Understanding the Church of the Second Century: American Research and Teaching 1890-1940

Thomas H. Olbricht

Professor Currie in his eagerness for insight was an avid student of church history, and, as his published works indicate, felt especially at home in the documents of the first and second centuries. The ideas of those within and outside the church were well-known to Currie. Interest in the study of the history of the ancient church, and especially interest in the momentous events of the second century, have come to the fore slowly but steadily in scholarly circles in the United States. By and large, however, the history of the teaching of church history has been ignored. The one study of significance is Henry Warner Bowden's *Church History in the Age of Science.*[1] This book offers a subtitle "Historiographical Patterns in the United States 1876-1918," an apt description of the contents. The aim of this essay is to fill some of the gap by tracing the teaching of early church history in America from the beginning, following it through the epoch of generalized study, and concluding by looking at the career and emphases of certain scholars of the period (1890-1940) in which the study of the history of the second century became a specialized field.

The writing of history has an ancient and revered heritage. The Assyrian Chronicles, the narrative of David's succession, Thucydides' "The Peloponnesian Wars," or the Histories of Tacitus offer ample testimony. As an academic discipline, however, the study of history is only about two centuries old. The medieval university made no provision for the teaching of history. Even in the renaissance, the study of Greek and Latin classics was the primary avenue through which classical history was investigated.

Some interest in oriental history was expressed here and there, but chiefly as it impinged upon the study of the Old Testament.

History first attained academic status in the German university of the eighteenth century, and foremost at the University of Göttingen due to the work of Johann Mosheim, regarded as the father of modern church history. Between 1810-1830 the flowering of historical studies, however, burst forth in Berlin through the scholarship of Johann A. W. Neander, Barthold Georg Niebuhr, and Leopold von Ranke. Von Ranke more than anyone else influenced subsequent historiography and advanced the methodological presuppositions of objectivity, accuracy, and scientific thoroughness. Scientific history was to be achieved through rigorously examining original documents from a critical posture. Von Ranke also scrutinized the means through which the historian could eliminate his prejudices. Though the French and British contributed to historical investigation, the Germans poured the methodological foundations upon which American academic historiography was built.

Harvard, the first American College, reflected its European heritage. According to Samuel Eliot Morison, "There is no mention of History, as such, in the College Laws of 1655, or in the programme of 1723."[2] History was read, but for leisure and in order to acquire knowledge of the world. The first professor of history in America was Ezra Stiles, appointed at Yale as President and Professor of Ecclesiastical History in 1778.[3] The first professorship of non-ecclesiastical history resulted from the appointment of Jared Sparks at Harvard in 1839.[4] Sparks initiated new teaching methods by doing away with recitations on textbooks. Instead he gave lectures and assigned readings. Fifty years later his approach became standard. Following the Civil War instruction in history in the colleges flowered with the appointments of Henry W. Torrey at Harvard, Francis Lieber at Columbia, and Andrew D. White at the University of Michigan. All three had been educated in Germany and reflected German historiography.

The first American "seminary" (now seminar) in history was established by Charles Kendall Adams at the University of Michigan. Adams spent the years 1867-68 in Germany and returned to Michigan excited by the prospect of forming a German-style seminar. In Germany the seminar emerged as the means through which a professor gave specialized training to the more advanced students. The first such *seminare* was established by Friedrich August Wolf in philology at Halle in 1787. The first historical seminar was conducted at Königsberg in 1832.[5] In 1869 Adams began his seminar at Michigan, but it was 1880 before it passed beyond a rudimentary state. In the meantime, The Johns Hopkins University, established in 1876, became one of the pioneers in American doctoral graduate studies. It was there that the famous historical seminar of Henry B. Adams commenced, a seminar which became the model for graduate training in history in America. W. Stull Holt gives schematic peripheries to these developments:

> By 1900 the profession of historical scholarship was in the third stage of its transit from western Europe. Forty years earlier there had been no such profession and the few historians in the country were lawyers or clergy or gentlemen with leisure to devote to their avocation of studying and writing history. Twenty years earlier the new profession emerged in the persons of eleven professors of history. Between 1880 and 1900 the profession became firmly established. There were at the beginning of the new century something over one hundred professors of history and more significantly there were a number of graduate schools for the training of new recruits.[6]

Americans were about half a century behind Germany in initiating history as an academic discipline. Church history, or ecclesiastical history as it was commonly called, was, however, in advance of secular history on both continents. The teaching of church history preceded the founding of seminaries in America (for example, at Yale), but systematic and perennial instruction awaited their appearance. The first permanently located, completely structured seminary in America was founded at Andover in 1807, Princeton followed in 1812, Harvard in 1816, and Yale in 1822. Each of these schools offered courses in church history from their founding or shortly thereafter. The courses surveyed large expanses of history and were usually taught by former clergymen who had little training in historiography. The observations of Ephraim Emerton, professor of church history at Harvard Divinity School at the close of the nineteenth century, are instructive, but reflect his bias as to the merits of the sort of history done by Philip Schaff whose work will be discussed below:

> I was one of the earliest in this company of ardent youths who came home to challenge the academic world of America to give them a chance. When I began my service in 1876 the conditions of historical instruction in America had but one encouraging aspect, namely, that there was a great work to do and very few workmen ready to do it....

As to church history, the situation was, I think, a little better. The very necessities of theological controversy compelled a certain familiarity with at least the great fundamental documents of the Christian faith. It meant a good deal that the first history of the church to be written with a truly historical purpose, the still useful treatise of Neander, should be translated by an American scholar as early as 1847 and should be widely accepted as the basis of instruction in theological schools.[7]

Further insight into the teaching of church history during the nineteenth century may be obtained by considering the training and interest of the history faculties at four particular seminaries differing in confession and region: Andover (Congregational, 1807), Gettysburg (Lutheran, 1826), Meadville (Unitarian, 1844), and Princeton (Presbyterian, 1812).

James Murdock (1776-1856) was the first professor of ecclesiastical history listed in the Andover *General Catalogue*.[8] In 1815 he became professor at the University of Vermont where he taught until being appointed at Andover in 1819. He had no specialized training, but developed a deep interest in church history. He was dismissed from Andover four years later because he objected to replacing ecclesiastical history in the curriculum with sacred rhetoric. Murdock was succeeded by another minister, Ralph Emerson, a distant cousin of Ralph Waldo Emerson. He in turn was followed in 1853 by William Greenough Thayer Shedd (1820-1894) who later moved to Union Theological Seminary (1862) where he taught sacred rhetoric and then theology.[9] Upon Shedd's departure for Union, Egbert Coffin Smyth (1829-1904) became his successor.[10] In 1862 Smyth studied for a year at Berlin and Halle, and then was appointed Brown Professor of Ecclesiastical History at Andover, where he continued until his death. Smyth thereby anticipated the droves of students who flocked to Germany after the Civil War.

Samuel Simon Schmucher (1799-1873) was the first instructor in church history and one of the founders of Gettysburg Theological Seminary.[11] Schmucher was followed by Charles Philip Krauth (1797-1867) who was essentially self-taught except that he studied medicine for a short period at the University of Maryland.[12] He first served as Professor of Biblical and Oriental Literature, but later (1850-1867) as Professor of Biblical Philology and Ecclesiastical History.[13] The first professor designated in the discipline of church history was Milton Valentine (1825-1906).[14] He also served for a time as president of Gettysburg College and in 1884 became professor of theology. As at Andover, the church historians at Gettysburg lacked specialized training and often transferred to other teaching assignments.

Frederic Huidekoper (1817-1892) taught at Meadville in 1844 when it opened as a school for western Unitarians and churchmen of the Christian connection.[15] He taught New Testament for a time, but finally only church history. Huidekoper, unlike most early American church historians, turned out at least two books representing original scholarship.[16] Interestingly, he rejected the Mosaic authorship of the Pentateuch and in 1857 published a work on Genesis identifying Elohist and Yahwist sources. Something of the character of Huidekoper's approach, essentially representative of the time, is contained in the Meadville catalogues. The 1845-46 catalogue mentions the use of Murdock's translation of Mosheim.[17] Over the years other readings were added and a few years after the end of Huidekoper's career the Catalogue (1884-85) presented the following course description:

> The Course in the History of Christianity begins with the Junior-Middle year. Allen's *Christian History* and Smith's *Ecclesiastical History* will be used as text books. The movement and events of Christian history will be studied in the lives of their leaders and representatives, and themes will be required upon the great men and epochs of the Christian church. Mc-Clintock and Strong's *Cyclopoedia,* Smith's *Dictionaries,* Milman's *History of Christianity,* Robertson's *History of the Christian Church,* and Huidekoper's *Judaism at Rome,* are among the works to which students will be referred.[18]

Princeton Theological Seminary from its commencement had a professor of church history in Samuel Miller (1769-1850), one of the founders.[19] Miller was a prolific writer.[20] He was succeeded by James W. Alexander who only lived a year, whereupon Joseph Addison Alexander (1809-1860) assumed the office.[21] The latter produced several commentaries, but wrote very little church history. James C. Moffat (1811-1890) was appointed in 1861.[22]

Though not at one of the four seminaries singled out in the review, Philip Schaff must be mentioned as the most important nineteenth-century church historian in America. He was the founding president of The American Society of Church History.[23] His most ambitious work was his *History of the Christian Church* in seven volumes which went through a number of editions.[24] His work was detailed and sometimes undigested, but competent. Bowden has written at length on Schaff's view of church history, referring to Schaff's approach as a "theological Discipline." Later writers deprecated his efforts as not being strictly scientific. Schaff himself wrote of his approach:

> A church history without the life of Christ glowing through its pages could give us at best only the picture of a temple stately and imposing from without, but vacant and dreary within, a mummy in praying posture perhaps and covered with trophies, but withered and unclean: such a history is not worth the trouble of writing or reading. Let the dead bury their dead; we prefer to live among the living, and to record the immortal thoughts and deeds of Christ in and through his people, rather than dwell upon the outer hulls, the trifling accidents and temporary scaffolding of history, or give too much prominence to Satan and his infernal tribe, whose works Christ came to destroy.[25]

Perhaps Schaff's greatest contribution was as editor of a number of projects, including *The American Church History Series* (1893-1897), *The Creeds of Christendom* (1877), *Religious Encyclopoedia* (1882-1884), and *The Nicene and Post-Nicene Fathers* (1886-1894). Sydney Ahlstrom has written of Schaff, "Though not an influential interpreter of the American religious tradition, Schaff probably did more than any other church historian to establish the 'historical standpoint' in the American mind."[26]

For the first seventy years, then, those involved in teaching church history in America for the most part trained themselves. Church history as a broad review of the church's life was taught in many seminaries,[27] using European texts of various sorts. After 1875 teachers trained in Germany began to enter the ranks. These too tended to teach general history, but from them flowed an ever-increasing stream of publications. While their interpretive works have long since receded, the greatest contribution was to the translation of materials, some of which are still in use.[28] The historical developments of the second century were treated, therefore, in the context of a larger course on the history of the early church.

In America specialized studies of the history of the second century were to await the development of graduate programs in the universities and degrees beyond the B.D. or its equivalents. Even at the beginning of the last quarter of the nineteenth century, work beyond the B.A. in the university or in the professional schools of law, medicine, and theology, were informal extensions of undergraduate instruction. It was only after the Civil War that graduate work was actually undertaken, though it had been discussed and halfheartedly tried prior to that time. The real impetus occurred when The Johns Hopkins University was founded as a graduate school after the pattern of German higher education.[29] In the 1880s an increasing number of Americans attended German universities and returned home to interject their specialized study into the graduate programs of America.

The emerging pattern of specialization led those teaching in American seminaries to more specific interests. Doctoral programs developed, especially in seminaries on or near university campuses with accelerating graduate programs. This new climate created the interest, the professors, and the tools with which to address particular problems and periods in church history, such as the second century. The earliest signs of specialized courses concentrating on the second century began to appear in the 1890s. The formulation and jelling of such programs continued over the next fifty years, so that an examination of the curricula and the scholarly work of the period from 1890-1940 provides considerable insight into the development of research in America on the church of the second century.

The earliest specialized courses on the second century appear to have been offered at Princeton Theological Seminary. The first were listed in the 1894-95 catalogue as "Extra-curricular Courses." These were taken after the completion of required courses and represented a step in the direction of graduate study beyond the B.D. The 1898 catalogue listed "Postapostolic Literature" by Dr. Purvey. "The Apostolic Fathers" was offered by Professor William Park Armstrong in 1905-06[30] and "Patristic Church History" and "Patristic Apologists" by Professor John De Witt.[31] These courses were more like guided studies, since subsequent catalogues listed one student enrolled in each.

In the 1910-11 catalogue, the earliest announcements of Yale Divinity School available to me, Williston Walker offered a course entitled "Christian Literature from Clement of Rome to Eusebius." The catalogue described the enrollment as "elective primarily for Graduates"[32] and outlined the content of the course in detail:

Special attention will be paid to the writings and the doctrinal and historical significance of the "Apostolic Fathers," Justin Martyr, Irenaeus, Tertullian, Clement of Alexandria, Origen, Novatian, Cyprian, and Eusebius. A considerable portion of their works will be read, using English translations as a basis.

The same course is listed again in 1915-16 and 1920-21 with Walker as professor. In 1925, after Walker's death, Roland H. Bainton was listed as instructor. In 1930-31 the course disappeared and was replaced by Erwin Goodenough's "The Early Church," described as follows:

> Seminar course requiring a working knowledge of Greek, Latin, French, and German. The specific subject studied will vary from year to year. For 1930-31 it will be Second Century Christianity.[33]

The 1935 catalogue did not contain this Seminar, but Goodenough offered "Readings in Hellenism, Hellenistic Judaism, and Early Christianity," which was still listed in the 1940-41 catalogue.[34]

At Harvard Divinity School Emerton developed a seminar in the Medieval church as early as 1895. But specialized work in the second century was to await the arrival of Kirsopp Lake twenty years later. The 1895-96 announcement listed Professor Emerton's "seminary," "Advanced Study and Research in connection with the Seminary in Mediaeval History."[35] In 1914, Lake arrived at Harvard from the University of Leiden and in that same year offered, "History of Early Christian Literature outside of the New Testament." This course was listed in 1919-20 and 1928-29. The last listing also contained an announcement that "Special instruction in Church History for advanced students will be given by Professor Lake for the Early Period."[36]

These specialized courses largely appeared at seminaries where doctoral programs existed. Other seminaries could not afford the luxury of either time or faculty. The Meadville catalogue for 1921-22, for example, listed four offerings in church history: ancient, mediaeval, reformation, and nineteenth century, all taught by Professor Christie. But where offered, these graduate seminars nurtured future scholars and provided incentive for publication.

When attention is turned from the curricula to the scholars, further insight is gained. A number of American scholars from 1890 to 1940 gave consideration to the second century, though not exclusively. Not all were American born, and fewer American trained. Among the most influential in order of birth were: George Foot Moore (1851-1931),[37] Frederick John Foakes-Jackson (1855-1941),[38] Williston Walker (1860-1922),[39] Arthur Cushman McGiffert (1861-1933), Edgar J. Goodspeed (1871-1962),[40] Kirsopp Lake (1872-1946), Shirley Jackson Case (1872-1947), Roy J. Deferrari (1890-   ),[41] Erwin Ramsdell Goodenough (1893-1965), A. D. Nock (1902-1963),[42] and Cyril C. Richardson (1909-1976).[43]

Six of the eleven professors were born in America, four in England, and one in Canada. One of the Britishers as well as the Canadian took advanced degrees in the United States. Of the nine American born or trained, all except Roy J. Deferrari took a degree in Germany or studied there. Only the three Britishers who took their degrees in England, Foakes-Jackson, Lake, and Nock, failed to study in Germany. The favorite German universities were Leipzig, Marburg, and Berlin. The American schools attended were Union, Yale, Chicago, and the Catholic University. Their works included indexes, translations, monographs, and general overviews and texts. Some of these works remain as major contributions to the study of the second-century church.[44]

Most of the specialized work on the second century was done by scholars at Union, Harvard, Chicago, and Yale. Two other centers should be mentioned, the Catholic University of America where numerous studies on specific patristic topics were completed, and Hartford Theological Seminary where Chester David Hartranft, E. C. Richardson, and Matthew Riddle expended considerable effort editing and translating texts.[45] Nonetheless, the work of Arthur Cushman McGiffert, Kirsopp Lake, Shirley Jackson Case, and Erwin R. Goodenough, who taught respectively at Union, Harvard, Chicago, and Yale, was the most significant. Each was a pioneer in his own specialty in America, while Case and Goodenough were trailblazers on the international scene as well. They each differed in their concerns; McGiffert with theology, Lake in historical backgrounds, Case in social structures, and Goodenough with hellenistic Jewish backgrounds, the multiplex nature of which reflects the character of American second-century studies in these years. Each of the four mirrored continental intellectual movements, especially McGiffert and Lake. Case and Goodenough were more individualistic, especially the latter. Case carried into his research on the second century the Chicago-school methodologies already pioneered in New Testament by Shailer Mathews. While differing, each made important contributions to the study of the church in the second century.

Arthur C. McGiffert, whose career is identified with Union Theological Seminary, was the first American scholar to specialize at least in part in the second-century church.[46] McGiffert's contributions were in the history of doctrine and the emergence of creeds. His discussions extended into the modern period, but most of his efforts were expended on the early church. His books tended to be thematic, for example, *God of the Early Christians*[47] and *The*

Social Triumph of the Ancient Church.[48] His greatest achievements, however, were *The Apostles' Creed* [49] and *A History of Christian Thought.*[50]

McGiffert's historiography represented a shift among American church historians toward scientific history. Schaff had highlighted the sacred mission of the institutional church, the liturgy, the confessions, and ecumenism. On the one hand, McGiffert emphasized objectivity, even when counter to the historian's own theological commitments.

> To study an organism in its antecedents and in its genesis, to trace the course of its growth, to examine it in the varied relations which it has sustained to its environment at successive states of its career, to search for the forces within and without which have served to make it what it is; to do it all, not with the desire of supporting one's own theory or of undermining the theory of another, but in order to understand the organism more thoroughly...this is the historic method, and this is the way we study the church today.[51]

On the other hand, he rejected objective historiography, such as that of Williston Walker. He argued that a historian is not simply an annalist, but must bring to bear upon history his insight and constructive genius.[52] This meant that as an objective historian McGiffert was not adverse to pursuing theological presuppositions such as those of liberal theology, specifically "a scientific naturalism, an emphasis on the simple gospel of Jesus, and a concern for the good of society."[53]

In terms of an overarching interpretation, a friend observed that McGiffert viewed Christianity in three unequal time periods, the first prior to institutions when the Spirit of God acted freely, the second manifesting a closed Canon and apostolic authoritarianism, then modern times when once again the Spirit moved freely in human conscience.[54] The common link throughout is Jesus who is recognized in some fashion as central by all Christians. Despite this commonality, McGiffert, unlike Schaff, located numerous variations, if not contradictions, and observed that there existed "no such thing as Christianity in general." Bowden concluded:

> Although much of his work described fundamental changes in the content of various Christianities, in the last analysis he still thought that, at rare moments in the history of western religion, some individuals had succeeded in regaining the basic essence of which Jesus was the best exemplar.[55]

Much like Harnack, for McGiffert Jesus was the most important figure in Christianity, and central to the teaching of Jesus is God as father who likewise is the father of Jesus' brethren. Life was to be expended in "love and service of one's fellows."[56] Paul's teachings in contrast were "totally at variance with Christ's" since Paul conceived God as remote and wrathful, humans as depraved and unable to improve themselves, salvation as an undeserved gift, and life as something to be devoted to otherworldly concerns.

Like others before and after, McGiffert considered Marcion the pivotal figure in second-century Christianity. He understood the Apostles' Creed as formulated for the specific purpose of combating Marcion.[57] He was also attentive to the influence of Paul upon the second century, which he held to be more attenuated than one might expect. "Though Paul was the greatest thinker in the early church his thought was not generally understood and his interpretation of Christianity was not widely accepted."[58] McGiffert saw an essential agreement in Paul and John that Christianity is a religion of personal salvation rather than a Jewish Messianic movement. The only apostolic father of this persuasion was Ignatius.

> The letters naturally contain no systematic statement of Ignatius' Christian beliefs, and yet there runs through them a very definite conception of Christianity, a genuinely mystical conception, which allies him to Paul and John and distinguishes him sharply from all the other so-called Apostolic Fathers....To Ignatius as to Paul and John Christianity was a religion of personal salvation.[59]

But then even John and Ignatius had differences with Paul:

> ... particularly the rejection of Paul's dualism by both John and Ignatius and their insistence that salvation is for the flesh as well as the spirit and that the Christian life is a life of obedience to the law of God....[60]

In the other fathers, according to McGiffert, Christianity was "a divine law by keeping which a man may win eternal reward and escape eternal punishment."[61] The apologists professed much the same except they emphasized the ethical. Irenaeus performed the feat of wedding the mysticism of Paul, John, and Ignatius with the legalism of the rest of the church.

> Before his time, as we have seen, two streams of thought ran side by side within the Christian church, the one predominantly mystical, the other legal. The great significance of Irenaeus

lies in the fact that he felt the influence of both these tendencies and in his interpretation of Christianity combined the
mystical and legal elements in such a way as to give them a
permanent place in Christian theology.[62]

McGiffert did not found "a school," though he trained a number
of scholars. His interpretive work suffered with the demise of
liberalism and the emergence of dialectical theology. His book on
the Apostles' Creed remains, however, a solid piece of scholarship.
He, perhaps more than anyone else, paved the way for scholars to
interpret church history in the manner they believed warranted by
the evidence rather than according to confessional positions and
doctrinal commitments.

Kirsopp Lake, a Britisher, was appointed professor at Harvard in
1914 where he remained until retirement in 1948.[63] Lake was
especially noted as a textual critic, palaeographer, archaeologist,
and an authority on Jewish and Hellenistic backgrounds for Paul
and Acts.[64] He also did considerable work on the second century,
especially in the translation of texts. Already noted was that he
offered a seminar on the second century for almost twenty years.
His translations of *The Apostolic Fathers* and Eusebius' *The
Ecclesiastical History* in the Loeb Classical Library edition continue
to serve the scholarly community.[65] In these works, Lake's comments are almost altogether historical and textual, revealing virtually nothing of his larger presuppositions. In general his concerns
were much less theological than those of McGiffert.[66]

The interpretive presuppositions of Lake may, however, be
found in a thin volume *Landmarks in the History of Early Christianity*,
the Haskell Foundation lectures at Oberlin in 1919.[67] Lake identified his procedure with a history of religions approach. He proposed that a religion comes into being as "a combination of synthesis of older forms of thought with little new in its
composition."[68] As the new religion makes its way into its environment, the best elements remain while the worst disappear.
Thereupon, newer elements of a higher quality are assimilated.
"But the process never really stopped; from beginning to end new
elements were constantly absorbed and old elements dropped. For
religion lives through the death of religions."[69] Christianity commenced in this pattern. It was conceived in Judaism and was content with such gestation, but Judaism forced the issue by its refusal
to recognize the cult of the emperor, resulting in the destruction of
Jerusalem in 70 C.E. The Christians henceforth found themselves
more and more interfacing with the Graeco-Roman world.

Nevertheless in the end the inevitable synthesis between Judaism and Greek thought was accomplished, though the official world was unable to bring it about. The small and at first despised sect of Christians was driven out of the Synagogue and forced into contact with the heathen world, at first probably against its will....When their fellow-countrymen refused to hear they turned to the Gentiles and there ensued rapidly the abandonment of Jewish practice and the assimilation of Greek and Graeco-Oriental thought.

From that time on the history of Christianity might be written as a series of syntheses with the thought and practice of the Roman world, beginning with the circumference and moving to the center.[70]

From this orientation, Lake identified a series of syntheses through which Christianity moved. First of all, it absorbed the Graeco-Oriental cults. Added to the Jewish worship of God was the longing of lower socio-economic classes for salvation initiated by a Lord, divine by nature. "Christianity became the Jewish contribution to the Oriental cults, offering, as the Synagogue never did, private salvation by supernatural means to all who were willing to accept it."[71] A second synthesis was thereafter accomplished especially in Ephesus, but possibly elsewhere. In this city claims for private salvation were wed with Greek philosophy. "It asked what was the philosophic explanation of its Lord, and it hit on the device of identifying him with the Logos—a phrase common to several types of philosophy though used in quite different meanings."[72] This synthesis passed through the Gnostic groups, but unsuccessfully, and reached its fruition in the Alexandrian theologians Clement and Origen, resulting in "the triumphant construction of a system which really reconciled in part and seemed to reconcile entirely the Christian cult and the later Platonic metaphysics."[73] A third synthesis resulted from Platonized Christianity conflated with Stoicism, the latter characterized by Lake as on the "border ground between metaphysics and ethics."[74] The culmination of these syntheses was obtained when Ambrose struggled with the ethics of Cicero in a series of sermons. This synthesis of the ethics of Jesus and Cicero made possible the acceptance "by one another of Christianity and the Empire."[75] The centuries that followed were occupied with working out the implications of these three major syntheses.

Unlike McGiffert and those influenced by Harnack and Ritschl, Lake negated the view that the simple religion of Jesus was Christianity's highest form. Much after the manner of Hegel, he visualized later syntheses as superior stages.

It is a great record of great achievement, for no one who studies the history of religions with any degree of sympathetic insight can doubt but that each synthesis was a real step in progress towards the unification of aspiration with knowledge which it is the task of theologians to bring about, and to express as clearly as they may.[76]

Second-century Christianity was therefore not a corrupted form but a stage on the way to even higher attainment.

Much like McGiffert, Lake formed no school, though Goodenough was his student. Goodenough recognized indebtedness to George Foot Moore but said little about Lake. Lake's contributions, however, have outlasted those of either McGiffert or Case. We have already noted his translations. In addition, his work on the New Testament period abides. Ernst Haenchen in his monumental *The Acts of the Apostles* acknowledged that "The treasures of *The Beginnings of Christianity* have been consulted again and again."[77]

Shirley Jackson Case completed his B.D. (1901) and Ph.D. (1906) at Yale.[78] In 1908 he was appointed professor of New Testament interpretation at Chicago, in part, no doubt, because of his sympathy with the major thrusts of the Chicago school. In 1917 he received an added appointment in early church history and in 1923 was made chairman of the church history department. In that office he created one of the most distinguished departments in the country with church historians of repute in all areas.

The Chicago school was noted for its emphasis on the socio-historical method of investigation and an epistemology of experience.[79] "Professor Case's distinct contribution to the Chicago school was to refine its socio-historical method and apply it vigorously and rigorously to early Christian beginnings."[80] Case concluded that by his time the literary analysis had gone as far as possible in its major conclusions, and that New Testament scholars should now turn to the "Christian literature out of which the New Testament came."

Instead of concentrating exclusively upon the New Testament documents, one presses inquiry on the more remote Christian society within which the writings arose and were finally assembled into a collection to be used for purposes of propaganda and control. The attempt to re-examine the New Testament in the light of this social setting carries interpretation on to the most recent phase in its history.[81]

Case published a number of works which traversed the second century. His most influential book, *The Evolution of Early Christianity*[82] is crucial in ascertaining the presuppositions from which he worked, while *The Social Origins of Christianity* extends his observations into the second century. Case called for a developmental interpretation of Christianity, asserting that only this perspective is possible for modern man. In the past, Case observed, Christianity had mostly been looked upon as unchangeable. Roman Catholics tended to argue that throughout its history the church remained the same. Protestants, in contrast, assumed that the first-century church was one in thought and life, but up until the Reformation was afflicted by a series of apostasies. Certain moderns appeared open to the idea of development; for example, the Catholic Modernists and the Hegelians. But in the view of Case, the Modernist Catholics at the start posited a static element, namely, "...the gospel spirit which has remained unchanged through the ages," even if they did admit that all the details have changed.[83] The Hegelians faithfully searched for evolution in Christianity, but one initiated from without, so that Christianity was "essentially the reproduction of a set of ideas divinely determined beforehand."[84] Case rejected an irreducible minimum of genuine essence since it gave attention to only "a partial definition of certain phases which have appeared in the historical career of the movement."[85] So he concluded:

> Christianity can be ultimately and comprehensively conceived only in the development sense, as the product of actual persons working out their religious problems in immediate contact with their several worlds of reality, the process being renewed in the religious experience of each new generation.[86]

Case came to a position much like that of Lake but did not emphasize dialectical aspects of that development, nor did he stress the emergence of higher forms.

With respect to the second century, Case's interest was the manner in which the church worked out its particular concerns and tasks. This century seemed neither superior nor inferior to other Christian centuries. Case was more interested in an objective scrutiny of the dynamics of development than assigning a rank to the qualities. It is clear, however, that Case considered modern Christianity with its social concerns at a higher stage, though its lofty attainment was possible only because of the *Zeitgeist* of the modern age. He had no criticism of the second century for its negligence in social concern.

Case identified a contrast in the church of the first and second centuries. In the first century, Paul's "Spirit directed churches" were a major force, but they were already beginning to fade in the latter part of the century. The demise of Pauline proclivities resulted from the growing need in the second century for "social consolidation, and for the gradual upbuilding of social structure."[87] Concretely, these had to do with church organization, the authority of the old traditions, that is, the Old Testament, and later the uniquely Christian experiences revolving about Jesus, hence the Canon of the New Testament, the apostolic succession of bishops, and the turning away from the Christian expectation of the early return of Christ to the enhancing of economic, social, and intellectual positions. During this period also surfaced a heightening of the institutional sacredness attached to the Lord's Supper.[88] While the tasks of the second century may seem irrelevant to the needs of modern man, still a study of this century can be "a very genuine source of inspiration" as one examines the manner in which religious people "sought to realize their desires within that area of experience and attainment commonly termed religion."[89] Case trained numerous students, but dialectical theology overshadowed his unique contributions as he himself grew aware.[90] In recent times, interest in a socio-historical approach to early Christianity has revived. Although many of Case's specific conclusions are no longer viable, his basic presuppositions have regained respectability, but not because Case himself is being read. Those who share Case's concerns would do well to retrace with him the trails he blazed even though improvements must precede cutting a new thruway.

Erwin Ramsdell Goodenough was appointed to the faculty of Yale in 1923 where initially he taught history and later history of religions.[91] His first interests were the second century, but he dropped back to the first century to explore the roots and never returned in the manner he himself anticipated.[92] Early in his career Goodenough taught a seminar on the second-century church at Yale. At this time he had recently published his doctoral dissertation on Justin Martyr.[93] In the process of completing this study, Goodenough came upon the question which was to occupy the rest of his life. In his own words, "How then could Christianity so early and quickly have been hellenized?"[94]

Goodenough decided even then that such assimilation was not a dramatic and sudden upheaval. The antagonism of the Jews, and hence the early Christians, for hellenistic ways was too deep-seated. So, as he struggled with the thought of Justin, he concluded:

If that leisurely fusion with paganism did not take place in Christianity, then it must have been antecedently prepared for early Christians in a Judaism (not *all* Judaism) which had in a gradual way come to be hellenized....So if we had no evidence for a hellenized Judaism at all we should have had to invent it, I early concluded, to make the origin of Christianity historically conceivable.[95]

To pursue his commitment Goodenough wrote a number of works on Philo and commenced his monumental effort to examine the Jewish symbols in the Graeco-Roman period so as to locate these gradual hellenistic acculturations. Upon completion these studies totaled eleven volumes, the last published in 1964. With his magnum opus finished, Goodenough turned to the work for which these volumes established the backdrop, "the history of early Christianity," but death precluded these long cherished hopes.[96]

Goodenough accepted the early hellenization of Christianity as the presupposition for his investigations. He found hellenism not only in John and Hebrews as did most scholars of the 1920s, but also in Paul. He charged that his Yale colleague Frank Porter missed the essential interest of Paul "which was to experience what in Greek tradition we should call the Orphic escape from the body or flesh to the soul or spirit, a dream of escape which is nowhere in the synoptic tradition ascribed to Jesus."[97] Paul was not alone, since these concerns are also found in John, eliciting the conclusion that a common hellenization was already present in Christianity for which Judaism had already laid the groundwork.

Goodenough's one book which reflects the manner in which he understood the second century was his study of Justin. Being challenged to locate the sources of Justin's allegories, Goodenough concluded that they could only have been generated from a common Jewish milieu that had already incorporated many hellenistic elements. Reflecting on his dissertation, Goodenough wrote:

That Justin, in the way dear to philological fancy, was writing with the text of Philo in mind did not at all appear: but that he was writing with a very similar tradition in mind was indisputable, and much more important than his having the text of Philo before him, for it indicated a widespread Judaism similar to that of Philo on which Justin could draw, a tradition which turned the Old Testament stories into revelations of the nature of the Logos, and made the pattern of religion the pagan one of appropriation of and union with this Logos rather than the typical Jewish one of obedience. So I suggested at the end of the dissertation that the hellenization of Christianity had been made possible because Jews in the pagan world had opened doors through which pagan notions had come into their Judaism; that when such Jews became Christians these notions were already at home in their minds as a part of their Judaism itself, and so at once became a part of their Christianity.[98]

Because of his own self-professed paganism, Goodenough had no apparent preference for second-century Christianity over any other century.[99] He seemed content to describe the developmental elements in Christianity and cared little for assigning relative merit to the various viewpoints found therein. His main contribution lay with his excursions into the Jewish and hellenistic backgrounds to second-century Christianity. Though Goodenough trained a number of students, his concerns were so individualistic that none followed explicitly in his steps.

This study has shown that instruction in the history of the second-century church began in America in the nineteenth century as a component part of generalized instruction in church history. Early in the twentieth century, work became more specialized and seminars on the second century ensued. Publications of various sorts heralded the accelerating scholarship. Both tools for the study of the primary texts and interpretation of the times appeared. Of these, many of the tools remain as standards while the interpretations have tended to drop by the wayside. Even now American scholarship awaits a monumental and classic study on the second-century church. It appears that the pragmatic concerns of American culture continue to influence all phases of academic study, even the seemingly esoteric field of ancient church history. Born to meet a particular need—the training of ministers—and maintained, because it provided useful comment from the past upon the present, the study of the history of the second century remains primarily the effort of those seeking to correct and nurture the church.

NOTES

1. Warner Bowden, *Church History in the Age of Science* (Chapel Hill: The University of North Carolina Press, 1971); Bowden's bibliography, 247-54, reveals the paucity of work in this area.
2. Samuel Elliot Morison, *Harvard College in the Seventeenth Century* (Cambridge: Harvard University Press, 1936) 2.265.
3. Roland H. Bainton, *Yale and the Ministry* (New York: Harper & Brothers, 1957) 186.

4. Charles H. Haskins, "History," *A Cyclopedia of Education,* ed Paul Monroe (New York: MacMillan, 1914) 3.284.

5. Charles Augustus Briggs, *History of the Study of Theology* (New York: Charles Scribner's Sons, 1919) 187. Cf. Jurgen Herbst, *The German Historical School in American Scholarship* (Ithaca: Cornell University Press, 1965) 34-36, and Bowden, *Church History,* 9-15.

6. W. Stull Holt, "Historical Scholarship," *American Scholarship,* ed Merle Curti (New York: Russell & Russell, 1953) 86.

7. Ephraim Emerton, "History in Theological Education," *Theological Study Today* (Chicago: University of Chicago Press, 1921) 121-33. The work to which Emerton referred is: August Neander, *General History of the Christian Religion and Church,* 4 vols (Boston: Crocker and Brewster, 1847-51). The translator was Joseph Torrey (1797-1867) who was born in Rowley, Mass., and graduated from Dartmouth in 1816 and Andover Theological Seminary in 1819. He taught at the University of Vermont in 1827. In 1828-29 he was in Europe, visiting Berlin, where he became acquainted with Schleiermacher and at Halle where he was befriended by Tholuck. He was president of Vermont from 1862-66.

8. *General Catalogue of the Theological Seminary Andover, Mass. 1808-1908* (Boston: Thomas Todd, 1908) 16. Murdock was born in Westbrook, Conn. and graduated from Yale in 1797. He was appointed Brown Professor of Sacred Rhetoric and Ecclesiastical History at Andover in 1819. He translated J. L. von Mosheim's *Institutes of Ecclesiastical History* which was published in New Haven in 1832 in three volumes. He provided such copious notes that the publication was almost an independent treatment. *Dictionary of American Biography* (New York: Charles Scribner's Sons, 1934) 13.342. (Hereafter cited *DAB*)

9. Born in Acton, Mass., Shedd graduated from the University of Vermont in 1839 and Andover in 1843. He served as a minister, then taught at Vermont in English literature, then at Auburn Seminary in sacred rhetoric. *DAB* 17.56. While teaching at Andover (1854-62) Shedd published his *Lectures Upon the Philosophy of History* (Andover: W. F. Draper, 1856).

10. Born in Brunswick, Maine, and educated at Bowdoin College and Bangor Theological Seminary (1835), he studied at Andover and taught rhetoric and oratory at Bowdoin. *DAB* 17.374. His published works include *The Prevalent View in the Ancient Church of the Purpose of the Death of Jesus Christ* (Boston: Usher, 1900).

11. Born at Hagerstown, Maryland, Schmucker graduated from the University of Pennsylvania (1819) and Princeton Theological Seminary (1820). *DAB* 16.443.

12. Born at New Goshenhoppen, Pa. *DAB* 10.501.

13. Abdel Ross Wentz, *Gettysburg Lutheran Theological Seminary* (Harrisburg: The Evangelical Press, 1964) 1.332f.

14. Valentine was born near Uniontown, Maryland, graduated from Gettysburg College in 1846 and the seminary in 1852. He served various churches until 1866 when he was appointed Professor of Biblical and Ecclesiastical History at the seminary. *DAB* 19.141.

15. Thomas H. Olbricht, "Christian Connexion and Unitarian Relations 1800-1844," *Restoration Quarterly* 9 (1966) 160-86.

16. Huidekoper was born in Meadville and educated at Harvard. Because of failing eyesight he traveled to Europe visiting the universities of Geneva, Leipzig, and Berlin attending lectures in history, literature, and biblical studies. There he had personal contact with Cousin, Picot, Neander and De Wette. Returning to America he completed his theological studies at Harvard in 1843. *DAB* 9.358. His two books impinging on the second century were *The Belief of the First Three Centuries Concerning Christ's Mission to the Underworld* (Boston: Crosby, Nichols, 1854) and *Judaism at Rome* (New York: J. Miller, 1876).

17. *The Catalogue of the Officers and Students,* 1845-46 (Meadville: Lewis L. Lord, 1845) 7. Blindness forced Huidekoper to retire in the late 1870s.

18. *The Catalogue of the Officers and Students,* 1884-85 (Meadville: Lewis L. Lord, 1884) 13.

19. A native of Dover, Delaware, Miller studied mostly at home, but after a year at the University of Pennsylvania took a degree. His theological training was with various noted ministers after which he was ordained. He preached in New York for a number of years, then in 1813 was appointed professor of church history and government at Princeton, which position he held until 1850. *DAB* 12.636.

20. His singular effort at church history was *Brief Retrospect of the Eighteenth Century,* 2 vols (New York: T. & J. Swords, 1803).

21. Joseph Alexander graduated from the college in 1826 at 15. He spent time in private study, taught at the college, and after a year of study at Halle (1834) taught at the seminary. He was first professor of oriental and biblical literature. In 1851 he was transferred to the chair of biblical and ecclesiastical history, which chair he occupied until 1859 a year before his death. *DAB* 1.173.

22. Moffat was born in Scotland and was essentially self-trained except that upon migrating to America in 1833 entered Princeton. He served as a tutor at Princeton and Yale, then taught at Lafayette and Miami in Oxford, Ohio, followed by eight years at Princeton in the college. *DAB* 13.75. His published works included *Outlines on Church History* (Princeton: C. S. Robinson, 1875), and *The Church in Scotland* (Philadelphia: Presbyterian Board of Publication, 1882).

23. Born in Chur, Switzerland, in 1819, Schaff died in New York in 1893. Schaff studied at Tübingen, Halle, and Berlin, where he attended the lectures of Neander. He received his theology degree in 1841. In 1842 he was a *Privatdozent* at the University of Berlin. In 1843 he was appointed a professor at Mercersburg Theological Seminary. He resigned in 1865 and joined the faculty of Union Theological Seminary in 1870. *DAB* 16.417. On Schaff's historiography see Bowden, *Church History,* 31-68.

24. Philip Schaff, *History of the Christian Church* (New York: Charles Scribner's Sons, 1882-1910).

25. *Ibid.,* 1.vi.

26. Sydney E. Ahlstrom, *A Religious History of the American People* (New Haven: Yale University Press, 1972) 8f, n 14. Ahlstrom also called Schaff's book, *What is Church History? A Vindication of the Idea of Historical Development* (Philadelphia: J. B. Lippincott, 1846) "a milestone in the history of American historical theology," 618.

27. The offerings at Drew Theological Seminary in 1867, the year it opened, are fairly typical of the manner in which the general history of the church was spread over the three-year curriculum:
Junior Year: History of the Old Covenant; Life of Jesus; Apostolic age.
Middle Year: Church History to the Reformation; History of Doctrines; Christian Archaeology.
Senior Year: Church History (Reformation to present time); Comparative Symbolics; History of Doctrines; History of Missions; Statistics.
James Richard Joy, *The Teachers of Drew 1867-1942* (Madison, N. J.: Drew University, 1942) 10f. Cf. *The Princeton Theological Seminary Catalogue* for 1858-59 in which Biblical and Ecclesiastical History are listed for each of the three years. The Harvard Divinity School announcement of 1895-96, 12f, also has a three-part division, but with somewhat different time spans: "1. The first Eight Christian Centuries, 2. The Middle Ages from Charlemagne to Dante, 3. The Era of the Reformation in Europe."

28. E.g., A. C. Coxe (1818-1896), born in Mendham, N. J., graduated from the University of the City of New York and from General Theological Seminary, consecrated Episcopalian bishop of Western New York in 1865, produced a revised edition of *The Ante-Nicene Fathers. DAB* 4. 484. Numerous Americans were involved in the translation of works included in *A Select Library of the Nicene and Post-Nicene Fathers of the Christian Church,* eds P. Schaff and H. Wace (Buffalo: The Christian Literature Company, 1 ser 1886-1889, 2 ser 1890-1900) such as: Tabbot W. Chambers, A. C. Coxe, F. B. Davenport, J. Rendel Harris, C. D. Hartranft, A. C. McGiffert, E. C. Moore, L. L. Paine, E. C. Richardson, Matthew Riddle, and G. F. Seymour.

29. Richard J. Storr, *The Beginnings of Graduate Education in America* (Chicago: The Univerity of Chicago Press, 1953). Cf. Bernard Berelson, *Graduate Education in the United States* (New York: McGraw Hill 1960) 9-42.

30. Armstrong was born in 1874, A. B. Princeton, 1894, A. M. 1896, B. D. 1897, Marburg 1897, Berlin 1897-98, Erlangen 1898. He became a professor at Princeton in 1903. *Who's Who* 1916-17, 66.

31. DeWitt was born in 1842, A. B. Princeton 1861, A. M. 1864, professor of church history at Princeton beginning in 1892. *Who's Who,* 1910-11, 516.

32. *Yale Divinity School,* 1910-11, 41.

33. *Yale Divinity School,* 1930-31, 24.

34. *Yale Divinity School,* 1934-35, 31; 1940-41, 29.

35. *Harvard Divinity School,* 1895-96, 12. Ephraim Emerton (1851-1935) was born in Salem, Mass. He received the A. B. at Harvard in 1871. In 1874-75 he was at Leipzig in history, then for two years at Berlin. He received the doctorate at Leipzig in 1877. He taught at Harvard until 1882 at which time he was appointed to a chair in church history at Harvard Divinity School. He was one of the founders of the American Historical Association in 1884. *DAB* sup. 1.285. Bowden, *Church History,* 94-114, has a lengthy analysis of his historiography.

36. *Harvard Divinity School,* 1928-29, 17.

37. Moore was born in West Chester, Pa., graduated from Yale in 1872, and Union Theological Seminary in 1877. He spent most of 1885 in

Germany, and again in 1909-10 where he was exchange professor. *DAB* 13.124. His special contribution was in the area of second-century Judaism, *Judaism in the First Centuries of the Christian Era, the Age of the Tannaim,* 3 vols (Cambridge: Harvard University Press, 1927-30).

38. Born in Ipswich, England, Foakes-Jackson took his degree from Trinity College, Cambridge in 1879, and the B.D. in 1903. He taught at Cambridge until 1916 when at 61 he accepted the Briggs graduate professorship of Christian institutions at Union Theological Seminary where he taught until retirement in 1934 at the age of 79. *Dictionary of National Biography*, 1941-50, 426. His works which pertain to the second century are: *Christian Difficulties in the Second and Twentieth Centuries; A Study of Marcion* (Cambridge: W. Heffer & Sons, 1903), *Studies in the Life of the Early Church* (London: Hodder & Stoughton, 1924) and *The History of the Christian Church From the Earliest Times to A.D. 461* (Cambridge: J. Hall, 1891).

39. Walker was born in Portland, Maine. He graduated from Amherst in 1883, took the B.D. from Hartford Theological Seminary in 1886, and received the Ph.D. in history from the University of Leipzig in 1888. He taught at Bryn Mawr, Hartford Theological Seminary (1892-1901) and then at Yale where he remained until his death. *DAB* 19.366. Walker taught courses in early church history at Yale, but most of his publications were on European and American Calvinism. His one work covering the second century was his widely acclaimed *A History of the Christian Church* (New York: Charles Scribner, 1918).

40. Born in Quincy, Goodspeed attended the University of Chicago and graduated from Denison University in 1890. He studied at Yale, but took his B.D. (1897) and Ph.D. (1898) at Chicago. The following two years he spent in study, mostly with Harnack at Berlin, and in the Near East, looking for ancient manuscripts. *The National Cyclopaedia of American Biography,* 52.481. (Hereafter cited *NCAB*) His contribution to second-century studies was in the area of indexes, translations and interpretations. Worthy of special mention here are *Index patristicus: Sive clavis patrum apostolicorum operum* (Leipzig: J. C. Hinrichs, 1907) and *Index apologeticus: Sive clavis Iustini Martyris operum aliorumque apologetarum pristinorum* (Leipzig: J. C. Hinrichs, 1912), *Die Ältesten Apologeten* (Göttingen: Vandenhoeck & Ruprecht, 1914), and *Apostolic Fathers: An American Translation* (Chicago: University of Chicago Press, 1950). Most of these works are still valuable tools.

41. Defarrari was born in Stoneham, Mass. He received the A.B. from Dartmouth in 1912 and the M.A. and Ph.D. from Princeton. He became a professor at the Catholic University of America in 1918. His main contribution has been in editing series: *Catholic University Patristic Studies* 100 vols (Washington: Catholic University of America, 1922-45) and *The Fathers of the Church* (New York: Cima Publishing Co., 1947).

42. Nock was born in Plymouth, England, and received the B.A. from Trinity College, Cambridge in 1922 and the M.A. in 1926. He lectured in classics at Cambridge. From 1930 he taught at Harvard until his death. *Who Was Who,* 4.705. His major contribution to second-century studies was *Corpus Hermeticum,* ed A. D. Nock, French tr A. J. Festugiere; 4 vols (Paris: Société d'edition 1945-54). Also of impor-

tance are his *Conversion* (London: Oxford University Press, 1933) and *Early Gentile Christianity and Its Hellenistic Background* (New York: Harper & Row, 1964).

43. Richardson was born in London, received his B.A. at the University of Saskatchewan in 1930, and a Licentiate in theology in 1931. He received the S.T.M. from Union Theological Seminary in 1932, and the Th. D. in 1934. He spent 1933 at Göttingen and 1935 in Basel. He was associated with Union from 1934 until his death. *Who's Who in America,* 1974-75, 2578. Two of his works should be noted, *The Christianity of Ignatius of Antioch* (New York: Columbia University Press, 1935) and *Early Christian Fathers,* LCC 1 (Philadelphia: The Westminster Press, 1953).

44. Various translations of the writings of second-century churchmen were printed in America prior to 1890, but these were mostly reprints of British works translated and edited by Britishers. Examples are Titus Flavius Clemens, *Christian Doctrine and Practice in the Second Century,* ed & tr C. F. Cornwallis (Philadelphia: Lea and Blanchard, 1846); *The Genuine Epistles of the Apostolical Fathers,* ed & tr William Wake (New York: Stanford and Swords, 1850); and *Epistles of Ignatius,* ed W. K. Clementson (Portland: Cay and Fraser, 1831; Troy: N. Tuttle, 1834). Two exceptions were *The Select Works of Tertullian,* ed F. A. March (New York: Harper & Brothers, 1876) and *Justin Martyr,* ed Basil L. Gildersleeve (New York: Harper and Brothers, 1877).

45. Hartranft (1839-1914) was born in Pennsylvania and graduated from the University of Pennsylvania in 1861, then from Brunswick Theological Seminary in 1864. In 1878 he was called to the Hartford Theological Seminary as professor of ecclesiastical history. *DAB* 8.367. Richardson (1860-1939) was born in Woburn, Mass. A. B. Amherst 1880, graduated from Hartford Theological Seminary in 1883, and later received his Ph.D. from Washington and Jefferson in 1887. He returned to Hartford Theological Seminary in 1884 where he served as Librarian and Professor of Bibliography until 1890. He then moved to Princeton University where he labored from 1890 to 1925. *Who Was Who in America,* 1.1030. Riddle (1836-1916) was born in Pittsburgh, and graduated from Jefferson College in 1852. He was a student at Western Theological Seminary, Pittsburgh 1853-55, but graduated from New Brunswick in 1859. He studied in Germany in 1860-61. He was elected professor of New Testament exegesis at Hartford Theological Seminary in 1871 where he served until 1887. In 1887 he returned to Western as professor. *DAB* 15.592.

46. Born in New York, McGiffert received the A.B. degree from Western Reserve University in 1882, and the B.D. from Union in 1885. He studied in Berlin for a year, then took his doctorate under Adolf Harnack at Marburg in 1888. He also spent extended periods in France and Italy. He was a professor of church history at Lane Theological Seminary in Cincinnati from 1888-1893. In 1893 he was elected Schaff's successor at Union, which position he held until his retirement in 1927. *DAB* sup. 1.527.

47. A. C. McGiffert, *God of the Early Christians* (Edinburgh: T. & T. Clark, 1924).

48. A. C. McGiffert, *The Social Triumph of the Ancient Church* (New York: Harper & Brothers, 1933).

49. A. C. McGiffert, *The Apostles' Creed* (New York: Charles Scribner's Sons, 1932).

50. A. C. McGiffert, *A History of Christian Thought,* 2 vols (New York: Charles Scribner's Sons, 1932).

51. A. C. McGiffert, "The Historical Study of Christianity," *Bibliotheca Sacra* 50 (1893) 152.

52. Bowden, *Church History,* 145f.

53. *Ibid.,* 159.

54. Ambrose W. Vernon, "Arthur Cushman McGiffert," *Hibbert Journal* 32 (1934) 286.

55. Bowden, *Church History,* 161.

56. A. C. McGiffert, "Was Jesus or Paul the Founder of Christianity?" *American Journal of Theology* 13 (1909) 18-20.

57. McGiffert, *The Apostles' Creed,* 13.

58. McGiffert, *A History of Christian Thought,* I 30.

59. *Ibid.,* 37.

60. *Ibid.,* 44.

61. *Ibid.,* 95.

62. *Ibid.,* 132.

63. Lake was born in Southhampton, England, and educated at Lincoln College, Oxford. From 1904-1914 he was professor ordinarius of early Christian literature and New Testament exegesis at the University of Leiden. While at Leiden he, with his wife, published the photographic facsimile of Codex Sinaiticus Petropolitanus: The New Testament, The Epistle of Barnabas, and the Shepherd of Hermas. *Dictionary of National Biography,* 1941-50, 466.

64. Aside from his textual studies the greatest work of Lake may be found in the volumes which he and Foakes-Jackson edited: *The Beginnings of Christianity,* 5 vols (London: Macmillan and Co., 1920-33).

65. *The Apostolic Fathers,* 2 vols (Cambridge: Harvard University Press, 1912-13) and Eusebius' *The Ecclesiastical History* (Cambridge: Harvard University Press, 1926).

66. Lake's son made the remark that his father's first interests were sociological. He later turned to history and exegesis never having much interest in theology. *Quantulacumque,* eds Robert P. Casey, Silva Lake, Agnes K. Lake (London: Christophers, 1937) vii.

67. Kirsopp Lake, *Landmarks in the History of Early Christianity* (London: Macmillan and Co., 1920).

68. *Ibid.,* 1.

69. *Ibid.*

70. *Ibid.,* 7-8.

71. *Ibid.,* 8. He obviously therefore did not seek to explain first-century Christianity as syncretistic in origin as did the more radical German *Religionsgeschichte* School.

72. *Ibid.,* 9.

73. *Ibid.*

74. *Ibid.*

75. *Ibid.,* 10.

76. *Ibid.,* 10-11.

77. Ernst Haenchen, *The Acts of the Apostles* (Philadelphia: The Westminster Press, 1971) vii.

78. Case received the A.B. degree from Acadia University, Nova Scotia in 1893, and the M.A. in 1896. He taught for two years at Cobb Divinity

School, Bates College, as professor of philosophy and the history of religion. In 1910 he spent several months at the University of Marburg. *NCAB* 36.152.

79. C. Harvey Arnold, *Near the Edge of Battle* (Chicago: Divinity School Association, 1966).
80. *Ibid.,* 49.
81. Shirley Jackson Case, *The Social Origins of Christianity* (Chicago: The University of Chicago Press, 1923) 24.
82. Shirley Jackson Case, *The Evolution of Early Christianity* (Chicago: The University of Chicago Press, 1914). On the importance of this book see *Environmental Factors in Christian History,* eds John Thomas McNeill, Matthew Spinka, and Harold R. Willoughby (Chicago: The University of Chicago Press, 1939) x. Other books by Case discussing the second century are *The Social Origins of Christianity, Studies in Early Christianity* (New York: The Century Company, 1928), *Makers of Christianity from Jesus to Charlemagne* (New York: H. Holt & Co., 1934), *The Social Triumph of the Ancient Church* (New York: Harper and Brothers, 1933), and *The Origins of Christian Supernaturalism* (Chicago: The University of Chicago Press, 1946).
83. Case, *The Evolution,* 21.
84. *Ibid.,* 12.
85. *Ibid.,* 25.
86. *Ibid.*
87. Case, *The Social Origins,* 164.
88. *Ibid.,* 161-207.
89. *Ibid.,* 252.
90. Case, *The Origins of Christian Supernaturalism,* v.
91. A native of Brooklyn, he received his B.A. from Hamilton College in 1915. He worked in graduate programs at Columbia and Drew Theological Seminary, and in 1917 received the S.T.B. from Garrett Biblical Institute. He was at Harvard from 1917-1920 where he studied with George Foot Moore and Lake. He received the D. Phil. from Oxford in 1923. While in Europe he spent about a year in Germany and shorter periods in France, Belgium, Holland, and Switzerland. *NCAB* 52.67. After retiring at Yale in 1959 he taught at Brandeis and Radcliffe. Cf. *Religions in Antiquity,* ed Jacob Neusner (Leiden: E. J. Brill, 1968) 1-2.
92. Neusner, *Religions in Antiquity,* 14-16.
93. Erwin R. Goodenough, *The Theology of Justin Martyr* (Jena: Walter Biedermann, 1923).
94. Erwin R. Goodenough, *Jewish Symbols in the Greco-Roman Period* (New York: Pantheon Books, Inc. 1953) 1.3.
95. Goodenough, *Jewish Symbols,* 1.5.
96. Neusner, *Religions in Antiquity,* 15.
97. Goodenough, *Jewish Symbols,* 1.5.
98. *Ibid.,* 1.6.
99. Neusner, *Religions in Antiquity,* 5.

The "Logic" of Canon-making and the Tasks of Canon-criticism

Albert C. Outler

The renewed discussions about the biblical canon and to what Professor J. A. Sanders has termed "canonical-criticism"[1] received warm welcome from Professor Stuart Currie. These discussions, at least in part, seemed to him to turn attention back to the text in its canonical form and, therefore, to the more existential questions of the early Christians. While modern scholarship too long has belabored such matters as dating, sequence, authorship, etc. (questions inherited from nineteenth-century historiography), the early Christians were wrestling with their special history, including the unexpected prolongation of history itself, for which they were ill-prepared, in human terms at least. They had originated as a Jewish sect with a Jewish cult-hero and although they had soon been ex-communicated from their Jewish matrix on account of their Messianic claims and message, they never abandoned their claims to their Jewish heritage. At the same time, they were a "new" religion, deeply involved in the process of "hellenization" (language, race, acculturation, etc.). Here, their pressing tempta-tions and dangers were assimilation and syncretism. On both sides, when they were not ignored (the usual case), they were misunderstood and even persecuted (as an "illicit religion"). Their *kerygma*—about Jesus Christ crucified and risen—was, as they soon discovered, a *skandalon* to orthodox Jews (i.e., a seduction to idolatry) and a *morian* to thoughtful "Greeks" (i.e., a blank absurdity). Professor Currie once remarked that Stephen's martyr-dom could be taken as a symbol of the Christian dilemma—a "hellenized" spokesman for a group caught between their Jewish-Messianic-apocalyptic heritage and the hellenistic *milieu* in which survival seemed doubtful.

I would not presume to claim Currie's agreements with any of my own reflections on "canon-criticism"—even though we did agree that it was a promising new horizon of inquiry in NT studies and in early church history. What I am confident of is that he would have been interested in such a project, and encouraging. It is in this confidence that I venture a series of comments on this "sub-discipline" of both NT and church history—which means that it falls only partially within my own field.

One place to begin the consideration of this problem of "canon" is with the fact that, traditionally, its discussion has been largely polemical in its contexts. More specifically, it was a function of the Protestant-Catholic quarrels about the rival rôles of Scripture and the church[2]—and, then, of the Enlightenment rejection of both rôles in favor of the authority of autonomous, critical judgment.[3] Echoes of this polemical history still reverberate in essays as contemporary as Kurt Aland, *The Problem of the New Testament Canon,*[4] Hans von Campenhausen, *The Formation of the Christian Bible,*[5] and A. C. Sundberg's "revisionist" proposal in *The Interpreter's Dictionary of the Bible,* Supplemental Volume.[6]

One of the bonuses of the new ecumenical situation, however, has been the transvaluation of almost all the issues that were in contention in the sixteenth century—with a new awareness among Protestants as to the hermeneutical importance of "Tradition"[7] and with corresponding "rediscoveries" among Roman Catholics of reformulated conceptions of the primacy of Scripture.[8] The old debates had centered around what Professor Sanders speaks of as the pole of "stabilization." The new insights relate to our heightened awareness of the *adaptability* that is also reflected in the canon-making process.[9] Thus canon-criticism can focus more clearly than other types of "criticism" on the "logic" of the canon-makers in their struggles for a valid sense of identity and differentiation in the self-understanding of the Christian community in its hellenistic *milieu.*

C. F. Evans' epigram ("Christianity is unique among the world religions in being born with a Bible in its cradle"[10]) oversimplifies a complex situation since that cradle "Bible" had not yet been officially "canonized."[11] But Evans' point is crucial for the "logic" of canon-making; viz., that the basic elements of what the Christians would call the "OT" (the Torah, the Prophets and the Psalter) were already "stabilized" as authoritative precipitates of oral traditions—and thus could serve the emerging Christian community in a multi-leveled way. First of all, it was a rehearsal, for the strange motley of Christians, of their common history as "children of God's covenant" and special subjects within God's providence in human history. Thus, it helped define their claims to the biblical heritage as fulfilled and transformed by God's Torah and grace incarnated in Jesus Christ. They understood that Judaism had never been merely "a religion of the book" but rather a tradition of prophetic or rabbinical interpretation of both ancient texts and contemporary experience. Pharisaic Judaism (destined for the crucial role in Judaism's survival after the catastrophes of 70 and 135) was a tradition of *"tannaim,"* whose interpretations were rooted in the Torah (and therefore stable) and yet also addressed to constantly changing circumstances (and therefore adaptable). Their distinction between halakah (case-law) and haggadah (insight)[12] enabled them to codify their "patterns of obedience to Torah" in a flexible way and yet also to enliven their interpretations of religious existence in the face of radical change ("how to sing the Lord's song in a strange land [Ps 137:4]—wherever the "strange land" might be). This was the Judaism that did in fact survive down through all the tragic centuries.

The problem of survival for the Christians, however, was different in more ways than one. Yet they also had need of a "canon" of holy Scripture to aid in their struggles for survival. As a consequence of their transformations of the concept of *Torah* (e.g., the rejection of "ceremonial law," etc.), the role of "case-law" was drastically reduced and transferred to the oral counsel of church leaders. This, however, meant that the Christian equivalents of Jewish haggadah was correspondingly enhanced. More and more (despite their "hellenism," by race and culture), the Christians reaffirmed their continuity with the OT heritage; this was the issue at stake in the Marcionite controversy, despite the attractions of Marcion's agapist "reforms." And yet, these same "hellenists" had a unique "story" (*logon*) about Jesus of Nazareth as "Lord and Savior to the glory of God the Father" which was linked to a vision (partly eschatological, partly institutional!) of a universal human community in a fragmented human family—i.e., the *Katholikos*. Here they were in unequal competition with the great Augustan vision of *lex et pax Romana*.[13] Judaism was forced inward; Christianity was forced outward. Their respective temptations (isolation versus assimilation) were obvious: their respective biblical canons (and their common "logic") served them equally well.

Canon-making, then, was a decisive force in the emergence of the *Katholikos*. Nobody set out—or even was appointed—to write this piece of "canonical literature" or that. Only "enthusiasts" claimed immediate literal inspiration by the Holy Spirit.[14] And yet inspired literature was produced in and for the churches, was recognized as authentic and authoritative and was put to use in the churches—for rehearsals of their roots and origins, for the tasks of proclamation and catechesis, as substance for their lections and liturgies. This literature, thus produced, had begun its "canonical" *functions* as early as Clement of Rome, Justin and Melito of Sardis. Its proto-canonical form is reflected, in different ways, in the Marcionite crisis and Tertullian, in Irenaeus and in Tatian's *Diatessaron* (based, as it was, on a fourfold quarternion already in proto-canonical form).[15] It is this history of function *and* form that supplies the program for canon-criticism—and one need not disparage any of the traditional inquiries of form-, redaction- and genre-criticism in order to agree that this would be a significant *addition* to the tasks of conventional "NT introduction" and early church history surveys. There is a legitimate role for "micro-criticism." There is an equally legitimate one for "macro-criticism"—i.e., the effort to comprehend the NT as a whole (i.e., as canon).

One of the more obvious elements in this inquiry would be a pondering of the fact that all proto-canonical lists are headed by the "gospels" (or, as in the cases of Marcion and Tatian, by one "gospel"). The ruling motive here would not be to solve "The Synoptic Problem" (which I regard as formally insoluble on methodological grounds), nor to smooth out the tangles in "Fourth Gospel" criticism. Canon-criticism raises such prior questions (for example) as why the Gospels are styled as "according to" whomever (*kata*) instead of "by" (*dia*)? What does this imply as to the early Christian understanding of the genre and function of "the gospel"? Or again, why does "The Gospel according to Matthew" stand at the head of *all* the listings of "the holy quarternion" (as Eusebius calls it)? Why is it the most frequently quoted of all the gospels—in the patristic church and later, till the eighteenth century at least? Partial answers to this last question turn upon Matthew's evident twin-intentions: (1) to identify Jesus of Nazareth as God's Messiah truly come and (2) to differentiate the new movement, based upon *this* claim, from Pharisaic Judaism. It may or may not have been written in "Hebrew";[16] what mattered was that it was both "Jewish" and anti-Pharisaic. It bears a clear analogy to the canonical form of the OT and underscores the continuities between Torah and Christ, Prophets and the parables, the Psalter and Christian worship. Part of its "logical" function, therefore, was to provide the Christians with a self-justification of the rift between the church and synagogue and to reinforce their own eschatological views.

It is not necessary for canon-criticism to take on a partisan role in the renewed debate between the defenders of "Markan priority" and the advocates of alternative views (e.g., the "Griesbach hypothesis").[17] Again, it turns to the prior question: what was the "logic" in the canon-makers' minds in their placement of Mark directly after Matthew (with some interesting exceptions)?[18] Papias' explanation here is clearly a summary of an established tradition—that Mark is a version of the memorabilia of Peter.[19] Canon-criticism would, therefore, read Mark, in the first instance, as a terse, episodic rehearsal of the same story as that in Matthew—but with a special focus on the Passion (i.e., on its christological and soteriological implications). Was it, as tradition claimed, especially suited to the needs of a Jewish-Christian community in Rome? Was it a main source for Irenaeus' notions of "impassibility," etc.? How much of a correlation may be found between Mark's "style" and what we know of the earliest Christian liturgies?

The "logic" of "the Gospel according to Luke" is fairly obvious (whatever one's judgment of Professor Conzelmann's ingenious reconstructions of the redactor's theology[20]). A "hellenized" Christian movement needed its own "etiology," a credible account of its Jewish origins *and* of its universal appeal, a firm linkage between the salvation-history of Israel *and* of their own salvation-history—plus an exposition of the unique role of Jesus Christ in the whole scope of God's redemptive purposes and action. They needed a reformulation of the problem of the Parousia. Especially, they needed to have the words *and* deeds of Jesus—and their interdependent meanings—shown forth as a coherent whole. Luke's *logon* meets these needs, as if custom-crafted—and it is in the light of such considerations that Luke may be read "canonically."

A rather different aspect of the "logic" of canon-making appears in the otherwise inexplicable sundering of Acts away from Luke's *proton logon* (Acts 1:1) by the addition of a *fourth* gospel—from a later date and with a different perspective. There are as many interpretations of "the Gospel according to John" as there have been commentators[21]—and canon-criticism need not pretend it can reduce this confusion by much. But it could consider how like and unlike the Fourth Gospel is to the first—especially on the point of the schism between church and synagogue. On the other front ("hellenization"), one should ask about the likeness and unlikeness of the Fourth Gospel to early gnostic interpretations of "the Christ-Event." Was it an orthodox alternative to "false gnosticism" (as Irenaeus and Clement of Alexandria claimed)? Or, take another interesting question, especially fitting for canon-criticism: why was John 13 ignored as the dominical institution of yet another sacrament—by the same church that had taken Matt 26:17 so seriously? Or yet again, canon-criticism would recognize the continuities between the Johannine perspective and the special tradition in Eastern Christianity of "participation"—*metousia theou*.[22]

"The Acts of the Apostles," once separated from its *proton logon*, seems to have found its place with the "catholic epistles" in some of the proto-canonical lists.[23] But its "logical" function as a bridge between "the stories" of Jesus and the Pauline interpretations of that story gradually prevailed and became stabilized. Acts might be seen as a haggadic development of important Christian presuppositions: e.g., how deeply rooted the Christian movement was in *Jerusalem*(!), how the divine charter for a *universal* gospel had come through Peter rather than Paul—and yet how Paul had flowered in his rôle as the divinely ordained "apostle to the Gentiles," with a special interpretation of a "common gospel."

This might then help to explain why the Pauline corpus was placed after the Four Gospels and Acts, with no obvious interest in the strict historical sequence of its units.[24] Along with this indifference as to sequence there was also a flexible view of the limits of the corpus.

No one supposed that Romans was Paul's *first* letter; everyone recognized it as his most comprehensive exposition of the Christian *Mysterium Salutis,* as he understood it. From the beginning—and all the more after the Marcionite crisis—the *Katholikos* needed Paul's incomparable understanding of the cosmic history of salvation (from the First through the Second Adam, from the human fall to Christ's *apocatastasis,* etc.). This, for them, was its "logical" function. The canon-makers had discovered that, without the Gospels and Acts, the Pauline *kerygma* could be understood as having shallow roots in history (2 Cor 5:16).[25] Equally, however, the Gospels alone, without their Pauline interpretations, would scarcely have sustained the church's need for a theology that was truly catholic, evangelical and reformable all at the same time. This need became ever more acute as Christianity plunged more deeply into its *Auseinandersetzungen* with other religions and religious philosophies. Only in some such context do the theological innovations of men like Irenaeus, Tertullian, Clement of Alexandria and Origen become intelligible.

Possible tasks for canon-criticism multiply as one moves to "the miscellaneous writings" and to the large mass of writings finally excluded from the Canon (some with legitimate reluctance). Thus far, at least, I find this a less exigent project—and less interesting. The clear exception is an adequate canonical-critical analysis of Hebrews and the Apocalypse. Hebrews, especially, seems to me never to have been explored as carefully as it deserves, and its significance for the history of christological thought has been seriously underestimated.[26]

A rather different task for canon-criticism—and a very complicated one—is the reconsideration of the *historical* basis for the idea of "a canon within the Canon." One understands some of the

modern motives behind such a notion: e.g., as a safeguard against
the levelling tendencies of "fundamentalism" and "proof-texting,"
as an attempt to rescue Jesus' own words and deeds from the over-
burden of his ecclesiastical redactors, as a bulwark against ecclesial
claims to arbitrary authority in interpretation, etc. One knows
something of the history of this idea—such questions as Luther's
famous Christocentrism and the larger question as to whether all
canonical Scripture is equally inspired and all extra-canonical
Scripture equally *un*inspired! But it is rather less our business—in
canon-criticism, at least—to pass judgment on the canon-makers'
judgments and rather more to understand their "logic" and the
functions of the process. In any case, it is required of us that we try
to see the whole Canon in its functional terms and its units in those
same terms. And this would make for new perspectives (and, one
might hope, new interest!) in NT "introductions" and early church
history "surveys."

The historiographical advantage of such an approach would come
from its directing the modern reader's efforts more directly to the
"life and times" of the early Christian communities, to understand
more emphatically their struggles to identify themselves, to explain
themselves and to differentiate themselves from Judaism, on the
one hand, and from popular religion (including civil religion), on
the other. It was their christologies and soteriologies that defined
their distance from Judaism; it was their common life in the Body
of Christ—in the great *passa* traditions of Israel—that marked them
off from the Greek *thiasoi* and their esoteric rites.[27]

That these are not merely historical excursions may be seen in
their equivalent in contemporary life—in the "Christian" West, at
least—in the ongoing estrangements between so many Jews and
Christians (despite all superficial amiabilities) and the "explosion"
of secular supernaturalisms (in various self-salvation movements).
We are still very far from sufficient probing of the relevance of the
original schism between church and synagogue (and Paul's agoniz-
ing reflections on it) for a fruitful understanding of the scandalous
history of Christian victimizations of the Jews. Without a clear
perspective here, the prospects for real progress in the Christian-
Jewish dialogue are blurred, at best. And it should be obvious by
now that no such perspective in this field can be achieved by
Jewish or Christian scholars working alone. What is needed is a
program of collaborative *historical* reconstruction—with canon-
criticism as one of the important sub-disciplines in such an inquiry.

There is still much "unfinished business" in the study of popular
religion in the Graeco-Roman world and the "place" of Christianity
in that world—and no adequate explanation of the fact that it was

the only popular religion that survived and finally merged with the civil religion of the Empire. Modern analogies here are unmistakable—and the modern problems of interaction, assimilation and differentiation are startlingly similar. The question of a Christian "canon" has, therefore, been reopened (even if this is unacknowledged officially), and the problems of the rôle and authority of Scripture in the church have been altered in more ways than have been fully faced. To the traditional question of a canon *within* the Canon has been added as an alternative one: an open canon subject to cultural adaptations and additions. Canon-criticism would help illuminate these "parallels," especially as they relate to the crucial issues of Christian self-identification in a "post-Christian society," to borrow a popular phrase, however misleading it may be (when was there ever a *"Christian* society" for ours to be "post" to?).

The final problem I'm inclined to mention has plagued Western Christianity since the Reformation at least: viz., "hellenization," "development"—and their presumed synonym, "corruption"—in the Christian movement after its loss of its pristine "apostolic" purity. Was "catholic Christianity" hopelessly corrupted as it "developed"?[28] Or was the "hellenized" *Katholikos* a legitimate continuation of the movement that began with Jesus? Here the ways divide—between those for whom the "simplicity," "purity" and validity of NT Christianity are somehow normative and recoverable only from the Scriptures but *not* tradition (this view is the essence of *pietism*, even when formulated by sophisticated "critics") and those for whom the historical experience of the Christian community—tragically flawed though it has *always* been—constitutes an integral element in both the history of salvation and in the *ethos* of the Christian community today.[29]

In one form or another, Christians have professed the canonical Scriptures (of the Old and New Testaments) to constitute their "sole rule of faith and practice"[30] or, alternatively, "the real *norma non normata* in the Church for all time.[31] The Protestant slogan about *sola Scriptura* encapsulates a profound but partial truth since the fact is unavoidable that, speaking historically, *Scriptura nunquam sola est.* What is more, as Dryden observed (among others), the appeal to Scripture as the court of final resort has never succeeded more than partially in reducing controversy or upholding the stabilization of doctrine.[32] The question of the interdependence between an exegete's subjective "canon" and his working hermeneutics is as slippery as an eel—for the notion of a hermeneutics without presuppositions is either pretentious or illusory (or both). Whenever the issue of canon-criticism is approached without critical analysis ("from kiver to kiver") the unavoidable result has been bibl*icism* and proof-texting (both profoundly anti-historical). Over on the other extreme, whenever the biblical reader is encouraged to respond chiefly in terms of "what speaks to him," the results can be no better than high-minded confusion.

The tilt of liberal biblical interpretation—since Simon, Ernesti and Semler—has been toward the subjective ("romantic") pole. Wesley had spoken of a fourfold criterion for doctrine—canonical Scripture (conceived always as a whole) as its font, tradition as its historical experimentation, reason as its referee in conceptualization and "Christian experience" as its existential appropriation. Since then, as two centuries have worn on, we have seen this holistic vision fragmented and its fragments atomized. The study of Scripture has turned toward "micro-criticism"; our recollection of tradition has been selective; reason has descended into rationalizations; and the stress on "experience" has nudged individuals and groups toward the Christian equivalent of narcissism.[33]

Canon-criticism is, of course, no panacea for any of these tendencies nor a sufficient substitute in itself for any of the existing biblical and historical disciplines. But it might help turn our inquiries in new directions, with a fresh set of queries and nuances that could affect both the substance and spirit of the "introductions" and "surveys" that upcoming generations could use for orientation. That is to say, they could then focus on the processes by which the church came by its "canon," how Christians understood themselves in whatever "age" they lived in, how they acted out their callings under the guidance of Scripture *and* community. And this would pose, in a different light and spirit, the question as to whether or not the canonical Scripture (with or without the Apocrypha?) "containeth all things necessary to salvation, so that whatsoever is not read therein, nor may be proved thereby, is not to be *required* of any man that it should be believed as an article of the Faith or be thought requisite or necessary to salvation."[34]

People accustomed to the enterprise of canon-criticism might very well reconsider the iconographic tradition of the *etoimasia*—i.e., the custom of enthroning the Gospels in the midst of solemn Christian assemblies (from congregations to General Councils) as a sign and agency of Christ's presence and "presidency"—"wherever two or three (or a thousand) are gathered..."[35] This symbolism could serve to remind Christians "of every rank and station" in the church, that the church was designed to be governed, not by its hierarchy, on the one hand, or by majority vote on questions of faith and practice, on the other, but by the Scripture and by the Spirit who bears witness to the centrality of Christ in the Scriptures and in our lives.

These Scriptures are, of course, open to the most rigorous historical-literary analysis and to the profoundest rational reflection. What must not be stultified in the process, however, is a lively sense of the Bible *as a whole*—as the irreplaceable deposit of faithful and authentic witnesses to the self-revelations of God in history—and in Jesus of Nazareth as the sum and substance of that self-revelation. If canon-criticism could stir and support this sense, it would serve the generations still to come in their tasks of recapitulating the Christian past and projecting the Christian future. It was to this end that Thomas Cranmer taught us to pray:

> Blessed Lord, who hast caused all holy Scriptures to be written for our learning; Grant that we may in such wise *hear* them, *read, mark, learn* and *inwardly digest* them, that by patience and comfort of thy holy Word, we may embrace and ever hold fast, the blessed hope of everlasting life....[36] (Italics mine.)

NOTES

1. Those familiar with J. A. Sanders, "A Call to Canonical Criticism" (*Torah and Canon* [Philadelphia, Pa.: Fortress, 1972] x-xx), will recognize that this present essay is a brief response to that "call." For further elaboration of Sanders' pioneering proposal, cf. his chapter, "Adaptability for Life," in G. Ernest Wright's memorial volume, *Magnalia Dei, the Mighty Acts of God: Essays on the Bible and Archaeology* (Garden City, New York: Doubleday, 1976) 531-60. The notes and bibliography are especially useful. Sanders prefers the phrase, "canonical-criticism," in line with such analogs as "biblical," "historical," "exegetical," etc. I prefer the more compact phrase, "canon-criticism," in line with other closer analogs (e.g., "text-," "form-," "redaction-," "genre-criticism," etc.). Nothing substantive that I know of turns on this option. The literature in the conventional field of "text and canon" is too vast (and familiar) to justify a listing here: the traditional approach is still best represented by B. F. Westcott, *A General Survey of the History of the Canon of the New Testament,* 7th ed (London: Macmillan, 1896); one of the best of the "revisionist" approaches is A. C. Sundberg's two articles, "Canon of the NT" and "Muratorian Fragment," *IDBS* (Nashville: Abingdon, 1976) 136-40, 609-10.

2. Trent's first anathema (following its official "list of the sacred books received by this Synod" [including the OT and Apoc]) is aimed at those "who receive not as sacred and canonical the aforesaid books *entire with all their parts...*" (Fourth Session, 1546)—a repudiation, among other things, of Protestant exclusions of the Apoc and of Luther's notion of a selective (i.e., Christocentric) canon *within* the Canon. Trent then added a decree establishing the Vulgate as "approved in the Church," so that "no one is to dare or presume to reject it under

any pretext whatever" (cf. P. Schaff, *The Creeds of Christendom* [New York; Harper and Brothers, 1977] 2.82; see also Denzinger-Schönmetzer, *Enchiridion Symbolorum* [Rome: Herder, 1957] 279-80. The Reformed tradition also rejected the Apoc and some (e.g., Musculus) went on to disparage such books as 2 Pet, 2 and 3 John, Jude, Heb and Rev (cf. Heinrich Heppe, *Reformed Dogmatics* [London: Allen & Unwin, 1950] 12-14).

3. This, of course, was Kant's definition of "enlightenment"; cf. "What Is Enlightenment?," *Critique of Practical Reason and Other Writings in Moral Philosophy,* ed L. W. Beck (Chicago: University of Chicago, 1949) 286-87.

4. Kurt Aland, *The Problem of the New Testament Canon* (London: A. R. Mowbray, 1962) 27-33.

5. Hans von Campenhausen, *The Formation of the Christian Bible* (Philadelphia, Pa.: Fortress, 1972) 333.

6. A. C. Sundberg, "Canon of the NT," 137: "It is now imperative to develop an alternative hypothesis (to the traditional one) and with it to write a revised history of the NT canon." Sundberg denies that the OT was "canonized" (i.e., closed) before C.E. 90 and argues that the NT canon was not closed until after the middle of the fourth century. Notice how consistently he correlates the notion of "canon" itself with the problem of its "closure." This discourages proper attention to "canon" as *process.*

7. Cf. *The Old and the New in the Church: Studies in Ministry and Worship, The World Council of Churches Commission on Faith & Order,* eds G. W. H. Lampe and David M. Paton (London: SCM, 1961), especially the articles by K. E. Skydsgaard, "Tradition as an Issue in Contemporary Theology," 20-35, and J. J. Pelikan, "Overcoming History by History," 36-42. See also, "The Renewal of the Christian Tradition," *Faith and Order Findings,* ed Paul S. Minear (London: SCM, 1963) 7-27. A more recent discussion by Professor Skydsgaard, "The Flaming Center, *Or* The Core of Tradition," is included in *Our Common History as Christians,* eds John Deschner, Leroy Howe, and Klaus Penzel (New York: Oxford, 1975) 3-22. The most extensive and perceptive Roman Catholic study of this problem is Yves M.-J. Congar, *Tradition and Traditions* (New York: Macmillan, 1966).

8. It will be remembered that the original draft of the Constitution on Revelation of Vatican II (ch 2) was entitled, "The Two Sources of Revelation" (i.e., Scripture *and* Tradition). One of the most significant of all the developments in the Council's work was the recasting of both the title of the chapter and the concept of the rôle of Scripture in "revelation." Cf. "Dogmatic Constitution on Divine Revelation," *Documents of Vatican II,* eds Walter M. Abbot and Joseph Gallagher (New York: Guild, 1966), ch 3, ¶¶11-13.

9. Cf. *Magnalia Dei,* 531 ("The concept of canon is located in the tension between two poles: stability and adaptability; but [previous] discussions ... have dealt almost exclusively with the former and rarely with the latter....hermeneutics must be viewed as the mid-term of the axis which lies between stability and adaptability.")

10. *The Cambridge History of the Bible,* ed P. Ackroyd, C. Evans (Cambridge: University Press, 1970) 1.232.

11. This would happen later, *after* the destruction of Jerusalem and *after*

the schism between synagogue and church; cf. D. N. Freedman's article on "Canon of the OT," *IDBS* 130-36.

12. I.e., between (1) the consensus of rabbinical judgments in matters of law and casuistry (first in the oral tradition and later in the Mishnah and Talmud) and (2) the far larger body of non-juridical interpretations of Scripture. Haggadah (aggadah) included narratives, legends, parables, poems, polemics, exhortations and moral tales, all with an edifying aim, of explaining "the ways of God to man." Cf. Louis Ginzberg, *On Jewish Law and Lore* (Philadelphia: Jewish Publication Society of America, 1955). Is it more than an intriguing speculation that the NT writings were haggadic in spirit and form—in *self-conscious* distinction from halakah (instances of which are significantly sparse—e.g., Acts 15:6-29, 1 Tim 3:2-13, etc.)? Even the Pastorals are distinctively haggadic in style and spirit—as also the Pauline epistles.

13. Cf. the Christian vision in Col 3:11, Gal 3:28 and Phil 2:9-11. The best summary of the classical vision may be found in C. N. Cochrane's *Christianity and Classical Culture* (New York: Oxford, 1944), Part 1, ch 1 (*"Pax Augusta"*) and ch 2 (*"Romanitas"*).

14. Cf. Paul's modesty on such a point in 1 Cor 7:40.

15. This crucial case is significant on several levels. Tatian had the fourfold gospels before him (mid-second century!); he intended to supplant the four separate versions with a single one *on principle.* His redaction was widely popular in Syria but circulated also from Persia to Britain. The *Katholikos* took extreme measures to suppress it (Theodoret [P G 83:372] is said to have collected two hundred copies from within his own diocese to destroy them!) and was successful to the extent that no intact manuscript of the *Diatessaron* is extant. For a fuller summary of this story, cf. B. F. Westcott, *A General Survey of the History of the Canon of the New Testament,* seventh edition (New York: Macmillan, 1896) 328-31. For the surviving fragments of the text, cf. Arthur Vööbus, *Studies in the History of the Gospel Text in Syriac* (Louvain: L. Durbecq, 1951).

16. This is Papias' testimony, in Eusebius, *Ecclesiastical History,* 3. 39. 16. It has long been customary in critical circles to accept Eusebius' low opinion of Papias ("a man of exceedingly small intelligence...") as ground for depreciating the validity of his reported "facts." But Eusebius' bias is clearly based on his negative views of Papias' chiliasm, and this scarcely justifies a dismissal of the substantive data in the "Expositions of the Dominical Oracles." Barring disproof (or some alternative testimony), we have no clearer ground for dismissing Papias' allegement of an Aramaic Matthew than we have for a similar judgment on Eusebius himself (especially of his miscomprehension of Nicea and his sycophancy vis-à-vis Constantine!).

17. The dominant view since B. H. Streeter, *The Four Gospels; A Study of Origins Treating of the Manuscript Tradition, Sources, Authorship and Dates* (London: Macmillan, 1924) has taken Markan priority for granted. In the past fifteen years this consensus has been challenged by William R. Farmer, *The Synoptic Problem* (New York: Macmillan, 1964), by David Dungan, "Mark—The Abridgement of Matthew and Luke," *Jesus and Man's Hope* (Pittsburgh, Pa.: Pittsburgh Theological Seminary, 1970) 51-97, by E. P. Sanders *The Tendencies of the Synoptic Tradition* (Cambridge: Cambridge University, 1969) and by Dom Bernard Orchard, *Matthew, Luke and Mark* (Manchester: Koinonia,

1976). More recently, Fr. Orchard and others have revived the hypothesis of J. J. Griesbach who regarded Mark as an epitome of Matthew and Luke—and therefore as *third* in the gospel-order. Griesbach's comment that *"Primus, quod sciamus, Augustinus, Marcum tanquam pedissequum et breviatorem subsecutum esse Matthaeum iudicavit* (he cites *De consensu Evangeliorum* [sic!], Libr. 1, cap. 2) ignores the fact Eusebius cites this canonical order from Origen. Even if Hanson's dubious contention that Origen had no concept of a New Testament Canon (in *Origen's Doctrine of Tradition* [1954], 140) were allowed, Eusebius' list antedates Augustine's by more than a full half century at least. Cf. *Opuscula Academica*, ed J. P. Gabler (Jena, 1825) 2. 359.

18. E.g., Irenaeus, *Against Heresies*, 3. 9. 7, where the order is Matt, Luke, Mark, John. See also Clement of Alexandria's *Hypotyposes* (reported in Eusebius, *Ecclesiastical History*, 6. 14. 5-7).

19. Cf. Eusebius, *ibid.*

20. Cf. W. C. Robinson, Jr., "Luke, Gospel of," *IDBS*, 558-60.

21. Cf. D. M. Smith, "John, Gospel of, " *IDBS*, 482-86.

22. The roots of this are in the original Johannine mysticism, but its flowering may be seen in Gregory of Nyssa and his disciples; cf. David L. Balás, *Metousia Theou: Man's Participation in God's Perfections According to St. Gregory of Nyssa* (Rome: Herder, 1966).

23. Cf. No. 4, The Canon of Cyril of Jerusalem, and No. 7, The Canon of the Council of Laodicea, in *Some Early Lists of the Books of the New Testament*, ed F. W. Grosheide (Leiden: E. J. Brill, 1948).

24. This question of sequence is currently being contested by Bishop J. A. T. Robinson, *Redating the New Testament* (Philadelphia: Westminster, 1976) but with inconclusive results, thus far at least.

25. The "place" of the "historical Jesus" in the Pauline Christology is a complex and obscure problem. But that it has required one degree of allegorizing or another may be seen in Augustine's *On Christian Doctrine*, ch 34, ¶38, where the Corinthian text is interpreted to mean that we should "pass over...temporal things (i.e., Jesus 'after the flesh') and struggle to attain unto Himself, who has freed our nature from the bondage of temporal things" (i.e., history).

26. The lack of major rôle for Hebrews in the history of hermeneutics is a standing puzzle since, next to the Gospels themselves, no other book in the NT is as crucial for the development of a "two-natures" christology; Professor Samuel Sandmel once spoke of it, in conversation, as "a fifth Gospel." It appears regularly in the Eastern lists (with Origen's famous disavowal that only God knew who wrote it; cf. Eusebius, *Ecclesiastical History*, 6. 25. 13-14), but in at least two of the Western lists it is omitted altogether ("The Cheltenham Canon" and the Codex Claromontanus).

27. Cf. the detailed and persuasive analysis of this in Georg Kretschmar, "Christliches Passa im 2. Jahrhundert und die Ausbildung der Christlichen Theologie," *Recherches de Science Religieuse* (1972) 60. 287-323.

28. Martin Werner, *The Formation of Christian Dogma* (London: Adam & Charles Black, 1957) has pushed this thesis to its extreme, but he is only more of a partisan spokesman than most in a long tradition.

29. The "classic" here, of course, is J. H. Newman, *An Essay on the Development of Christian Doctrine* (New York: Longmans, Green,

1949). The contemporary problematic is best summed up by J. J. Pelikan, *Development of Christian Doctrine* (New Haven: Yale University, 1969), and *Historical Theology: Continuity and Change in Christian Doctrine* (New York: Corpus, 1971).

30. Cf. "The Epitome of The Formula of Concord" (1580) in *The Book of Concord,* ed T. G. Tappert (Philadelphia: Mühlenberg, 1959) 464: The Scriptures "are the only rule and norm to which all doctrines and teachers alike must be appraised and judged...."

31. Paul Neuenzeit, art. "Canon" in *Sacramentum Mundi,* 1. 256, expounding *Dei Verbum* (the *Constitution on Revelation* of the Second Vatican Council, ¶¶24-25); cf. 252-57.

32. Cf. *Religio Laici* (1682), 400-16, and *The Hind and the Panther* (1687) 2. 150-55;

>   For did not Arius first, Socinus now
>   The Son's eternal Godhead disavow?
>   And did these not by Gospel texts alone
>   Condemn our doctrine and maintain their own?
>   Have not all heretics the same pretence,
>   To plead the Scriptures in their own defence?

33. For a secular comment on this trend, cf. *The Narcissistic Condition: A Fact of Our Lives and Times,* ed Marie Coleman Nelson (New York: Human Sciences, 1977).

34. Art. 6, Thirty-Nine Articles, Book of Common Prayer. Note here the *limiting concept* of biblical authority.

35. Cf. Romeo de Maio, *The Book of the Gospels at the Oecumenical Councils* (Rome: Biblioteca Apostolica Vaticana, 1963).

36. The Collect for the Second Sunday in Advent, *BCP.*

Stuart Dickson Currie

Biography and Bibliography

A Brother Beloved

Thomas W. Currie, Jr.

Stuart Dickson Currie was born October 20, 1922 in Austin, Texas, the third child of Thomas White Currie and Jeannette Roe Currie. He grew up on the campus of Austin Presbyterian Theological Seminary, only a short three blocks from The University of Texas. Just before he was born his father had been made president of the Seminary. Stuart's early schooling was at Wooldridge School at 24th and Nueces, a unit of the Austin Independent School District.

The Curries had come to Texas from Caswell County, North Carolina, some 75 years before Stuart was born. David Mitchell Currie and one of his seven sisters settled in Falls County between Durango and Lott. David M. Currie was a farmer. He and his family were part of the Carolina Presbyterian Church. The congregation was later moved to Lott, but the earlier location can still be identified by the cemetery. David M. Currie had nine children by his wife, Ira Ione White Currie and, later, four by his second wife, Irene Morgan Currie. The fourth child of the first group was Thomas White Currie, born January 23, 1879. This son in 1903 entered Austin College at Sherman, Texas. After being graduated in 1907 he stayed on for a year to teach chemistry while one of the professors was on leave. In 1908 he entered Austin Presbyterian Theological Seminary and in 1911 received a B.D. while at the same time earning at The University of Texas an M.A. He was employed as secretary of the University Y.M.C.A. and in 1911 also began to teach Bible at the Seminary.

Jeannette, the third daughter of Theodore Hart Roe and his wife, Elizabeth Walker Dickson Roe, was born August 16, 1884 in Fort Worth, Texas. Shortly thereafter the family moved to Colorado City, Texas where Mr. Roe managed a lumberyard. The family was active in the Presbyterian church there. To help earn her way through The University of Texas, Jeannette once worked as a tutor on a ranch near Snyder, Texas, and later took a job as a teacher in Richmond, Texas. While she was at The University, she resided in a dormitory known for many years as "The Woman's Building." It

was early on the morning of August 26, 1913 in the church in
Colorado City that she and Tom Currie were married.

For a time the couple were guests in the home of Dr. and Mrs.
T. R. Sampson. Dr. Sampson had been the first president and at the
time was a professor at Austin Presbyterian Theological Seminary.
Soon, however, the Curries moved and occupied the residence at
2621 Speedway, one of the homes provided by the Seminary for its
teachers. Tom Currie continued his connection with the Seminary
for the rest of his life, serving as president from 1922 until his death
in 1943.

In order to keep the Seminary afloat financially during the Great
Depression, Dr. Currie accepted the call of the Session of Highland
Park Presbyterian Church, Dallas to become Stated Supply while
continuing his five-day weekly schedule at the Seminary. Stuart
was ten years old at the time. Jeannette and the three younger
children, David, Stuart, and Bettie, moved to 4412 Potomac, Dallas.
In the fall of 1936 Stuart went to study at the Choate School, Wall-
ingford, Connecticut. While there he won honors in modern
languages.

In the fall of 1940 Stuart entered The University of Texas at
Austin. He matriculated in Dean H. T. Parlin's Plan II and worked
toward a B.A. degree. The Plan II afforded those who were enrolled
in it an opportunity to be exposed to excellent teachers early in
their studies and enabled them to concentrate in certain preferred
areas if they chose. At one point, Dr. Currie offered to pay for
whatever books Stuart would read and add to his personal library.

On the fifth of September 1942, Stuart was married in Itasca,
Texas, to Sara Files. Her parents, Sidney and Janie Files, were long-
time residents of Itasca in Hill County. Mr. Files was manager of
the Itasca Cotton Manufacturing Company, and the Files family
had for many years been benefactors of the Presbyterian Children's
Home just east of Itasca. To Stuart and Sara were born two
daughters, Helen and Grace, and two sons, Kenneth Files and Mark
Stuart.

After Stuart's first two years in The University of Texas, in 1942,
he entered Austin Seminary as candidate for the B.D. degree and
carried on his studies simultaneously, receiving both the B.D. from
the Seminary and the B.A. from The University in the spring of
1945. In April of that year he was licensed and, two months later,
ordained and installed by the Presbytery of Mid-Texas of the
Presbyterian Church, U.S. as pastor of the First Presbyterian
Church, Haskell, Texas. He also served as stated supply in the First
Presbyterian Church, Rochester, Texas.

A pastorate in west Texas is likely to give one some memorable impressions. Haskell is 156 miles west and a little north of Fort Worth in the dry upper basin of the Brazos River. In his description of a day taken up with remote business in this lonely cattle country, Stuart included a cross section of what is vividly and sometimes painfully autobiographic.

Procul Negotiis

"Preacher? John Rand. I've got to move some cattle tomorrow. Be glad to have you along."

"Fine. I'd like to come. Where shall I meet you?"

"Oh I'll come by for you about six."

"No need for that. I'll be at your place at six."

Next morning the preacher got up earlier than necessary. He put on old pants, a worn white shirt—he didn't own a colored one—and horsehide shoes. Knowing the Texas sun, he tied a handkerchief around his neck. But he had no hat.

They ate breakfast in a little cafe on the square—John Rand, the preacher, and Ben, John's hand. After breakfast John bought three plugs of tobacco, and they piled in the pickup. Five miles out on the hard-top they turned off south. Last time the preacher had been along this road was coming back from a Fourth of July picnic. A sudden rain had made the road slick, and he remembered watching the speedometer jump crazily up to 25 or 30 as the wheels spun. He had been a little uneasy, worrying about getting stuck miles from town with a car full of youngsters. He was a little uneasy this morning. He had never herded cattle before; in fact, he had only been on a horse half a dozen times in his life. But he had made his offer, and he meant to stick by it.

Being a preacher has its difficulties—especially for a cub just out of seminary taking his first church in a little West Texas town. He had heard a story about one man who had served the church before him. Jackson, his name was. He, too, had come there straight from seminary, green and cocky. They had asked him to be toastmaster for the Chamber of Commerce banquet, and he had accepted readily. Introducing the lawyer who was to speak, Jackson had told one of the numerous stories about lawyers going to hell. But the lawyer went him one better. He said, "Well, I'd rather be a lawyer and know I'm going to hell, than a Presbyterian preacher and not know where in the hell I am going." Jackson had been driven to cover for three days; but the experience had helped make a man of him.

Sometimes the preacher wondered if he did know where he was going. He wanted to help people. He enjoyed preaching. But it was hard. Sunday after Sunday to open God's Word, to show the demands of righteousness, to sharpen consciences. It made him feel he was always accusing people—good, friendly

people, men and women who had asked him to come among
them and help them. It was a heavy burden for a cub of
twenty-three. He liked these people and he wanted their
friendship. So he had made his offer: he would help anyone
anytime with anything they needed done. He had made the offer because he felt helpless. A word of comfort to a new-made
widow, separated by sudden death from the intimate compan-
ion of thirty years—such words were hard to come by, and
young as he was, he spoke them with diffidence. But taking
eggs to market seemed like really helping. Not many took his
offer seriously; but some did. He had helped paint a house for
one man, chopped cotton for another, clerked an hour or so for
a merchant who had to take his son to the doctor.

On the way out of town Rand told him what they had to do.
They were going to get all the cattle together and drive them
down to the creek for water. (It had not rained since the Fourth
of July, and the tanks were just mudpuddles surrounded by
black aureols of sun-cracked earth.) Then they had to cut out a
few calves for vaccination.

Not a very ambitious program, thought the preacher. But
then it is easy for a preacher to become overwhelmed with a
sense of the enormous seriousness of his calling, where every
day is spent in the service of eternity, every contact weighted
with a sense of divine purpose. Besides, he had looked forward
to today as an adventure; and so it was to him. But for Rand it
was just the day's work. Cattle must have water every day;
they must be inoculated.

First of all they saddled the horses. The horse they gave the
preacher was walking gingerly. He had a big bruise on his
chest. Apparently he had got in with the mares the night
before, and one of them had kicked him. Before the day was
out this nearly ruined the preacher. The horse just wouldn't
walk as fast as the others, and the preacher had to jog most of
the time to keep up.

They started out from the stable, rounded up a few strays
which were standing mournfully around the dry tank, and
herded them over to the west pasture where the other cattle
were. Rand called it a pasture, but in fact it was nothing more
than a mesquite thicket, better suited to goats than to cattle.
The first real job was to search the whole thicket and round up
the cattle. The men separated and began beating the bounds of
the tract, driving the animals toward the gate. Back off in the
southwest corner the preacher came across the carcass of a
yearling. Nothing was left but bones and hide, and just enough
putrid flesh to draw all the flies in the county. The preacher
found the sight moving. It reminded him of Horace's ode in
which the poet speaks of the kid he will sacrifice to the spring
at Bandusia—a kid whose swelling horn-buds foretell a life of

love and battles never to be won, forestalled by death.

As they converged on the gate he told Rand of the yearling. John said the worms had killed it. That was why he wanted to vaccinate the calves.

By now the sun was getting hot, and the saddle hard. The preacher was glad to get down and hold the gate while John and Ben punched the cattle through. John gave him a plug of tobacco. They had left all their drinking water at the truck, and there's nothing like tobacco to keep thirst at bay.

Finally all the cattle were through the gate, and they started toward the creek, moving along a barely discernible trail. This part of the ranch was typical of the eastern half of the county: thin, blanched, short grass barely covering the gray soil through which, here and there, the underlying limestone was visible. The cattle moved eagerly now, with no need for herding. When they reached the creek, the men dismounted. First they watered their horses, then moved up-stream and slaked their own thirst from the brown stream. While the cattle drank, Rand told the preacher how wild turkey used to abound there until men hunted them all down, even, toward the last, shooting them at roost by the light of a full moon.

They got the cattle together again and started back, headed this time for the east pasture. John and Ben made a few good-natured jibes at the preacher's restlessness. By now he had taken to standing in the stirrups as long as he could, then sitting first on one side, then on the other. His horse would walk a while and then have to be urged into a jog to catch up.

The preacher rode on ahead to open the gate. As he passed the cattle he saw one cow with what looked like a white balloon protruding from its rump. Puzzled for a moment, he recognized it at last for an amniotic sac. He wanted very much to see the calf born, and resolved to keep the heifer in sight. He told Rand about it.

Now they were in a sown pasture, the highest spot on the place, rising toward the north and forming a horizon barely a mile away. The pasture was incredibly green, its deeper roots still drawing moisture from the subsoil while the native grass was nearly gone. Overhead was a Texas sky—a thin, hot blue, relieved by scattered clouds on two levels: a high bank of cirrus, small as ripples on a beach, icy; and far below row after row of fluffy cumulus, coming up from the Gulf, looking like cotton ready for picking. The heat was palpable; it weighed on the back and shoulders, the hair was hot to the touch.

Ben went back for the pickup, and they sat in its meager shade while they ate their sandwiches and drank the welcome warm water from a burlap-covered jug. For perhaps a quarter hour they lay under the mesquite trees and watched the clouds. To the preacher the thin leaves of the mesquite looked like lines on graph paper, the branches like the axes; and the clouds moving past satisfied the equation, $x = y$.

John got out the medicine and the hypodermic needle, and they went back to the cattle. As they passed one corner of the pasture the preacher saw the new-born calf. He had missed the birth. The cow was still licking its calf; but the calf, unlike the babies the preacher knew, was already ambulatory. Rand told him it wouldn't be many days until the calf was eating grass.

Ben and the preacher were assigned to get the cattle milling, moving around slowly in a rough circle. Rand rode into the circle time and again to cut out the calves. When he had one cut out, Ben would go with him some distance from the herd, rope the calf, and hold it while Rand wielded the needle. The preacher had plenty of time to look around as he rode his slow circle. He saw the cow nudging its calf along, the afterbirth trailing on the ground behind the cow until another animal stepped on it and it pulled loose. Ben said that most of the time the cow ate the afterbirth, but he reckoned all the moving around had distracted the critter. The preacher was glad it had.

Off toward the north edge of the pasture the mares were running free. Rand kept them mostly for the pleasure of having them around. Of course he bred them; but they were never ridden and had never worked. They were beautiful to watch in their carefree grace. They ran for the fun of it, with an easy, flowing gait, heads high, manes streaming in the wind, silhouetted against the sky. The preacher was glad there was no way of telling which mare it was whose proud defiance had caused his misery, for they were fair to behold. He thought Jonathan Swift's Houyhnhnms should have seemed stodgy and matronly beside these sylphs.

The cattle suffered by comparison. Slow, cumbersome, their jaws working sideways, their eyes vacant. They had to be cared for.

The work was done and they went back to town. Mutual thanks and goodbyes, and the preacher went back to the manse, walking in a rather unusual gait. He tried halfheartedly to find some deep meaning in the day, something that might be useful in a sermon. He thought about the dead yearling and the new-born calf. He thought about the vaccination. The cattle, the cow-ponies, the mares. But his heart wasn't in it. It had been a glorious day. That night his nose was pink; the next day it was like leather. Two weeks later it peeled.[1]

In 1947 the preacher and his family came to Taylor, Texas, for a two-year pastorate. From 1949 to 1954 they were in Fulton, Missouri. While serving as pastor there Mr. Currie also taught freshman Bible in Westminster College. His inclination toward teaching became more and more pronounced. In 1954, at the encouragement of Dr. Roland M. Frye, Mr. Currie began study at the Graduate Institute of Liberal Arts of Emory University, Atlanta, Georgia. The subject of his dissertation was, *"Koinonia* in Christian Literature to 200 A.D." Several years later, in 1962, the completed work won first place from the Christian Research Foundation.

Not only did Mr. Currie toil in his own academic pursuits while he was in Atlanta, but his facility in languages became an avenue to widening acquaintance among theologians. In 1956 Charles Scribner's Sons published a book by Oscar Cullmann, professor in Basel and Paris, under the title, *The State in the New Testament.* In the foreword to this book the author included the following sentences: "Grateful recognition is due also to Reverend Stuart D. Currie, who during my stay at Emory University in Georgia as guest professor, was of invaluable help in the preparation of the English manuscript. His deep theological understanding greatly facilitated our work together."[2]

For the five years from 1956-1961 Mr. Currie was Chairman of the Department of Bible, Religion, and Philosophy at Queens College, Charlotte, North Carolina. In 1959 he received that school's first Distinguished Professor Award. In addition to his teaching responsibilities, he was frequently called on to supply pulpits in the Charlotte area. All the while he continued work on his dissertation. Whenever he finished a chapter the family would celebrate with a loaf of homemade bread.

In 1961 he was called to Austin Presbyterian Theological Seminary as Assistant Professor of Church History. In 1964 he became Professor of New Testament Language and Exegesis.

The Faculty Editions of the Austin Presbyterian Theological Seminary *Bulletin* soon began to publish his special studies. One of these which appeared in September 1962 was entitled "A Peculiar People." It is an exploration of the unique understanding of man displayed in the Scripture. There is the contrast between the recognition scene in Book 19 of *The Odyssey* and the account of Abraham's offering of Isaac in Genesis 22: in the former there is drama and vivid detail, while in the latter there is almost no detail, but nevertheless a far more compelling drama because of a soul battling in crucial decision precipitated by the command of the divine Visitant. The author averred, "The reality of the individual is the anguish of decision in the moment of visitation."[3] He concluded:

> Faith in the God who visits man, that solitary individual in the moment of decision, is the channel through which flows the

grace which gives meaning to the inescapable privacy of existence, which renders sweet our inevitable involvement with our neighbor and makes of him a brother, and renders it possible—in spite of nature, fate or fortune, tides of history, pomp or empire, threat of death—to find our real world, the realm of our existence, to be none other than the kingdom of God.[4]

Addressing another issue, a practical matter that was of no little trouble to the church of the 1960s, Dr. Currie commented on the supposed rift between the clergy and the laity and where to look for the remedy. He held:

We are a people with a service to render to God's world. We understand it is our task and our dignity to be charged with proclamation of God's Gospel and Kingdom, his Sovereignty and Grace; we know we are called to bear witness to Christ's Lordship through obedient discipleship in our workaday world and in merciful service and godly friendship toward all who inhabit that world which God so loved; and we recognize that we have been charged to invite and welcome all God's elect into full membership in that people who want instruction, who have a fellowship to realize, and a praise to perfect in order to be equipped to render service to God's world. The guise of that Gospel toward the world is grace, but discipline toward the saints. So we pray to Christ for his gift of a pastor who with the help of those chosen from among us will exercise us in the godly discipline of the Gospel. Only such gracious training in the law of love can make us graceful witnesses.[5]

In the area of aids to worship, the Joint Committee on Worship of the United Presbyterian Church, U.S.A. and the Presbyterian Church, U.S. issued a "Lectionary for the Christian Year" for experimental use in 1964 and Dr. Currie's comments on it appeared in the Faculty *Bulletin* of April the next year under the title, "Never on Sunday." After paying tribute to the usefulness of a lectionary and to the hours of toil expended by the committee on this particular effort, Dr. Currie itemized the startling number of what might be thought of as most striking, illuminating, and beneficial passages which were omitted from Sunday readings. For instance, no reading was indicated on any Sunday that would have included the Beatitudes or the Crucifixion, the parable of the Prodigal Son, nor ever any selection from any of the 150 psalms. With no discourtesy and with a light touch of humor he noted the incongruity with Reformed tradition illustrated once and again in the new Lectionary.[6]

Dr. Currie's inaugural address, delivered October 4, 1966, two years after he had become Professor, was entitled, "Isaiah 63,9 and the Transfiguration in Mark."[7] As he remarked, this "study undertakes to examine the Markan account against its historical background and to show what formative influence Isaiah 63,9 may have exercised upon the tradition as it came to Mark." The lecture suggested the consequences of the Gospel of Mark having been written prior to the time it was evident that the Jewish community at large, and not simply its leaders in Jerusalem, would not recognize Jesus as God incarnate. Dr. Currie intimated that appropriate as were the titles of Savior, Rabbi, Lord, King, prophet, Messiah (Christ), Son of Man, none of these was adequate. The message of the Transfiguration in Mark is that Jesus was to be distinguished from Elijah and Moses, that he was God's only, his beloved son, to be identified as the deity. The first sentence in Mark reads: "The beginning of the gospel of Jesus Christ, the son of God." As Jesus breathed his last, the centurion conceded, "Truly this man was the son of God!" (Marginal reading, the N.E.B.) Between these two confessions is the main body of the Gospel in which the disciples sought for Jesus' true identity. The Transfiguration brings Peter and James and John to the conviction so forcibly expressed in Isaiah 63,9, "It was no envoy, no angel, but he himself that delivered them; he himself ransomed them...." Thus, no small element in the motive for writing the Gospel of Mark may have been to produce a tract for the times in the hope that contemporary Jews could be persuaded to see in Jesus of Nazareth the fulfillment of Isaiah 63,9.

On another level Dr. Currie's gifts were manifest. The Board of Christian Education of the Presbyterian Church, U.S. in the 1960s was producing the Covenant Life Curriculum. Dr. Currie wrote one of the texts to be used in the elementary grades, *The Beginnings of the Church.*[8] Here, starting with Abraham, he carried the story of the church through the ages, ending where Acts closes, with Paul in Rome. Few books for elementary grades so faithfully and vividly tell the story with such an economy of words and with such disarming simplicity. And yet, there were reflected here some of the sophisticated benefits of modern scholarship.

One of the best examples of Dr. Currie's gifts in the study and interpretation of scripture was to be found in a Teacher's Guide[9] published by the Geneva Press for use by teachers of 7th and 8th graders. Here he suggested approaches to the study of the Bible calculated to aid students in understanding the significance of the facts as recorded, the message for us in the interdependence of the Old and New Testaments, the pertinence for us in the variations in similar stories of their order, or of the inclusion or omission of various details.

Evident in the church at large during this decade was an increasing interest in the third Person of the Trinity and in the gifts of the Spirit. The theme of the World Alliance of Reformed Churches meeting in Frankfurt Germany in 1964 was "Come, Creator Spirit." Dr. Currie wrote a study of "Speaking in Tongues"[10] which reviewed early extra-scriptural evidence and concluded that since no light was shed on the precise character of *glōssais lalein* as used in the New Testament, it was not possible to say whether that phrase might be correctly applied to modern "speaking in tongues" phenomena. Further, he concluded that early non-canonical sources offered no support for Christians giving firsthand account of having been enabled by the Spirit to speak a human language not previously learned, nor being enabled by the Spirit to speak a non-human language. The early church regarded "dark sayings uttered ecstatically" with great diffidence, counting as crucial in the matter the spirit of the speaker and the orderly subjection to the brethren in the Lord.

Two years later (in 1967) Dr. Currie published an inquiry into "Jesus and the Spirit." There he noted, "Nothing in the Synoptic records implies that 'speaking in tongues' should have been expected to be a normal concomitant of baptism or a common feature of Christian devotions."[11] In the Fourth Gospel the work of the Spirit principally showed how inseparable were the Spirit of God and the words of Christ. Dr. Currie brought his paper to a close with the observation: "The records carefully examined leave little room for supposing (Jesus Christ) created the impression of a wonder-worker, and even less that he was remembered as the paragon of all pneumatics."[12]

Dr. Currie took part in the dialogue between Orthodox and Reformed traditions. Three consultations occurred, May 2, 3, 1968 at Princeton Theological Seminary, April 18, 19, 1969 at Hellenic College, Brookline, Massachusetts, and May 13, 14, 1970 again at Princeton Theological Seminary. A volume presenting papers from the discussions included one by Dr. Currie entitled, "The Christian Community in the Second Century."[13] It was a study of the use and significance of the word *ekklēsia* in Pauline letters and in the second-century Christian writings. He found that whereas the *ekklēsia* and the Body of Christ were quite distinguishable concepts for Paul, they tended in the next century to be mingled, if not fused in a grand metaphysical idea personified as Mother, Teacher, Execututrix.

February 9, 10, 1972 found Dr. Currie as the L. W. Anderson

lecturer at The Presbyterian College of McGill University, Montreal, Canada. The subject was "Good News in Samaria. The Simon Magus Episode: Acts 8, lb-25. Essays in Interpretation and Preaching." The first lecture suggested three different ways of approaching the study of the passage. It was a story about power. It was the description of an open possibility. It was a stylistic oddity. The second lecture defined a sermon: "A sermon is an address based on Scripture which furnishes to its hearers no occasion for negative response to what it calls for that is not a stumbling at the scandal of the Gospel."[14] The third address is a sermon from the text: "Now when the apostles at Jerusalem heard that Samaria had received the Word of God, they sent to them Peter and John, who came down and prayed for them that they might receive the Holy Spirit." (Acts 8:14-15) At the outset there is an examination of man as part of a ruptured and chaotic society, then of man as singular, lonely. What does the Holy Spirit do in each instance?

> The word first came to the broken society of the Twelve—a company like our own, rent by betrayal, failure, envy, fear and hankering for power. And it came simultaneously (so John tells us) with the experience which convinced them that God had vindicated by deliverance from death that One whose food was to do not his own, but his Father's will, who had given up his life for his friends. The company formed by the appearance of the risen Lord persists by means of and for the sake of proclamation of that resurrection. And by the grace of God who raised Christ Jesus from the dead there now exists in the midst of our broken human societies a Gathering where the possibilities of healing the past and creating a future are present because of the activity of that Spirit whose office it is to release, renew, and create.
>
> The word of that proclamation is addressed also severally and specifically to the lonely centers of human life, offering in the words 'Receive the Holy Spirit!' the spirit of adoption whereby the once forlorn now finds his loneliness broken by the new word placed upon his lips: 'Abba, Father!'[15]

The sermon notes that in the New Testament the Lord Jesus, and he only, uses the imperative, "receive the Holy Spirit" because he only can deliver what he offers. The Holy Spirit sometimes comes unexpectedly as in the household of Cornelius. It is appropriate for preachers and hearers of the Word to look forward to receiving the Holy Spirit and to pray that they and others may receive the Holy Spirit. But the Holy Spirit cannot be coerced to do our will nor to conform to our time table.[16] The Holy Spirit may convict of sin, bring consolation and peace and life.

...they prayed as men who took his word for it who said, 'If you, bad as you are, know how to give good gifts to your children, how much more will your Father in heaven give the Holy Spirit to those who ask him'....They prayed for the scandalous gift of which one may say there is no prudence nor merit in asking for it, no honor or preferment implied in its bestowal. Even when it is sought it comes unbidden; though we cannot live without it, we cannot get it for the life of us.[17]

So the author summarized his discourse and closed it with a prayer:

[This sermon] has had no imperative to utter, no blandishments to offer, no inducements to hold out, no threats to make. It has not asked that you take the speaker's word for anything. It has not set out to prove or to explain.

It has spoken of loneliness—of having to live alone, like it or not; of having to call one's self one's own.

It has spoken of plasticity—of having to live as a mere specimen of a species, like it or not; of having nothing to call one's own.

It has spoken of the Holy Spirit—Spirit of adoption and of brotherhood, of freedom and of service, of joy and of peace.

It has spoken of the possibility that one may have it within one's power to receive that Spirit over which one can have no power.

It has spoken of the possibility that there may be an unbroken chain of prayer offered on behalf of men by men on whose behalf prayer has been offered that they may receive the Holy Spirit.

My hearer, if you do not count yourself among those who know the joy of that Spirit, may nothing—especially nothing in this discourse—conceal from you the scandal that you may receive by believing what cannot be had by achieving.

My hearer, if you consider that you have the Spirit of Christ, may nothing—especially nothing in this discourse—conceal from you the scandal that it is only by the preaching of the Word and prayer in behalf of others that Good News is heard in Samaria.

And now, my brothers, I intend to pray. I invite you to follow as I go before in these words which, though they are of my choosing, may as well—if you choose—be ours:

"Lord, we pray thee that thy grace may always prevent and follow us, and make us continually to be given to all good works; through Jesus Christ our Lord." (Collect for the Seventeenth Sunday after Trinity, BCP 1549).

"God hath spoken once; twice have I heard this; that power belongeth unto God. Also unto thee, O Lord, belongeth mercy; for thou renderest to every man according to his work" (Psalm 62,11f). Surely it is of thy lovingkindness, O Lord, that thou dost render to each man according to his work; it is of thy justice that thou wilt not spare us from thy mercy; it is of thy power that thou wilt not defend us from thy love.

We acknowledge and confess, O Lord, that we have been drawn to this place as men who love power and desire acclaim of men, as those who have entertained the temptation to try to use the power of thy Word to bend men to our will. We confess that we have been drawn to this place because we yearn to be looked upon as those who can give help and counsel, consolation and strength and thereby receive the thanks of and gain power over men. Deliver us not from thy mercy, but graciously grant us so to love thy power as that we may pray for thy justice and vengeance upon us, reforming the temper and disposition of our hearts. We pray to receive thy Holy Spirit.

We give thanks to thee, O Lord, for all God-conquered men whom this world has found unconquerable, who have (like Philip) stood firm in the strength which thou dost supply to those whom thou hast taught not to trust in themselves nor in princes nor in horses: continue to them thy Holy Spirit.

We pray for those who stand in danger of thy power: for churchmen who offer the gifts of thy grace as though they were the rewards of mammon, and who urge men to actions of obedience by promising reward or threatening the need of insurance against thy justice; for those who recommend piety for the sake of obtaining or preserving worldly advantage—for all, in short, who offer the holy on a pragmatic platter. For those who envy the Lordship of Christ: for all ad men and shills who aim to control the hearts of men by pandering and enticement. For all calculating users of violence, ruthless wielders of economic power, reckless exciters of popular passion. We pray that they may receive thy Holy Spirit.

Half-masted and half-mastered ourselves, O Lord, we who yearn for thy sovereignty but will not yield thee unqualified allegiance dare not so much as to offer our prayers untutored by thy lovingkindness. We remember the rebuke deserved by James and John the sons of Zebedee when they proposed to invoke thy fire upon a village of the Samaritans; so we presume to offer this our prayer only in the name and for the sake and under the correction of that Son of man who came not to destroy men's lives but to save them, not to kill but to heal.

So now "we beseech thee, Almighty God, let our souls enjoy this their desire, to be enkindled by thy Spirit, that being filled as lamps, by the divine Gift, we may shine like blazing lights before the presence of thy son Christ at his coming; Through the same Jesus Christ our Lord. Amen." (Gelasian Sacramentary).[18]

In these words came illumination which, though they might have been ignited by the sparks of controversy, were surely blown upon and sustained by Him who speaks and who is that lamp to our feet and light to our pathway.

Another area which engaged Dr. Currie's attention can be noted in the "Biblical Studies for a Seminar on Sexuality and the Human Community." Lectures on this subject were delivered January 18-20, 1971 at Perkins School of Theology of Southern Methodist University at the request of the Committee on Continuing Education, Synod of Texas, United Presbyterian Church, U.S.A. and were published the same year. The first lecture examined the tale recounted in Judges 19-21, illustrative of the nightmarish barbarities of an agglomeration of individuals in which everyone did what was right in his own eyes. Lust and vengeance went unchecked by societal or other sanctions. The second and third lectures studied certain passages in 1 Corinthians 6 and in Mark and Matthew. The fourth discourse was a brief word on preaching from the Bible about sex. It may not be amiss to surmise that Dr. Currie's advice to his students on preaching may be found in capsule form here:

In the examples used I have tried to show some of the methods I find to be involved in "doing one's home work" in preparation for preaching. One tries one's best to wait upon the text and hear it out, to look at it, back off from it, ask why what's said here is said this way and not some other. One looks for the unusual: for sentences completed in unanticipated ways, for apparently "oblique" considerations advanced as if the writer were sure of their weight and acceptance. In 1 Peter 3,7 we read that husbands are to live considerately with their wives. Well, of course! So they won't nag or eat crackers in bed or burn the eggs. But that's not what follows in the text: "seeing that you are joint heirs of the gift of life, to the end that your prayers may not be hindered." Now I ask you, what kind of reason is that! And yet it is in the Scripture's capacity to surprise, startle, and shock that one finds the best evidence of its peculiar and distinctive claim to be the occasion of insights not invented by human curiosity. So one looks not just for the course of action or the attitude recommended, but even more closely for the considerations advanced in connection with the counsel.

The few passages we have examined here on this occasion suggest several themes which run through the Biblical literature: chastity, courtesy, continuity, and commitment. One may suppose that where the Bible is taken seriously human reflection on the proprieties of sexual intercourse, for example, will not be limited to weighing "what is right in one's own eyes" at a given moment; that other interests will be seen to be at stake than just what seems at the moment agreeable to "two consenting adults"—especially when the claims of one generation upon another are weighed; that the only offerers to be trusted are those whose disinterested commitment toward the receiver has been exhibited.

Listening for "what the Bible has to say about sex" and preparing to preach from the Bible about sex will surely require study of many other passages of Scripture. We have not even begun to list those passages which celebrate the joys of those whose mutual life in the flesh is lived within the compass of obedient trust in God. It was this worshipping community which cherished The Song of Songs. It was in this worshipping community that one prophet was forbidden to marry, another forbidden to grieve at the death of his beloved wife, another bidden to buy back and re-win a wife who had been false to him (Have you ever tried to imagine the task of a movie director undertaking to instruct actors how to represent the scene as Hosea and Gomer walk toward home from the place of her repurchase?)—and all as a part of the message and the obedience and the mission entrusted to the community of faith, faith in the God who is the Father of our Lord Jesus Christ.

The Nestle edition of the Greek New Testament which many of us use bears on its opening page a quotation from Johannes Bengel: Te totum applica ad textum: rem totam applica ad te—"Apply your whole self to the text: the whole matter apply to yourself." I take this to mean for us that we are advised to bring to the study of the Scripture a whole twentieth-century man with all his questions, doubts, lingo, hang-ups, superstitions, and tastes and with his own private store of scars, mementos, trinkets, and treasures from his personal pilgrimage. A man who sees himself reflected in the fun-house mirrors of the movies, the commercials, the ads, and the Sunday supplements; whose ears ring with casual conversation as well as the currently popular records; who feels his own pulse and heartbeat in the novels and plays and poems of his contemporaries. But the next thing that must happen is, that when we know that man well enough to recognize him on sight, we must tell him to keep quiet, to hold his peace while we try to listen to the ancient text in terms of its own century's setting of hopes and fears and questions and outlook. Then when we have done our best to hear the text in its own tone and temper and interest, we must undertake to let it speak to that twentieth-century man who's been left cooling his heels. After that, we are ready to start to work preparing to file with our listeners the latest correspondent's report from the scene of the Good News.[19]

To enumerate the civic duties in Austin and beyond, the ties of friendship in the University Presbyterian Church where Dr. Currie and his family worshipped, and in many congregations, campuses, and conference grounds across the land would extend this chapter beyond its appointed limits. But it must be said that, although he never had been in any branch of the military, he was appointed to and served from July 1967 until his death as a member of Austin Draft Board Number 119. Dr. and Mrs. Currie had been appointed Danforth Associates when he had taught at Queens College, Charlotte, and the connection was severed only by his death. He was the Presbyterian Bible Chair at The University of Texas, Austin. Without remuneration he taught one section of Old Testament one semester (Bible 305) and one section of New Testament (Bible 301) the next from September 1965 till April 1975.

At the Seminary he came to have primary responsibility for Student Aid and a more than ordinary concern for the finances of the theologs and their families. He was as faithful in chapel as in his classes, and it was a rare sight indeed to see him dependent on a hymnbook for any verse. Indeed, when he was on the archeological expeditions at Shechem with Prescott H. Williams, Jr. in 1966 and 1968 he discharged, among other chores, the duty of being the hymnbook for the devotional periods of the group. He seemed to know all the stanzas by heart. He habitually read Scripture from the Greek, and if it were aloud, his hearers might wonder, from the easy flow and the perfect English, which new translation he was using.

He loved the land. He was more than an amateur naturalist. He could give the common and the scientific names of all the trees and shrubs around his home. He could set a good pace tramping up some of the steep slopes in the Rocky Mountain National Park, so far from being winded as all the while to be playing tunes on his harmonica. His camera captured many a treasured moment. Often in Austin it was possible to see his figure with a knapsack of books and papers on his back covering the two and half miles from his home at 3305 Jamesborough to the Seminary on his bicycle. He also got relief from his desk by enjoying exercise on the handball court in the basement of the McMillan Building. After his left wrist was broken it healed a little less than perfectly, and thereafter, he was frequently able to give the little black ball a particularly sinister twist.

Dr. Currie was the first resident professor at Austin Seminary to deliver the Mid-winter lecture series bearing his father's name. The title chosen for this series in 1973 was "The Word of the Lord, the Word of God, and the Preaching of the Word."[20]

The discourses included reflections on the nature of God's call to the Gospel ministry. There is a study of prophecy in the Old and in the New Testaments and then of prophecy and the significance of Jesus, together with an examination of three passages in which Paul describes his method and purpose in preaching (1 Cor 2:1-5; 2 Cor 4:1-6; 10:1-6).

The closing section illustrates the author's conception of preaching. One of the especially appealing thumbnail sermons is from the texts, Mark 12:41-44 and Mark 14:3-11. The matter of stewardship is treated in the light that shines forth from the record of the widow's mite and of the woman who poured expensive ointment on Jesus' head in the house of Simon the Leper. Here were two women, names unknown, who with uncalculating, prodigal abandon gladly gave what they had to the temple. The appeal implicit was that to him who had replaced the temple as the center of our worship we might be inspired to a like stewardship.

The chapel at the Seminary was a focal point for Dr. Currie. He found in it a congenial place of worship. When it was erected the communion table was attached to the base of the reredos in the chancel. As the years went by there was increasing sentiment for the communion table to be located much nearer the transept in order to allow for the minister to have the table between himself and the congregation, more in the Reformed tradition. Without disturbing the original furniture, Dr. Currie took the initiative in commissioning and donating the new, movable communion table, together with two prayer desks. From sketches by Mary Gaines, the woodwork and carving were executed by Johannes C. Scholze, the artist who earlier had done the shields of the Lamb and the Apostles above the entrance from the narthex into the nave.

The sole adornment of the table was the leaf and the cluster of the Vine. On one prayer desk was the symbol of John Calvin, the hand offering the heart. On the other was the picture of a spade plunged into the Scripture. The first symbol is derived from Calvin's reply to Farel as he finally acceded to repeated calls to return to Geneva: "My heart as offered up to God I present in sacrifice." (*Opera* X, 400) The second is derived from Calvin's comment, "Prayer digs

out those treasures which the gospel of the Lord discovers to our
faith."(*Inst* III xx 2)

The new furnishings were first used at a communion service
September 4, 1974. One of the hymns chosen by Dr. Currie was the
1874 poem by William Bright:

> And now, O Father, mindful of the love
>   That bought us, once for all, on Calvary's Tree,
> And having with us Him that pleads above,
>   We here present, we here spread forth to Thee
> That only offering perfect in Thine eyes,
>   That one true, pure, immortal sacrifice.
>
> Look, Father, look on His anointed face,
>   And only look on us as found in Him;
> Look not on our misusing of Thy grace,
>   Our prayer so languid, and our faith so dim:
> For lo! between our sins and their reward
>   We set the passion of Thy Son our Lord.
>
> And so we come: O draw us to Thy feet,
>   Most patient Saviour, who canst love us still;
> And by this food, so awful and so sweet,
>   Deliver us from every touch of ill;
> In Thine own service make us glad and free,
>   And grant us never more to part with Thee.[21]

At the peak of his powers, and, so far as those closest to him
knew, in robust good health, Dr. Currie entered the Seminary
handball court for a little exercise the afternoon of Tuesday, April
15, 1975. The game had hardly begun when Dr. Currie collapsed.
On the court and at Brackenridge Hospital efforts to arouse him
proved futile.

The service in the chapel conducted by the family's pastor,
Roland P. Perdue, of the University Presbyterian Church, was one
of doxologies in word and music. Dr. Currie's influence did not end
with his death. His own family continued in strength: Sara, an elder
in University Church, Associate School Psychologist with the
Austin Independent School District; Helen, college English teacher,
and her husband Larry Foster, Associate Professor of Management
in the School of Business at Michigan State; Grace, trustee and
elder in the Presbyterian Church, language arts teacher in
Appalachia High School, with her attorney husband, Bill Bradshaw
in Big Stone Gap, Virginia; Kenneth, recent Rice University
graduate with Master of Business and Public Administration,

employed by Merichem Co., and his wife, Pam, realtor in Houston; and Mark, an intern in Internal Medicine at Duke University Medical School, Durham, North Carolina.

As one beholden to Dr. Currie as a brother, I am quite unable to find words adequate to describe the admiration and the debt owed for the years of kin and friendship. He forgave with such grace one might suppose he had sensed no reason to have noticed an offense. He responded to appeals for help as naturally as if a request had been unnecessary. His word and conduct were the very definition of courtesy. His awesome intellect was no barrier.

Shortly after Dr. Currie's death the Seminary *Bulletin* carried some memories from the pen of a colleague, George S. Heyer, Jr., one of those who saw many facets of Dr. Currie's personality.

At the thought of Stuart Currie a crowd of memories arise, witnesses to the many-sidedness of the man. All deserve recognition, but I must discriminate among them and I have decided to concentrate upon more personal recollections, saying less regarding the contributions that he made to our school. In any case, I do not know how I could so much as suggest the depth and diversity of these contributions. No facet of the Seminary's life remained untouched by his influence, and I cannot yet imagine the place without him. We all leaned on him in matters both small and large, and he never disappointed us. But chiefly it is a singular and utterly unique person whom I remember. I hope that my remarks recapture that person, at least in outline.

I recall Stuart's intense love for language and languages. Whether he was composing a limerick in Latin, translating a Psalm from Hebrew, analyzing a delicate problem in exegesis, or discoursing upon some issue that touched the life of the Seminary, he employed language with that blend of elegance, precision, and freedom which marks a true master of this precious instrument. Words delighted him. Some months ago a son of mine developed an unexpected fondness for palindromes, and I went to ask Stuart if he could furnish me with some. He promptly sat down, wrote out thirty or so (in English, Latin, and Greek!), and passed them along to me. Walking across the campus and reading such gems as ''Lewd did I live and evil I did dwel'' and ''Sit on a potato pan, Otis,'' I rocked with laughter, and I am sure that those who saw me decided that I had at last come unhinged. But it was typical of Stuart to share his delight with those around him. Few persons have been as richly endowed as Stuart Currie, and fewer still have shared so liberally the fruits of their talents.

I also remember drives across country with Stuart. They were non-stop affairs! He did acknowledge the necessary inconvenience of pausing occasionally to provide the car with gas, but, to him, this constituted the sole valid reason for stopping. In Texas, these trips were also lessons in the geography and history of the state. Once, on the way back to Austin from San Angelo, we passed a hill with a peculiar tapered shape, rising to a flat, cut-off summit. Stuart was bothered that he did not know its name. The next morning I found on my office a note, which said simply, "Smoothing Iron Mountain."

To him, I am certain, "Smoothing Iron" was a far better name than merely "Iron" or even "Flatiron." It was redolent of the past, of history, of other times, into which Stuart, as an historian, was able to project himself—even to live—by virtue of his most sensitive imagination and the sharp tools that, as a professional scholar, he had refined. I myself saw in him no conflict between his incredible learning on the one hand and his simplicity of outlook on the other. He did not hanker for the past, however intimately he knew it. He was a conservative, in the most proper sense of that term; one who deeply believed that the achievements of the past must not be wasted in the present. Upon that conviction not only the Church but civilization itself depends.

Stuart never wasted anything. I have spoken of trips taken with him. On one of these, he said to me, "I always make this trip with the feeling that I might not pass this way again." In similar fashion he lived all his days. Each one afforded to him that unique opportunity which, indeed, would *not* come again. Each one of these the Lord in *his* own time had provided, and, were we to waste them, why then we should be not only spendthrifts but also unfaithful. Stuart kept us all on our mettle, whether by his diligence in chapel and classroom or as a competitor on the handball court, where he suffered the attack that proved fatal. Now, of course, he will not come our way again, and a great light has vanished from our midst. But we remember its brightness and we shall carry on.[22]

The acknowledgment card sent from the family in response to expressions of sympathy had on it a collage of line sketches by Mark Currie. At the left was a portrait of Dr. Currie, then an open Bible showing the words, "with thanksgiving." These were followed by an aardvark (the first animal in the dictionary, a picture of which decorated Dr. Currie's study door), and an owl. Just above these figures is a sketch of four peaks in the Rocky Mountain National Park: Chiquita, Ypsilon, Fairchild, and Hagues. Above all is depicted the tower of Austin Seminary Chapel. Within appear the words:

STUART DICKSON CURRIE
October 20, 1922   April 15, 1975
"I will lift up mine eyes unto the hills...my help
cometh from the Lord, which made heaven and earth."
"Death is swallowed up in victory."
Thank you for weeping with us at Stuart's death,
rejoicing with us in his life.

HIS FAMILY

NOTES

1. Private undated paper in the hands of T.W.C., Jr.
2. Oscar Cullmann, *The State in the New Testament* (New York: Charles Scribner's Sons, 1956) viii, ix.
3. Stuart D. Currie, "A Peculiar People," *Austin Presbyterian Theological Seminary Bulletin,* Faculty Edition, LXXVIII (September 1962) 13.
4. *Ibid.,* 33.
5. Stuart D. Currie, "Clergy and Laity," *Austin Presbyterian Theological Seminary Bulletin,* Faculty Edition, LXXIX (April 1964) 43.
6. Stuart D. Currie, "Never on Sunday," *Austin Presbyterian Theological Seminary Bulletin,* Faculty Edition, LXXX (April 1965) 27-33.
7. Stuart D. Currie, "Isaiah 63, 9 and the Transfiguration in Mark," *Austin Presbyterian Theological Seminary Bulletin,* Faculty Edition, LXXXII (November 1966) 7-34.
8. Stuart D. Currie, *The Beginnings of the Church* (Richmond, Virginia: The CLC Press, 1966).
9. *Teacher's Guide, Revised, For Use With Sourcebooks and Other Study Materials, Grades 7-8, Year I,* ed Virginia Creps (Philadelphia: The Geneva Press, 1971, 1973). According to a letter to T.W.C., Jr. dated July 26, 1977, from David Ng, the original editor, the author of "The Teacher's Study" for Units 1-5 (pp 47-54, 77-87, 107-116, 141-151,171-178) was Stuart D. Currie. The above volume is in possession of David Ng, Austin Presbyterian Theological Seminary, Austin, Texas.
10. Stuart D. Currie, "Speaking in Tongues," *Interpretation* XIX (July 1965) 274-94.
11. Stuart D. Currie, "Jesus and the Spirit," *Austin Presbyterian Theological Seminary Bulletin,* Faculty Edition, LXXXIII (November 1967) 27.
12. *Ibid.,* 41.
13. Stuart D. Currie, "The Christian Community in the Second Century," *The New Man, An Orthodox and Reformed Dialogue,* eds John Meyendorff and Joseph McLelland (New Brunswick, N. J.: Agora Brooks, 1973; copyright by Standard Press) 92-106.
14. Stuart D. Currie, *Good News in Samaria* (Montreal: The Presbyterian College, 1972) 26-27.
15. *Ibid.,* 46-47.
16. *Ibid.,* 48.
17. *Ibid.,* 51.
18. *Ibid.,* 52-55.

19. Stuart D. Currie, "Biblical Studies for a Seminar on Sexuality and the Human Community," *Austin Presbyterian Theological Seminary Bulletin*, Faculty Edition, LXXXVII (November 1971) 56-57.

20. Stuart D. Currie, *The Word of the Lord, The Word of God, and the Preaching of the Word*. Unpublished mimeographed typescript in the possession of Sara Files (Mrs. S. D.) Currie, Austin, Texas.

21. *The Church Hymnary, Revised Edition,* authorized for use in public worship by The Church of Scotland *et al.* (London: Oxford University Press, 1931) 101, #320.

22. George S. Heyer, Jr., "As I Knew Him," *Austin Presbyterian Theological Seminary Bulletin* XC (May 1975).

WRITTEN WORKS
STUART DICKSON CURRIE

BOOKS:

The Beginnings of the Church. Richmond, Virginia: The CLC Press, 1966.

Good News in Samaria. Montreal, Canada: The Presbyterian College, McGill University, February 9-10, 1972.

Koinonia in Christian Literature to 200 A.D. Microfilm, University of Michigan, Ann Arbor, Michigan, 1962.

ARTICLES:

"A Peculiar People," *Austin Presbyterian Theological Seminary Bulletin,* Faculty Edition LXXVIII (September 1962) 3-34.

"*Koinonia* in Paul's Covenant Vocabulary," *Austin Presbyterian Theological Seminary Bulletin,* Faculty Edition, LXXVIII (March 1963) 5-13.

"Clergy and Laity," *Austin Presbyterian Theological Seminary Bulletin,* Faculty Edition LXXIX (April 1964) 36-44.

"Matthew 5:39a—Resistance or Protest?" *The Harvard Theological Review,* 57, 2 (April 1964) 140-145.

"Never on Sunday," *Austin Presbyterian Theological Seminary Bulletin,* LXXX (April 1965) 27-33.

"Speaking in Tongues," *Interpretation XIX (July 1965) 274-294.*

"Isaiah 63, 9 and the Transfiguration in Mark," *Austin Presbyterian Theological Seminary Bulletin,* Faculty Edition LXXXII (November 1966) 7-36.

"Jesus and the Spirit," *Austin Presbyterian Theological Seminary Bulletin,* Faculty Edition LXXXIII (November 1967) 17-44.

"Hope in Its Biblical Settings," *Austin Presbyterian Theological Seminary Bulletin,* Faculty Edition LXXXIV (April 1969) 29-39.

"Biblical Studies for a Seminar on Sexuality and the Human Community," *Austin Presbyterian Theological Seminary Bulletin,* Faculty Edition LXXXVII (November 1971) 1-60.

"The Christian Community in the Second Century," *The New Man, An Orthodox and Reformed Dialogue,* eds John Meyendorff and Joseph McLelland. New Brunswick, N.J.: Agora Books, 1973.

"The Teacher's Study," Units 1-5, *Teachers Guide, Revised, For Use With Sourcebooks and Other Study Materials, Grades 7-8, Year I*, ed Virginia Creps (Philadelphia: The Geneva Press, 1971, 1973) 47-54, 77-87, 107-116, 141-151, 171-178.

"A Declaration of Faith," *Austin Presbyterian Theological Seminary Bulletin*, Faculty Edition XC (November 1974) 5-9.

UNPUBLISHED:

"Procul Negotiis"

The Word of the Lord, the Word of God, and the Preaching of the Word. 1973.

"Spiro T. Agnew, March 31, 2984" (Archeological Spoof).

Easter Devotional Booklet (April 3-10, 1977). Mimeographed. Austin, Texas: University Presbyterian Church.

Translation of Latin in Introduction to K. Aland, *Synopsis Quattuor Evangeliorum*. Stuttgart: Württembergische Bibelanstalt, 1964.

Index to Biblical Texts

Index to Other Primary Sources

Index to Authors of Secondary Sources

Abbreviations
Ancient Authors and Sources

Aug	Augustine
C adv leg et proph	*Contra adversarium legis et prophetarum*
Enarr in Ps	*Enarrationes in Psalmos*
Quaest in Hept	*Quaestionum in Heptateuchum*
Aphrahat *Hom*	Aphrahat, *Homilies (Demonstrations)*
Ap Const	*The Apostolic Constitution*
Barn	The Epistle of Barnabas
1-2 Clem	1-2 Clement
Clem	Clement of Alexandria
Ecl	*Eclogae ex Scripturis propheticis*
Paed	*Paedagogus*
Strom	*Stromata*
Cyp	Cyprian
Test	*Testimonia ad Quirinum*
Dialogue	Justin, *Dialogue with Trypho*
Did	Didache
Didas	*Didascolia Apostolorum*
Ep, Epp	*Epistola, Epistolae*
Fr	*Fragmenta*
HE	Eusebius, *Historica Ecclesiastica*
Ign	Ignatius
Magn	Letter to the Magnesians
Phld	Letter to the Philadelphians
Smyrn	Letter to the Smyrnaeans
Trall	Letter to the Trallians
Iren	Irenaeus
Adv haer	*Adversus haereses*
Muson	Musonius
Ep Pancrat	*Epistola Pancratidae*
Orig	Origen
C Cels	*Contra Celsum*
Comm Joh	*Commentary on John*
Comm Matt	*Commentary on Matthew*
Comm Rom	*Commentary on Romans*
De or	*De oratione libellus*
De princ	*De principiis*
Ep to Africanus	*Epistola ad Africanum*
Exh ad mart	*Exhortatio ad martyrium*
In Ex hom	*Homiliae in Exodum*
In Num hom	*Homiliae in Numeros*
Plea	Athenagoras, *A Plea for the Christians*
Ps-Clem	Pseudo-Clementines
Hom	*Homilien*
Recogn	*Recognitiones*
Ps-Cyp	Pseudo-Cyprian
Adv Iudaeos	*Adversus Iudaeos*
Or	*Orationes*

Tert   Tertullian

Ad ux   *Ad uxorem*

Adv Herm   *Adversus Hermogenem*

Adv Iud   *Adversus Iudaeos*

Adv Marc; AM   *Adversus Marcionem*

Adv Prax   *Adversus Praxean*

Apol   *Apologeticus*

De Anima   *De Anima*

De Ieiun   *De Ieiunio*

De monog   *De monogamia*

De or   *De oratione*

De praesc haer   *De praescriptione haereticorum*

De pud   *De pudicita*

Res carn   *De resurrectione mortuorum (carnis)*

Virg vel   *De virginibus velandis*

Periodicals, Reference Works, and Serials

AJT	*American Journal of Theology*
BKAT	Biblischer Kommentar: Altes Testament
BSac	*Bibliotheca Sacra*
CCL	Corpus Christianorum. Series Latina.
DAB	*Dictionary of American Biography*
EBib	Etudes bibliques (EtBib)
EvT	*Evangelische Theologie (EvTh)*
GCS	Griechische christliche Schriftsteller
GRBS	*Greek, Roman, and Byzantine Studies*
HibJ	*Hibbert Journal*
HNTC	Harper's NT Commentaries
HTR	*Harvard Theological Review*
ICC	International Critical Commentary
IDB	G. A. Buttrick (ed), *Interpreter's Dictionary of the Bible*
IDBS	Supplementary volume to *IDB*
Int	*Interpretation*
JAAR	*Journal of the American Academy of Religion*
JBL	*Journal of Biblical Literature*
JR	*Journal of Religion*
JTS	*Journal of Theological Studies*
L.-S.-J.	Liddell-Scott-Jones, *Greek-English Lexicon*
NCAB	*The National Cyclopaedia of American Biography*
NovT	*Novum Testamentum*
NPNF	Nicene and Post-Nicene Fathers
NTD	Das Neue Testament Deutsch
NTS	*New Testament Studies*
Or	*Orientalia (Rome)*
PG	J. Migne, *Patrologia graeca*
RBen	*Revue bénédictine*
RNT	Regensburger Neues Testament
RSV	*Revised Standard Version*
SBLMS	SBL Monograph Series
SBT	Studies in Biblical Theology
SJT	*Scottish Journal of Theology*
ST	*Studia theologica (StTh)*
SVF	H. von Arnim, *Stoicorum Veterum Fragmenta* (1903-)
TDNT	G. Kittel and G. Friedrich (eds) *Theological Dictionary of the New Testament*
TDOT	G. Botterweck and H. Ringgren (eds) *Theological Dictionary of the Old Testament*
TS	*Theological Studies*
TU	Texte und Untersuchungen
TWNT	G. Kittel and G. Friedrich (eds), *Theologisches Wörtenbuch zum Neuen Testament (ThWNT)*
TZ	*Theologische Zeitschrift (ThZ)*
VC	*Vigiliae christianae*
W.-H.	C. Wachsmuth and O. Hense (eds), Stobaeus
ZKG	*Zeitschrift für Kirchengeschichte*
ZNW	*Zeitschrift für die neutestamentliche Wissenschaft*
ZTK	*Zeitschrift für Theologie und Kirche (ZThK)*